Swinburne:
Selected Poetry and Prose

Swinburne:
Selected Poetry and Prose

Edited and Introduced by John D. Rosenberg

PROFESSOR OF ENGLISH, COLUMBIA UNIVERSITY

The Modern Library
NEW YORK

Library of Congress Catalog Card Number: 68–12407

The Introduction to this
volume originally appeared
in *Victorian Studies*.

Manufactured in the United States of America

THE MODERN LIBRARY is published by
Random House, Inc.

✥ ❧ Preface

Swinburne is probably the most important unread poet in English today. Much of his major poetry remains unknown and inaccessible, and the small body of his anthologized verse does not, for the most part, do him justice. Even when his finest poetry is before us, the critical canons of the past half century have virtually incapacitated us from responding to it. The modern reader tends to feel much closer to an early seventeenth-century lyric than to a poem of Swinburne—not because the one is necessarily better than the other, but because his sensibility lies open to the Metaphysical poets and shut to the Victorian. The intent of this anthology is to suggest in its introduction, and to demonstrate by its selections, that Swinburne can deeply engage the intelligent reader, once he perceives what Swinburne was attempting to create: a poetry as highly colored yet intentionally diffuse as the equally radical art of J. M. W. Turner.

In selecting from Swinburne's sizable output, I have favored the intrinsically vital over the merely representative. Several familiar titles have been dropped, and half a dozen major poems, not previously recognized as such, are here anthologized for the first time. Swinburne the critic and novelist is also represented, for he was very versatilely and vitally a man of letters as well as a poet. I regret the exclusion of Swinburne's letters, but priorities of space and the recent, admirable edition by Cecil Lang must serve as my excuse. The letters offer a remarkable glimpse of Swinburne, who must have been the most entirely eccentric of entirely sane men. A brief sketch of his life may be found in the Chronology at the end of this volume.

For the text of the poetry, I have gone to the 1904 Chatto & Windus collected *Poems,* which is more accurate than the "standard" Bonchurch Edition. With the exception of *Lesbia Brandon*, first published in 1952, the prose is taken from the Bonchurch Edition, collated, where possible, with earlier editions.

I am indebted to my wife Barbara, my friend Carl Woodring, and my editor Berenice Hoffman for suggestions which have made the critical introduction more nearly just. My student Beth K. Helsinger assisted very substantially in annotating the volume and in all the stages of its preparation. It is also pleasant to acknowledge the generosity of the American Council of Learned Societies, whose fellowship assistance enabled me to devote my undivided energies to the study of Swinburne.

J. D. R.

NEW YORK, 1967

◄᷄ ᷄᷄᷄ᶿ᷆᷾ *Introduction*

Swinburne is a poet not of natural objects but of natural energies—of winds and surging waters. His scale is macrocosmic, his
focus less upon the small celandine than upon the spines of
mountains, less upon things seen than forces felt. At times he is
nearly a blind poet, all tongue and ear and touch. His poetry
moves away from the art of painting and toward the art of
music; after reading Swinburne one retains not an image but a
tonality and a rhythm.

Traditionally, the English poet has prided himself on particu-
larity, which English criticism has exalted as the clearest sign of
genius. Donne's "bracelet of bright haire about the bone" has
dazzled the critics for half a century. The modern reader's very
conception of poetry has been shaped by the practices of the
Metaphysical poets and by Keats's dictum that the poet must
have "distinctness for his luxury." We are at a loss in reading a
poet who, like Swinburne, is diffuse not by default but by design.

From the perspective of Keats's principles, Gerard Manley
Hopkins is in the main stream of nineteenth-century verse and
Swinburne is the eccentric. For Hopkins' attempt to etch in
words the dappled individuality of things was as much a cul-
tural as a personal concern. Hopkins was simply an extreme
exponent of the impulse to render with absolute accuracy the
distinct profusion of nature itself. One recognizes the same impulse in the splendid exactitude of Tennyson's verse and Ruskin's prose, in the bright, crowded, microscopically accurate
foliage of the Pre-Raphaelites, in Browning's eft, queer, creeping
things, or, for that matter, in the solid clutter of any Victorian
mantelpiece.

Memory betrays us into believing Swinburne to be far more

ornate than he is. Dismissed as overlush and decadent, he is in point of diction the most *austere* of the greatly gifted poets of his century. Early in his career he evokes the heady, Pre-Raphaelite scent of oversweet violets, but in his greatest poetry Swinburne is more starkly monosyllabic than Wordsworth. The knight doomed to a sexually joyless service in "Laus Veneris" craves death in a stanza containing thirty-seven sparse words, all but four of them monosyllables:

> Ah yet would God this flesh of mine might be
> Where air might wash and long leaves cover me,
>   Where tides of grass break into foam of flowers,
> Or where the wind's feet shine along the sea.

Edmund Wilson condemns Swinburne for his "generalizing visageless monosyllables"; I would praise him as the supreme master in English of the bleak beauty of little words.

Wilson has argued that Swinburne the poet is a nullity and that his true gifts lay with the novel, in which he escapes the monotonous vocabulary of his verse: "He can never surprise or delight by a colloquial turn of phrase, a sharply observed detail, a magical touch of color." [1] This might be helpful if it were true, which it is not, or if it were reasonable to condemn Swinburne for not succeeding in what he did not attempt to do. If there are few sudden glories in his verse, they are suppressed in the interests of a more sustained harmony. Great art, he believed, does not vex or fret the beholder with "mere brilliance of point and sharpness of stroke, and such intemperate excellence as gives astonishment the precedence of admiration: such beauties as strike you and startle and go out." [2] Hopkins pushes language as far as it can go toward pointedness and sharpness of stroke; Swinburne moves it with equal daring in the opposite direction, diffusing where Hopkins concentrates, generalizing

[1] *The Novels of A. C. Swinburne,* with an Introduction by Edmund Wilson, pp. 24–25.
[2] "Matthew Arnold's New Poems," *The Complete Works of Algernon Charles Swinburne* (Bonchurch Edition), Vol. XV, p. 77. For a fuller discussion of Swinburne "On Fixities and Definites: The Use of Detail in Art," see Chapter IV of Robert L. Peters' *The Crowns of Apollo* (1965).

where Hopkins specifies. Together, they are the linguistic bravos of Victorian verse.

By diffuseness, however, I mean something very different from vagueness. The vague poet cannot see or speak clearly—in short, is not a poet. Swinburne is often called vague, but no one who has read his best poetry closely could ever accuse him of imprecision or carelessness with words. T. S. Eliot did not look closely enough at a famous chorus of Swinburne and charged him with laxity:

> Before the beginning of years
>   There came to the making of man
> Time, with a gift of tears;
>   Grief, with a glass that ran. . . .

The verses appear to make a "tremendous statement, like statements made in our dreams," Eliot writes of this chorus from *Atalanta in Calydon;* "when we wake up we find that the 'glass that ran' would do better for time than for grief, and that the gift of tears would be as appropriately bestowed by grief as by time." [3]

The reversed verses that Eliot prefers—time with an hourglass, grief with tears—are trite, and Swinburne wisely avoided them. But he had more positive reasons for overturning our expectation, as immediately becomes clear if we complete Eliot's truncated quotation:

> . . . Grief, with a glass that ran;
> Pleasure, with pain for leaven;
>   Summer, with flowers that fell;
> Remembrance fallen from heaven,
>   And madness risen from hell;
> Strength without hands to smite;
>   Love that endures for a breath:
> Night, the shadow of light,
>   And life, the shadow of death.

The chorus, like the play it mirrors, is about the terrible am-

3 "Swinburne as Poet," *Selected Essays* (1951), p. 326.

biguity of the gods' gifts to men. We are given the bittersweet gift of time, but it passes even as it is given, and hence our tears; yet the pangs of grief also fade with the hours, like the summer blossom. As we read the lines, we are half aware of the conventional imagery underlying them, our mind reacting as does our ear to a departure from regular rhythm, half hearing the normal beat and half hearing the eccentric.

Swinburne constantly breaks down our habitual word associations, but the rupture is so slight that we scarcely notice it. The kind of gentle dislocation that Eliot condemned in the chorus from *Atalanta* gives to Swinburne's poetry the quality of a prolonged, mildly mixed metaphor, a quality which Eliot himself brilliantly exploited in his own poetry. This sense of disorientation, together with Swinburne's insistent, mesmeric meters, induces a surrealist heightening of consciousness that we associate with dreaming and that Swinburne realized with beautiful daring in "The Leper," a ballad about a necrophiliac monk who makes love to the remnants of his lady. Grotesquely explicit, the poem is also inexplicably lovely, like the disintegrating lady, "sweeter than all sweet." [4] The word *sweet* floats like a perfume throughout "The Leper." It recurs most often at those moments when the sense of the poem is most repugnant, sweet sound and fetid sense miraculously counterpoised through thirty-five stanzas.

Swinburne's adjectives, as with *sweet* in "The Leper," have a way of detaching themselves from the nouns they adjoin and modifying instead whole lines or stanzas. He deliberately suppresses the specifying, limiting function of the adjective in order to discharge its meaning through the total poem. The search for

---

[4] In its original version, entitled "A Vigil," the poem is strongly reminiscent of the Pre-Raphaelite manner of Rossetti and Morris. Swinburne radically revised "The Leper," adding the motif of disease, at about the time (1862) he published in the *Spectator* an essay in praise of *Les Fleurs du Mal*. The revision may in part have been inspired by a desire to emulate Baudelaire, whose strong, acrid subject matter, Swinburne wrote, demands a "supreme excellence of words." One sentence from the Baudelaire essay might stand as an epigraph for "The Leper": "Thus, even of the loathsomest bodily putrescence and decay he can make some noble use; pluck out its meaning and secret, even its beauty, in a certain way, from actual carrion." (*Works*, XIII, 421.)

le mot juste is, in the young Swinburne at least, the search for *le ton juste*, for the word which will not stick like a burr in the consciousness but serve unnoticed as a supporting note in a chord of color. Hence the intentional blandness of his diction, and his overfondness for generalizing modifiers like *bright, sad, light, glad*, and *sweet*. Swinburne's earlier, Pre-Raphaelite imitations are especially rich in such diction and should be read as *études* in verbal coloration. The opening lines of "A Ballad of Life," the first of the *Poems and Ballads* of 1866, offer the reader a conditioning exercise in those lightly limiting adjectives and bland plural nouns[5] that enable Swinburne to arrange words as if they were pigments, or notes in a scale. Pairs of *glads, sweets*, and *sads* resolve themselves into a single neutral chord, as muted as a flame rained upon:

> I found in dreams a place of wind and flowers,
>> Full of *sweet* trees and colour of *glad* grass,
>> In midst whereof there was
> A lady clothed like summer with *sweet* hours.
> Her beauty, fervent as a fiery moon,
>> Made my blood burn and swoon
>> Like a flame rained upon.
> Sorrow had filled her shaken eyelids' blue,
> And her mouth's *sad* red heavy rose all through
>> Seemed *sad* with *glad* things gone.

In these flawless minor lyrics—"A Ballad of Life," "Hermaphro-

---

[5] Cf. the remarkable ninth stanza of "The Garden of Proserpine," in which *all* of the thirteen nouns are plural:

> There go the loves that wither,
>> The old loves with wearier wings;
> And all dead years draw thither,
>> And all disastrous things;
> Dead dreams of days forsaken,
> Blind buds that snows have shaken,
> Wild leaves that winds have taken,
>> Red strays of ruined springs.

The poem illustrates Swinburne's mastery of the music of enervation; the blurring, generic plurals, the muted imagery, and the feminine rhymes all evoke the pause of being "when the spirit, without fear or hope . . . thirsts only after the perfect sleep" (Swinburne's note).

ditus," "A Match," "Before the Mirror," "The Roundel"—language takes on a life independent of any ostensible subject. Words, severed from the soil of things, send out aerial roots of their own.

One seems to be overhearing an exquisitely beautiful voice singing at a distance; the melody carries, but the words come muffled, as if in a foreign tongue:

> If love were what the rose is,
>   And I were like the leaf,
> Our lives would grow together
> In sad or singing weather,
> Blown fields or flowerful closes,
>   Green pleasure or grey grief;
> If love were what the rose is,
>   And I were like the leaf.
>
>   · · · · ·
>
> If you were queen of pleasure,
>   And I were king of pain,
> We'd hunt down love together,
> Pluck out his flying-feather,
> And teach his feet a measure,
>   And find his mouth a rein;
> If you were queen of pleasure,
>   And I were king of pain.
>   ("A Match")

Self-engendered, self-contained, the poem is inspired not by the emotion of love but by the emotion of poetry itself.

All that Swinburne learned in composing these exercises in verbal color he put to use in the much later and more ambitious *Tristram of Lyonesse* (1882). The "Prelude" to *Tristram* usually makes its way into the anthologies, but the rest of the poem is virtually unread, although it is one of the great erotic poems in English. *Tristram* is undervalued largely because the wrong demands have been made upon it. As narrative or as a drama of action the poem inevitably disappoints, in precisely the ways that Wagner's *Tristan und Isolde* disappoints. In both of these essentially *lyrical* re-creations of the legend, action and characterization are wholly subordinate to the all-absorbing theme of love. Just as there are no independent arias in *Tristan,* so there are no striking images in Swinburne's *Tristram* that are not repeated as leitmotifs and thus reabsorbed into the enveloping texture of the verse. The Londoner who read Swinburne's poem upon its publication in 1882 and then, just one month later, heard the English première of Wagner's music drama might well have felt a certain *déjà entendu.*[6]

From its opening lines to its close, *Tristram of Lyonesse* is about four lips that "become one burning mouth." As so often in Swinburne, the "image" is more tactile than visual. It first appears when Tristram and Iseult drink the potion; it recurs in a series of variants, most notably in Tristram's praise of "the mute clear music of her amorous mouth," a line whose enunciation moves the mouth into the position of a kiss. The image closes the poem as Iseult bows her head over the dead Tristram, "And their four lips became one silent mouth."

Although love is doomed, bleak, sick and sterile in almost all of Swinburne's poetry, in *Tristram* one senses his unique exultation in portraying sex that is fulfilled, however fated. Perhaps it is *because* the lovers are so clearly foredoomed that he could write so richly of their fulfillment. In this central legend symbolizing the love-sickness of the Western world, Swinburne creates by far his healthiest love poetry:

> Only with stress of soft fierce hands she prest
> Between the throbbing blossoms of her breast
> His ardent face, and through his hair her breath
> Went quivering as when life is hard on death;

[6] When Swinburne began the poem in 1869, in emulation of what he liked to call Tennyson's "Morte d'Albert," he wrote to Edward Burne-Jones that the thought of Wagner's music "ought to abash but does stimulate me." (*The Swinburne Letters,* ed. Cecil Y. Lang, II, 51.) He also planned to write a poem in French on the Prelude to *Tristan* some ten years before the English première of the opera. (See *Letters,* II, 183.) Two excellent discussions of the Wagnerian elements in Swinburne occur in Elliott Zuckerman's *The First Hundred Years of Wagner's Tristan* and Samuel Chew's *Swinburne.*

And with strong trembling fingers she strained fast
His head into her bosom; till at last,
Satiate with sweetness of that burning bed,
His eyes afire with tears, he raised his head
And laughed into her lips; and all his heart
Filled hers; then face from face fell, and apart
Each hung on each with panting lips, and felt
Sense into sense and spirit in spirit melt.

These lines occur in Canto II, "The Queen's Pleasance," the poem's great *Liebesnacht* in which rest at last gains mastery "in the lovely fight of love and sleep." All of nature is absorbed into the passion of love, until the perfumed air seems an extension of the lovers' breath, the soft grass an extension of their bodies. The erotic interpenetration of nature and man is one of the poem's pervasive motifs, most remarkably realized in lines from Canto I describing a spring sunrise and the parallel dawning of womanhood in Iseult. Images of light, heat, florescence and flame all fuse into a single Turnerian chord of color, as Iseult herself comes to full flower under the "august great blossom" of the sun:

                          . . . she felt
Through her own soul the sovereign morning melt,
And all the sacred passion of the sun;
And as the young clouds flamed and were undone
About him coming, touched and burnt away
In rosy ruin and yellow spoil of day,
The sweet veil of her body and corporal sense
Felt the dawn also cleave it, and incense
With light from inward and with effluent heat
The kindling soul through fleshly hands and feet.
And as the august great blossom of the dawn
Burst, and the full sun scarce from sea withdrawn
Seemed on the fiery water a flower afloat,
So as a fire the mighty morning smote
Throughout her, and incensed with the influent hour

Her whole soul's one great mystical red flower
Burst, and the bud of her sweet spirit broke
Rose-fashion, and the strong spring at a stroke
Thrilled, and was cloven, and from the full sheath came
The whole rose of the woman red as flame:
And all her Mayday blood as from a swoon
Flushed, and May rose up in her and was June.

II

Swinburne concluded *Tristram of Lyonesse* with a final verse paragraph that, to my knowledge, has no precedent in any version of the legend. King Mark builds the lovers a stone chapel at the sea's edge, and in their death the lovers undergo a second doom. For the waves shatter the chapel and the sea closes over their uncoffined bones. Fulfilled love in Swinburne pays the penalty of double death.

The association of love with death is the underlying theme of almost all of Swinburne's major poetry. He is of course best known for a variant on that theme—the pain implicit in all pleasure. Virtually incapable of using the word *pleasure* without its alliterative opposite, Swinburne is undeniably sadomasochistic, but this lurid aspect of his lyricism has obscured his true achievement. His greatest love poetry is addressed not to those literary ladies with sharp teeth—Dolores, Faustine, and the rest—but to his bitter, salt mother the sea, and to those bleakly beautiful, ravaged margins of earth that yield their substance to her.

Swinburne is the laureate of barrenness in all its forms. I find myself further from the essential matter of his poetry when I learn, as his critics stress of late, that he was fond of being whipped, than when I read his nobly sad letter congratulating Edmund Gosse on his marriage:

> I suppose it must be the best thing that can befall a man to win and keep the woman that he loves while yet young; at any rate I can congratulate my friend on his good hap without any too jealous afterthought of the

reverse experience which left my own young manhood
'a barren stock.' [7] . . .

The signs of that "reverse experience" are everywhere in
Swinburne's poetry. In the autobiographical "Thalassius," for
example, Swinburne tells of his painful encounter with the
young god of Love. Terrifyingly transformed, Love "waxes immeasurable" and from his erected height says to the poet:

> O fool, my name is sorrow;
> Thou fool, my name is death.

Of course, Swinburne's trauma in love would not have so
scarred him were it not for an antecedent disposition toward
being bruised. His peculiar vulnerability and ambivalence to
pain express themselves in the figure of the *femme fatale* who
dominates all of his early writing.[8] Although she is a familiar

---

[7] *Letters,* III, 51. Cecil Lang has shown that Swinburne's disappoint-
ment in love occurred sometime between 1862–65, when he was in his
mid-twenties, and that the probable cause was the marriage of his
cousin Mary Gordon, with whom he was much in love, to Colonel Disney
Leith. See Lang's "Swinburne's Lost Love," *PMLA,* LXXIV (1959), pp.
123–30.

[8] Swinburne's biographers have made too much of his reading of
Sade's *Justine* in 1862 as the "source" of the algolagnia in *Poems and
Ballads,* First Series. Over a decade earlier, as a schoolboy freshly arrived
at Eton, Swinburne wrote a pseudo-Elizabethan drama describing, in
part, the tortures of the Christian martyrs in Imperial Rome:

SULPITIUS: What music will the creaking of the rack
              Make to his heart
PAMPHILIUS: My soul shall welcome it
              As the sweet strain that ushers me to bliss. . . .
                      Fetch more irons
              Hotter than these that tear me; pour fresh oils
              On the flames that consume my flesh; away!
              Can you not force one shriek? what are your gods
              That cannot torture?
                  (See Georges Lafourcade, *La Jeunesse de Swinburne,*
                  II, 119.)

Despite the frankly sadistic content of such poetry, one can never be
certain if Swinburne intends merely to shock the reader, or if he is
exressing his profoundest impulses. Nor can we draw a clear line between
his "literary" and his "actual" experiences. A book read could be more
real to him than a face seen. Swinburne's grief over the marriage of his
cousin Mary Gordon was, I am sure, one of the most intense experiences
of his life: as intense, that is, as his love of the sea, or of the works of
Sade and Victor Hugo.

type in nineteenth-century literature, this "fair fearful Venus made of deadly foam" [9] objectifies Swinburne's personal sense of the deathliness of desire and the desirability of death. The hero of *Chastelard* (1865), for example, commits the curiously passive indiscretion of watching Mary Stuart disrobe, in order to compel her to behead him. In an ecstasy of self-prostration, Chastelard says to his Queen:

> Stretch your throat that I may kiss all round
> Where mine shall be cut through; suppose my mouth
> The axe-edge to bite so sweet a throat in twain
> With bitter iron, should not it turn soft
> As lip is soft to lip?
>
> (V, ii)

Chastelard is too specialized in theme and derivative in style to engage the general reader, although as an exercise in unrelenting eroticism, this mid-Victorian *Salomé* retains the power to shock. In *Atalanta* Swinburne steps outside the torrid circle of his obsessions and creates a world as bright, virginal and swift as *Chastelard* is sick with too many roses. Yet he still manages to use the myth of the virgin huntress as a vehicle for his private sensibility. Atalanta is a *frigid* Venus who destroys her lover Meleager as mercilessly as Aphrodite destroys Hippolytus.[10]

No tact is fine enough to discriminate among all the various shades in Swinburne's portrait of love. At times he takes a schoolboy's hot delight simply in handling the theme. At times he writes like a patrician revolutionary attacking sexual prudery as John Stuart Mill attacked intellectual conformity. Occasionally love serves him as an excuse for embroidering rhymes in which birds or flowers would do as well. But the theme can

---

[9] *Chastelard*, Act V, Scene ii.
[10] See Mario Praz' *The Romantic Agony*, 2nd ed. (1951), pp. 225–26. Atalanta is indirectly, Althaea directly, responsible for Meleager's death, the play offering the unusual spectacle of both mistress and mother in the roles of *femmes fatales*. Convinced Freudians might make something of the added fact that when Meleager presents Atalanta with the hairy spoil of the wild boar, she laughs in his face. Cf. Swinburne's self-description in "Thalassius" as "a manchild with an ungrown God's desire."

get out of hand, as in "Anactoria," in which he writes with morbid power of the pleasures of inflicting pain:

> I would find grievous ways to have thee slain,
> Intense device, and superflux of pain;
> Vex thee with amorous agonies, and shake
> Life at thy lips, and leave it there to ache;
> Strain out thy soul with pangs too soft to kill,
> Intolerable interludes, and infinite ill;
> Relapse and reluctation of the breath,
> Dumb tunes and shuddering semitones of death.
>
> . . . . .
>
> Ah that my lips were tuneless lips, but pressed
> To the bruised blossom of thy scourged white breast!
> Ah that my mouth for Muses' milk were fed
> On the sweet blood thy sweet small wounds had bled!
> That with my tongue I felt them, and could taste
> The faint flakes from thy bosom to thy waist!
> That I could drink thy veins as wine, and eat
> Thy breasts like honey! that from face to feet
> Thy body were abolished and consumed,
> And in my flesh thy very flesh entombed!
>
> . . . . .
>
> Would I not plague thee dying overmuch?
> Would I not hurt thee perfectly? not touch
> Thy pores of sense with torture, and make bright
> Thine eyes with bloodlike tears and grievous light?
> Strike pang from pang as note is struck from note,
> Catch the sob's middle music in thy throat,
> Take thy limbs living, and new-mould with these
> A lyre of many faultless agonies?

The horror of the last couplet is heightened by its exquisite verbal wit, as faultless as Marvell's green thought in a green shade.

The passion in "Anactoria" goes well beyond Swinburne's desire throughout *Poems and Ballads* to *épater le bourgeois*. Only in two or three prose passages of *Lesbia Brandon* does one sense the same overwhelming pressure toward personal release, the same breathing closeness of the author to his text. Elsewhere in *Poems and Ballads* Swinburne handles similar themes in cooler tones. Poems whose sadism and anti-theism aroused or shocked generations of readers seem today to veer away from blasphemy toward burlesque. Yet Swinburne's death occasioned a sermon by the Vice Dean of Canterbury Cathedral on ,the need of Christ's blood itself to wash away "the pollution which Swinburne's poetry introduced into English literature." [11]

Instead of pollution, I find a certain innocence in Swinburne's perversity. As in his letters, with their Etonian slang and naughty allusions to the Divine Marquis, his eroticism is often more infantile than immoral. Perhaps critical judgment is so unsettled over Swinburne because he is at once a great poet of the solitude of loving and a precocious schoolboy making off-color rhymes. Nor does it simplify matters that he is possibly the most gifted parodist and mimic in English. Swinburne in jest often appears most in earnest, and his apparent earnestness is often a jest, as in his hymn to Notre Dame des Sept Douleurs:

> Could you hurt me, sweet lips, though I hurt you?
> Men touch them, and change in a trice
> The lilies and languors of virtue
> For the raptures and roses of vice;
> Those lie where thy foot on the floor is,
> These crown and caress thee and chain,
> O splendid and sterile Dolores,
> Our Lady of Pain.

· · · · ·

[11] *Letters*, VI, 231. Cf. Thomas Hardy's description, in "A Singer Asleep," of the first effects of Swinburne's poetry upon high Victorian culture:

> —It was as though a garland of red roses
> Had fallen about the hood of some smug nun
> When irresponsibly dropped as from the sun,
> In fulth of numbers freaked with musical closes,
> Upon Victoria's formal middle time
> His leaves of rhythm and rhyme.

Thou wert fair in the fearless old fashion,
    And thy limbs are as melodies yet,
And move to the music of passion
    With live and lascivious regret.
What ailed us, O gods, to desert you
    For creeds that refuse and restrain?
Come down and redeem us from virtue,
    Our Lady of Pain.

In this litany of a sadomasochist's lust, Dolores presides over the marriage of Pleasure and Pain in a ceremony that suggests a black mass. Beneath the deftly controlled surface, one recognizes several of the major themes of *Poems and Ballads:* the intricate connection of pleasure and pain; the dual desire to experience and inflict suffering; a will to fall prey to the destructive sexual force of woman, and the fear of so falling; a need for total self-abasement and a counterimpulse to rebel; a deeply religious reverence before a mystery, and as profound a desire to blaspheme.

God is the supreme sadist in *Poems and Ballads.* Swinburne defies Him eloquently and delightedly: "Him would I reach, him smite, him desecrate," he writes in "Anactoria" of the God who grinds men in order to feed the mute, melancholy lust of heaven. At times Swinburne's poetry of pure defiance achieves a Job-like integrity; at times it suggests a schoolboy's provoking his headmaster to lay on the rod. This anti-theist verse never succeeds as great poetry, although it is often great rhetoric, as in the "Hymn to Proserpine," with its lament for the conquest of the pagan world by the pale Galilean.

Swinburne's rebellion against the tyrant God finds its complement in his worship of man. One recalls that this blasphemer of the pieties of his age once arrived at a dinner party bearing a footstool, so that he could pay proper homage to Robert Browning. In his verse, as in his life, Swinburne was both rigidly defiant and pliantly responsive, self-exultant and self-abasing, a rebel and a mimic. His long sequence of poems of praise begins with tributes to Walter Savage Landor and Victor Hugo in

Poems and Ballads and ends, some fifty years later, with his
humble effusions to the babies of Wimbledon Common.[12]

Swinburne's second volume of poems, *Songs before Sunrise*
(1871), is in all apparent respects the opposite of *Poems and
Ballads*. Erotic verses give way to marching songs in praise of
Italian liberation. We leave the sultry atmosphere of the boudoir
and breathe instead the bracing air of the *Risorgimento;* our
Lady of Liberty displaces our Lady of Pain. Yet the two ladies
inspire in Swinburne similar emotions of self-prostration and
worship. In "The Oblation," for example, he addresses Liberty
as if she were a stern lover under whose feet he craves to be
trampled:

> All things were nothing to give
>   Once to have sense of you more,
>   Touch you and taste of you sweet,
> Think you and breathe you and live,
>   Swept of your wings as they soar,
>   Trodden by chance of your feet.

The sincerity of Swinburne's attachment to the goddess of Liberty is unassailable, although he composed many of his odes to
her while walking to a brothel where he paid to be flogged.

The fault with *Songs before Sunrise* and its companion volume, *Songs of Two Nations* (1875), is not their covert pathology
but their dullness. Dolores and Faustine at least could bite, but

---

[12] A few lines of Reginald Harewood, the autobiographical hero
of *Love's Cross-Currents,* illuminate the connection in Swinburne's poetry
between his sadomasochism and his hero-worship; the passage is pat-
terned on the—for Swinburne—voluptuous metaphor of a flogging on
all fours:

> When I fall in with a nature and powers above me, I cannot
> help going down before it. I do like admiring; service of one's
> masters must be good for one, it is so perfectly pleasant . . . I
> feel my betters in my blood; they send a heat and sting all
> through one at first sight. And the delight of feeling small and
> giving in when one does get sight of them is beyond words—it
> seems to me all the same whether they beat one in wisdom and
> great gifts and power . . . or just in being beautiful. It is just
> as reasonable to worship one sort as the other; they are all one's
> betters, and were made for one to come down on one's knees to,
> clearly enough. (*Novels*, pp. 162–63.)

Lady Liberty merely bores. Perhaps the themes of sexual humiliation and theological defiance in *Poems and Ballads* are intrinsically richer than the parallel themes of hero-worship and political rebellion in *Songs before Sunrise*. At any rate, the abstract diction, the manic, trumpet-blast tone, the rhetorical straining— "O soul, O God, O glory of liberty"—soon exhaust the reader's capacity to respond.

With startling self-knowledge, Swinburne anticipated the cause of his relative failure in *Songs before Sunrise*.[13] "There is I think room for a book of songs of the European revolution," he wrote to William Michael Rossetti on beginning the volume, "and if sung as thoroughly as Hugo or as Whitman would sing them, they ought to ring for some time to some distance of echo. The only fear is that one may be disabled by one's desire—made impotent by excess of strain." [14] The love of liberty was one of the most abiding and intense emotions that Swinburne knew. His rhetorical excess in *Songs before Sunrise* marks his ineffectual effort to translate great conviction into great art.

III

All that is forced or febrile in *Songs before Sunrise* achieves quiet fulfillment in the *Poems and Ballads* of 1878. In the first series of *Poems and Ballads,* one felt the exuberance of genius discovering itself; in the second series the voice has achieved self-mastery and sings in chaste magnificence. The volume appeared during the grimmest period of Swinburne's life, when he

---

[13] "Failure" is too harsh a term. There are at least a dozen distinguished poems in the volume, among them "Super Flumina Babylonis," "Hertha," "Before a Crucifix," "Hymn of Man," "Genesis," "Christmas Antiphones," "Siena," "Cor Cordium," "Tiresias," "On the Downs," "Messidor," and " 'Non Dolet.' " But none of these reaches the standard set in *Poems and Ballads*, 1866, by "Laus Veneris" and "The Triumph of Time" and attained again in *Poems and Ballads*, 1878, by "A Forsaken Garden" and "A Vision of Spring in Winter." I should add that other critics disagree with my tepid estimate of *Songs before Sunrise*, among them T. Earle Welby and Swinburne himself. Welby's *A Study of Swinburne* (New York, 1926) remains the most perceptive analysis in English of Swinburne's poetry.

[14] *Letters*, I, 268.

lived alone in London in suicidal dissipation. One senses the
solitude, but none of the squalor. In the splendid elegies to dead
poets interspersed through *Poems and Ballads,* Swinburne seems
to lay his own youth to rest and prepare to retire from the exercise of his highest powers. One year after the volume was published, he was removed from his rooms in Great James Street by
his friend Theodore Watts-Dunton and taken to live at Putney.
For thirty years their home at "No. 2, The Pines," served Swinburne as a kind of suburban sanitorium. "The Pines" became
the tomb of a great poet and the birthplace of a distinguished
man of letters who wrote on Shakespeare and Victor Hugo,
Marlowe and Mary, Queen of Scots. One of the finest lyrics in
Poems and Ballads is entitled "A Vision of Spring in Winter";
the volume itself is a prevision of Swinburne's long winter, seen
from the last moment of his spring.

The leitmotif of *Poems and Ballads* is the triumph of time
over love, over life, and over the generative powers of earth and
man. These are Swinburne's essential themes, and *Poems and
Ballads,* 1878, is remarkable only in that it plays upon them
more persistently and with his subtlest music. The sadomasochist verses of *Poems and Ballads,* First Series, are less the heart
of Swinburne's poetic matter than a variation on this larger
theme of the forces in nature that divide and destroy us. "Laus
Veneris," "The Leper," and "Anactoria" are extreme cases of
the classic Swinburne situation in which lovers are, so to speak,
disjointed. Once in the First Series—in "The Triumph of Time"
—and once in the Second Series—in "A Forsaken Garden"—all
of these elements meet in perfect balance. They are Swinburne's
archetypical lyrics, adjacent stanzas of a single, larger poem.

In both poems one feels the full force of loss, and the
counterforce of its acceptance. This stoicism of the heart, which
falls short of bitterness on the one hand, and the sentimentality
of unresisted regret on the other, is the defining note of Swinburne's love poetry. It is struck in the opening stanza of "The
Triumph of Time," in which the propulsive rush of the meter
paces time's triumph over the lovers, changing all things except
the fact of their separation:

> Before our lives divide for ever,
>   While time is with us and hands are free,
> (Time, swift to fasten and swift to sever
>   Hand from hand, as we stand by the sea)
> I will say no word that a man might say
>   Whose whole life's love goes down in a day;
> For this could never have been; and never
>   Though the gods and the years relent, shall be.

I mentioned the lovers in "The Triumph of Time," but, remarkably, there are scarcely any lovers in Swinburne's poetry. There is much passion but little conjunction; emotion is felt but not communicated and not returned. Swinburne has mistakenly acquired the reputation of an erotic poet; he is rather the poet of love's impossibility. Perhaps that is why, even in his most sensual verses, one feels a peculiar innocence, just as in his most moving love poetry one feels a profound barrenness:

> It will grow not again, this fruit of my heart,
>   Smitten with sunbeams, ruined with rain.
> The singing seasons divide and depart,
>   Winter and summer depart in twain.
> It will grow not again, it is ruined at root,
> The bloodlike blossom, the dull red fruit;
> Though the heart yet sickens, the lips yet smart,
>   With sullen savour of poisonous pain.

All of Swinburne's finer love poetry is set by the sea—the cold, clean "mother-maid" who is more palpable than the ever-shadowy girl who refuses, or is unaware of, the poet's love. The return to the sea in "The Triumph of Time" occurs near the poem's end, in three stanzas more strange than Swinburne's critics have yet acknowledged:

> I will go back to the great sweet mother,
>   Mother and lover of men, the sea.
> I will go down to her, I and none other,
>   Close with her, kiss her and mix her with me;
> Cling to her, strive with her, hold her fast:

O fair white mother, in days long past
Born without sister, born without brother,
   Set free my soul as thy soul is free.

O fair green-girdled mother of mine,
   Sea, that art clothed with the sun and the rain,
Thy sweet hard kisses are strong like wine,
   Thy large embraces are keen like pain.
Save me and hide me with all thy waves,
Find me one grave of thy thousand graves,
Those pure cold populous graves of thine
   Wrought without hand in a world without stain.

I shall sleep, and move with the moving ships,
   Change as the winds change, veer in the tide;
My lips will feast on the foam of thy lips,
   I shall rise with thy rising, with thee subside;
Sleep, and now know if she be, if she were,
Filled full with life to the eyes and hair,
As a rose is fulfilled to the roseleaf tips
   With splendid summer and perfume and pride.

The lines are at once infantile—"save me and hide me"—and
overwhelming. One recalls that Swinburne's earliest memory
was of shrieking with delight as his father tossed him headfirst
into the waves. Fifty years later he wrote to his sister of the
ecstasy he felt in swimming off the Sussex Downs:

> I ran like a boy, tore off my clothes, and hurled myself
> into the water. And it was but for a few minutes—but I
> was in Heaven! The whole sea was literally golden as
> well as green—it was liquid and living sunlight in which
> one lived and moved and had one's being. And to feel
> that in deep water is to feel—as long as one is swimming
> out, if only a minute or two—as if one was in another
> world of life, and one far more glorious than even Dante
> ever dreamed of in his Paradise. (*Letters*, III, 12; V, 275.)

That paradise held many pleasures, among them the pleasure
of death—that primordial return to "the great sweet mother,"

whose rocking rhythms Swinburne captures in lines that, like some fluid lullaby, mix the image of love-making with the image of drowning: "My lips will feast on the foam of thy lips,/I shall rise with thy rising, with thee subside." The passage is animistic in its primitiveness of emotion. The decadent, verbally sophisticated Swinburne was in another part of his being pre-civilized, a wind-worshiper and a sea-worshiper whose poetry springs from sources more antique than words.

In "A Forsaken Garden," as in "The Triumph of Time," this fusion of the artificial with the aboriginal achieves a fragile power. The setting is an eighteenth-century garden gone to seed and thorn. A faint, salt-sprayed scent of faded flowers and ghostly lovers hovers over the opening stanzas. It is springtime, but neither leaves nor loves will bloom again in this rocky wasteland poised over the sea. The actual garden that inspired the imagined garden of the poem was on the Isle of Wight, where Swinburne spent the springs of his childhood in a setting of near-tropical luxuriance. In late summer the Swinburnes drove north to the family seat at Capheaton, Northumberland, where the bare moors, gray seas, and autumnal summits must have seemed, to the young Swinburne, like winter suddenly overlaid upon spring. The two seasons became forever fixed in his mind in their sudden proximity and sharpness of contrast, so that he could scarcely feel the one without its opposite. The sea that rolls through the great closing stanzas of "A Forsaken Garden" is a chill, northern sea, a blast of death bringing a second ruin, as in *Tristram of Lyonesse*,[15] to a rich but ravaged landscape:

> All are at one now, roses and lovers,
>   Not known of the cliffs and the fields and the sea.
> Not a breath of the time that has been hovers
>   In the air now soft with a summer to be.
> Not a breath shall there sweeten the seasons hereafter
>   Of the flowers or the lovers that laugh now or weep,

[15] The setting recurs a third time, with the same macabre beauty, in "By the North Sea," p. 270, below.

When as they that are free now of weeping and laughter
  We shall sleep.

Here death may deal not again for ever;
  Here change may come not till all change end.
From the graves they have made they shall rise up never,
  Who have left nought living to ravage and rend.
Earth, stones, and thorns of the wild ground growing,
  While the sun and the rain live, these shall be;
Till a last wind's breath upon all these blowing
  Roll the sea.

Till the slow sea rise and the sheer cliff crumble,
  Till terrace and meadow the deep gulfs drink,
Till the strength of the waves of the high tides humble
  The fields that lessen, the rocks that shrink,
Here now in his triumph where all things falter,
  Stretched out on the spoils that his own hand spread,
As a god self-slain on his own strange altar,
  Death lies dead.

As in all of his most powerful verse, Swinburne writes here not
of time present, but of a time immemorially before time, or of
the eternity that follows time. The steady pulse of the monosyllables, the starkness of the diction, the open generalized barrenness of the setting—"earth, stones, and thorns"—evoke some
primordial drama of the elements, as though nature suddenly
shed the coloration of millennia and resolved back into earth,
water, fire, and wind. The lifeless landscape is charged with
hidden life, only to make its final ravagement the more complete: the wind breathes, the rocks shrink, the sea rises, the
gulfs drink, the fields are humbled. The wreck is so total that
Death itself, with nothing mutable left to prey upon, lies dead.
The personification ought to ring hollow—a poetical flourish in
an elemental landscape. But this touch of artifice makes more
awesome the larger, cosmic death that Swinburne heard blowing through nature like a low bone-shaking rumble and that he
here evokes in the form of the wind's last breath rolling sea
over earth in the final Deluge.

One hears the same elemental music in "At a Month's End," another lyric of doomed love in *Poems and Ballads,* Second Series. The lovers, no longer in love, stand by night at the sea's edge and watch the serried spears of the waves storm toward the shore:

> Hardly we saw the high moon hanging,
>   Heard hardly through the windy night
> Far waters ringing, low reefs clanging,
>   Under wan skies and waste white light.
>
> With chafe and change of surges chiming,
>   The clashing channels rocked and rang
> Large music, wave to wild wave timing,
>   And all the choral water sang.

The lapsed love plays itself out against a background of alliterative choiring of the elements. Drifting clouds, waves, gulls, wind, the earth's margins, these are the phenomena on which Swinburne's senses instinctually fix, the background of earth against which his people stand, dwarfed and apart:

> Across, aslant, a scudding sea-mew
>   Swam, dipped, and dropped, and grazed the sea:
> And one with me I could not dream you;
>   And one with you I could not be.
>
> As the white wing the white wave's fringes
>   Touched and slid over and flashed past—
> As a pale cloud a pale flame tinges
>   From the moon's lowest light and last—
>
> As a star feels the sun and falters,
>   Touched to death by diviner eyes—
> As on the old gods' untended altars
>   The old fire of withered worship dies—
>   . . . . .
> So once with fiery breath and flying
>   Your winged heart touched mine and went,

> And the swift spirits kissed, and sighing,
> Sundered and smiled and were content.

The lovers in "At a Month's End" [16] seem not only lost to each other but eclipsed by the larger motions of nature around them. Always in Swinburne the pure, fluid power of wind and sea sweeps everything before it, just as the cataclysmic rush of avalanche and inundation obliterates the paltry human figures in J. M. W. Turner's *Val d'Aosta*. Like Turner, too, Swinburne finds in the vast undifferentiated sea the visible emblem of his genius, with its exaltation of energy over form, infinite nuance over discrete detail. One stanza from "At a Month's End" might have come from Turner's own catalogue descriptions of his seascapes:

> Faint lights fell this way, that way floated,
> Quick sparks of sea–fire keen like eyes
> From the rolled surf that flashed, and noted
> Shores and faint cliffs and bays and skies.

One recognizes in both artists the same sophisticated virtuosity, alongside an enormous responsiveness to the aboriginal forces of nature. Swinburne's landscapes, like Turner's, abstract all the

[16] Swinburne may have drawn the closing stanzas directly from personal experience. For over a month during the winter of 1867–68, in the most caricaturable of the many caricaturable incidents of his life, the diminutive Swinburne was encouraged by Dante Gabriel Rossetti to have an affair with Adah Isaacs Menken, a full-bodied international charmer, circus-rider, and poetess. The two became most companionable, but not proper lovers, Miss Menken finally remarking to Rossetti, "I can't make him understand that biting's no use!" (See *Letters,* VI, 246). It seems likely that she loomed in Swinburne's mind as the ample panther in the following lines, which are so strikingly different in tone from the earlier stanzas quoted above:

> But I, who leave my queen of panthers,
> As a tired honey-heavy bee
> Gilt with sweet dust from gold-grained anthers
> Leaves the rose-chalice, what for me?

> From the ardours of the chaliced centre,
> From the amorous anthers' golden grime,
> That scorch and smutch all wings that enter,
> I fly forth hot from honey-time.

sharp, divisible aspects of nature into an elemental luminosity
and motion, such as God might have beheld on completing the
Creation:

> . . . one clear hueless haze of glimmering hues
> The sea's line and the land's line and the sky's.
>
> ("Thalassius")

"Indistinctness is my forte," Turner retorted to a patron who
chided him for vagueness, a fault which modern critics still im-
pute to Turner's early admirer, Swinburne.[17] Both men practice
a highly structured art that has nonetheless freed itself from the
canons of conventional representation. No single word in a
Swinburne poem quite corresponds to a given thing, just as no
single dab of paint on a Turner canvas corresponds to a natural
object; the correspondence is always between the total configuration of the poem or painting and the total configuration of
nature. The adjective floating freely away from its substantive
in a Swinburne poem is equivalent to the blob of pigment that
is neither sea nor foam nor sky, but all of these, in a Turner
painting. Such an art prizes color over outline, light over form,
music over meaning. Its concern, as Swinburne wrote of poetry,
but might as well have written of Impressionism in general, "is
rather to render the effect of a thing than the thing itself."[18] I
had read the following lines from *Atalanta in Calydon* many
times before they actually sprang into focus as a splendid rendering not of the thing itself, but of its effect upon the sun-dazed
beholder. Althaea describes the bright blur of approaching hunters, as they ride between her and the slanted morning light:

> . . . for sharp mixed shadow and wind
> Blown up between the morning and the mist,
> With steam of steeds and flash of bridle or wheel,
> And fire, and parcels of the broken dawn,
> And dust divided by hard light, and spears

---

[17] For Swinburne's admiration of Turner—"I was brought up on
him . . . and simply revel in everything of his"—see *Letters,* III, 11; V,
216, 254, 258; VI, 72, 118, and 152, n.

[18] "Notes on the Text of Shelley," *Works,* XV, 380.

> That shine and shift as the edge of wild beasts' eyes,
> Smite upon mine; so fiery their blind edge
> Burns, and bright points break up and baffle day.

Swinburne's love of mixed effects gives to his descriptive verse much of its Turnerian quality. His poetry is charged with the tension of delicately poised opposites: shadows thinned by light, lights broken by shade, sunset passing into moonrise, sea merging with sky. He is obsessed by the moment when one thing shades off into its opposite, or when contraries fuse, as in "Hermaphroditus," one of his earliest and finest poems. Yet apart from his profound esthetic affinity with Turner, there is the unique idiosyncrasy of Swinburne himself, who was equipped with superb senses, each of which must have transmitted a peculiar counterpoint. This basic, polarizing rhythm runs through his being and manifests itself in his compulsive use of alliterating antitheses in prose and verse. Much in Swinburne that has been criticized as mere mannerism—paradox, alliteration, elaborate antithesis—strikes me as deriving from his deepest impulses, although the question of "sincerity" is always vexing in his verse. In a sense, Swinburne *perceived* in paradoxes, and his recurrent synesthetic images express perfectly that passing of pain into pleasure, bitter into sweet, loathing into desire, which lay at the root of his profoundest experiences. He loves nature best in her moments of transition, as if drawn to dusk and dawn as the day's hermaphrodisms:

> Over two shadowless waters, adrift as a pinnace in peril,
>> Hangs as in heavy suspense, charged with irresolute
>> light,
> Softly the soul of the sunset upholden awhile
>> on the sterile
>> Waves and wastes of the land, half repossessed
>> by the night.
>
> ("Evening on the Broads")

His imagery of these times of change is most mixed and rich, as when, in "Evening on the Broads," he fuses touch, sound, and sight to describe twilight at sea as "a molten music of colour";

and in a line from "Laus Veneris" that is wisest not to gloss at all, the knight is maddened by erotic fumes rising from "the sea's panting mouth of *dry* desire."

At times Swinburne will elaborate a single antithesis into an entire poem. "A Vision of Spring in Winter" is a beautifully poised evocation of life arising from dormancy as the poet himself declines from spring toward winter; the countermovements of rebirth and loss are as delicately juxtaposed as the snowdrop set in the vanishing snow at the poem's opening. Muted antithesis is also at the heart of "Ave Atque Vale," an elegy to Baudelaire in which Swinburne uncannily evokes the mixed, sweetly-acrid scent of *Les Fleurs du Mal*.[19] The elegaic convention of strewing flowers takes on sudden, sensuous reality as one *smells* the very leaves of Baudelaire's book, the paradoxical

> Half-*faded fiery* blossoms, *pale* with *heat*
> And full of *bitter* summer, but more *sweet*
> To thee than the gleanings of a northern shore . . .

The poem pays its subject the high tribute of perfect imitation. At its close we move away from the bitter-sweet scent of *Les Fleurs du Mal* to the chill smell of the earth that is to receive the poet's body. There is no "far-off divine event" to lighten grief, no advance to pastures new; only death, and this grim tribute of one great poet to another:

> For thee, O now a silent soul, my brother,
> Take at my hands this garland, and farewell.
> Thin is the leaf, and chill the wintry smell,
> And chill the solemn earth, a fatal mother,
> With sadder than the Niobean womb,
> And in the hollow of her breasts a tomb.
> Content thee, howsoe'er, whose days are done;

[19] Cf. Swinburne's parallel attempt to suggest the flavor of Villon's life and verse in "A Ballad of François Villon." This tribute to a poet who created beauty out of a life of depravity illustrates Swinburne's most extreme use of balanced antithetical adjectives. The line "Villon, our *sad bad glad mad* brother's name" recurs four times in four stanzas. The refrain frames a poem whose diction recalls Swinburne's tonal use of adjectives in "A Ballad of Life."

> There lies not any troublous thing before,
> Nor sight nor sound to war against thee more,
> For whom all winds are quiet as the sun,
> All waters as the shore.

IV

Only once again, in *Tristram of Lyonesse,* did Swinburne achieve the sustained excellence of *Poems and Ballads,* Second Series. He continued to publish volumes of verse into our own century, but for the most part the later poetry is a peculiarly vacant sort of versage that exists still-born in a world of its own. One thinks of Swinburne's increasing deafness at Putney, and somehow the poetry suggests a muted soliloquy. The saddest lines in all of Swinburne appear in "A Midsummer Holiday" (1884), dedicated to Watts-Dunton. The setting is indistinguishable from those great, bleak earlier lyrics of the sea's encroachments on the land; here, however, the sea has shrunk to a suburban pond reflecting the ghost of a dead poet:

> Friend, the lonely land is bright for you and me
> All its wild ways through: but this methinks is best,
> Here to watch how kindly time and change agree
> Where the small town smiles, a warm still sea-side nest.

Yet there are moments of astonishing strength in late Swinburne. Much of "By the North Sea," more of the unknown "Evening on the Broads," all of "A Nympholept"[20] defeat one's impulse to impose a curve of growth, flowering, and decline upon the actual pattern of his creativity. Swinburne always wrote a good deal of dead and silly verse, rather more of both

---

[20] Swinburne has been poorly served by anthologists. In glancing through a dozen selections of his poems, I have come across only one which includes "A Nympholept"—the greatest and strangest of his later lyrics. To read it is to experience the terror and "splendid oppression of nature at noon which found utterance of old in words of such singular and everlasting significance as panic and nympholepsy" (Swinburne's note). Nowhere else does the pagan purity of Swinburne's apprehension of nature come across so starkly. The poem *embodies* the pantheism for which Swinburne expounds the theologic and philosophic basis in "Hertha," the "Hymn of Man," and "Genesis."

toward the end of his career. That his most lifeless poetry is in all formal respects—meter, diction, and subject—virtually indistinguishable from his greatest poetry is one of the mysteries of his art. His genius is extraordinary above all for its *intermittency;* the verse-making engine spins constantly for half a century, but the surges of engaged power are sudden and unpredictable. Tennyson called him "a reed through which all things blow into music." Sometimes the melody carries; often it does not. Swinburne had a curious passion for monotony, which was undoubtedly linked to his love of bleak, monochromatic effects. Out of this love came his most powerful poetry; out of it also came whole poems too like his own description of the Dunwich coast:

> Miles, and miles, and miles of desolation!
> Leagues on leagues on leagues without a change!
> ("By the North Sea")

One's final reservation toward Swinburne has to do with a certain arrested development. Wordsworth's genius flowers, then endlessly wanes: *Tintern Abbey* unfolds an organic evolution of growths, losses, and gains. Neither Swinburne nor his verse seems to undergo much change; a single note is struck early and held obsessively long. The reader wants a richer range of subject, more nuance of idea. Swinburne composes by compounding, not synthesizing. Too often, his method is merely quantitative: "I have added yet four more jets of boiling and gushing infamy to the perennial and poisonous fountain of Dolores." [21] One wishes that his eccentric genius could have retained all its power while ridding itself of rigidity and repetitiveness. It did not, and the death of development in Swinburne may have been as large a loss to English poetry as the physical death of Keats.

[21] *Letters,* I, 122.

❧ Contents

Contents

Prose

Poetry

Atalanta in Calydon

A TRAGEDY

Τοὺς ζῶντας εὖ δρᾶν · κατθανὼν δὲ πᾶς ἀνὴρ
Γῆ καὶ σκιά · τὸ μηδὲν εἰς οὐδὲν ῥέπει
Eur. *Fr. Mel.* 20 (537)*

The Argument

Althæa, daughter of Thestius and Eurythemis, queen of Calydon, being with child of Meleager her first-born son, dreamed that she brought forth a brand burning; and upon his birth came the three Fates and prophesied of him three things, namely these; that he should have great strength in his hands, and good fortune in this life, and that he should live no longer when the brand then in the fire were consumed: wherefore his mother plucked it forth and kept it by her. And the child being a man grown sailed with Jason after the fleece of gold, and won himself great praise of all men living; and when the tribes of the north and west made war upon Ætolia, he fought against their army and scattered it. But Artemis, having at the first stirred up these tribes to war against Œneus king of Calydon, because he had offered sacrifice to all the gods saving her alone, but her he had forgotten to honour, was yet more wroth because of the destruction of this army, and sent upon the land of Calydon a wild boar which slew many and wasted all their increase, but him could none slay, and many went against him and perished. Then were all the chief men of Greece gathered together, and

---

* "The living treat well; for, dying, every man is earth and shadow; nothing to nothing descends."

among them Atalanta daughter of Iasius the Arcadian, a virgin;
for whose sake Artemis let slay the boar, seeing she favoured
the maiden greatly; and Meleager having despatched it gave the
spoil thereof to Atalanta, as one beyond measure enamoured of
her; but the brethren of Althæa his mother, Toxeus and Plexippus, with such others as misliked that she only should bear off
the praise whereas many had borne the labour, laid wait for her
to take away her spoil; but Meleager fought against them and
slew them: whom when Althæa their sister beheld and knew
to be slain of her son, she waxed for wrath and sorrow like as
one mad, and taking the brand whereby the measure of her
son's life was meted to him, she cast it upon a fire; and with
the wasting thereof his life likewise wasted away, that being
brought back to his father's house he died in a brief space; and
his mother also endured not long after for very sorrow; and
this was his end, and the end of that hunting.

THE PERSONS

CHIEF HUNTSMAN	TOXEUS
CHORUS	PLEXIPPUS
ALTHÆA	HERALD
MELEAGER	MESSENGER
ŒNEUS	SECOND MESSENGER
ATALANTA	

CHIEF HUNTSMAN

Maiden, and mistress of the months* and stars
Now folded in the flowerless fields of heaven,
Goddess whom all gods love with threefold heart,
Being treble in thy divided deity,
A light for dead men and dark hours, a foot
Swift on the hills as morning, and a hand
To all things fierce and fleet that roar and range
Mortal, with gentler shafts than snow or sleep;
Hear now and help and lift no violent hand,
But favourable and fair as thine eye's beam　　　　10

---

* Artemis, invoked in her triple aspect as Luna, mother of months;
Diana, goddess of chastity and the hunt; and Hecate, deity of the dead.

Hidden and shown in heaven; for I all night
Amid the king's hounds and the hunting men
Have wrought and worshipped toward thee; nor shall man
See goodlier hounds or deadlier edge of spears;
But for the end, that lies unreached at yet
Between the hands and on the knees of gods.
O fair-faced sun, killing the stars and dews
And dreams and desolation of the night!
Rise up, shine, stretch thine hand out, with thy bow
Touch the most dimmest height of trembling heaven,   20
And burn and break the dark about thy ways,
Shot through and through with arrows; let thine hair
Lighten as flame above that flameless shell
Which was the moon, and thine eyes fill the world
And thy lips kindle with swift beams; let earth
Laugh, and the long sea fiery from thy feet
Through all the roar and ripple of streaming springs
And foam in reddening flakes and flying flowers
Shaken from hands and blown from lips of nymphs
Whose hair or breast divides the wandering wave   30
With salt close tresses cleaving lock to lock,
All gold, or shuddering and unfurrowed snow;
And all the winds about thee with their wings,
And fountain-heads of all the watered world;
Each horn of Acheloüs, and the green
Euenus, wedded with the straitening sea.
For in fair time thou comest; come also thou,
Twin-born with him, and virgin, Artemis,
And give our spears their spoil, the wild boar's hide,
Sent in thine anger against us for sin done   40
And bloodless altars without wine or fire.
Him now consume thou; for thy sacrifice
With sanguine-shining steam divides the dawn,
And one, the maiden rose of all thy maids,
Arcadian Atalanta, snowy-souled,
Fair as the snow and footed as the wind,
From Ladon and well-wooded Mænalus
Over the firm hills and the fleeting sea

Hast thou drawn hither, and many an armèd king,
Heroes, the crown of men, like gods in fight.   50
Moreover out of all the Ætolian land,
From the full-flowered Lelantian pasturage
To what of fruitful field the son of Zeus*
Won from the roaring river and labouring sea
When the wild god shrank in his horn and fled
And foamed and lessened through his wrathful fords
Leaving clear lands that steamed with sudden sun,
These virgins with the lightening of the day
Bring thee fresh wreaths and their own sweeter hair,
Luxurious locks and flower-like mixed with flowers,   60
Clean offering, and chaste hymns; but me the time
Divides from these things; whom do thou not less
Help and give honour, and to mine hounds good speed,
And edge to spears, and luck to each man's hand.

CHORUS

When the hounds of spring are on winter's traces,
   The mother of months in meadow or plain
Fills the shadows and windy places
   With lisp of leaves and ripple of rain;
And the brown bright nightingale amorous
Is half assuaged for Itylus,**   70
For the Thracian ships and the foreign faces,
   The tongueless vigil, and all the pain.

Come with bows bent and with emptying of quivers,
   Maiden most perfect, lady of light,
With a noise of winds and many rivers,
   With a clamour of waters, and with might;
Bind on thy sandals, O thou most fleet,
Over the splendour and speed of thy feet;
For the faint east quickens, the wan west shivers,
   Round the feet of the day and the feet of the night.   80

---

    * Hercules defeated the river god Acheloüs, who had taken the form
of a bull, and cut off one of his horns. Cf. l. 35, above.
    ** See note to "Itylus," p. 111.

Where shall we find her, how shall we sing to her,
    Fold our hands round her knees, and cling?
O that man's heart were as fire and could spring to her,
    Fire, or the strength of the streams that spring!
For the stars and the winds are unto her
As raiment, as songs of the harp-player;
For the risen stars and the fallen cling to her,
    And the southwest-wind and the west-wind sing.

For winter's rains and ruins are over,
    And all the season of snows and sins;   90
The days dividing lover and lover,
    The light that loses, the night that wins;
And time remembered is grief forgotten,
And frosts are slain and flowers begotten,
And in green underwood and cover
    Blossom by blossom the spring begins.

The full streams feed on flower of rushes,
    Ripe grasses trammel a travelling foot,
The faint fresh flame of the young year flushes
    From leaf to flower and flower to fruit;   100
And fruit and leaf are as gold and fire,
And the oat is heard above the lyre,
And the hoofèd heel of a satyr crushes
    The chestnut-husk at the chestnut-root.

And Pan by noon and Bacchus by night,
    Fleeter of foot than the fleet-foot kid,
Follows with dancing and fills with delight
    The Mænad and the Bassarid;*
And soft as lips that laugh and hide
The laughing leaves of the trees divide,   110
And screen from seeing and leave in sight
    The god pursuing, the maiden hid.

* Frenzied followers of Bacchus.

The ivy falls with the Bacchanal's hair
   Over her eyebrows hiding her eyes;
The wild vine slipping down leaves bare
   Her bright breast shortening into sighs;
The wild vine slips with the weight of its leaves,
But the berried ivy catches and cleaves
To the limbs that glitter, the feet that scare
   The wolf that follows, the fawn that flies.   120

ALTHÆA

What do ye singing? what is this ye sing?

CHORUS

Flowers bring we, and pure lips that please the gods,
And raiment meet for service: lest the day
Turn sharp with all its honey in our lips.

ALTHÆA

Night, a black hound, follows the white fawn day,
Swifter than dreams the white flown feet of sleep;
Will ye pray back the night with any prayers?
And though the spring put back a little while
Winter, and snows that plague all men for sin,
And the iron time of cursing, yet I know   130
Spring shall be ruined with the rain, and storm
Eat up like fire the ashen autumn days.
I marvel what men do with prayers awake
Who dream and die with dreaming; any god,
Yea the least god of all things called divine,
Is more than sleep and waking; yet we say,
Perchance by praying a man shall match his god.
For if sleep have no mercy, and man's dreams
Bite to the blood and burn into the bone,
What shall this man do waking? By the gods,   140
He shall not pray to dream sweet things to-night,
Having dreamt once more bitter things than death.

CHORUS

Queen, but what is it that hath burnt thine heart?
For thy speech flickers like a blown-out flame.

ALTHÆA

Look, ye say well, and know not what ye say;
For all my sleep is turned into a fire,
And all my dreams to stuff that kindles it.

CHORUS

Yet one doth well being patient of the gods.

ALTHÆA

Yea, lest they smite us with some four-foot plague.

CHORUS

But when time spreads find out some herb for it.   150

ALTHÆA

And with their healing herbs infect our blood.

CHORUS

What ails thee to be jealous of their ways?

ALTHÆA

What if they give us poisonous drinks for wine?

CHORUS

They have their will; much talking mends it not.

ALTHÆA

And gall for milk, and cursing for a prayer?

CHORUS

Have they not given life, and the end of life?

ALTHÆA

Lo, where they heal, they help not; thus they do,
They mock us with a little piteousness,
And we say prayers, and weep; but at the last,
Sparing awhile, they smite and spare no whit.   160

CHORUS

Small praise man gets dispraising the high gods:
What have they done that thou dishonourest them?

ALTHÆA

First Artemis for all this harried land
I praise not, and for wasting of the boar
That mars with tooth and tusk and fiery feet
Green pasturage and the grace of standing corn
And meadow and marsh with springs and unblown leaves,
Flocks and swift herds and all that bite sweet grass,
I praise her not; what things are these to praise?

CHORUS

But when the king did sacrifice, and gave   170
Each god fair dues of wheat and blood and wine,
Her not with bloodshed nor burnt-offering
Revered he, nor with salt or cloven cake;
Wherefore being wroth she plagued the land; but now
Takes off from us fate and her heavy things.
Which deed of these twain were not good to praise?
For a just deed looks always either way
With blameless eyes, and mercy is no fault.

ALTHÆA

Yea, but a curse she hath sent above all these
To hurt us where she healed us; and hath lit   180
Fire where the old fire went out, and where the wind
Slackened, hath blown on us with deadlier air.

CHORUS

What storm is this that tightens all our sail?

ALTHÆA

Love, a thwart sea-wind full of rain and foam.

CHORUS

Whence blown, and born under what stormier star?

ALTHÆA

Southward across Euenus from the sea.

CHORUS

Thy speech turns toward Arcadia like blown wind.

ALTHÆA

Sharp as the north sets when the snows are out.

CHORUS

Nay, for this maiden hath no touch of love.

ALTHÆA

I would she had sought in some cold gulf of sea   190
Love, or in dens where strange beasts lurk, or fire,
Or snows on the extreme hills, or iron land
Where no spring is; I would she had sought therein
And found, or ever love had found her here.

CHORUS

She is holier than all holy days or things,
The sprinkled water or fume of perfect fire;
Chaste, dedicated to pure prayers, and filled
With higher thoughts than heaven; a maiden clean,
Pure iron, fashioned for a sword; and man
She loves not; what should one such do with love?   200

ALTHÆA

Look, you, I speak not as one light of wit,
But as a queen speaks, being heart-vexed; for oft
I hear my brothers wrangling in mid hall,
And am not moved; and my son chiding them,
And these things nowise move me, but I know
Foolish and wise men must be to the end,
And feed myself with patience; but this most,
This moves me, that for wise men as for fools
Love is one thing, an evil thing, and turns
Choice words and wisdom into fire and air.   210
And in the end shall no joy come, but grief,
Sharp words and soul's division and fresh tears
Flower-wise upon the old root of tears brought forth,
Fruit-wise upon the old flower of tears sprung up,
Pitiful sighs, and much regrafted pain.
These things are in my presage, and myself
Am part of them and know not; but in dreams
The gods are heavy on me, and all the fates
Shed fire across my eyelids mixed with night,
And burn me blind, and disilluminate   220
My sense of seeing, and my perspicuous soul
Darken with vision; seeing I see not, hear
And hearing am not holpen, but mine eyes
Stain many tender broideries in the bed
Drawn up about my face that I may weep
And the king wake not; and my brows and lips
Tremble and sob in sleeping, like swift flames
That tremble, or water when it sobs with heat
Kindled from under; and my tears fill my breast
And speck the fair dyed pillows round the king   230
With barren showers and salter than the sea,
Such dreams divide me dreaming; for long since
I dreamed that out of this my womb had sprung
Fire and a firebrand; this was ere my son,
Meleager, a goodly flower in fields of fight,
Felt the light touch him coming forth, and wailed

Childlike; but yet he was not; and in time
I bare him, and my heart was great; for yet
So royally was never strong man born,
Nor queen so nobly bore as noble a thing   240
As this my son was: such a birth God sent
And such a grace to bear it. Then came in
Three weaving women, and span each a thread,
Saying This for strength and That for luck, and one
Saying Till the brand upon the hearth burn down,
So long shall this man see good days and live.
And I with gathered raiment from the bed
Sprang, and drew forth the brand, and cast on it
Water, and trod the flame bare-foot, and crushed
With naked hand spark beaten out of spark   250
And blew against and quenched it; for I said,
These are the most high Fates that dwell with us,
And we find favour a little in their sight,
A little, and more we miss of, and much time
Foils us; howbeit they have pitied me, O son,
And thee most piteous, thee a tenderer thing
Than any flower of fleshly seed alive.
Wherefore I kissed and hid him with my hands,
And covered under arms and hair, and wept,
And feared to touch him with my tears, and laughed;   260
So light a thing was this man, grown so great
Men cast their heads back, seeing against the sun
Blaze the armed man carven on his shield, and hear
The laughter of little bells along the brace
Ring, as birds singing or flutes blown, and watch,
High up, the cloven shadow of either plume
Divide the bright light of the brass, and make
His helmet as a windy and wintering moon
Seen through blown cloud and plume-like drift, when ships
Drive, and men strive with all the sea, and oars   270
Break, and the beaks dip under, drinking death;
Yet was he then but a span long, and moaned
With inarticulate mouth inseparate words,
And with blind lips and fingers wrung my breast

Hard, and thrust out with foolish hands and feet,
Murmuring; but those grey women with bound hair
Who fright the gods frighted not him; he laughed
Seeing them, and pushed out hands to feel and haul
Distaff and thread, intangible; but they
Passed, and I hid the brand, and in my heart   280
Laughed likewise, having all my will of heaven.
But now I know not if to left or right
The gods have drawn us hither; for again
I dreamt, and saw the black brand burst on fire
As a branch bursts in flower, and saw the flame
Fade flower-wise, and Death came and with dry lips
Blew the charred ash into my breast; and Love
Trampled the ember and crushed it with swift feet.
This I have also at heart; that not for me,
Not for me only or son of mine, O girls,   290
The gods have wrought life, and desire of life,
Heart's love and heart's division; but for all
There shines one sun and one wind blows till night.
And when night comes the wind sinks and the sun,
And there is no light after, and no storm,
But sleep and much forgetfulness of things.
In such wise I gat knowledge of the gods
Years hence, and heard high sayings of one most wise,
Eurythemis my mother, who beheld
With eyes alive and spake with lips of these   300
As one on earth disfleshed and disallied
From breath or blood corruptible; such gifts
Time gave her, and an equal soul to these
And equal face to all things; thus she said.
But whatsoever intolerable or glad
The swift hours weave and unweave, I go hence
Full of mine own soul, perfect of myself,
Toward mine and me sufficient; and what chance
The gods cast lots for and shake out on us,
That shall we take, and that much bear withal.   310
And now, before these gather to the hunt,

I will go arm my son and bring him forth,
Lest love or some man's anger work him harm.

CHORUS

Before the beginning of years
   There came to the making of man
Time, with a gift of tears;
   Grief, with a glass that ran;
Pleasure, with pain for leaven;
   Summer, with flowers that fell;
Remembrance fallen from heaven, 320
   And madness risen from hell;
Strength without hands to smite;
   Love that endures for a breath:
Night, the shadow of light,
   And life, the shadow of death.
And the high gods took in hand
   Fire, and the falling of tears,
And a measure of sliding sand
   From under the feet of the years;
And froth and drift of the sea; 330
   And dust of the labouring earth;
And bodies of things to be
   In the houses of death and of birth;
And wrought with weeping and laughter,
   And fashioned with loathing and love,
With life before and after
   And death beneath and above,
For a day and a night and a morrow,
   That his strength might endure for a span
With travail and heavy sorrow, 340
   The holy spirit of man.

From the winds of the north and the south
   They gathered as unto strife;
They breathed upon his mouth,
   They filled his body with life;

Eyesight and speech they wrought
   For the veils of the soul therein,
A time for labour and thought,
   A time to serve and to sin;*
They gave him light in his ways,   350
   And love, and a space for delight,
And beauty and length of days,
   And night, and sleep in the night.
His speech is a burning fire;
   With his lips he travaileth;
In his heart is a blind desire,
   In his eyes foreknowledge of death;
He weaves, and is clothed with derision;
   Sows, and he shall not reap;
His life is a watch or a vision   360
   Between a sleep and a sleep.

MELEAGER

O sweet new heaven and air without a star,
Fair day, be fair and welcome, as to men
With deeds to do and praise to pluck from thee.
Come forth a child, born with clear sound and light,
With laughter and swift limbs and prosperous looks;
That this great hunt with heroes for the hounds
May leave thee memorable and us well sped.

ALTHÆA

Son, first I praise thy prayer, then bid thee speed;
But the gods hear men's hands before their lips,   370
And heed beyond all crying and sacrifice
Light of things done and noise of labouring men.
But thou, being armed and perfect for the deed,
Abide; for like rain-flakes in a wind they grow,
The men thy fellows, and the choice of the world,

---

   * Cf. *Ecclesiastes* 3:1–4: "To every thing there is a season. . . . A time to weep and a time to laugh; a time to mourn and a time to dance." The whole chorus recreates the rich, fatalistic despair of *Ecclesiastes*.

Bound to root out the tuskèd plague, and leave
Thanks and safe days and peace in Calydon.

MELEAGER

For the whole city and all the low-lying land
Flames, and the soft air sounds with them that come;
The gods give all these fruit of all their works.   380

ALTHÆA

Set thine eye thither and fix thy spirit and say
Whom there thou knowest; for sharp mixed shadow and
     wind
Blown up between the morning and the mist,
With steam of steeds and flash of bridle or wheel,
And fire, and parcels of the broken dawn,
And dust divided by hard light, and spears
That shine and shift as the edge of wild beasts' eyes,
Smite upon mine; so fiery their blind edge
Burns, and bright points break up and baffle day.

MELEAGER

The first, for many I know not, being far off,   390
Peleus and Larissæan, couched with whom
Sleeps the white sea-bred wife and silver-shod,
Fair as fled foam, a goddess; and their son
Most swift and splendid of men's children born,
Most like a god, full of the future fame.

ALTHÆA

Who are these shining like one sundered star?

MELEAGER

Thy sister's sons, a double flower of men.

ALTHÆA

O sweetest kin to me in all the world,
O twin-born blood of Leda, gracious heads
Like kindled lights in untempestuous heaven,   400

Fair flower-like stars on the iron foam of fight,
With what glad heart and kindliness of soul,
Even to the staining of both eyes with tears
And kindling of warm eyelids with desire,
A great way off I greet you, and rejoice
Seeing you so fair, and moulded like as gods.
Far off ye come, and least in years of these,
But lordliest, but worth love to look upon.

MELEAGER

Even such (for sailing hither I saw far hence,
And where Eurotas hollows his moist rock   410
Nigh Sparta with a strenuous-hearted stream)
Even such I saw their sisters; one swan-white,
The little Helen, and less fair than she
Fair Clytæmnestra, grave as pasturing fawns
Who feed and fear some arrow; but at whiles,
As one smitten with love or wrung with joy,
She laughs and lightens with her eyes, and then
Weeps; whereat Helen, having laughed, weeps too,
And the other chides her, and she being chid speaks
    nought,
But cheeks and lips and eyelids kisses her,   420
Laughing; so fare they, as in their bloomless bud
And full of unblown life, the blood of gods.

ALTHÆA

Sweet days befall them and good loves and lords,
And tender and temperate honours of the hearth,
Peace, and a perfect life and blameless bed.
But who shows next an eagle wrought in gold,
That flames and beats broad wings against the sun
And with void mouth gapes after emptier prey?

MELEAGER

Know by that sign the reign of Telamon
Between the fierce mouths of the encountering brine   430
On the strait reefs of twice-washed Salamis.

ALTHÆA

For like one great of hand he bears himself,
Vine-chapleted, with savours of the sea,
Glittering as wine and moving as a wave.
But who girt round there roughly follows him?

MELEAGER

Ancæus, great of hand, an iron bulk,
Two-edged for fight as the axe against his arm,
Who drives against the surge of stormy spears
Full-sailed; him Cepheus follows, his twin-born,
Chief name next his of all Arcadian men.   440

ALTHÆA

Praise be with men abroad; chaste lives with us,
Home-keeping days and household reverences.

MELEAGER

Next by the left unsandalled foot know thou
The sail and oar of this Ætolian land,
Thy brethren, Toxeus and the violent-souled
Plexippus, over-swift with hand and tongue;
For hands are fruitful, but the ignorant mouth
Blows and corrupts their work with barren breath.

ALTHÆA

Speech too bears fruit, being worthy; and air blows down
Things poisonous, and high-seated violences,   450
And with charmed words and songs have men put out
Wild evil, and the fire of tyrannies.

MELEAGER

Yea, all things have they, save the gods and love.

ALTHÆA

Love thou the law and cleave to things ordained.

MELEAGER

Law lives upon their lips whom these applaud.

ALTHÆA

How sayest thou these? what god applauds new things?

MELEAGER

Zeus, who hath fear and custom under foot.

ALTHÆA

But loves not laws thrown down and lives awry.

MELEAGER

Yet is not less himself than his own law.

ALTHÆA

Nor shifts and shuffles old things up and down.   460

MELEAGER

But what he will remoulds and discreates.

ALTHÆA

Much, but not this, that each thing live its life.

MELEAGER

Nor only live, but lighten and lift up higher.

ALTHÆA

Pride breaks itself, and too much gained is gone.

MELEAGER

Things gained are gone, but great things done endure.

ALTHÆA

Child, if a man serve law through all his life
And with his whole heart worship, him all gods
Praise; but who loves it only with his lips,

And not in heart and deed desiring it
Hides a perverse will with obsequious words, 470
Him heaven infatuates and his twin-born fate
Tracks, and gains on him, scenting sins far off,
And the swift hounds of violent death devour.
Be man at one with equal-minded gods,
So shall he prosper; not through laws torn up,
Violated rule and a new face of things.
A woman armed makes war upon herself,
Unwomanlike, and treads down use and wont
And the sweet common honour that she hath,
Love, and the cry of children, and the hand 480
Trothplight and mutual mouth of marriages.
This doth she, being unloved; whom if one love,
Not fire nor iron and the wide-mouthed wars
Are deadlier than her lips or braided hair.
For of the one comes poison, and a curse
Falls from the other and burns the lives of men.
But thou, son, be not filled with evil dreams,
Nor with desire of these things; for with time
Blind love burns out; but if one feed it full
Till some discolouring stain dyes all his life, 490
He shall keep nothing praiseworthy, nor die
The sweet wise death of old men honourable,
Who have lived out all the length of all their years
Blameless, and seen well-pleased the face of gods,
And without shame and without fear have wrought
Things memorable, and while their days held out
In sight of all men and the sun's great light
Have gat them glory and given of their own praise
To the earth that bare them and the day that bred,
Home friends and far-off hospitalities, 500
And filled with gracious and memorial fame
Lands loved of summer or washed by violent seas,
Towns populous and many unfooted ways,
And alien lips and native with their own.
But when white age and venerable death
Mow down the strength and life within their limbs,

Drain out the blood and darken their clear eyes,
Immortal honour is on them, having past
Through splendid life and death desirable
To the clear seat and remote throne of souls,　　510
Lands indiscoverable in the unheard-of west,
Round which the strong stream of a sacred sea
Rolls without wind for ever, and the snow
There shows not her white wings and windy feet,
Nor thunder nor swift rain saith anything,
Nor the sun burns, but all things rest and thrive;
And these, filled full of days, divine and dead,
Sages and singers fiery from the god,
And such as loved their land and all things good
And, best beloved of best men, liberty,　　520
Free lives and lips, free hands of men free-born,
And whatsoever on earth was honourable
And whosoever of all the ephemeral seed,
Live there a life no liker to the gods
But nearer than their life of terrene days.
Love thou such life and look for such a death.
But from the light and fiery dreams of love
Spring heavy sorrows and a sleepless life,
Visions not dreams, whose lids no charm shall close
Nor song assuage them waking; and swift death　　530
Crushes with sterile feet the unripening ear,
Treads out the timeless vintage; whom do thou
Eschewing embrace the luck of this thy life,
Not without honour; and it shall bear to thee
Such fruit as men reap from spent hours and wear,
Few men, but happy; of whom be thou, O son,
Happiest, if thou submit thy soul to fate,
And set thine eyes and heart on hopes high-born
And divine deeds and abstinence divine.
So shalt thou be toward all men all thy days　　540
As light and might communicable, and burn
From heaven among the stars above the hours,
And break not as a man breaks nor burn down:
For to whom other of all heroic names

Have the gods given his life in hand as thine?
And gloriously hast thou lived, and made thy life
To me that bare thee and to all men born
Thankworthy, a praise for ever; and hast won fame
When wild wars broke all round thy father's house,
And the mad people of windy mountain ways   550
Laid spears against us like a sea, and all
Ætolia thundered with Thessalian hoofs;
Yet these, as wind baffles the foam, and beats
Straight back the relaxed ripple, didst thou break
And loosen all their lances, till undone
And man from man they fell; for ye twain stood
God against god, Ares and Artemis,
And thou the mightier; wherefore she unleashed
A sharp-toothed curse thou too shalt overcome;
For in the greener blossom of thy life   560
Ere the full blade caught flower, and when time gave
Respite, thou didst not slacken soul nor sleep,
But with great hand and heart seek praise of men
Out of sharp straits and many a grievous thing,
Seeing the strange foam of undivided seas
On channels never sailed in, and by shores
Where the old winds cease not blowing, and all the night
Thunders, and day is no delight to men.

CHORUS

Meleager, a noble wisdom and fair words
The gods have given this woman; hear thou these.   570

MELEAGER

O mother, I am not fain to strive in speech
Nor set my mouth against thee, who art wise
Even as they say and full of sacred words.
But one thing I know surely, and cleave to this;
That though I be not subtle of wit as thou
Nor womanlike to weave sweet words, and melt
Mutable minds of wise men as with fire,
I too, doing justly and reverencing the gods,

Shall not want wit to see what things be right.
For whom they love and whom reject, being gods,　　580
There is no man but seeth, and in good time
Submits himself, refraining all his heart.
And I too as thou sayest have seen great things;
Seen otherwhere, but chiefly when the sail
First caught between stretched ropes the roaring west,
And all our oars smote eastward, and the wind
First flung round faces of seafaring men
White splendid snow-flakes of the sundering foam,
And the first furrow in virginal green sea
Followed the plunging ploughshare of hewn pine,　　590
And closed, as when deep sleep subdues man's breath
Lips close and heart subsides; and closing, shone
Sunlike with many a Nereid's hair, and moved
Round many a trembling mouth of doubtful gods,
Risen out of sunless and sonorous gulfs
Through waning water and into shallow light,
That watched us; and when flying the dove was snared
As with men's hands, but we shot after and sped
Clear through the irremeable Symplegades;*
And chiefliest when hoar beach and herbless cliff　　600
Stood out ahead from Colchis, and we heard
Clefts hoarse with wind, and saw through narrowing reefs
The lightning of the intolerable wave
Flash, and the white wet flame of breakers burn
Far under a kindling south-wind, as a lamp
Burns and bends all its blowing flame one way;
Wild heights untravelled of the wind, and vales
Cloven seaward by their violent streams, and white
With bitter flowers and bright salt scurf of brine;
Heard sweep their sharp swift gales, and bowing birdwise　610
Shriek with birds' voices, and with furious feet
Tread loose the long skirts of a storm; and saw

---

*Irremeable: admitting of no return. Symplegades: two great,
floating rocks that perpetually clashed against each other. Jason, after
releasing a dove that flew ahead of his ship, passed between the Symplegades on his quest for the Golden Fleece.

The whole white Euxine clash together and fall
Full-mouthed, and thunderous from a thousand throats:
Yet we drew thither and won the fleece and won
Medea, deadlier than the sea; but there
Seeing many a wonder and fearful things to men
I saw not one thing like this one seen here,
Most fair and fearful, feminine, a god,
Faultless; whom I that love not, being unlike,   620
Fear, and give honour, and choose from all the gods.

ŒNEUS

Lady, the daughter of Thestius, and thou, son,
Not ignorant of your strife nor light of wit,
Scared with vain dreams and fluttering like spent fire,
I come to judge between you, but a king
Full of past days and wise from years endured.
Nor thee I praise, who art fain to undo things done:
Nor thee, who art swift to esteem them overmuch.
For what the hours have given is given, and this
Changeless; howbeit these change, and in good time   630
Devise new things and good, not one thing still.
Us have they sent now at our need for help
Among men armed a woman, foreign born,
Virgin, not like the natural flower of things
That grows and bears and brings forth fruit and dies;
Unlovable, no light for a husband's house,
Espoused; a glory among unwedded girls,
And chosen of gods who reverence maidenhood.
These too we honour in honouring her; but thou,
Abstain thy feet from following, and thine eyes   640
From amorous touch; nor set toward hers thine heart,
Son, lest hate bear no deadlier fruit than love.

ALTHÆA

O king, thou art wise, but wisdom halts; and just,
But the gods love not justice more than fate,
And smite the righteous and the violent mouth,
And mix with insolent blood the reverent man's,

And bruise the holier as the lying lips.
Enough; for wise words fail me, and my heart
Takes fire and trembles flamewise, O my son,
O child, for thine head's sake; mine eyes wax thick,   650
Turning toward thee, so goodly a weaponed man,
So glorious; and for love of thine own eyes
They are darkened, and tears burn them, fierce as fire,
And my lips pause and my soul sinks with love.
But by thine hand, by thy sweet life and eyes,
By thy great heart and these clasped knees, O son,
I pray thee that thou slay me not with thee.
For there was never a mother woman-born
Loved her sons better; and never a queen of men
More perfect in her heart toward whom she loved.   660
For what lies light on many and they forget,
Small things and transitory as a wind o' the sea,
I forget never; I have seen thee all thine years
A man in arms, strong and a joy to men
Seeing thine head glitter and thine hand burn its way
Through a heavy and iron furrow of sundering spears;
But always also a flower of three suns old,
The small one thing that lying drew down my life
To lie with thee and feed thee; a child and weak,
Mine, a delight to no man, sweet to me.   670
Who then sought to thee? who gat help? who knew
If thou wert goodly? nay, no man at all.
Or what sea saw thee, or sounded with thine oar,
Child? or what strange land shone with war through thee?
But fair for me thou wert, O little life,
Fruitless, the fruit of mine own flesh, and blind,
More than much gold, ungrown, a foolish flower.
For silver nor bright snow nor feather of foam
Was whiter, and no gold yellower than thine hair,
O child, my child; and now thou art lordlier grown,   680
Not lovelier, nor a new thing in mine eyes,
I charge thee by thy soul and this my breast,
Fear thou the gods and me and thine own heart,
Lest all these turn against thee; for who knows

What wind upon what wave of altering time
Shall speak a storm and blow calamity?
And there is nothing stabile in the world
But the gods break it; yet not less, fair son,
If but one thing be stronger, if one endure,
Surely the bitter and the rooted love   690
That burns between us, going from me to thee,
Shall more endure than all things. What dost thou,
Following strange loves? why wilt thou kill mine heart?
Lo, I talk wild and windy words, and fall
From my clear wits, and seem of mine own self
Dethroned, dispraised, disseated; and my mind,
That was my crown, breaks, and mine heart is gone,
And I am naked of my soul, and stand
Ashamed, as a mean woman; take thou thought:
Live if thou wilt, and if thou wilt not, look,   700
The gods have given thee life to lose or keep,
Thou shalt not die as men die, but thine end
Fallen upon thee shall break me unaware.

MELEAGER

Queen, my whole heart is molten with thy tears,
And my limbs yearn with pity of thee, and love
Compels with grief mine eyes and labouring breath;
For what thou art I know thee, and this thy breast
And thy fair eyes I worship, and am bound
Toward thee in spirit and love thee in all my soul.
For there is nothing terribler to men   710
Than the sweet face of mothers, and the might.
But what shall be let be; for us the day
Once only lives a little, and is not found.
Time and the fruitful hour are more than we,
And these lay hold upon us; but thou, God,
Zeus, the sole steersman of the helm of things,
Father, be swift to see us, and as thou wilt
Help: or if adverse, as thou wilt, refrain.

CHORUS

We have seen thee, O Love, thou art fair; thou art goodly,
        O Love;
Thy wings make light in the air as the wings of a dove.*   720
Thy feet are as winds that divide the stream of the sea;
Earth is thy covering to hide thee, the garment of thee.
Thou art swift and subtle and blind as a flame of fire;
Before thee the laughter, behind thee the tears of desire;
And twain go forth beside thee, a man with a maid;
Her eyes are the eyes of a bride whom delight makes afraid;
As the breath in the buds that stir is her bridal breath:
But Fate is the name of her; and his name is Death.

For an evil blossom was born
    Of sea-foam and the frothing of blood,   730
        Blood-red and bitter of fruit,
            And the seed of it laughter and tears,
    And the leaves of it madness and scorn;
        A bitter flower from the bud,
            Sprung of the sea without root,
                Sprung without graft from the years.

The weft of the world was untorn
    That is woven of the day on the night,
    The hair of the hours was not white
Nor the raiment of time overworn,   740
    When a wonder, a world's delight,
A perilous goddess was born;
    And the waves of the sea as she came
Clove, and the foam at her feet,
        Fawning, rejoiced to bring forth
        A fleshly blossom, a flame
Filling the heavens with heat
        To the cold white ends of the north.

* In this chorus describing the birth of Aphrodite, Swinburne
alludes, with a certain perverse appropriateness, to *The Song of Solomon:*
"Behold, thou art fair, my love; behold, thou art fair; thou hast doves'
eyes within thy locks (4:1)."

And in air the clamorous birds,
   And men upon earth that hear   750
Sweet articulate words
     Sweetly divided apart,
   And in shallow and channel and mere
The rapid and footless herds,
     Rejoiced, being foolish of heart.

For all they said upon earth,
   She is fair, she is white like a dove,
     And the life of the world in her breath
Breathes, and is born at her birth;
   For they knew thee for mother of love,   760
     And knew thee not mother of death.

What hadst thou to do being born,
   Mother, when winds were at ease,
As a flower of the springtime of corn,
   A flower of the foam of the seas?
For bitter thou wast from thy birth,
   Aphrodite, a mother of strife;
For before thee some rest was on earth,
     A little respite from tears,
   A little pleasure of life;   770
For life was not then as thou art,
     But as one that waxeth in years
Sweet-spoken, a fruitful wife;
     Earth had no thorn, and desire
No sting, neither death any dart;
   What hadst thou to do amongst these,
     Thou, clothed with a burning fire,
Thou, girt with sorrow of heart,
   Thou, sprung of the seed of the seas
As an ear from a seed of corn,   780
     As a brand plucked forth of a pyre,
As a ray shed forth of the morn,
   For division of soul and disease,

For a dart and a sting and a thorn?
What ailed thee then to be born?

Was there not evil enough,
   Mother, and anguish on earth
   Born with a man at his birth,
Wastes underfoot, and above
   Storm out of heaven, and dearth   790
Shaken down from the shining thereof,
     Wrecks from afar overseas
   And peril of shallow and firth,
     And tears that spring and increase
   In the barren places of mirth,
That thou, having wings as a dove,
   Being girt with desire for a girth,
     That thou must come after these,
That thou must lay on him love?

Thou shouldst not so have been born: 800
   But death should have risen with thee,
   Mother, and visible fear,
     Grief, and the wringing of hands,
And noise of many that mourn;
   The smitten bosom, the knee
   Bowed, and in each man's ear
     A cry as of perishing lands,
A moan as of people in prison,
   A tumult of infinite griefs;
     And thunder of storm on the sands,   810
     And wailing of wives on the shore;
And under thee newly arisen
   Loud shoals and shipwrecking reefs,
     Fierce air and violent light;
     Sail rent and sundering oar,
     Darkness, and noises of night;
Clashing of streams in the sea,
   Wave against wave as a sword,

Clamour of currents, and foam;
Rains making ruin on earth, 820
Winds that wax ravenous and roam
As wolves in a wolfish horde;
Fruits growing faint in the tree,
And blind things dead in their birth;
Famine, and blighting of corn,
When thy time was come to be born.

All these we know of; but thee
Who shall discern or declare?
In the uttermost ends of the sea
The light of thine eyelids and hair, 830
The light of thy bosom as fire
Between the wheel of the sun
And the flying flames of the air?
Wilt thou turn thee not yet nor have pity,
But abide with despair and desire
And the crying of armies undone,
Lamentation of one with another
And breaking of city by city;
The dividing of friend against friend,
The severing of brother and brother; 840
Wilt thou utterly bring to an end?
Have mercy, mother!

For against all men from of old
Thou hast set thine hand as a curse,
And cast out gods from their places.
These things are spoken of thee.
Strong kings and goodly with gold
Thou hast found out arrows to pierce,
And made their kingdoms and races
As dust and surf of the sea. 850
All these, overburdened with woes
And with length of their days waxen weak,
Thou slewest; and sentest moreover

Upon Tyro an evil thing,*
Rent hair and a fetter and blows
    Making bloody the flower of the cheek,
        Though she lay by a god as a lover,
            Though fair, and the seed of a king.
For of old, being full of thy fire,
    She endured not longer to wear   860
        On her bosom a saffron vest,
            On her shoulder an ashwood quiver;
Being mixed and made one through desire
    With Enipeus, and all her hair
        Made moist with his mouth, and her breast
            Filled full of the foam of the river.

ATALANTA

Sun, and clear light among green hills, and day
Late risen and long sought after, and you just gods
Whose hands divide anguish and recompense,
But first the sun's white sister, a maid in heaven,   870
On earth of all maids worshipped—hail, and hear,
And witness with me if not without sign sent,
Not without rule and reverence, I a maid
Hallowed, and huntress holy as whom I serve,
Here in your sight and eyeshot of these men
Stand, girt as they toward hunting, and my shafts
Drawn; wherefore all ye stand up on my side,
If I be pure and all ye righteous gods,
Lest one revile me, a woman, yet no wife,
That bear a spear for spindle, and this bow strung   880
For a web woven; and with pure lips salute
Heaven, and the face of all the gods, and dawn
Filling with maiden flames and maiden flowers
The starless fold o' the stars, and making sweet
The warm wan heights of the air, moon-trodden ways
And breathless gates and extreme hills of heaven.

* Tyro was seduced by Poseidon in the form of the river–god
Enipeus, with whom she had fallen in love; afterwards she was cruelly
mistreated.

Whom, having offered water and bloodless gifts,
Flowers, and a golden circlet of pure hair,
Next Artemis I bid be favourable
And make this day all golden, hers and ours,   890
Gracious and good and white to the unblamed end.
But thou, O well-beloved, of all my days
Bid it be fruitful, and a crown for all,
To bring forth leaves and bind round all my hair
With perfect chaplets woven for thine of thee.
For not without the word of thy chaste mouth,
For not without law given and clean command,
Across the white straits of the running sea
From Elis even to the Acheloïan horn,
I with clear winds came hither and gentle gods,   900
Far off my father's house, and left uncheered
Iasius, and uncheered the Arcadian hills
And all their green-haired waters, and all woods
Disconsolate, to hear no horn of mine
Blown, and behold no flash of swift white feet.

MELEAGER

For thy name's sake and awe toward thy chaste head,
O holiest Atalanta, no man dares
Praise thee, though fairer than whom all men praise,
And godlike for thy grace of hallowed hair
And holy habit of thine eyes, and feet   910
That make the blown foam neither swift nor white
Though the wind winnow and whirl it; yet we praise
Gods, found because of thee adorable
And for thy sake praiseworthiest from all men:
Thee therefore we praise also, thee as these,
Pure, and a light lit at the hands of gods.

TOXEUS

How long will ye whet spears with eloquence,
Fight, and kill beasts dry-handed with sweet words?
Cease, or talk still and slay thy boars at home.

PLEXIPPUS

Why, if she ride among us for a man,   920
Sit thou for her and spin; a man grown girl
Is worth a woman weaponed; sit thou here.

MELEAGER

Peace, and be wise; no gods love idle speech.

PLEXIPPUS

Nor any man a man's mouth woman-tongued.

MELEAGER

For my lips bite not sharper than mine hands.

PLEXIPPUS

Nay, both bite soft, but no whit softly mine.

MELEAGER

Keep thine hands clean; they have time enough to stain.

PLEXIPPUS

For thine shall rest and wax not red to-day.

MELEAGER

Have all thy will of words; talk out thine heart.

ALTHÆA

Refrain your lips, O brethren, and my son,   930
Lest words turn snakes and bite you uttering them.

TOXEUS

Except she give her blood before the gods
What profit shall a maid be among men?

PLEXIPPUS

Let her come crowned and stretch her throat for a knife,
Bleat out her spirit and die, and so shall men

Through her too prosper and through prosperous gods,
But nowise through her living; shall she live
A flower-bud of the flower-bed, or sweet fruit
For kisses and the honey-making mouth,
And play the shield for strong men and the spear?   940
Then shall the heifer and her mate lock horns,
And the bride overbear the groom, and men
God; for no less division sunders these;
Since all things made are seasonable in time,
But if one alter unseasonable are all.
But thou, O Zeus, hear me that I may slay
This beast before thee and no man halve with me
Nor woman, lest these mock thee, though a god,
Who hast made men strong, and thou being wise be held
Foolish; for wise is that thing which endures.   950

ATALANTA

Men, and the chosen of all this people, and thou,
King, I beseech you a little bear with me.
For if my life be shameful that I live,
Let the gods witness and their wrath; but these
Cast no such word against me. Thou, O mine,
O holy, O happy goddess, if I sin
Changing the words of women and the works
For spears and strange men's faces, hast not thou
One shaft of all thy sudden seven that pierced
Seven through the bosom or shining throat or side,*   960
All couched about one mother's loosening knees,
All holy born, engraffed of Tantalus?
But if toward any of you I am overbold
That take thus much upon me, let him think
How I, for all my forest holiness,
Fame, and this armed and iron maidenhood,
Pay thus much also; I shall have no man's love
For ever, and no face of children born

* The children of Niobe, daughter of Tantalus, were slain, seven by
the spears of Artemis and seven by Apollo, when Niobe boasted of them
to Leto, mother of Artemis and Apollo.

Or feeding lips upon me or fastening eyes
For ever, nor being dead shall kings my sons   970
Mourn me and bury, and tears on daughters' cheeks
Burn; but a cold and sacred life, but strange,
But far from dances and the back-blowing torch,
Far off from flowers or any bed of man,
Shall my life be for ever: me the snows
That face the first o' the morning, and cold hills
Full of the land-wind and sea-travelling storms
And many a wandering wing of noisy nights
That know the thunder and hear the thickening wolves—
Me the utmost pine and footless frost of woods   980
That talk with many winds and gods, the hours
Re-risen, and white divisions of the dawn,
Springs thousand-tongued with the intermitting reed
And streams that murmur of the mother snow—
Me these allure, and know me; but no man
Knows, and my goddess only. Lo now, see
If one of all you these things vex at all.
Would God that any of you had all the praise
And I no manner of memory when I die,
So might I show before her perfect eyes   990
Pure, whom I follow, a maiden to my death.
But for the rest let all have all they will;
For is it a grief to you that I have part,
Being woman merely, in your male might and deeds
Done by main strength? yet in my body is throned
As great a heart, and in my spirit, O men,
I have not less of godlike. Evil it were
That one a coward should mix with you, one hand
Fearful, one eye abase itself; and these
Well might ye hate and well revile, not me.   1000
For not the difference of the several flesh
Being vile or noble or beautiful or base
Makes praiseworthy, but purer spirit and heart
Higher than these meaner mouths and limbs, that feed,
Rise, rest, and are and are not; and for me,
What should I say? but by the gods of the world

And this my maiden body, by all oaths
That bind the tongue of men and the evil will,
I am not mighty-minded, nor desire
Crowns, nor the spoil of slain things nor the fame;   1010
Feed ye on these, eat and wax fat; cry out,
Laugh, having eaten, and leap without a lyre,
Sing, mix the wind with clamour, smite and shake
Sonorous timbrels and tumultuous hair,
And fill the dance up with tempestuous feet,
For I will none; but having prayed my prayers
And made thank-offering for prosperities,
I shall go hence and no man see me more.
What thing is this for you to shout me down,
What, for a man to grudge me this my life   1020
As it were envious of all yours, and I
A thief of reputations? nay, for now,
If there be any highest in heaven, a god
Above all thrones and thunders of the gods
Throned, and the wheel of the world roll under him,
Judge he between me and all of you, and see
If I transgress at all: but ye, refrain
Transgressing hands and reinless mouths, and keep
Silence, lest by much foam of violent words
And proper poison of your lips ye die.   1030

ŒNEUS

O flower of Tegea, maiden, fleetest foot
And holiest head of women, have good cheer
Of thy good words: but ye, depart with her
In peace and reverence, each with blameless eye
Following his fate; exalt your hands and hearts,
Strike, cease not, arrow on arrow and wound on wound,
And go with gods and with the gods return.

CHORUS

Who hath given man speech? or who hath set therein
A thorn for peril and a snare for sin?
For in the word his life is and his breath,   1040

And in the word his death,
That madness and the infatuate heart may breed
  From the word's womb the deed
And life bring one thing forth ere all pass by,
Even one thing which is ours yet cannot die—
Death. Hast thou seen him ever anywhere,
Time's twin-born brother, imperishable as he
Is perishable and plaintive, clothed with care
  And mutable as sand,
But death is strong and full of blood and fair   1050
And perdurable and like a lord of land?
Nay, time thou seest not, death thou wilt not see
Till life's right hand be loosened from thine hand
  And thy life-days from thee.
For the gods very subtly fashion
  Madness with sadness upon earth:
Not knowing in any wise compassion,
  Nor holding pity of any worth;
And many things they have given and taken,
  And wrought and ruined many things;   1060
The firm land have they loosed and shaken,
  And sealed the sea with all her springs;
They have wearied time with heavy burdens
  And vexed the lips of life with breath:
Set men to labour and given them guerdons,
  Death, and great darkness after death:
Put moans into the bridal measure
  And on the bridal wools a stain;
And circled pain about with pleasure,
  And girdled pleasure about with pain;   1070
And strewed one marriage-bed with tears and fire
For extreme loathing and supreme desire.

What shall be done with all these tears of ours?
  Shall they make watersprings in the fair heaven
To bathe the brows of morning? or like flowers
Be shed and shine before the starriest hours,
  Or made the raiment of the weeping Seven?

Or rather, O our masters, shall they be
Food for the famine of the grievous sea,
   A great well-head of lamentation   1080
Satiating the sad gods? or fall and flow
Among the years and seasons to and fro,
   And wash their feet with tribulation
And fill them full with grieving ere they go?
   Alas, our lords, and yet alas again,
Seeing all your iron heaven is gilt as gold
   But all we smite thereat in vain;
Smite the gates barred with groanings manifold,
   But all the floors are paven with our pain.
Yea, and with weariness of lips and eyes,   1090
With breaking of the bosom, and with sighs,
   We labour, and are clad and fed with grief
And filled with days we would not fain behold
And nights we would not hear of; we wax old,
   All we wax old and wither like a leaf.
We are outcast, strayed between bright sun and moon;
   Our light and darkness are as leaves of flowers,
Black flowers and white, that perish; and the noon
   As midnight, and the night as daylight hours.
   A little fruit a little while is ours,   1100
      And the worm finds it soon.

But up in heaven the high gods one by one
   Lay hands upon the draught that quickeneth,
Fulfilled with all tears shed and all things done,
   And stir with soft imperishable breath
   The bubbling bitterness of life and death,
And hold it to our lips and laugh; but they
Preserve their lips from tasting night or day,
   Lest they too change and sleep, the fates that spun,
The lips that made us and the hands that slay;   1110
   Lest all these change, and heaven bow down to none,
Change and be subject to the secular sway
   And terrene revolution of the sun.
Therefore they thrust it from them, putting time away.

I would the wine of time, made sharp and sweet
   With multitudinous days and nights and tears
   And many mixing savours of strange years,
Were no more trodden of them under feet,
   Cast out and spilt about their holy places:
That life were given them as a fruit to eat   1120
And death to drink as water; that the light
Might ebb, drawn backward from their eyes, and night
   Hide for one hour the imperishable faces.
That they might rise up sad in heaven, and know
Sorrow and sleep, one paler than young snow,
   One cold as blight of dew and ruinous rain;
Rise up and rest and suffer a little, and be
Awhile as all things born with us and we,
   And grieve as men, and like slain men be slain.

For now we know not of them; but one saith   1130
   The gods are gracious, praising God; and one,
When hast thou seen? or hast thou felt his breath
   Touch, nor consume thine eyelids as the sun,
Nor fill thee to the lips with fiery death?
   None hath beheld him, none
Seen above other gods and shapes of things,
Swift without feet and flying without wings,
Intolerable, not clad with death or life,
   Insatiable, not known of night or day,
The lord of love and loathing and of strife   1140
   Who gives a star and takes a sun away;
Who shapes the soul, and makes her a barren wife
   To the earthly body and grievous growth of clay;
Who turns the large limbs to a little flame
   And binds the great sea with a little sand;
Who makes desire, and slays desire with shame;
   Who shakes the heaven as ashes in his hand;
Who, seeing the light and shadow for the same,
   Bids day waste night as fire devours a brand,
Smites without sword, and scourges without rod;   1150
   The supreme evil, God.

Yea, with thine hate, O God, thou hast covered us,
  One saith, and hidden our eyes away from sight,
And made us transitory and hazardous,
  Light things and slight;
Yet have men praised thee, saying, He hath made man thus,
  And he doeth right.
Thou hast kissed us, and hast smitten; thou hast laid
Upon us with thy left hand life, and said,
Live: and again thou hast said, Yield up your breath,   1160
And with thy right hand laid upon us death.
Thou hast sent us sleep, and stricken sleep with dreams,
  Saying, Joy is not, but love of joy shall be;
Thou hast made sweet springs for all the pleasant streams,
  In the end thou hast made them bitter with the sea.
Thou hast fed one rose with dust of many men;
  Thou hast marred one face with fire of many tears;
Thou hast taken love, and given us sorrow again;
  With pain thou hast filled us full to the eyes and ears.
Therefore because thou art strong, our father, and we   1170
  Feeble; and thou art against us, and thine hand
Constrains us in the shallows of the sea
  And breaks us at the limits of the land;
Because thou hast bent thy lightnings as a bow,
  And loosed the hours like arrows; and let fall
Sins and wild words and many a wingèd woe
  And wars among us, and one end of all;
Because thou hast made the thunder, and thy feet
  Are as a rushing water when the skies
Break, but thy face as an exceeding heat   1180
  And flames of fire the eyelids of thine eyes;
Because thou art over all who are over us;
  Because thy name is life and our name death;
Because thou art cruel and men are piteous,
  And our hands labour and thine hand scattereth;
Lo, with hearts rent and knees made tremulous,
  Lo, with ephemeral lips and casual breath,
    At least we witness of thee ere we die
That these things are not otherwise, but thus;

That each man in his heart sigheth, and saith, 1190
   That all men even as I,
All we are against thee, against thee, O God most high.

   But ye, keep ye on earth
   Your lips from over-speech,
Loud words and longing are so little worth;
   And the end is hard to reach.
For silence after grievous things is good,
   And reverence, and the fear that makes men whole,
And shame, and righteous governance of blood,
   And lordship of the soul. 1200
But from sharp words and wits men pluck no fruit,
And gathering thorns they shake the tree at root;
For words divide and rend;
But silence is most noble till the end.

ALTHÆA

I heard within the house a cry of news
And came forth eastward hither, where the dawn
Cheers first these warder gods that face the sun
And next our eyes unrisen; for unaware
Came clashes of swift hoofs and trampling feet
And through the windy pillared corridor 1210
Light sharper than the frequent flames of day
That daily fill it from the fiery dawn;
Gleams, and a thunder of people that cried out,
And dust and hurrying horsemen; lo their chief,
That rode with Œneus rein by rein, returned.
What cheer, O herald of my lord the king?

HERALD

Lady, good cheer and great; the boar is slain.

CHORUS

Praised be all gods that look toward Calydon.

ALTHÆA

Good news and brief; but by whose happier hand?

HERALD

A maiden's and a prophet's and thy son's.   1220

ALTHÆA

Well fare the spear that severed him and life.

HERALD

Thine own, and not an alien, hast thou blest.

ALTHÆA

Twice be thou too for my sake blest and his.

HERALD

At the king's word I rode afoam for thine.

ALTHÆA

Thou sayest he tarrieth till they bring the spoil?

HERALD

Hard by the quarry, where they breathe, O queen.

ALTHÆA

Speak thou their chance; but some bring flowers and crown
These gods and all the lintel, and shed wine,
Fetch sacrifice and slay; for heaven is good.

HERALD

Some furlongs northward where the brakes begin   1230
West of that narrowing range of warrior hills
Whose brooks have bled with battle when thy son
Smote Acarnania, there all they made halt,
And with keen eye took note of spear and hound,
Royally ranked; Laertes island-born,

The young Gerenian Nestor, Panopeus,
And Cepheus and Ancæus, mightiest thewed,
Arcadians; next, and evil-eyed of these,
Arcadian Atalanta, with twain hounds
Lengthening the leash, and under nose and brow   1240
Glittering with lipless tooth and fire-swift eye;
But from her white braced shoulder the plumed shafts
Rang, and the bow shone from her side; next her
Meleager, like a sun in spring that strikes
Branch into leaf and bloom into the world,
A glory among men meaner; Iphicles,
And following him that slew the biform bull
Pirithous, and divine Eurytion,
And, bride-bound to the gods, Æacides.
Then Telamon his brother, and Argive-born   1250
The seer and sayer of visions and of truth,
Amphiaraus; and a four-fold strength,
Thine, even thy mother's and thy sister's sons.
And recent from the roar of foreign foam
Jason, and Dryas twin-begot with war,
A blossom of bright battle, sword and man
Shining; and Idas, and the keenest eye
Of Lynceus, and Admetus twice-espoused,
And Hippasus and Hyleus, great in heart.
These having halted bade blow horns, and rode   1260
Through woods and waste lands cleft by stormy streams,
Past yew-trees and the heavy hair of pines,
And where the dew is thickest under oaks,
This way and that; but questing up and down
They saw no trail nor scented; and one said,
Plexippus, Help, or help not, Artemis,
And we will flay thy boarskin with male hands;
But saying, he ceased and said not that he would,
Seeing where the green ooze of a sun-struck marsh
Shook with a thousand reeds untunable,   1270
And in their moist and multitudinous flower
Slept no soft sleep, with violent visions fed,
The blind bulk of the immeasurable beast.

And seeing, he shuddered with sharp lust of praise
Through all his limbs, and launched a double dart.
And missed; for much desire divided him,
Too hot of spirit and feebler than his will,
That his hand failed, though fervent; and the shaft,
Sundering the rushes, in a tamarisk stem
Shook, and stuck fast; then all abode save one,   1280
The Arcadian Atalanta; from her side
Sprang her hounds, labouring at the leash, and slipped,
And plashed ear-deep with plunging feet; but she
Saying, Speed it as I send it for thy sake,
Goddess, drew bow and loosed; the sudden string
Rang, and sprang inward, and the waterish air
Hissed, and the moist plumes of the songless reeds
Moved as a wave which the wind moves no more.
But the boar heaved half out of ooze and slime
His tense flank trembling round the barbèd wound,   1290
Hateful; and fiery with invasive eyes
And bristling with intolerable hair
Plunged, and the hounds clung, and green flowers and
        white
Reddened and broke all round them where they came.
And charging with sheer tusk he drove, and smote
Hyleus; and sharp death caught his sudden soul,
And violent sleep shed night upon his eyes.
Then Peleus, with strong strain of hand and heart,
Shot; but the sidelong arrow slid, and slew
His comrade born and loving countryman,   1300
Under the left arm smitten, as he no less
Poised a like arrow; and bright blood brake afoam,
And falling, and weighed back by clamorous arms,
Sharp rang the dead limbs of Eurytion.
Then one shot happier, the Cadmean seer,
Amphiaraus; for his sacred shaft
Pierced the red circlet of one ravening eye
Beneath the brute brows of the sanguine boar,
Now bloodier from one slain; but he so galled   1310
Sprang straight, and rearing cried no lesser cry

Than thunder and the roar of wintering streams
That mix their own foam with the yellower sea;
And as a tower that falls by fire in fight
With ruin of walls and all its archery,
And breaks the iron flower of war beneath,
Crushing charred limbs and molten arms of men;
So through crushed branches and the reddening brake
Clamoured and crashed the fervour of his feet,
And trampled, springing sideways from the tusk,　　　　1320
Too tardy a moving mould of heavy strength,
Ancæus; and as flakes of weak-winged snow
Break, all the hard thews of his heaving limbs
Broke, and rent flesh fell every way, and blood
Flew, and fierce fragments of no more a man.
Then all the heroes drew sharp breath, and gazed,
And smote not; but Meleager, but thy son,
Right in the wild way of the coming curse
Rock-rooted, fair with fierce and fastened lips,
Clear eyes, and springing muscle and shortening limb—　　1330
With chin aslant indrawn to a tightening throat,
Grave, and with gathered sinews, like a god,—
Aimed on the left side his well-handled spear
Grasped where the ash was knottiest hewn, and smote,
And with no missile wound, the monstrous boar
Right in the hairiest hollow of his hide
Under the last rib, sheer through bulk and bone,
Deep in; and deeply smitten, and to death,
The heavy horror with his hanging shafts
Leapt, and fell furiously, and from raging lips　　　　1340
Foamed out the latest wrath of all his life.
And all they praised the gods with mightier heart,
Zeus and all gods, but chiefliest Artemis,
Seeing; but Meleager bade whet knives and flay,
Strip and stretch out the splendour of the spoil;
And hot and horrid from the work all these
Sat, and drew breath and drank and made great cheer
And washed the hard sweat off their calmer brows.
For much sweet grass grew higher than grew the reed,

And good for slumber, and every holier herb,   1350
Narcissus, and the low-lying melilote,
And all of goodliest blade and bloom that springs
Where, hid by heavier hyacinth, violet buds
Blossom and burn; and fire of yellower flowers
And light of crescent lilies, and such leaves
As fear the Faun's and know the Dryad's foot;
Olive and ivy and poplar dedicate,
And many a well-spring overwatched of these.
There now they rest; but me the king bade bear
Good tidings to rejoice this town and thee.   1360
Wherefore be glad, and all ye give much thanks,
For fallen is all the trouble of Calydon.

ALTHÆA

Laud ye the gods; for this they have given is good,
And what shall be they hide until their time.
Much good and somewhat grievous hast thou said,
And either well; but let all sad things be,
Till all have made before the prosperous gods
Burnt-offering, and poured out the floral wine.
Look fair, O gods, and favourable; for we
Praise you with no false heart or flattering mouth,   1370
Being merciful, but with pure souls and prayer.

HERALD

Thou hast prayed well; for whoso fears not these,
But once being prosperous waxes huge of heart,
Him shall some new thing unaware destroy.

CHORUS

O that I now, I too were
By deep wells and water-floods,
Streams of ancient hills, and where
All the wan green places bear
Blossoms cleaving to the sod,
Fruitless fruit, and grasses fair,   1380
Or such darkest ivy-buds

As divide thy yellow hair,
Bacchus, and their leaves that nod
Round thy fawnskin brush the bare
Snow-soft shoulders of a god;
There the year is sweet, and there
Earth is full of secret springs,
And the fervent rose-cheeked hours,
Those that marry dawn and noon,
There are sunless, there look pale   1390
In dim leaves and hidden air,
Pale as grass or latter flowers
Or the wild vine's wan wet rings
Full of dew beneath the moon,
And all day the nightingale
Sleeps, and all night sings;
There in cold remote recesses
That nor alien eyes assail,
Feet, nor imminence of wings,
Nor a wind nor any tune,
Thou, O queen and holiest,   1400
Flower the whitest of all things,
With reluctant lengthening tresses
And with sudden splendid breast
Save of maidens unbeholden,
There art wont to enter, there
Thy divine swift limbs and golden
Maiden growth of unbound hair,
Bathed in waters white,
Shine, and many a maid's by thee
In moist woodland or the hilly   1410
Flowerless brakes where wells abound
Out of all men's sight;
Or in lower pools that see
All their marges clothed all round
With the innumerable lily,
Whence the golden-girdled bee
Flits through flowering rush to fret
White or duskier violet,

Fair as those that in far years
With their buds left luminous   1420
And their little leaves made wet,
From the warmer dew of tears,
Mother's tears in extreme need,
Hid the limbs of Iamus,
Of thy brother's seed;
For his heart was piteous
Toward him, even as thine heart now
Pitiful toward us;
Thine, O goddess, turning hither
A benignant blameless brow;   1430
Seeing enough of evil done
And lives withered as leaves wither
In the blasting of the sun;
Seeing enough of hunters dead,
Ruin enough of all our year,
Herds and harvests slain and shed,
Herdsmen stricken many an one,
Fruits and flocks consumed together,
And great length of deadly days.
Yet with reverent lips and fear   1440
Turn we toward thee, turn and praise
For this lightening of clear weather
And prosperities begun.
For not seldom, when all air
As bright water without breath
Shines, and when men fear not, fate
Without thunder unaware
Breaks, and brings down death.
Joy with grief ye great gods give,
Good with bad, and overbear   1450
All the pride of us that live,
All the high estate,
As ye long since overbore,
As in old time long before,
Many a strong man and a great,
All that were.

> But do thou, sweet, otherwise,
> Having heed of all our prayer,
> Taking note of all our sighs;
> We beseech thee by thy light, 1460
> By thy bow, and thy sweet eyes,
> And the kingdom of the night,
> Be thou favourable and fair;
> By thine arrows and thy might
> And Orion overthrown;
> By the maiden thy delight,
> By the indissoluble zone
> And the sacred hair.

MESSENGER

Maidens, if ye will sing now, shift your song,
Bow down, cry, wail for pity; is this a time 1470
For singing? nay, for strewing of dust and ash,
Rent raiment, and for bruising of the breast.

CHORUS

What new thing wolf-like lurks behind thy words?
What snake's tongue in thy lips? what fire in the eyes?

MESSENGER

Bring me before the queen and I will speak.

CHORUS

Lo, she comes forth as from thank-offering made.

MESSENGER

A barren offering for a bitter gift.

ALTHÆA

What are these borne on branches, and the face
Covered? no mean men living, but now slain
Such honour have they, if any dwell with death. 1480

MESSENGER

Queen, thy twain brethren and thy mother's sons.

ALTHÆA

Lay down your dead till I behold their blood
If it be mine indeed, and I will weep.

MESSENGER

Weep if thou wilt, for these men shall no more.

ALTHÆA

O brethren, O my father's sons, of me
Well loved and well reputed, I should weep
Tears dearer than the dear blood drawn from you
But that I know you not uncomforted,
Sleeping no shameful sleep, however slain,
For my son surely hath avenged you dead.   1490

MESSENGER

Nay, should thine own seed slay himself, O queen?

ALTHÆA

Thy double word brings forth a double death.

MESSENGER

Know this then singly, by one hand they fell.

ALTHÆA

What mutterest thou with thine ambiguous mouth?

MESSENGER

Slain by thy son's hand; is that saying so hard?

ALTHÆA

Our time is come upon us: it is here.

CHORUS

O miserable, and spoiled at thine own hand.

ALTHÆA

Wert thou not called Meleager from this womb?

CHORUS

A grievous huntsman hath it bred to thee.

ALTHÆA

Wert thou born fire, and shalt thou not devour?   1500

CHORUS

The fire thou madest, will it consume even thee?

ALTHÆA

My dreams are fallen upon me; burn thou too.

CHORUS

Not without God are visions born and die.

ALTHÆA

The gods are many about me; I am one.

CHORUS

She groans as men wrestling with heavier gods.

ALTHÆA

They rend me, they divide me, they destroy.

CHORUS

Or one labouring in travail of strange births.

ALTHÆA

They are strong, they are strong; I am broken, and these
        prevail.

CHORUS

The god is great against her; she will die.

ALTHÆA

Yea, but not now; for my heart too is great.   1510
I would I were not here in sight of the sun.
But thou, speak all thou sawest, and I will die.

MESSENGER

O queen, for queenlike hast thou borne thyself,
A little word may hold so great mischance.
For in division of the sanguine spoil
These men thy brethren wrangling bade yield up
The boar's head and the horror of the hide
That this might stand a wonder in Calydon,
Hallowed; and some drew toward them; but thy son
With great hands grasping all that weight of hair   1520
Cast down the dead heap clanging and collapsed
At female feet, saying This thy spoil not mine,
Maiden, thine own hand for thyself hath reaped,
And all this praise God gives thee: she thereat
Laughed, as when dawn touches the sacred night
The sky sees laugh and redden and divide
Dim lips and eyelids virgin of the sun,
Hers, and the warm slow breasts of morning heave,
Fruitful, and flushed with flame from lamp-lit hours,
And maiden undulation of clear hair   1530
Colour the clouds; so laughed she from pure heart,
Lit with a low blush to the braided hair,
And rose-coloured and cold like very dawn,
Golden and godlike, chastely with chaste lips,
A faint grave laugh; and all they held their peace,
And she passed by them. Then one cried Lo now,
Shall not the Arcadian shoot out lips at us,
Saying all we were despoiled by this one girl?
And all they rode against her violently
And cast the fresh crown from her hair, and now   1540

They had rent her spoil away, dishonouring her,
Save that Meleager, as a tame lion chafed,
Bore on them, broke them, and as fire cleaves wood
So clove and drove them, smitten in twain; but she
Smote not nor heaved up hand; and this man first,
Plexippus, crying out This for love's sake, sweet,
Drove at Meleager, who with spear straightening
Pierced his cheek through; then Toxeus made for him,
Dumb, but his spear spake; vain and violent words.
Fruitless; for him too stricken through both sides   1550
The earth felt falling, and his horse's foam
Blanched thy son's face, his slayer; and these being slain,
None moved nor spake; but Œneus bade bear hence
These made of heaven infatuate in their deaths,
Foolish; for these would baffle fate, and fell.
And they passed on, and all men honoured her,
Being honourable, as one revered of heaven.

ALTHÆA

What say you, woman? is all this not well done?

CHORUS

No man doth well but God hath part in him.

ALTHÆA

But no part here; for these my brethren born   1560
Ye have no part in, these ye know not of
As I that was their sister, a sacrifice
Slain in their slaying. I would I had died for these;
For this man dead walked with me, child by child,
And made a weak staff for my feebler feet
With his own tender wrist and hand, and held
And led me softly and shewed me gold and steel
And shining shapes of mirror and bright crown
And all things fair; and threw light spears, and brought
Young hounds to huddle at my feet and thrust   1570
Tame heads against my little maiden breasts
And please me with great eyes; and those days went

And these are bitter and I a barren queen
And sister miserable, a grievous thing
And mother of many curses; and she too,
My sister Leda, sitting overseas
With fair fruits round her, and her faultless lord,
Shall curse me, saying A sorrow and not a son,
Sister, thou barest, even a burning fire,
A brand consuming thine own soul and me.   1580
But ye now, sons of Thestius, make good cheer,
For ye shall have such wood to funeral fire
As no king hath; and flame that once burnt down
Oil shall not quicken or breath relume or wine
Refresh again; much costlier than fine gold,
And more than many lives of wandering men.

CHORUS

O queen, thou hast yet with thee love-worthy things,
Thine husband, and the great strength of thy son.

ALTHÆA

Who shall get brothers for me while I live?
Who bear them? who bring forth in lieu of these?   1590
Are not our fathers and our brethren one,
And no man like them? are not mine here slain?
Have we not hung together, he and I,
Flowerwise feeding as the feeding bees,
With mother-milk for honey? and this man too,
Dead, with my son's spear thrust between his sides,
Hath he not seen us, later born than he,
Laugh with lips filled, and laughed again for love?
There were no sons then in the world, nor spears,
Nor deadly births of women; but the gods   1600
Allowed us, and our days were clear of these.
I would I had died unwedded, and brought forth
No swords to vex the world; for these that spake
Sweet words long since and loved me will not speak
Nor love nor look upon me; and all my life
I shall not hear nor see them living men.

But I too living, how shall I now live?
What life shall this be with my son, to know
What hath been and desire what will not be,
Look for dead eyes and listen for dead lips,   1610
And kill mine own heart with remembering them,
And with those eyes that see their slayer alive
Weep, and wring hands that clasp him by the hand?
How shall I bear my dreams of them, to hear
False voices, feel the kisses of false mouths
And footless sound of perished feet, and then
Wake and hear only it may be their own hounds
Whine masterless in miserable sleep,
And see their boar-spears and their beds and seats
And all the gear and housings of their lives   1620
And not the men? shall hounds and horses mourn,
Pine with strange eyes, and prick up hungry ears,
Famish and fail at heart for their dear lords,
And I not heed at all? and those blind things
Fall off from life for love's sake, and I live?
Surely some death is better than some life,
Better one death for him and these and me
For if the gods had slain them it may be
I had endured it; if they had fallen by war
Or by the nets and knives of privy death   1630
And by hired hands while sleeping, this thing too
I had set my soul to suffer; or this hunt,
Had this despatched them under tusk or tooth
Torn, sanguine, trodden, broken; for all deaths
Or honourable or with facile feet avenged
And hands of swift gods following, all save this,
Are bearable; but not for their sweet land
Fighting, but not a sacrifice, lo these
Dead; for I had not then shed all mine heart
Out at mine eyes: then either with good speed,   1640
Being just, I had slain their slayer atoningly,
Or strewn with flowers their fire and on their tombs
Hung crowns, and over them a song, and seen
Their praise outflame their ashes: for all men,

All maidens, had come thither, and from pure lips
Shed songs upon them, from heroic eyes
Tears; and their death had been a deathless life;
But now, by no man hired nor alien sword,
By their own kindred are they fallen, in peace,
After much peril, friendless among friends,   1650
By hateful hands they loved; and how shall mine
Touch these returning red and not from war,
These fatal from the vintage of men's veins,
Dead men my brethren? how shall these wash off
No festal stains of undelightful wine,
How mix the blood, my blood on them, with me,
Holding mine hand? or how shall I say, son,
That am no sister? but by night and day
Shall we not sit and hate each other, and think
Things hate-worthy? not live with shamefast eyes,   1660
Brow-beaten, treading soft with fearful feet,
Each unupbraided, each without rebuke
Convicted, and without a word reviled
Each of another? and I shall let thee live
And see thee strong and hear men for thy sake
Praise me, but these thou wouldest not let live
No man shall praise for ever? these shall lie
Dead, unbeloved, unholpen, all through thee?
Sweet were they toward me living, and mine heart
Desired them, but was then well satisfied,   1670
That now is as men hungered; and these dead
I shall want always to the day I die.
For all things else and all men may renew;
Yea, son for son the gods may give and take,
But never a brother or sister any more.

CHORUS

Nay, for the son lies close about thine heart,
Full of thy milk, warm from thy womb, and drains
Life and the blood of life and all thy fruit,
Eats thee and drinks thee as who breaks bread and eats,
Treads wine and drinks, thyself, a sect of thee;   1680

And if he feed not, shall not thy flesh faint?
Or drink not, are not thy lips dead for thirst?
This thing moves more than all things, even thy son,
That thou cleave to him; and he shall honour thee,
Thy womb that bare him and the breasts he knew,
Reverencing most for thy sake all his gods.

ALTHÆA

But these the gods too gave me, and these my son,
Not reverencing his gods nor mine own heart
Nor the old sweet years nor all venerable things,
But cruel, and in his ravin like a beast,   1690
Hath taken away to slay them: yea, and she
She the strange woman, she the flower, the sword,
Red from spilt blood, a mortal flower to men,
Adorable, detestable—even she
Saw with strange eyes and with strange lips rejoiced,
Seeing these mine own slain of mine own, and me
Made miserable above all miseries made,
A grief among all women in the world,
A name to be washed out with all men's tears.

CHORUS

Strengthen thy spirit; is this not also a god,   1700
Chance, and the wheel of all necessities?
Hard things have fallen upon us from harsh gods,
Whom lest worse hap rebuke we not for these.

ALTHÆA

My spirit is strong against itself, and I
For these things' sake cry out on mine own soul
That it endures outrage, and dolorous days,
And life, and this inexpiable impotence.
Weak am I, weak and shameful; my breath drawn
Shames me, and monstrous things and violent gods.
What shall atone? what heal me? what bring back   1710
Strength to the foot, light to the face? what herb
Assuage me? what restore me? what release?

What strange thing eaten or drunken, O great gods,
Make me as you or as the beasts that feed,
Slay and divide and cherish their own hearts?
For these ye show us; and we less than these
Have not wherewith to live as all these things
Which all their lives fare after their own kind
As who doth well rejoicing; but we ill,
Weeping or laughing, we whom eyesight fails,   1720
Knowledge and light of face and perfect heart,
And hands we lack, and wit; and all our days
Sin, and have hunger, and die infatuated.
For madness have ye given us and not health,
And sins whereof we know not; and for these
Death, and sudden destruction unaware.
What shall we say now? what thing comes of us?

CHORUS

Alas, for all this all men undergo.

ALTHÆA

Wherefore I will not that these twain, O gods,
Die as a dog dies, eaten of creeping things,   1730
Abominable, a loathing; but though dead
Shall they have honour and such funereal flame
As strews men's ashes in their enemies' face
And blinds their eyes who hate them: lest men say,
"Lo how they lie, and living had great kin,
And none of these hath pity of them, and none
Regards them lying, and none is wrung at heart,
None moved in spirit for them, naked and slain,
Abhorred, abased, and no tears comfort them:"
And in the dark this grieve Eurythemis,   1740
Hearing how these her sons come down to her
Unburied, unavenged, as kinless men,
And had a queen their sister. That were shame
Worse than this grief. Yet how to atone at all
I know not; seeing the love of my born son,
A new-made mother's new-born love, that grows

From the soft child to the strong man, now soft
Now strong as either, and still one sole same love,
Strives with me, no light thing to strive withal;
This love is deep, and natural to man's blood,   1750
And ineffaceable with many tears.
Yet shall not these rebuke me though I die,
Nor she in that waste world with all her dead,
My mother, among the pale flocks fallen as leaves,
Folds of dead people, and alien from the sun;
Nor lack some bitter comfort, some poor praise,
Being queen, to have borne her daughter like a queen,
Righteous; and though mine own fire burn me too,
She shall have honour and these her sons, though dead.
But all the gods will, all they do, and we   1760
Not all we would, yet somewhat; and one choice
We have, to live and do just deeds and die.

CHORUS

Terrible words she communes with, and turns
Swift fiery eyes in doubt against herself,
And murmurs as who talks in dreams with death.

ALTHÆA

For the unjust also dieth, and him all men
Hate, and himself abhors the unrighteousness,
And seeth his own dishonour intolerable.
But I being just, doing right upon myself,
Slay mine own soul, and no man born shames me.   1770
For none constrains nor shall rebuke, being done,
What none compelled me doing; thus these things fare.
Ah, ah, that such things should so fare; ah me,
That I am found to do them and endure,
Chosen and constrained to choose, and bear myself
Mine own wound through mine own flesh to the heart
Violently stricken, a spoiler and a spoil,
A ruin ruinous, fallen on mine own son.
Ah, ah, for me too as for these; alas,
For that is done that shall be, and mine hand   1780

Full of the deed, and full of blood mine eyes,
That shall see never nor touch anything
Save blood unstanched and fire unquenchable.

CHORUS

What wilt thou do? what ails thee? for the house
Shakes ruinously; wilt thou bring fire for it?

ALTHÆA

Fire in the roofs, and on the lintels fire.
Lo ye, who stand and weave, between the doors,
There; and blood drips from hand and thread, and stains
Threshold and raiment and me passing in
Flecked with the sudden sanguine drops of death.   1790

CHORUS

Alas that time is stronger than strong men,
Fate than all gods: and these are fallen on us.

ALTHÆA

A little since and I was glad; and now
I never shall be glad or sad again.

CHORUS

Between two joys a grief grows unaware.

ALTHÆA

A little while and I shall laugh; and then
I shall weep never and laugh not any more.

CHORUS

What shall be said? for words are thorns to grief.
Withhold thyself a little and fear the gods.

ALTHÆA

Fear died when these were slain; and I am as dead,   1800
And fear is of the living; these fear none.

CHORUS

Have pity upon all people for their sake.

ALTHÆA

It is done now; shall I put back my day?

CHORUS

An end is come, an end; this is of God.

ALTHÆA

I am fire, and burn myself; keep clear of fire.

CHORUS

The house is broken, is broken; it shall not stand.

ALTHÆA

Woe, woe for him that breaketh; and a rod
Smote it of old, and now the axe is here.

CHORUS

Not as with sundering of the earth
Nor as with cleaving of the sea   1810
Nor fierce foreshadowings of a birth
    Nor flying dreams of death to be
Nor loosening of the large world's girth
And quickening of the body of night,
    And sound of thunder in men's ears
And fire of lightning in men's sight,
    Fate, mother of desires and fears,
    Bore unto men the law of tears;
But sudden, an unfathered flame,
    And broken out of night, she shone,   1820
She, without body, without name,
    In days forgotten and foregone;
And heaven rang round her as she came

Like smitten cymbals, and lay bare;
  Clouds and great stars, thunders and snows,
The blue sad fields and folds of air,
  The life that breathes, the life that grows,
  All wind, all fire, that burns or blows,
Even all these knew her: for she is great;
  The daughter of doom, the mother of death,   1830
The sister of sorrow; a lifelong weight
  That no man's finger lighteneth,
Nor any god can lighten fate;
A landmark seen across the way
  Where one race treads as the other trod;
An evil sceptre, an evil stay,
  Wrought for a staff, wrought for a rod,
  The bitter jealousy of God.

For death is deep as the sea,
  And fate as the waves thereof.   1840
Shall the waves take pity on thee
  Or the southwind offer thee love?
Wilt thou take the night for thy day
Or the darkness for light on thy way,
  Till thou say in thine heart Enough?
Behold, thou art over fair, thou art over wise;
The sweetness of spring in thine hair, and the light in
    thine eyes.
The light of the spring in thine eyes, and the sound in
    thine ears;
Yet thine heart shall wax heavy with sighs and thine
    eyelids with tears.
Wilt thou cover thine hair with gold, and with silver thy
    feet?   1850
Hast thou taken the purple to fold thee, and made thy
    mouth sweet?
Behold, when thy face is made bare, he that loved thee
    shall hate;
Thy face shall be no more fair at the fall of thy fate.

For thy life shall fall as a leaf and be shed as the rain;
And the veil of thine head shall be grief; and the crown
    shall be pain.

ALTHÆA

Ho, ye that wail, and ye that sing, make way
Till I be come among you. Hide your tears,
Ye little weepers, and your laughing lips,
Ye laughers for a little; lo mine eyes
That outweep heaven at rainiest, and my mouth   1860
That laughs as gods laugh at us. Fate's are we,
Yet fate is ours a breathing-space; yea, mine,
Fate is made mine for ever; he is my son,
My bedfellow, my brother. You strong gods,
Give place unto me; I am as any of you,
To give life and to take life. Thou, old earth,
That hast made man and unmade; thou whose mouth
Looks red from the eaten fruits of thine own womb;
Behold me with what lips upon what food
I feed and fill my body; even with flesh   1870
Made of my body. Lo, the fire I lit
I burn with fire to quench it; yea, with flame
I burn up even the dust and ash thereof.

CHORUS

Woman, what fire is this thou burnest with?

ALTHÆA

Yea to the bone, yea to the blood and all.

CHORUS

For this thy face and hair are as one-fire.

ALTHÆA

A tongue that licks and beats upon the dust.

CHORUS

And in thine eyes are hollow light and heat.

ALTHÆA

Of flame not fed with hand or frankincense.

CHORUS

I fear thee for the trembling of thine eyes.   1880

ALTHÆA

Neither with love they tremble nor for fear.

CHORUS

And thy mouth shuddering like a shot bird.

ALTHÆA

Not as the bride's mouth when man kisses it.

CHORUS

Nay, but what thing is this thing thou hast done?

ALTHÆA

Look, I am silent, speak your eyes for me.

CHORUS

I see a faint fire lightening from the hall.

ALTHÆA

Gaze, stretch your eyes, strain till the lids drop off.

CHORUS

Flushed pillars down the flickering vestibule.

ALTHÆA

Stretch with your necks like birds: cry, chirp as they.

CHORUS

And a long brand that blackens: and white dust.   1890

ALTHÆA

O children, what is this ye see? your eyes
Are blinder than night's face at fall of moon.
That is my son, my flesh, my fruit of life,
My travail, and the year's weight of my womb,
Meleager, a fire enkindled of mine hands
And of mine hands extinguished; this is he.

CHORUS

O gods, what word has flown out at thy mouth?

ALTHÆA

I did this and I say this and I die.

CHORUS

Death stands upon the doorway of thy lips,
And in thy mouth has death set up his house.   1900

ALTHÆA

O death, a little, a little while, sweet death,
Until I see the brand burnt down and die.

CHORUS

She reels as any reed under the wind,
And cleaves unto the ground with staggering feet.

ALTHÆA

Girls, one thing will I say and hold my peace.
I that did this will weep not nor cry out,
Cry ye and weep: I will not call on gods,
Call ye on them; I will not pity man,
Shew ye your pity. I know not if I live;
Save that I feel the fire upon my face   1910
And on my cheek the burning of a brand.
Yea the smoke bites me, yea I drink the steam
With nostril and with eyelid and with lip

Insatiate and intolerant; and mine hands
Burn, and fire feeds upon mine eyes; I reel
As one made drunk with living, whence he draws
Drunken delight; yet I, though mad for joy,
Loathe my long living and am waxen red
As with the shadow of shed blood; behold,
I am kindled with the flames that fade in him, 1920
I am swollen with subsiding of his veins,
I am flooded with his ebbing; my lit eyes
Flame with the falling fire that leaves his lids
Bloodless; my cheek is luminous with blood
Because his face is ashen. Yet, O child,
Son, first-born, fairest—O sweet mouth, sweet eyes,
That drew my life out through my suckling breast,
That shone and clove mine heart through—O soft knees
Clinging, O tender treadings of soft feet,
Cheeks warm with little kissings—O child, child, 1930
What have we made each other? Lo, I felt
Thy weight cleave to me, a burden of beauty, O son,
Thy cradled brows and loveliest loving lips,
The floral hair, the little lightening eyes,
And all thy goodly glory; with mine hands
Delicately I fed thee, with my tongue
Tenderly spake, saying, Verily in God's time,
For all the little likeness of thy limbs,
Son, I shall make thee a kingly man to fight,
A lordly leader; and hear before I die, 1940
"She bore the goodliest sword of all the world."
Oh! oh! For all my life turns round on me;
I am severed from myself, my name is gone,
My name that was a healing, it is changed,
My name is a consuming. From this time,
Though mine eyes reach to the end of all these things,
My lips shall not unfasten till I die.

SEMICHORUS

    She has filled with sighing the city,
       And the ways thereof with tears;

She arose, she girdled her sides,   1950
She set her face as a bride's;
She wept, and she had no pity;
     Trembled, and felt no fears.

SEMICHORUS

Her eyes were clear as the sun,
     Her brows were fresh as the day;
She girdled herself with gold,
Her robes were manifold;
But the days of her worship are done,
     Her praise is taken away.

SEMICHORUS

For she set her hand to the fire,   1960
     With her mouth she kindled the same;
As the mouth of a flute-player,
So was the mouth of her;
With the might of her strong desire
     She blew the breath of the flame.

SEMICHORUS

She set her hand to the wood,
     She took the fire in her hand;
As one who is nigh to death,
She panted with strange breath;
She opened her lips unto blood,   1970
     She breathed and kindled the brand.

SEMICHORUS

As a wood-dove newly shot,
     She sobbed and lifted her breast;
She sighed and covered her eyes,
Filling her lips with sighs;
She sighed, she withdrew herself not,
     She refrained not, taking not rest;

SEMICHORUS

But as the wind which is drouth,
   And as the air which is death,
As storm that severeth ships,   1980
Her breath severing her lips,
The breath came forth of her mouth
   And the fire came forth of her breath.

SECOND MESSENGER

Queen, and you maidens, there is come on us
A thing more deadly than the face of death;
Meleager the good lord is as one slain.

SEMICHORUS

Without sword, without sword is he stricken;
   Slain, and slain without hand.

SECOND MESSENGER

For as keen ice divided of the sun
His limbs divide, and as thawed snow the flesh   1990
Thaws from off all his body to the hair.

SEMICHORUS

He wastes as the embers quicken;
   With the brand he fades as a brand.

SECOND MESSENGER

Even while they sang and all drew hither and he
Lifted both hands to crown the Arcadian's hair
And fix the looser leaves, both hands fell down.

SEMICHORUS

With rending of cheek and of hair
   Lament ye, mourn for him, weep.

SECOND MESSENGER

Straightway the crown slid off and smote on earth,

First fallen; and he, grasping his own hair, groaned   2000
And cast his raiment round his face and fell.

SEMICHORUS

    Alas for visions that were,
       And soothsayings spoken in sleep.

SECOND MESSENGER

But the king twitched his reins in and leapt down
And caught him, crying out twice "O child" and thrice,
So that men's eyelids thickened with their tears.

SEMICHORUS

    Lament with a long lamentation,
       Cry, for an end is at hand.

SECOND MESSENGER

O son, he said, son, lift thine eyes, draw breath,
Pity me; but Meleager with sharp lips   2010
Gasped, and his face waxed like as sunburnt grass.

SEMICHORUS

    Cry aloud, O thou kingdom, O nation,
       O stricken, a ruinous land.

SECOND MESSENGER

Whereat king Œneus, straightening feeble knees,
With feeble hands heaved up a lessening weight,
And laid him sadly in strange hands, and wept.

SEMICHORUS

    Thou art smitten, her lord, her desire,
       Thy dear blood wasted as rain.

SECOND MESSENGER

And they with tears and rendings of the beard

Bear hither a breathing body, wept upon   2020
And lightening at each footfall, sick to death.

SEMICHORUS

Thou madest thy sword as a fire,
With fire for a sword thou art slain.

SECOND MESSENGER

And lo, the feast turned funeral, and the crowns
Fallen; and the huntress and the hunter trapped;
And weeping and changed faces and veiled hair.

MELEAGER

Let your hands meet
Round the weight of my head;
Lift ye my feet
As the feet of the dead;   2030
For the flesh of my body is molten, the limbs of it molten
as lead.

CHORUS

O thy luminous face,
Thine imperious eyes!
O the grief, O the grace,
As of day when it dies!
Who is this bending over thee, lord, with tears and
suppression of sighs?

MELEAGER

Is a bride so fair?
Is a maid so meek?
With unchapleted hair,
With unfilleted cheek,   2040
Atalanta, the pure among women, whose name is as
blessing to speak.

ATALANTA

> I would that with feet
>   Unsandalled, unshod,
> Overbold, overfleet,
>   I had swum not nor trod
> From Arcadia to Calydon northward, a blast of the envy
>   of God.

MELEAGER

> Unto each man his fate;
>   Unto each as he saith
> In whose fingers the weight
>   Of the world is as breath;   2050
> Yet I would that in clamour of battle mine hands had laid
>   hold upon death.

CHORUS

> Not with cleaving of shields
>   And their clash in thine ear,
> When the lord of fought fields
>   Breaketh spearshaft from spear,
> Thou art broken, our lord, thou art broken, with travail
>   and labour and fear.

MELEAGER

> Would God he had found me
>   Beneath fresh boughs!
> Would God he had bound me
>   Unawares in mine house,   2060
> With light in mine eyes, and songs in my lips, and a
>   crown on my brows!

CHORUS

> Whence art thou sent from us?
>   Whither thy goal?
> How art thou rent from us,
>   Thou that wert whole,

As with severing of eyelids and eyes, as with sundering
    of body and soul!

MELEAGER

      My heart is within me
        As an ash in the fire;
      Whosoever hath seen me,
        Without lute, without lyre,   2070
Shall sing of me grievous things, even things that were
    ill to desire.

CHORUS

      Who shall raise thee
        From the house of the dead?
      Or what man praise thee
        That thy praise may be said?
Alas thy beauty! alas thy body! alas thine head!

MELEAGER

      But thou, O mother,
        The dreamer of dreams,
      Wilt thou bring forth another
        To feel the sun's beams   2080
When I move among shadows a shadow, and wail by
    impassable streams?

ŒNEUS

      What thing wilt thou leave me
        Now this thing is done?
      A man wilt thou give me,
        A son for my son,
For the light of mine eyes, the desire of my life, the
    desirable one?

CHORUS

      Thou wert glad above others,
        Yea, fair beyond word;

Thou wert glad among mothers;
For each man that heard   2090
Of thee, praise there was added unto thee, as wings to
    the feet of a bird.

ŒNEUS

Who shall give back
Thy face of old years
With travail made black,
Grown grey among fears,
Mother of sorrow, mother of cursing, mother of tears?

MELEAGER

Though thou art as fire
Fed with fuel in vain,
My delight, my desire,
Is more chaste than the rain,   2100
More pure than the dewfall, more holy than stars are that
    live without stain.

ATALANTA

I would that as water
My life's blood had thawn,
Or as winter's wan daughter
Leaves lowland and lawn
Spring-stricken, or ever mine eyes had beheld thee made
    dark in thy dawn.

CHORUS

When thou dravest the men
Of the chosen of Thrace,
None turned him again
Nor endured he thy face   2110
Clothed round with the blush of the battle, with light
    from a terrible place.

ŒNEUS

    Thou shouldst die as he dies
     For whom none sheddeth tears;
    Filling thine eyes
     And fulfilling thine ears
With the brilliance of battle, the bloom and the beauty,
  the splendour of spears.

CHORUS

    In the ears of the world
     It is sung, it is told,
    And the light thereof hurled   2120
     And the noise thereof rolled
From the Acroceraunian snow to the ford of the fleece
  of gold.

MELEAGER

    Would God ye could carry me
     Forth of all these;
    Heap sand and bury me
     By the Chersonese
Where the thundering Bosphorus answers the thunder
  of Pontic seas.

ŒNEUS

    Dost thou mock at our praise
     And the singing begun
    And the men of strange days
     Praising my son   2130
In the folds of the hills of home, high places of Calydon?

MELEAGER

    For the dead man no home is;
     Ah, better to be
    What the flower of the foam is
     In fields of the sea,

That the sea-waves might be as my raiment, the
    gulf-stream a garment for me.

CHORUS

    Who shall seek thee and bring
      And restore thee thy day,
    When the dove dipt her wing
      And the oars won their way   2140
Where the narrowing Symplegades whitened the straits
    of Propontis with spray?

MELEAGER

    Will ye crown me my tomb
      Or exalt me my name,
    Now my spirits consume,
      Now my flesh is a flame?
Let the sea slake it once, and men speak of me sleeping
    to praise me or shame.

CHORUS

    Turn back now, turn thee,
      As who turns him to wake;
    Though the life in thee burn thee,
      Couldst thou bathe it and slake   2150
Where the sea-ridge of Helle hangs heavier, and east upon
    west waters break?

MELEAGER

    Would the winds blow me back
      Or the waves hurl me home?
    Ah, to touch in the track
      Where the pine learnt to roam
Cold girdles and crowns of the sea-gods, cool blossoms
    of water and foam!

CHORUS

    The gods may release
      That they made fast;

Thy soul shall have ease
    In thy limbs at the last;   2160
But what shall they give thee for life, sweet life that is
    overpast?

MELEAGER

Not the life of men's veins,
    Not of flesh that conceives;
But the grace that remains,
    The fair beauty that cleaves
To the life of the rains in the grasses, the life of the dews
    on the leaves.

CHORUS

Thou wert helmsman and chief;
    Wilt thou turn in an hour,
Thy limbs to the leaf,
    Thy face to the flower,   2170
Thy blood to the water, thy soul to the gods who divide
    and devour?

MELEAGER

The years are hungry,
    They wail all their days;
The gods wax angry
    And weary of praise;
And who shall bridle their lips? and who shall straiten
    their ways?

CHORUS

The gods guard over us
    With sword and with rod;
Weaving shadow to cover us,
    Heaping the sod,   2180
That law may fulfil herself wholly, to darken man's face
    before God.*

---

* A possible allusion to the Lord's commandment, just before He
speaks from a cloud of "thick darkness" on Mt. Sinai, that the people
gaze not upon Him (*Exodus* 19–20).

MELEAGER

O holy head of Œneus, lo thy son
Guiltless, yet red from alien guilt, yet foul
With kinship of contaminated lives,
Lo, for their blood I die; and mine own blood
For bloodshedding of mine is mixed therewith,
That death may not discern me from my kin.
Yet with clean heart I die and faultless hand,
Not shamefully; thou therefore of thy love
Salute me, and bid fare among the dead   2190
Well, as the dead fare; for the best man dead
Fares sadly; nathless I now faring well
Pass without fear where nothing is to fear
Having thy love about me and thy goodwill,
O father, among dark places and men dead.

ŒNEUS

Child, I salute thee with sad heart and tears,
And bid thee comfort, being a perfect man
In fight, and honourable in the house of peace.
The gods give thee fair wage and dues of death,
And me brief days and ways to come at thee.   2200

MELEAGER

Pray thou thy days be long before thy death,
And full of ease and kingdom; seeing in death
There is no comfort and none aftergrowth,
Nor shall one thence look up and see day's dawn
Nor light upon the land whither I go.
Live thou and take thy fill of days and die
When thy day comes; and make not much of death
Lest ere thy day thou reap an evil thing.
Thou too, the bitter mother and mother-plague
Of this my weary body—thou too, queen,   2210
The source and end, the sower and the scythe,
The rain that ripens and the drought that slays,
The sand that swallows and the spring that feeds,
To make me and unmake me—thou, I say,

Althæa, since my father's ploughshare, drawn
Through fatal seedland of a female field,
Furrowed thy body, whence a wheaten ear
Strong from the sun and fragrant from the rains
I sprang and cleft the closure of thy womb,
Mother, I dying with unforgetful tongue   2220
Hail thee as holy and worship thee as just
Who art unjust and unholy; and with my knees
Would worship, but thy fire and subtlety,
Dissundering them, devour me; for these limbs
Are as light dust and crumblings from mine urn
Before the fire has touched them; and my face
As a dead leaf or dead foot's mark on snow,
And all this body a broken barren tree
That was so strong, and all this flower of life
Disbranched and desecrated miserably,   2230
And minished all that god-like muscle and might
And lesser than a man's: for all my veins
Fail me, and all mine ashen life burns down.
I would thou hadst let me live; but gods averse,
But fortune, and the fiery feet of change,
And time, these would not, these tread out my life,
These and not thou; me too thou hast loved, and I
Thee; but this death was mixed with all my life,
Mine end with my beginning: and this law,
This only, slays me, and not my mother at all.   2240
And let no brother or sister grieve too sore,
Nor melt their hearts out on me with their tears,
Since extreme love and sorrowing overmuch
Vex the great gods, and overloving men
Slay and are slain for love's sake; and this house
Shall bear much better children; why should these
Weep? but in patience let them live their lives
And mine pass by forgotten: thou alone,
Mother, thou sole and only, thou not these,
Keep me in mind a little when I die   2250
Because I was thy first-born; let thy soul
Pity me, pity even me gone hence and dead,

Though thou wert wroth, and though thou bear again
Much happier sons, and all men later born
Exceedingly excel me; yet do thou
Forget not, nor think shame; I was thy son.
Time was I did not shame thee; and time was
I thought to live and make thee honourable
With deeds as great as these men's; but they live,
These, and I die; and what thing should have been   2260
Surely I know not; yet I charge thee, seeing
I am dead already, love me not the less,
Me, O my mother; I charge thee by these gods,
My father's, and that holier breast of thine,
By these that see me dying, and that which nursed,
Love me not less, thy first-born: though grief come,
Grief only, of me, and of all these great joy,
And shall come always to thee; for thou knowest,
O mother, O breasts that bare me, for ye know,
O sweet head of my mother, sacred eyes,   2270
Ye know my soul albeit I sinned, ye know
Albeit I kneel not neither touch thy knees,
But with my lips I kneel, and with my heart
I fall about thy feet and worship thee.
And ye farewell now, all my friends; and ye,
Kinsmen, much younger and glorious more than I,
Sons of my mother's sister; and all farewell
That were in Colchis with me, and bare down
The waves and wars that met us: and though times
Change, and though now I be not anything,   2280
Forget not me among you, what I did
In my good time; for even by all those days,
Those days and this, and your own living souls,
And by the light and luck of you that live,
And by this miserable spoil, and me
Dying, I beseech you, let my name not die.
But thou, dear, touch me with thy rose-like hands,
And fasten up mine eyelids with thy mouth,
A bitter kiss; and grasp me with thine arms,
Printing with heavy lips my light waste flesh,   2290

Made light and thin by heavy-handed fate,
And with thine holy maiden eyes drop dew,
Drop tears for dew upon me who am dead,
Me who have loved thee; seeing without sin done
I am gone down to the empty weary house
Where no flesh is nor beauty nor swift eyes
Nor sound of mouth nor might of hands and feet.
But thou, dear, hide my body with thy veil,
And with thy raiment cover foot and head,
And stretch thyself upon me and touch hands   2300
With hands and lips with lips: be pitiful
As thou art maiden perfect; let no man
Defile me to despise me, saying, This man
Died woman-wise, a woman's offering, slain
Through female fingers in his woof of life,
Dishonourable; for thou hast honoured me.
And now for God's sake kiss me once and twice
And let me go; for the night gathers me,
And in the night shall no man gather fruit.

ATALANTA

Hail thou: but I with heavy face and feet   2310
Turn homeward and am gone out of thine eyes.

CHORUS

Who shall contend with his lords
  Or cross them or do them wrong?
Who shall bind them as with cords?
  Who shall tame them as with song?
Who shall smite them as with swords?
  For the hands of their kingdom are strong.

A Ballad of Life

I found in dreams a place of wind and flowers,
  Full of sweet trees and colour of glad grass,

In midst whereof there was
A lady clothed like summer with sweet hours.
Her beauty, fervent as a fiery moon,
  Made my blood burn and swoon
    Like a flame rained upon.
Sorrow had filled her shaken eyelids' blue,
And her mouth's sad red heavy rose all through
    Seemed sad with glad things gone.   10

She held a little cithern by the strings,
  Shaped heartwise, strung with subtle-coloured hair
  Of some dead lute-player
That in dead years had done delicious things.
The seven strings were named accordingly;
    The first string charity,
      The second tenderness,
The rest were pleasure, sorrow, sleep, and sin,
And loving-kindness, that is pity's kin
      And is most pitiless.   20

There were three men with her, each garmented
  With gold and shod with gold upon the feet;
    And with plucked ears of wheat
The first man's hair was wound upon his head:
His face was red, and his mouth curled and sad;
    All his gold garment had
      Pale stains of dust and rust.
A riven hood was pulled across his eyes;
The token of him being upon this wise
      Made for a sign of Lust.   30

The next was Shame, with hollow heavy face
  Coloured like green wood when flame kindles it.
  He hath such feeble feet
They may not well endure in any place.
His face was full of grey old miseries,
    And all his blood's increase

Was even increase of pain.
The last was Fear, that is akin to Death;
He is Shame's friend, and always as Shame saith
    Fear answers him again.   40

My soul said in me; This is marvellous,
    Seeing the air's face is not so delicate
    Nor the sun's grace so great,
If sin and she be kin or amorous.
And seeing where maidens served her on their knees,
    I bade one crave of these
        To know the cause thereof.
Then Fear said: I am Pity that was dead.
And Shame said: I am Sorrow comforted.
        And Lust said: I am Love.   50

Thereat her hands began a lute-playing
    And her sweet mouth a song in a strange tongue;
    And all the while she sung
There was no sound but long tears following
Long tears upon men's faces, waxen white
    With extreme sad delight.
        But those three following men
Became as men raised up among the dead;
Great glad mouths open and fair cheeks made red
        With child's blood come again.   60

Then I said: Now assuredly I see
    My lady is perfect, and transfigureth
    All sin and sorrow and death,
Making them fair as her own eyelids be,
Or lips wherein my whole soul's life abides;
    Or as her sweet white sides
        And bosom carved to kiss.
Now therefore, if her pity further me,
Doubtless for her sake all my days shall be
        As righteous as she is.   70

Forth, ballad, and take roses in both arms,
    Even till the top rose touch thee in the throat
Where the least thornprick harms;
    And girdled in thy golden singing-coat,
Come thou before my lady and say this;
    Borgia, thy gold hair's colour burns in me,
        Thy mouth makes beat my blood in feverish rhymes;
    Therefore so many as these roses be,
        Kiss me so many times.
Then it may be, seeing how sweet she is,
    That she will stoop herself none otherwise
    Than a blown vine-branch doth,
    And kiss thee with soft laughter on thine eyes,
        Ballad, and on thy mouth.   80

≈{ }≈

Laus Veneris *

Asleep or waking is it? for her neck,
Kissed over close, wears yet a purple speck
    Wherein the pained blood falters and goes out;
Soft, and stung softly—fairer for a fleck.

But though my lips shut sucking on the place,
There is no vein at work upon her face;
    Her eyelids are so peaceable, no doubt
Deep sleep has warmed her blood through all its ways.

Lo, this is she that was the world's delight;
The old grey years were parcels of her might;   10
    The strewings of the ways wherein she trod
Were the twain seasons of the day and night.

---

* In this retelling of the Tannhäuser legend "In Praise of Venus,"
the doomed knight has returned to Venus after begging mercy from the
Pope for the sin of loving her. For Swinburne's comments on this and
other lyrics in *Poems and Ballads*, First Series, see his "Notes on Poems
and Reviews," p. 325 ff.

Lo, she was thus when her clear limbs enticed
All lips that now grow sad with kissing Christ,
   Stained with blood fallen from the feet of God,
The feet and hands whereat our souls were priced.

Alas, Lord, surely thou art great and fair.
But lo her wonderfully woven hair!
   And thou didst heal us with thy piteous kiss;
But see now, Lord; her mouth is lovelier.   20

She is right fair; what hath she done to thee?
Nay, fair Lord Christ, lift up thine eyes and see;
   Had now thy mother such a lip—like this?
Thou knowest how sweet a thing it is to me.

Inside the Horsel* here the air is hot;
Right little peace one hath for it, God wot;
   The scented dusty daylight burns the air,
And my heart chokes me till I hear it not.

Behold, my Venus, my soul's body, lies
With my love laid upon her garment-wise,   30
   Feeling my love in all her limbs and hair
And shed between her eyelids through her eyes.

She holds my heart in her sweet open hands
Hanging asleep; hard by her head there stands,
   Crowned with gilt thorns and clothed with flesh
      like fire,
Love, wan as foam blown up the salt burnt sands—

Hot as the brackish waifs of yellow spume
That shift and steam—loose clots of arid fume
   From the sea's panting mouth of dry desire;
There stands he, like one labouring at a loom.   40

    * Venus held court in a cavern within the Horselberg, the "Moun-
tain of Venus" in central Germany.

The warp holds fast across; and every thread
That makes the woof up has dry specks of red;
   Always the shuttle cleaves clean through, and he
Weaves with the hair of many a ruined head.

Love is not glad nor sorry, as I deem;
Labouring he dreams, and labours in the dream,
   Till when the spool is finished, lo I see
His web, reeled off, curls and goes out like steam.

Night falls like fire; the heavy lights run low,
And as they drop, my blood and body so   50
   Shake as the flame shakes, full of days and hours
That sleep not neither weep they as they go.

Ah yet would God this flesh of mine might be
Where air might wash and long leaves cover me,
   Where tides of grass break into foam of flowers,
Or where the wind's feet shine along the sea.

Ah yet would God that stems and roots were bred
Out of my weary body and my head,
   That sleep were sealed upon me with a seal,
And I were as the least of all his dead.   60

Would God my blood were dew to feed the grass,
Mine ears made deaf and mine eyes blind as glass,
   My body broken as a turning wheel,
And my mouth stricken ere it saith Alas!

Ah God, that love were as a flower or flame,
That life were as the naming of a name,
   That death were not more pitiful than desire,
That these things were not one thing and the same!

Behold now, surely somewhere there is death:
For each man hath some space of years, he saith,   70

A little space of time ere time expire,
A little day, a little way of breath.

And lo, between the sundawn and the sun,
His day's work and his night's work are undone;
   And lo, between the nightfall and the light,
He is not, and none knoweth of such an one.

Ah God, that I were as all souls that be,
As any herb or leaf of any tree,
   As men that toil through hours of labouring night,
As bones of men under the deep sharp sea.   80

Outside it must be winter among men;
For at the gold bars of the gates again
   I heard all night and all the hours of it
The wind's wet wings and fingers drip with rain.

Knights gather, riding sharp for cold; I know
The ways and woods are strangled with the snow;
   And with short song the maidens spin and sit
Until Christ's birthnight, lily-like, arow.

The scent and shadow shed about me make
The very soul in all my senses ache;   90
   The hot hard night is fed upon my breath,
And sleep beholds me from afar awake.

Alas, but surely where the hills grow deep,
Or where the wild ways of the sea are steep,
   Or in strange places somewhere there is death,
And on death's face the scattered hair of sleep.

There lover-like with lips and limbs that meet
They lie, they pluck sweet fruit of life and eat;
   But me the hot and hungry days devour,
And in my mouth no fruit of theirs is sweet.   100

No fruit of theirs, but fruit of my desire,
For her love's sake whose lips through mine respire;
   Her eyelids on her eyes like flower on flower,
Mine eyelids on mine eyes like fire on fire.

So lie we, not as sleep that lies by death,
With heavy kisses and with happy breath;
   Not as man lies by woman, when the bride
Laughs low for love's sake and the words he saith.

For she lies, laughing low with love; she lies
And turns his kisses on her lips to sighs,   110
   To sighing sound of lips unsatisfied,
And the sweet tears are tender with her eyes.

Ah, not as they, but as the souls that were
Slain in the old time, having found her fair;
   Who, sleeping with her lips upon their eyes,
Heard sudden serpents hiss across her hair.

Their blood runs round the roots of time like rain:
She casts them forth and gathers them again;
   With nerve and bone she weaves and multiplies
Exceeding pleasure out of extreme pain.   120

Her little chambers drip with flower-like red,
Her girdles, and the chaplets of her head,
   Her armlets and her anklets; with her feet
She tramples all that winepress of the dead.

Her gateways smoke with fume of flowers and fires,
With loves burnt out and unassuaged desires;
   Between her lips the steam of them is sweet,
The languor in her ears of many lyres.

Her beds are full of perfume and sad sound,
Her doors are made with music, and barred round   130

With sighing and with laughter and with tears,
With tears whereby strong souls of men are bound.

There is the knight Adonis that was slain;
With flesh and blood she chains him for a chain;
   The body and the spirit in her ears
Cry, for her lips divide him vein by vein.

Yea, all she slayeth; yea, every man save me;
Me, love, thy lover that must cleave to thee
   Till the ending of the days and ways of earth,
The shaking of the sources of the sea. 140

Me, most forsaken of all souls that fell;
Me, satiated with things insatiable;
   Me, for whose sake the extreme hell makes mirth,
Yea, laughter kindles at the heart of hell.

Alas thy beauty! for thy mouth's sweet sake
My soul is bitter to me, my limbs quake
   As water, as the flesh of men that weep,
As their heart's vein whose heart goes nigh to break.

Ah God, that sleep with flower-sweet finger-tips
Would crush the fruit of death upon my lips; 150
   Ah God, that death would tread the grapes of sleep
And wring their juice upon me as it drips.

There is no change of cheer for many days,
But change of chimes high up in the air, that sways
   Rung by the running fingers of the wind;
And singing sorrows heard on hidden ways.

Day smiteth day in twain, night sundereth night,
And on mine eyes the dark sits as the light;
   Yea, Lord, thou knowest I know not, having sinned,
If heaven be clean or unclean in thy sight. 160

Yea, as if earth were sprinkled over me,
Such chafed harsh earth as chokes a sandy sea,
   Each pore doth yearn, and the dried blood thereof
Gasps by sick fits, my heart swims heavily,

There is a feverish famine in my veins;
Below her bosom, where a crushed grape stains
   The white and blue, there my lips caught and clove
An hour since, and what mark of me remains?

I dare not always touch her, lest the kiss
Leave my lips charred. Yea, Lord, a little bliss,   170
   Brief bitter bliss, one hath for a great sin;
Nathless thou knowest how sweet a thing it is.

Sin, is it sin whereby men's souls are thrust
Into the pit? yet had I a good trust
   To save my soul before it slipped therein,
Trod under by the fire-shod feet of lust.

For if mine eyes fail and my soul takes breath,
I look between the iron sides of death
   Into sad hell where all sweet love hath end,
All but the pain that never finisheth.   180

There are the naked faces of great kings,
The singing folk with all their lute-playings;
   There when one cometh he shall have to friend
The grave that covets and the worm that clings.

There sit the knights that were so great of hand,
The ladies that were queens of fair green land,
   Grown grey and black now, brought unto the dust,
Soiled, without raiment, clad about with sand.

There is one end for all of them; they sit
Naked and sad, they drink the dregs of it,   190

Trodden as grapes in the wine-press of lust,
Trampled and trodden by the fiery feet.*

I see the marvellous mouth whereby there fell
Cities and people whom the gods loved well,
   Yet for her sake on them the fire gat hold,
And for their sakes on her the fire of hell.**

And softer than the Egyptian lote-leaf is,
The queen whose face was worth the world to kiss,
   Wearing at breast a suckling snake of gold;
And large pale lips of strong Semiramis,   200

Curled like a tiger's that curl back to feed;
Red only where the last kiss made them bleed;
   Her hair most thick with many a carven gem,
Deep in the mane, great-chested, like a steed.

Yea, with red sin the faces of them shine;
But in all these there was no sin like mine;
   No, not in all the strange great sins of them
That made the wine-press froth and foam with wine.

For I was of Christ's choosing, I God's knight,
No blinkard heathen stumbling for scant light;   210
   I can well see, for all the dusty days
Gone past, the clean great time of goodly fight.

I smell the breathing battle sharp with blows,
With shriek of shafts and snapping short of bows;
   The fair pure sword smites out in subtle ways,
Sounds and long lights are shed between the rows

---

    * Cf. *Isaiah* 63:2–3: "Wherefore art thou red in thine apparel, and
thy garments like him that treadeth in the winefat? I have trodden the
winepress alone; and of the people there was none with me: for I will
tread them in mine anger, and trample them in my fury; and their blood
shall be sprinkled upon my garments, and I will stain all my raiment."
    ** An allusion to Helen of Troy; the following two stanzas refer
to Cleopatra and to Queen Semiramis, legendary builder of Babylon.

Of beautiful mailed men; the edged light slips,
Most like a snake that takes short breath and dips
   Sharp from the beautifully bending head,
With all its gracious body lithe as lips   220

That curl in touching you; right in this wise
My sword doth, seeming fire in mine own eyes,
   Leaving all colours in them brown and red
And flecked with death; then the keen breaths like sighs,

The caught-up choked dry laughters following them,
When all the fighting face is grown a flame
   For pleasure, and the pulse that stuns the ears,
And the heart's gladness of the goodly game.

Let me think yet a little; I do know
These things were sweet, but sweet such years ago,   230
   Their savour is all turned now into tears;
Yea, ten years since, where the blue ripples blow,

The blue curled eddies of the blowing Rhine,
I felt the sharp wind shaking grass and vine
   Touch my blood too, and sting me with delight
Through all this waste and weary body of mine

That never feels clear air; right gladly then
I rode alone, a great way off my men,
   And heard the chiming bridle smite and smite,
And gave each rhyme thereof some rhyme again,   240

Till my song shifted to that iron one;
Seeing there rode up between me and the sun
   Some certain of my foe's men, for his three
White wolves across their painted coats did run.

The first red-bearded, with square cheeks—alack,
I made my knave's blood turn his beard to black;

The slaying of him was a joy to see:
Perchance too, when at night he came not back,

Some woman fell a-weeping, whom this thief
Would beat when he had drunken; yet small grief   250
   Hath any for the ridding of such knaves;
Yea, if one wept, I doubt her teen was brief.

This bitter love is sorrow in all lands,
Draining of eyelids, wringing of drenched hands,
   Sighing of hearts and filling up of graves;
A sign across the head of the world he stands,

As one that hath a plague-mark on his brows;
Dust and spilt blood do track him to his house
   Down under earth; sweet smells of lip and cheek,
Like a sweet snake's breath made more poisonous   260

With chewing of some perfumed deadly grass,
Are shed all round his passage if he pass,
   And their quenched savour leaves the whole soul weak,
Sick with keen guessing whence the perfume was.

As one who hidden in deep sedge and reeds
Smells the rare scent made where a panther feeds,
   And tracking ever slotwise the warm smell
Is snapped upon by the sweet mouth and bleeds,

His head far down the hot sweet throat of her—
So one tracks love, whose breath is deadlier,   270
   And lo, one springe and you are fast in hell,
Fast as the gin's grip of a wayfarer.

I think now, as the heavy hours decease
One after one, and bitter thoughts increase
   One upon one, of all sweet finished things;
The breaking of the battle; the long peace

Wherein we sat clothed softly, each man's hair
Crowned with green leaves beneath white hoods of vair;*
   The sounds of sharp spears at great tourneyings,
And noise of singing in the late sweet air.   280

I sang of love too, knowing nought thereof;
"Sweeter," I said, "the little laugh of love
   Than tears out of the eyes of Magdalen,
Or any fallen feather of the Dove.

"The broken little laugh that spoils a kiss,
The ache of purple pulses, and the bliss
   Of blinded eyelids that expand again—
Love draws them open with those lips of his,

"Lips that cling hard till the kissed face has grown
Of one same fire and colour with their own;   290
   Then ere one sleep, appeased with sacrifice,
Where his lips wounded, there his lips atone."

I sang these things long since and knew them not;
"Lo, here is love, or there is love, God wot,
   This man and that finds favour in his eyes,"
I said, "but I, what guerdon have I got?

"The dust of praise that is blown everywhere
In all men's faces with the common air;
   The bay-leaf that wants chafing to be sweet
Before they wind it in a singer's hair."   300

So that one dawn I rode forth sorrowing;
I had no hope but of some evil thing,
   And so rode slowly past the windy wheat
And past the vineyard and the water-spring,

Up to the Horsel. A great elder-tree
Held back its heaps of flowers to let me see

    * The fur of a variety of squirrel, used in trimming medieval robes.

The ripe tall grass, and one that walked therein,
Naked, with hair shed over to the knee.

She walked between the blossom and the grass;
I knew the beauty of her, what she was,   310
    The beauty of her body and her sin,
And in my flesh the sin of hers, alas!

Alas! for sorrow is all the end of this.
O sad kissed mouth, how sorrowful it is!
    O breast whereat some suckling sorrow clings,
Red with the bitter blossom of a kiss!

Ah, with blind lips I felt for you, and found
About my neck your hands and hair enwound,
    The hands that stifle and the hair that stings,
I felt them fasten sharply without sound.   320

Yea, for my sin I had great store of bliss:
Rise up, make answer for me, let thy kiss
    Seal my lips hard from speaking of my sin,
Lest one go mad to hear how sweet it is.

Yet I waxed faint with fume of barren bowers,
And murmuring of the heavy-headed hours;
    And let the dove's beak fret and peck within
My lips in vain, and Love shed fruitless flowers.

So that God looked upon me when your hands
Were hot about me; yea, God brake my bands   330
    To save my soul alive, and I came forth
Like a man blind and naked in strange lands

That hears men laugh and weep, and knows not whence
Nor wherefore, but is broken in his sense;
    Howbeit I met folk riding from the north
Towards Rome, to purge them of their souls' offence,

And rode with them, and spake to none; the day
Stunned me like lights upon some wizard way,
　　And ate like fire mine eyes and mine eyesight;
So rode I, hearing all these chant and pray,　　　　　　　　340

And marvelled; till before us rose and fell
White cursed hills, like outer skirts of hell
　　Seen where men's eyes look through the day to night,
Like a jagged shell's lips, harsh, untunable,

Blown in between by devils' wrangling breath;
Nathless we won well past that hell and death,
　　Down to the sweet land where all airs are good,
Even unto Rome where God's grace tarrieth.

Then came each man and worshipped at his knees
Who in the Lord God's likeness bears the keys　　　　　350
　　To bind or loose, and called on Christ's shed blood,
And so the sweet-souled father gave him ease.

But when I came I fell down at his feet,
Saying, "Father, though the Lord's blood be right sweet,
　　The spot it takes not off the panther's skin,
Nor shall an Ethiop's stain be bleached with it.*

"Lo, I have sinned and have spat out at God,
Wherefore his hand is heavier and his rod
　　More sharp because of mine exceeding sin,
And all his raiment redder than bright blood　　　　　360

"Before mine eyes; yea, for my sake I wot
The heat of hell is waxen seven times hot
　　Through my great sin." Then spake he some sweet
　　　　　word,
Giving me cheer; which thing availed me not;

* Cf. *Jeremiah* 13:23: "Can the Ethiopian change his skin, or the leopard his spots?"

Yea, scarce I wist if such indeed were said;
For when I ceased—lo, as one newly dead
   Who hears a great cry out of hell, I heard
The crying of his voice across my head.

"Until this dry shred staff, that hath no whit
Of leaf nor bark, bear blossom and smell sweet,   370
   Seek thou not any mercy in God's sight,
For so long shalt thou be cast out from it."

Yea, what if dried-up stems wax red and green,
Shall that thing be which is not nor has been?
   Yea, what if sapless bark wax green and white,
Shall any good fruit grow upon my sin?

Nay, though sweet fruit were plucked of a dry tree,
And though men drew sweet waters of the sea,
   There should not grow sweet leaves on this dead stem,
This waste wan body and shaken soul of me.   380

Yea, though God search it warily enough,
There is not one sound thing in all thereof;
   Though he search all my veins through, searching them
He shall find nothing whole therein but love.

For I came home right heavy, with small cheer,
And lo my love, mine own soul's heart, more dear
   Than mine own soul, more beautiful than God,
Who hath my being between the hands of her—

Fair still, but fair for no man saving me,
As when she came out of the naked sea   390
   Making the foam as fire whereon she trod,
And as the inner flower of fire was she.

Yea, she laid hold upon me, and her mouth
Clove unto mine as soul to body doth,

And, laughing, made her lips luxurious;
Her hair had smells of all the sunburnt south,

Strange spice and flower, strange savour of crushed fruit,
And perfume the swart kings tread underfoot
 For pleasure when their minds wax amorous,
Charred frankincense and grated sandal-root.   400

And I forgot fear and all weary things,
All ended prayers and perished thanksgivings,
 Feeling her face with all her eager hair
Cleave to me, clinging as a fire that clings

To the body and to the raiment, burning them;
As after death I know that such-like flame
 Small cleave to me for ever; yea, what care,
Albeit I burn then, having felt the same?

Ah love, there is no better life than this;
To have known love, how bitter a thing it is, 410
 And afterward be cast out of God's sight;
Yea, these that know not, shall they have such bliss

High up in barren heaven before his face
As we twain in the heavy-hearted place,
 Remembering love and all the dead delight,
And all that time was sweet with for a space?

For till the thunder in the trumpet be,
Soul may divide from body, but not we
 One from another; I hold thee with my hand,
I let mine eyes have all their will of thee, 420

I seal myself upon thee with my might,
Abiding alway out of all men's sight
 Until God loosen over sea and land
The thunder of the trumpets of the night.

EXPLICIT LAUS VENERIS.

The Triumph of Time

Before our lives divide for ever,
  While time is with us and hands are free,
(Time, swift to fasten and swift to sever
  Hand from hand, as we stand by the sea)
I will say no word that a man might say
Whose whole life's love goes down in a day;
For this could never have been; and never,
  Though the gods and the years relent, shall be.

Is it worth a tear, is it worth an hour,
  To think of things that are well outworn?   10
Of fruitless husk and fugitive flower,
  The dream foregone and the deed forborne?
Though joy be done with and grief be vain,
Time shall not sever us wholly in twain;
Earth is not spoilt for a single shower;
  But the rain has ruined the ungrown corn.

It will grow not again, this fruit of my heart,
  Smitten with sunbeams, ruined with rain.
The singing seasons divide and depart,
  Winter and summer depart in twain.   20
It will grow not again, it is ruined at root,
The bloodlike blossom, the dull red fruit;
Though the heart yet sickens, the lips yet smart,
  With sullen savour of poisonous pain.

I have given no man of my fruit to eat;
  I trod the grapes, I have drunken the wine.
Had you eaten and drunken and found it sweet,
  This wild new growth of the corn and vine,
This wine and bread without lees or leaven,

We had grown as gods, as the gods in heaven,*   30
Souls fair to look upon, goodly to greet,
   One splendid spirit, your soul and mine.

In the change of years, in the coil of things,
   In the clamour and rumour of life to be,
We, drinking love at the furthest springs,
   Covered with love as a covering tree,
We had grown as gods, as the gods above,
Filled from the heart to the lips with love,
Held fast in his hands, clothed warm with his wings,
   O love, my love, had you loved but me!   40

We had stood as the sure stars stand, and moved
   As the moon moves, loving the world; and seen
Grief collapse as a thing disproved,
   Death consume as a thing unclean.
Twain halves of a perfect heart, made fast
Soul to soul while the years fell past;
Had you loved me once, as you have not loved;
   Had the chance been with us that has not been.

I have put my days and dreams out of mind,
   Days that are over, dreams that are done.   50
Though we seek life through, we shall surely find
   There is none of them clear to us now, not one.
But clear are these things; the grass and the sand,
Where, sure as the eyes reach, ever at hand,
With lips wide open and face burnt blind,
   The strong sea-daisies feast on the sun.

The low downs lean to the sea; the stream,
   One loose thin pulseless tremulous vein,
Rapid and vivid and dumb as a dream,

---

   * Cf. *Genesis* 3:5: "For God doth know that in the day ye eat
[the fruit] thereof, then your eyes shall be opened, and ye shall be as
gods, knowing good and evil."

Works downward, sick of the sun and the rain;   60
No wind is rough with the rank rare flowers;
The sweet sea, mother of loves and hours,
Shudders and shines as the grey winds gleam,
    Turning her smile to a fugitive pain.

Mother of loves that are swift to fade,
    Mother of mutable winds and hours.
A barren mother, a mother-maid,
    Cold and clean as her faint salt flowers.
I would we twain were even as she,
Lost in the night and the light of the sea,   70
Where faint sounds falter and wan beams wade,
    Break, and are broken, and shed into showers.

The loves and hours of the life of a man,
    They are swift and sad, being born of the sea.
Hours that rejoice and regret for a span,
    Born with a man's breath, mortal as he;
Loves that are lost ere they come to birth,
Weeds of the wave, without fruit upon earth.
I lose what I long for, save what I can,
    My love, my love, and no love for me!   80

It is not much that a man can save
    On the sands of life, in the straits of time,
Who swims in sight of the great third wave
    That never a swimmer shall cross or climb.
Some waif washed up with the strays and spars
That ebb-tide shows to the shore and the stars;
Weed from the water, grass from a grave,
    A broken blossom, a ruined rhyme.

There will no man do for your sake, I think,
    What I would have done for the least word said.   90
I had wrung life dry for your lips to drink,
    Broken it up for your daily bread:

Body for body and blood for blood,
As the flow of the full sea risen to flood
That yearns and trembles before it sink,
  I had given, and lain down for you, glad and dead.

Yea, hope at highest and all her fruit,
  And time at fullest and all his dower,
I had given you surely, and life to boot,
  Were we once made one for a single hour.   100
But now, you are twain, you are cloven apart,
Flesh of his flesh, but heart of my heart;
And deep in one is the bitter root,
  And sweet for one is the lifelong flower.

To have died if you cared I should die for you, clung
  To my life if you bade me, played my part
As it pleased you—these were the thoughts that stung,
  The dreams that smote with a keener dart
Than shafts of love or arrows of death;
These were but as fire is, dust, or breath,   110
Or poisonous foam on the tender tongue
  Of the little snakes that eat my heart.

I wish we were dead together to-day,
  Lost sight of, hidden away out of sight,
Clasped and clothed in the cloven clay,
  Out of the world's way, out of the light,
Out of the ages of worldly weather,
Forgotten of all men altogether,
As the world's first dead, taken wholly away,
  Made one with death, filled full of the night.   120

How we should slumber, how we should sleep,
  Far in the dark with the dreams and the dews!
And dreaming, grow to each other, and weep,
  Laugh low, live softly, murmur and muse;
Yea, and it may be, struck through by the dream,

Feel the dust quicken and quiver, and seem
Alive as of old to the lips, and leap
  Spirit to spirit as lovers use.

Sick dreams and sad of a dull delight;
  For what shall it profit when men are dead   130
To have dreamed, to have loved with the whole soul's
    might,
  To have looked for day when the day was fled?
Let come what will, there is one thing worth,
To have had fair love in the life upon earth:
To have held love safe till the day grew night,
  While skies had colour and lips were red.

Would I lose you now? would I take you then,
  If I lose you now that my heart has need?
And come what may after death to men,
  What thing worth this will the dead years breed?   140
Lose life, lose all; but at least I know,
O sweet life's love, having loved you so,
Had I reached you on earth, I should lose not again,
  In death nor life, nor in dream or deed.

Yea, I know this well: were you once sealed mine,
  Mine in the blood's beat, mine in the breath,
Mixed into me as honey in wine,
  Not time, that sayeth and gainsayeth,
Nor all strong things had severed us then;
Not wrath of gods, nor wisdom of men,   150
Nor all things earthly, nor all divine,
  Nor joy nor sorrow, nor life nor death.

I had grown pure as the dawn and the dew,
  You had grown strong as the sun or the sea.
But none shall triumph a whole life through:
  For death is one, and the fates are three.
At the door of life, by the gate of breath,

There are worse things waiting for men than death;
Death could not sever my soul and you,
    As these have severed your soul from me.   160

You have chosen and clung to the chance they sent you,
    Life sweet as perfume and pure as prayer.
But will it not one day in heaven repent you?
    Will they solace you wholly, the days that were?
Will you lift up your eyes between sadness and bliss,
Meet mine, and see where the great love is,
And tremble and turn and be changed? Content you;
    The gate is strait; I shall not be there.*

But you, had you chosen, had you stretched hand,
    Had you seen good such a thing were done,   170
I too might have stood with the souls that stand
    In the sun's sight, clothed with the light of the sun;
But who now on earth need care how I live?
Have the high gods anything left to give,
Save dust and laurels and gold and sand?
    Which gifts are goodly; but I will none.

O all fair lovers about the world,
    There is none of you, none, that shall comfort me.
My thoughts are as dead things, wrecked and whirled
    Round and round in a gulf of the sea;   180
And still, through the sound and the straining stream,
Through the coil and chafe, they gleam in a dream,
The bright fine lips so cruelly curled,
    And strange swift eyes where the soul sits free.

Free, without pity, withheld from woe,
    Ignorant; fair as the eyes are fair.
Would I have you change now, change at a blow,
    Startled and stricken, awake and aware?

    * Cf. *Luke* 13:24: "Strive to enter in at the strait gate: for many, I say unto you, will seek to enter in, and shall not be able."

Yea, if I could, would I have you see
My very love of you filling me,   100
And know my soul to the quick, as I know
    The likeness and look of your throat and hair?

I shall not change you. Nay, though I might,
    Would I change my sweet one love with a word?
I had rather your hair should change in a night,
    Clear now as the plume of a black bright bird;
Your face fail suddenly, cease, turn grey,
Die as a leaf that dies in a day.
I will keep my soul in a place out of sight,
    Far off, where the pulse of it is not heard.   200

Far off it walks, in a bleak blown space,
    Full of the sound of the sorrow of years.
I have woven a veil for the weeping face,
    Whose lips have drunken the wine of tears;
I have found a way for the failing feet,
A place for slumber and sorrow to meet;
There is no rumour about the place,
    Nor light, nor any that sees or hears.

I have hidden my soul out of sight, and said
    "Let none take pity upon thee, none   210
Comfort thy crying; for lo, thou art dead,
    Lie still now, safe out of sight of the sun.
Have I not built thee a grave, and wrought
Thy grave-clothes on thee of grievous thought,
With soft spun verses and tears unshed,
    And sweet light visions of things undone?

"I have given thee garments and balm and myrrh,
    And gold, and beautiful burial things.
But thou, be at peace now, make no stir;
    Is not thy grave as a royal king's?   220
Fret not thyself though the end were sore;

Sleep, be patient, vex me no more.
Sleep; what hast thou to do with her?
  The eyes that weep, with the mouth that sings?"

Where the dead red leaves of the years lie rotten,
  The cold old crimes and the deeds thrown by,
The misconceived and the misbegotten,
  I would find a sin to do ere I die,
Sure to dissolve and destroy me all through,
That would set you higher in heaven, serve you   230
And leave you happy, when clean forgotten,
  As a dead man out of mind, am I.

Your lithe hands draw me, your face burns through me,
  I am swift to follow you, keen to see;
But love lacks might to redeem or undo me;
  As I have been, I know I shall surely be;
"What should such fellows as I do?" * Nay,
My part were worse if I chose to play;
For the worst is this after all; if they knew me,
  Not a soul upon earth would pity me.   240

And I play not for pity of these; but you,
  If you saw with your soul what man am I,
You would praise me at least that my soul all through
  Clove to you, loathing the lives that lie;
The souls and lips that are bought and sold,
The smiles of silver and kisses of gold,
The lapdog loves that whine as they chew,
  The little lovers that curse and cry.

There are fairer women, I hear; that may be;
  But I, that I love you and find you fair,   250
Who are more than fair in my eyes if they be,
  Do the high gods know or the great gods care?

  * Cf. *Hamlet*, Act III, Scene 1, lines 132–3: "What should such
fellows as I do, crawling between earth and heaven?"

Though the swords in my heart for one were seven,*
Would the iron hollow of doubtful heaven,
That knows not itself whether night-time or day be,
 Reverberate words and a foolish prayer?

I will go back to the great sweet mother,
 Mother and lover of men, the sea.
I will go down to her, I and none other,
 Close with her, kiss her and mix her with me;   260
Cling to her, strive with her, hold her fast:
O fair white mother, in days long past
Born without sister, born without brother,
 Set free my soul as thy soul is free.

O fair green-girdled mother of mine,
 Sea, that art clothed with the sun and the rain,
Thy sweet hard kisses are strong like wine,
 Thy large embraces are keen like pain.
Save me and hide me with all thy waves,
Find me one grave of thy thousand graves,   270
Those pure cold populous graves of thine
 Wrought without hand in a world without stain.

I shall sleep, and move with the moving ships,
 Change as the winds change, veer in the tide;
My lips will feast on the foam of thy lips,
 I shall rise with thy rising, with thee subside;
Sleep, and not know if she be, if she were,
Filled full with life to the eyes and hair,
As a rose is fulfilled to the roseleaf tips
 With splendid summer and perfume and pride.   280

This woven raiment of nights and days,
 Were it once cast off and unwound from me,
Naked and glad would I walk in thy ways,
 Alive and aware of thy ways and thee;

  * An allusion to the Seven Sorrows of the Virgin, symbolized by seven swords piercing the heart.

Clear of the whole world, hidden at home,
Clothed with the green and crowned with the foam,
A pulse of the life of thy straits and bays,
   A vein in the heart of the streams of the sea.

Fair mother, fed with the lives of men,
   Thou art subtle and cruel of heart, men say.   290
Thou hast taken, and shalt not render again;
   Thou art full of thy dead, and cold as they.
But death is the worst that comes of thee;
Thou art fed with our dead, O mother, O sea,
But when hast thou fed on our hearts? or when,
   Having given us love, hast thou taken away?

O tender-hearted, O perfect lover,
   Thy lips are bitter, and sweet thine heart.
The hopes that hurt and the dreams that hover,
   Shall they not vanish away and apart?   300
But thou, thou art sure, thou art older than earth;
Thou art strong for death and fruitful of birth;
Thy depths conceal and thy gulfs discover;
   From the first thou wert; in the end thou art.

And grief shall endure not for ever, I know.
   As things that are not shall these things be;
We shall live through seasons of sun and of snow,
   And none be grievous as this to me.
We shall hear, as one in a trance that hears,
The sound of time, the rhyme of the years;   310
Wrecked hope and passionate pain will grow
   As tender things of a spring-tide sea.

Sea-fruit that swings in the waves that hiss,
   Drowned gold and purple and royal rings.
And all time past, was it all for this?
   Times unforgotten, and treasures of things?
Swift years of liking and sweet long laughter,
That wist not well of the years thereafter

Till love woke, smitten at heart by a kiss,
  With lips that trembled and trailing wings? 320

There lived a singer in France of old *
  By the tideless dolorous midland sea.
In a land of sand and ruin and gold
  There shone one woman, and none but she.
And finding life for her love's sake fail,
Being fain to see her, he bade set sail,
Touched land, and saw her as life grew cold,
  And praised God, seeing; and so died he.

Died, praising God for his gift and grace:
  For she bowed down to him weeping, and said 330
"Live;" and her tears were shed on his face
  Or ever the life in his face was shed.
The sharp tears fell through her hair, and stung
Once, and her close lips touched him and clung
Once, and grew one with his lips for a space;
  And so drew back, and the man was dead.

O brother, the gods were good to you.
  Sleep, and be glad while the world endures.
Be well content as the years wear through;
  Give thanks for life, and the loves and lures; 340
Give thanks for life, O brother, and death,
For the sweet last sound of her feet, her breath,
For gifts she gave you, gracious and few,
  Tears and kisses, that lady of yours.

Rest, and be glad of the gods; but I,
  How shall I praise them, or how take rest?
There is not room under all the sky
  For me that know not of worst or best,
Dream or desire of the days before,

* Geoffrey Rudel, a twelfth-century Provençal poet, who, according to legend, fell in love, sight unseen, with the Countess of Tripoli and journeyed to his death to see her.

Sweet things or bitterness, any more.   350
Love will not come to me now though I die,
    As love came close to you, breast to breast.

I shall never be friends again with roses;
    I shall loathe sweet tunes, where a note grown strong
Relents and recoils, and climbs and closes,
    As a wave of the sea turned back by song.
There are sounds where the soul's delight takes fire,
Face to face with its own desire;
A delight that rebels, a desire that reposes;
    I shall hate sweet music my whole life long.   360

The pulse of war and passion of wonder,
    The heavens that murmur, the sounds that shine,
The stars that sing and the loves that thunder,
    The music burning at heart like wine,
An armed archangel whose hands raise up
All senses mixed in the spirit's cup
Till flesh and spirit are molten in sunder—
    These things are over, and no more mine.

These were a part of the playing I heard
    Once, ere my love and my heart were at strife;   370
Love that sings and hath wings as a bird,
    Balm of the wound and heft of the knife.
Fairer than earth is the sea, and sleep
Than overwatching of eyes that weep,
Now time has done with his one sweet word,
    The wine and leaven of lovely life.

I shall go my ways, tread out my measure,
    Fill the days of my daily breath
With fugitive things not good to treasure,
    Do as the world doth, say as it saith;   380
But if we had loved each other—O sweet,
Had you felt, lying under the palms of your feet,

The heart of my heart, beating harder with pleasure
    To feel you tread it to dust and death—

Ah, had I not taken my life up and given
    All that life gives and the years let go,
The wine and honey, the balm and leaven,
    The dreams reared high and the hopes brought low?
Come life, come death, not a word be said;
Should I lose you living, and vex you dead?   390
I never shall tell you on earth; and in heaven,
    If I cry to you then, will you hear or know?

Itylus *

Swallow, my sister, O sister swallow,
    How can thine heart be full of the spring?
      A thousand summers are over and dead.
What hast thou found in the spring to follow?
    What hast thou found in thine heart to sing?
      What wilt thou do when the summer is shed?

O swallow, sister, O fair swift swallow,
    Why wilt thou fly after spring to the south,
      The soft south whither thine heart is set?
Shall not the grief of the old time follow?   10
    Shall not the song thereof cleave to thy mouth?
      Hast thou forgotten ere I forget?

Sister, my sister, O fleet sweet swallow,
    Thy way is long to the sun and the south;
      But I, fulfilled of my heart's desire,

* Based on the myth of Philomela, raped by her brother-in-law, Tereus, King of Thrace, who cut out her tongue. Weaving the story into a tapestry, Philomela informed her sister, Procne, who in revenge killed her son Itylus and fed him to her husband Tereus. Procne fled as a swallow; Philomela, a nightingale.

Shedding my song upon height, upon hollow,
　　From tawny body and sweet small mouth
　　　Feed the heart of the night with fire.

I the nightingale all spring through,
　　O swallow, sister, O changing swallow,   20
　　　All spring through till the spring be done,
Clothed with the light of the night on the dew,
　　Sing, while the hours and the wild birds follow,
　　　Take flight and follow and find the sun.

Sister, my sister, O soft light swallow,
　　Though all things feast in the spring's guest-chamber,
　　　How hast thou heart to be glad thereof yet?
For where thou fliest I shall not follow,
　　Till life forget and death remember,
　　　Till thou remember and I forget.   30

Swallow, my sister, O singing swallow,
　　I know not how thou hast heart to sing.
　　　Hast thou the heart? is it all past over?
Thy lord the summer is good to follow,
　　And fair the feet of thy lover the spring:
　　　But what wilt thou say to the spring thy lover?

O swallow, sister, O fleeting swallow,
　　My heart in me is a molten ember
　　　And over my head the waves have met.
But thou wouldst tarry or I would follow,   40
　　Could I forget or thou remember,
　　　Couldst thou remember and I forget.

O sweet stray sister, O shifting swallow,
　　The heart's division divideth us.
　　　Thy heart is light as a leaf of a tree;
But mine goes forth among sea-gulfs hollow
　　To the place of the slaying of Itylus,
　　　The feast of Daulis, the Thracian sea.

O swallow, sister, O rapid swallow,
  I pray thee sing not a little space. 50
    Are not the roofs and the lintels wet?
The woven web that was plain to follow,
  The small slain body, the flowerlike face,
    Can I remember if thou forget?

O sister, sister, thy first-begotten!
  The hands that cling and the feet that follow,
    The voice of the child's blood crying yet
Who hath remembered me? who hath forgotten?
  Thou hast forgotten, O summer swallow,
    But the world shall end when I forget. 60

Anactoria *

My life is bitter with thy love; thine eyes
Blind me, thy tresses burn me, thy sharp sighs
Divide my flesh and spirit with soft sound,
And my blood strengthens, and my veins abound.
I pray thee sigh not, speak not, draw not breath;
Let life burn down, and dream it is not death.
I would the sea had hidden us, the fire
(Wilt thou fear that, and fear not my desire?)
Severed the bones that bleach, the flesh that cleaves,
And let our sifted ashes drop like leaves. 10
I feel thy blood against my blood: my pain
Pains thee, and lips bruise lips, and vein stings vein.
Let fruit be crushed on fruit, let flower on flower,
Breast kindle breast, and either burn one hour.
Why wilt thou follow lesser loves? are thine
Too weak to bear these hands and lips of mine?
I charge thee for my life's sake, O too sweet
To crush love with thy cruel faultless feet,

* For Swinburne's comments on this very free rendering of Sappho's ode to one of her favorites, see pp. 327–31.

I charge thee keep thy lips from hers or his,
Sweetest, till theirs be sweeter than my kiss: 20
Lest I too lure, a swallow for a dove,
Erotion or Erinna to my love.
I would my love could kill thee; I am satiated
With seeing thee live, and fain would have thee dead.
I would earth had thy body as fruit to eat,
And no mouth but some serpent's found thee sweet.
I would find grievous ways to have thee slain,
Intense device, and superflux of pain;
Vex thee with amorous agonies, and shake
Life at thy lips, and leave it there to ache;   30
Strain out thy soul with pangs too soft to kill,
Intolerable interludes, and infinite ill;
Relapse and reluctation of the breath,
Dumb tunes and shuddering semitones of death.
I am weary of all thy words and soft strange ways,
Of all love's fiery nights and all his days,
And all the broken kisses salt as brine
That shuddering lips make moist with waterish wine,
And eyes the bluer for all those hidden hours
That pleasure fills with tears and feeds from flowers,   40
Fierce at the heart with fire that half comes through,
But all the flowerlike white stained round with blue;
The fervent underlid, and that above
Lifted with laughter or abashed with love;
Thine amorous girdle, full of thee and fair,
And leavings of the lilies in thine hair.
Yea, all sweet words of thine and all thy ways,
And all the fruit of nights and flower of days,
And stinging lips wherein the hot sweet brine
That Love was born of burns and foams like wine,   50
And eyes insatiable of amorous hours,
Fervent as fire and delicate as flowers,
Coloured like night at heart, but cloven through
Like night with flame, dyed round like night with blue,
Clothed with deep eyelids under and above—
Yea, all thy beauty sickens me with love;

Thy girdle empty of thee and now not fair,
And ruinous lilies in thy languid hair.
Ah, take no thought for Love's sake; shall this be,
And she who loves thy lover not love thee?   60
Sweet soul, sweet mouth of all that laughs and lives,
Mine is she, very mine; and she forgives.
For I beheld in sleep the light that is
In her high place in Paphos, heard the kiss
Of body and soul that mix with eager tears
And laughter stinging through the eyes and ears;
Saw Love, as burning flame from crown to feet,
Imperishable, upon her storied seat;
Clear eyelids lifted toward the north and south,
A mind of many colours, and a mouth   70
Of many tunes and kisses; and she bowed,
With all her subtle face laughing aloud,
Bowed down upon me, saying, "Who doth thee wrong,
Sappho?" but thou—thy body is the song,
Thy mouth the music; thou art more than I,
Though my voice die not till the whole world die;
Though men that hear it madden; though love weep,
Though nature change, though shame be charmed to sleep.
Ah, wilt thou slay me lest I kiss thee dead?
Yet the queen laughed from her sweet heart and said: 80
"Even she that flies shall follow for thy sake,
And she shall give thee gifts that would not take,
Shall kiss that would not kiss thee" (yea, kiss me)
"When thou wouldst not"—when I would not kiss thee!
Ah, more to me than all men as thou art,
Shall not my songs assuage her at the heart?
Ah, sweet to me as life seems sweet to death,
Why should her wrath fill thee with fearful breath?
Nay, sweet, for is she God alone? hath she
Made earth and all the centuries of the sea,   90
Taught the sun ways to travel, woven most fine
The moonbeams, shed the starbeams forth as wine,
Bound with her myrtles, beaten with her rods,
The young men and the maidens and the gods?

Have we not lips to love with, eyes for tears,
And summer and flower of women and of years?
Stars for the foot of morning, and for noon
Sunlight, and exaltation of the moon;
Waters that answer waters, fields that wear
Lilies, and languor of the Lesbian air?   100
Beyond those flying feet of fluttered doves,
Are there not other gods for other loves?
Yea, though she scourge thee, sweetest, for my sake,
Blossom not thorns and flowers not blood should break.
Ah that my lips were tuneless lips, but pressed
To the bruised blossom of thy scourged white breast!
Ah that my mouth for Muses' milk were fed
On the sweet blood thy sweet small wounds had bled!
That with my tongue I felt them, and could taste
The faint flakes from thy bosom to the waist!   110
That I could drink thy veins as wine, and eat
Thy breasts like honey! that from face to feet
Thy body were abolished and consumed,
And in my flesh thy very flesh entombed!
Ah, ah, thy beauty! like a beast it bites,
Stings like an adder, like an arrow smites.
Ah sweet, and sweet again, and seven times sweet,
The paces and the pauses of thy feet!
Ah sweeter than all sleep or summer air
The fallen fillets fragrant from thine hair!   120
Yea, though their alien kisses do me wrong,
Sweeter thy lips than mine with all their song;
Thy shoulders whiter than a fleece of white,
And flower-sweet fingers, good to bruise or bite
As honeycomb of the inmost honey-cells,
With almond-shaped and roseleaf-coloured shells
And blood like purple blossom at the tips
Quivering; and pain made perfect in thy lips
For my sake when I hurt thee; O that I
Durst crush thee out of life with love, and die,   130
Die of thy pain and my delight, and be
Mixed with thy blood and molten into thee!

Would I not plague thee dying overmuch?
Would I not hurt thee perfectly? not touch
Thy pores of sense with torture, and make bright
Thine eyes with bloodlike tears and grievous light?
Strike pang from pang as note is struck from note,
Catch the sob's middle music in thy throat,
Take they limbs living, and new-mould with these
A lyre of many faultless agonies?   140
Feed thee with fever and famine and fine drouth,
With perfect pangs convulse thy perfect mouth,
Make thy life shudder in thee and burn afresh,
And wring thy very spirit through the flesh?
Cruel? but love makes all that love him well
As wise as heaven and crueller than hell.
Me hath love made more bitter toward thee
Than death toward man; but were I made as he
Who hath made all things to break them one by one,
If my feet trod upon the stars and sun   150
And souls of men as his have always trod,
God knows I might be crueller than God.
For who shall change with prayers or thanksgivings
The mystery of the cruelty of things?
Or say what God above all gods and years
With offering and blood-sacrifice of tears,
With lamentation from strange lands, from graves
Where the snake pastures, from scarred mouths of slaves,
From prison, and from plunging prows of ships
Through flamelike foam of the sea's closing lips—   160
With thwartings of strange signs, and wind-blown hair
Of comets, desolating the dim air,
When darkness is made fast with seals and bars,
And fierce reluctance of disastrous stars,
Eclipse, and sound of shaken hills, and wings
Darkening, and blind inexpiable things—
With sorrow of labouring moons, and altering light
And travail of the planets of the night,
And weeping of the weary Pleiads seven,
Feeds the mute melancholy lust of heaven?   170

Is not his incense bitterness, his meat
Murder? his hidden face and iron feet
Hath not man known, and felt them on their way
Threaten and trample all things and every day?
Hath he not sent us hunger? who hath cursed
Spirit and flesh with longing? filled with thirst
Their lips who cried unto him? who bade exceed
The fervid will, fall short the feeble deed,
Bade sink the spirit and the flesh aspire,
Pain animate the dust of dead desire,   180
And life yield up her flower to violent fate?
Him would I reach, him smite, him desecrate,
Pierce the cold lips of God with human breath,
And mix his immortality with death.
Why hath he made us? what had all we done
That we should live and loathe the sterile sun,
And with the moon wax paler as she wanes,
And pulse by pulse feel time grow through our veins?
Thee too the years shall cover; thou shalt be
As the rose born of one same blood with thee,   190
As a song sung, as a word said, and fall
Flower-wise, and be not any more at all,
Nor any memory of thee anywhere;
For never Muse has bound above thine hair
The high Pierian flower whose graft outgrows
All summer kinship of the mortal rose
And colour of deciduous days, nor shed
Reflex and flush of heaven about thine head,
Nor reddened brows made pale by floral grief
With splendid shadow from that lordlier leaf.   200
Yea, thou shalt be forgotten like spilt wine,
Except these kisses of my lips on thine
Brand them with immortality; but me—
Men shall not see bright fire nor hear the sea,
Nor mix their hearts with music, nor behold
Cast forth of heaven, with feet of awful gold
And plumeless wings that make the bright air blind,
Lightning, with thunder for a hound behind

Hunting through fields unfurrowed and unsown,
But in the light and laughter, in the moan 210
And music, and in grasp of lip and hand
And shudder of water that makes felt on land
The immeasurable tremor of all the sea,
Memories shall mix and metaphors of me.
Like me shall be the shuddering calm of night,
When all the winds of the world for pure delight
Close lips that quiver and fold up wings that ache;
When nightingales are louder for love's sake,
And leaves tremble like lute-strings or like fire;
Like me the one star swooning with desire 220
Even at the cold lips of the sleepless moon,
As I at thine; like me the waste white noon,
Burnt through with barren sunlight; and like me
The land-stream and the tide-stream in the sea.
I am sick with time as these with ebb and flow,
And by the yearning in my veins I know
The yearning sound of waters; and mine eyes
Burn as that beamless fire which fills the skies
With troubled stars and travailing things of flame;
And in my heart the grief consuming them 230
Labours, and in my veins the thirst of these,
And all the summer travail of the trees
And all the winter sickness; and the earth,
Filled full with deadly works of death and birth,
Sore spent with hungry lusts of birth and death,
Has pain like mine in her divided breath;
Her spring of leaves is barren, and her fruit
Ashes; her boughs are burdened, and her root
Fibrous and gnarled with poison; underneath
Serpents have gnawn it through with tortuous teeth 240
Made sharp upon the bones of all the dead,
And wild birds rend her branches overhead.
These, woven as raiment for his word and thought,
These hath God made, and me as these, and wrought
Song, and hath lit it at my lips; and me
Earth shall not gather though she feed on thee.

As a shed tear shalt thou be shed; but I—
Lo, earth may labour, men live long and die,
Years change and stars, and the high God devise
New things, and old things wane before his eyes   250
Who wields and wrecks them, being more strong than
    they—
But, having made me, me he shall not slay.
Nor slay nor satiate, like those herds of his
Who laugh and live a little, and their kiss
Contents them, and their loves are swift and sweet,
And sure death grasps and gains them with slow feet,
Love they or hate they, strive or bow their knees—
And all these end; he hath his will of these.
Yea, but albeit he slay me, hating me—
Albeit he hide me in the deep dear sea   260
And cover me with cool wan foam, and ease
This soul of mine as any soul of these,
And give me water and great sweet waves, and make
The very sea's name lordlier for my sake,
The whole sea sweeter—albeit I die indeed
And hide myself and sleep and no man heed,
Of me the high God hath not all his will.
Blossom of branches, and on each high hill
Clear air and wind, and under in clamorous vales
Fierce noises of the fiery nightingales,   270
Buds burning in the sudden spring like fire,
The wan washed sand and the waves' vain desire,
Sails seen like blown white flowers at sea, and words
That bring tears swiftest, and long notes of birds
Violently singing till the whole world sings—
I Sappho shall be one with all these things,
With all high things for ever; and my face
Seen once, my songs once heard in a strange place,
Cleave to men's lives, and waste the days thereof
With gladness and much sadness and long love.   280
Yea, they shall say, earth's womb has borne in vain
New things, and never this best thing again;
Borne days and men, borne fruits and wars and wine,

Seasons and songs, but no song more like mine.
And they shall know me as ye who have known me here,
Last year when I loved Atthis, and this year
When I love thee; and they shall praise me, and say
"She hath all time as all we have our day,
Shall she not live and have her will"—even I?
Yea, though thou diest, I say I shall not die.   290
For these shall give me of their souls, shall give
Life, and the days and loves wherewith I live,
Shall quicken me with loving, fill with breath,
Save me and serve me, strive for me with death.
Alas, that neither moon nor snow nor dew
Nor all cold things can purge me wholly through,
Assuage me nor allay me nor appease,
Till supreme sleep shall bring me bloodless ease;
Till time wax faint in all his periods;
Till fate undo the bondage of the gods,   300
And lay, to slake and satiate me all through,
Lotus and Lethe on my lips like dew,
And shed around and over and under me
Thick darkness and the insuperable sea.

Hymn to Proserpine

(*AFTER THE PROCLAMATION IN ROME OF THE
CHRISTIAN FAITH*)

*Vicisti, Galilæe.**

I have lived long enough, having seen one thing, that love
hath an end;

* "Thou hast conquered, O Galilean," said to be the dying words of
Julian the Apostate, Roman emperor (331–63).
    Proserpine (cf. the "Garden of Proserpine," p. 159), daughter of
Zeus and Demeter, the Earth Mother, was carried off to the underworld,
where she became Queen, and was allowed to return to earth each spring.
But Swinburne's Proserpine, as he writes in *Lesbia Brandon* (p. 389,
below), "was not the old Proserpine who comes and goes up and down
between Sicily and hell; she had never seen the sun."

Goddess and maiden and queen, be near me now and
  befriend.

Thou art more than the day or the morrow, the seasons
  that laugh or that weep;

For these give joy and sorrow; but thou, Proserpina, sleep.

Sweet is the treading of wine, and sweet the feet of the
  dove;

But a goodlier gift is thine than foam of the grapes or love.

Yea, is not even Apollo, with hair and harpstring of gold,

A bitter God to follow, a beautiful God to behold?

I am sick of singing: the bays burn deep and chafe: I am
  fain

To rest a little from praise and grievous pleasure and pain.   10

For the Gods we know not of, who give us our daily
  breath,

We know they are cruel as love or life, and lovely as death.

O Gods dethroned and deceased, cast forth, wiped out in
  a day!

From your wrath is the world released, redeemed from
  your chains, men say.

New Gods are crowned in the city; their flowers have
  broken your rods;

They are merciful, clothed with pity, the young
  compassionate Gods.

But for me their new device is barren, the days are bare;

Things long past over suffice, and men forgotten that
  were.

Time and the Gods are at strife; ye dwell in the midst
  thereof,

Draining a little life from the barren breasts of love.   20

I say to you, cease, take rest; yea, I say to you all, be at
  peace,

Till the bitter milk of her breast and the barren bosom
  shall cease.

Wilt thou yet take all, Galilean? but these thou shalt not
  take,

The laurel, the palms and the pæan, the breasts of the
  nymphs in the brake;

Breasts more soft than a dove's, that tremble with
    tenderer breath;
And all the wings of the Loves, and all the joy before
    death;
All the feet of the hours that sound as a single lyre,
Dropped and deep in the flowers, with strings that flicker
    like fire.
More than these wilt thou give, things fairer than all
    these things?
Nay, for a little we live, and life hath mutable wings.   30
A little while and we die; shall life not thrive as it may?
For no man under the sky lives twice, outliving his day.
And grief is a grievous thing, and a man hath enough of
    his tears:
Why should he labour, and bring fresh grief to blacken
    his years?
Thou hast conquered, O pale Galilean; the world has
    grown grey from thy breath;
We have drunken of things Lethean, and fed on the
    fulness of death.
Laurel is green for a season, and love is sweet for a day;
But love grows bitter with treason, and laurel outlives
    not May.
Sleep, shall we sleep after all? for the world is not sweet
    in the end;
For the old faiths loosen and fall, the new years ruin and
    rend.   40
Fate is a sea without shore, and the soul is a rock that
    abides;
But her ears are vexed with the roar and her face with
    the foam of the tides.
O lips that the live blood faints in, the leavings of racks
    and rods!
O ghastly glories of saints, dead limbs of gibbeted
    Gods!
Though all men abase them before you in spirit, and all
    knees bend,

I kneel not neither adore you, but standing, look to the
    end.

All delicate days and pleasant, all spirits and sorrows are
    cast

Far out with the foam of the present that sweeps to the
    surf of the past:

Where beyond the extreme sea-wall, and between the
    remote sea-gates,

Waste water washes, and tall ships founder, and deep   50
    death waits:

Where, mighty with deepening sides, clad about with the
    seas as with wings,

And impelled of invisible tides, and fulfilled of unspeak-
    able things,

White-eyed and poisonous-finned, shark-toothed and
    serpentine-curled,

Rolls, under the whitening wind of the future, the wave
    of the world.

The depths stand naked in sunder behind it, the storms
    flee away;

In the hollow before it the thunder is taken and snared
    as a prey;

In its sides is the north-wind bound; and its salt is of all
    men's tears;

With light of ruin, and sound of changes, and pulse of
    years:

With travail of day after day, and with trouble of hour
    upon hour;

And bitter as blood is the spray; and the crests are as   60
    fangs that devour:

And its vapour and storm of its steam as the sighing of
    spirits to be;

And its noise as the noise in a dream; and its depth as
    the roots of the sea:

And the height of its heads as the height of the utmost
    stars of the air:

And the ends of the earth at the might thereof tremble,
    and time is made bare.

Will ye bridle the deep sea with reins, will ye chasten
    the high sea with rods? *

Will ye take her to chain her with chains, who is older
    than all ye Gods?

All ye as a wind shall go by, as a fire shall ye pass and
    be past;

Ye are Gods, and behold, ye shall die, and the waves be
    upon you at last.

In the darkness of time, in the deeps of the years, in
    the changes of things,

Ye shall sleep as a slain man sleeps, and the world shall   70
    forget you for kings.

Though the feet of thine high priests tread where thy
    lords and our forefathers trod,

Though these that were Gods are dead, and thou being
    dead art a God,

Though before thee the throned Cytherean** be fallen,
    and hidden her head,

Yet thy kingdom shall pass, Galilean, thy dead shall go
    down to thee dead.

Of the maiden thy mother men sing as a goddess with
    grace clad around;

Thou art throned where another was king; where another
    was queen she is crowned.

Yea, once we had sight of another: but now she is queen,
    say these.

Not as thine, not as thine was our mother, a blossom of
    flowering seas,

Clothed round with the world's desire as with raiment,
    and fair as the foam,

And fleeter than kindled fire, and a goddess, and mother   80
    of Rome.

For thine came pale and a maiden, and sister to sorrow;
    but ours,

---

    * Cf. *Job* 38:8: "Who shut up the sea with doors, when it brake
forth . . . ?" Swinburne here ironically echoes the voice of Jehovah to
cast doubt on the authenticity of the Son.

    ** Venus-Aphrodite, born of the sea-foam off the isle of Cythera,
mother of Aeneas and Rome (line 80).

Her deep hair heavily laden with odour and colour of
    flowers,
White rose of the rose-white water, a silver splendour, a
    flame,
Bent down unto us that besought her, and earth grew
    sweet with her name.
For thine came weeping, a slave among slaves, and
    rejected; but she
Came flushed from the full-flushed wave, and imperial,
    her foot on the sea.
And the wonderful waters knew her, the winds and the
    viewless ways,
And the roses grew rosier, and bluer the sea-blue stream
    of the bays.
Ye are fallen, our lords, by what token? we wist that
    ye should not fall.
Ye were all so fair that are broken; and one more fair   90
    than ye all.
But I turn to her still, having seen she shall surely abide
    in the end;
Goddess and maiden and queen, be near me now and
    befriend.
O daughter of earth, of my mother, her crown and
    blossom of birth,
I am also, I also, thy brother; I go as I came unto
    earth.
In the night where thine eyes are as moons are in heaven,
    the night where thou art,
Where the silence is more than all tunes, where sleep
    overflows from the heart,
Where the poppies are sweet as the rose in our world,
    and the red rose is white,
And the wind falls faint as it blows with the fume of the
    flowers of the night,
And the murmur of spirits that sleep in the shadow of
    Gods from afar
Grows dim in thine ears and deep as the deep dim soul   100
    of a star,

In the sweet low light of thy face, under heavens untrod
    by the sun,
Let my soul with their souls find place, and forget what
    is done and undone.
Thou art more than the Gods who number the days of
    our temporal breath;
For these give labour and slumber; but thou, Proserpina,
    death.
Therefore now at thy feet I abide for a season in silence.
    I know
I shall die as my fathers died, and sleep as they sleep;
    even so.
For the glass of the years is brittle wherein we gaze for
    a span;
A little soul for a little bears up this corpse which is
    man.
So long I endure, no longer; and laugh not again, neither
    weep.
For there is no God found stronger than death; and   110
    death is a sleep.

Hermaphroditus

I

Lift up thy lips, turn round, look back for love,
    Blind love that comes by night and casts out rest;
    Of all things tired thy lips look weariest,
Save the long smile that they are wearied of.
Ah sweet, albeit no love be sweet enough,
    Choose of two loves and cleave unto the best,
    Two loves at either blossom of thy breast
Strive until one be under and one above.
Their breath is fire upon the amorous air,
    Fire in thine eyes and where thy lips suspire: 10
And whosoever hath seen thee, being so fair,

Two things turn all his life and blood to fire;
A strong desire begot on great despair,
  A great despair cast out by strong desire.

II

Where between sleep and life some brief space is,
  With love like gold bound round about the head,
  Sex to sweet sex with lips and limbs is wed,
Turning the fruitful feud of hers and his
To the waste wedlock of a sterile kiss;
  Yet from them something like as fire is shed   20
  That shall not be assuaged till death be dead,
Though neither life nor sleep can find out this.
Love made himself of flesh that perisheth
  A pleasure-house for all the loves his kin;
But on the one side sat a man like death,
  And on the other a woman sat like sin.
So with veiled eyes and sobs between his breath
  Love turned himself and would not enter in.

III

Love, is it love or sleep or shadow or light
  That lies between thine eyelids and thine eyes?   30
  Like a flower laid upon a flower it lies,
Or like the night's dew laid upon the night.
Love stands upon thy left hand and thy right,
  Yet by no sunset and by no moonrise
  Shall make thee man and ease a woman's sighs,
  Or make thee woman for a man's delight.
To what strange end hath some strange god made fair
  The double blossom of two fruitless flowers?
Hid love in all the folds of all thy hair,
  Fed thee on summers, watered thee with showers,   40
Given all the gold that all the seasons wear
  To thee that art a thing of barren hours?

IV

Yea, love, I see; it is not love but fear.

Nay, sweet, it is not fear but love, I know;
  Or wherefore should thy body's blossom blow
So sweetly, or thine eyelids leave so clear
Thy gracious eyes that never made a tear—
    Though for their love our tears like blood should flow,
    Though love and life and death should come and go,
So dreadful, so desirable, so dear?   50
Yea, sweet, I know; I saw in what swift wise
    Beneath the woman's and the water's kiss
    Thy moist limbs melted into Salmacis,*
And the large light turned tender in thine eyes,
And all thy boy's breath softened into sighs;
    But Love being blind, how should he know of this?

In the Orchard

(*PROVENÇAL BURDEN*)

Leave go my hands, let me catch breath and see;
Let the dew-fall drench either side of me;
  Clear apple-leaves are soft upon that moon
Seen sidelong like a blossom in the tree;
  Ah God, ah God, that day should be so soon.

The grass is thick and cool, it lets us lie.
Kissed upon either cheek and either eye,
  I turn to thee as some green afternoon
Turns toward sunset, and is loth to die;
  Ah God, ah God, that day should be so soon.   10

Lie closer, lean your face upon my side,
Feel where the dew fell that has hardly dried,
  Hear how the blood beats that went nigh to swoon;

---

* Hermaphroditus, son of Hermes and Aphrodite, was originally a handsome boy who, while bathing in the fountain of Salmacis, was indissolubly united by the gods with the nymph of the fountain, whose love he had rejected.

The pleasure lives there when the sense has died;
   Ah God, ah God, that day should be so soon.

O my fair lord, I charge you leave me this:
Is it not sweeter than a foolish kiss?
   Nay take it then, my flower, my first in June,
My rose, so like a tender mouth it is:
   Ah God, ah God, that day should be so soon.   20

Love, till dawn sunder night from day with fire,
Dividing my delight and my desire,
   The crescent life and love the plenilune,
Love me though dusk begin and dark retire;
   Ah God, ah God, that day should be so soon.

Ah, my heart fails, my blood draws back; I know,
When life runs over, life is near to go;
   And with the slain of love love's ways are strewn,
And with their blood, if love will have it so;
   Ah God, ah God, that day should be so soon.   30

Ah, do thy will now; slay me if thou wilt;
There is no building now the walls are built,
   No quarrying now the corner-stone is hewn,
No drinking now the vine's whole blood is spilt;
   Ah God, ah God, that day should be so soon.

Nay, slay me now; nay, for I will be slain;
Pluck thy red pleasure from the teeth of pain,
   Break down thy vine ere yet grape-gatherers prune,
Slay me ere day can slay desire again;
   Ah God, ah God, that day should be so soon.   40

Yea, with thy sweet lips, with thy sweet sword; yea,
Take life and all, for I will die, I say;
   Love, I gave love, is life a better boon?
For sweet night's sake I will not live till day;
   Ah God, ah God, that day should be so soon.

Nay, I will sleep then only; nay, but go.
Ah sweet, too sweet to me, my sweet, I know
    Love, sleep, and death go to the sweet same tune;
Hold my hair fast, and kiss me through it so.
    Ah God, ah God, that day should be so soon.   50

A Match

If love were what the rose is,
    And I were like the leaf,
Our lives would grow together
In sad or singing weather,
Blown fields or flowerful closes,
    Green pleasure or grey grief;
If love were what the rose is,
    And I were like the leaf.

If I were what the words are,
    And love were like the tune,   10
With double sound and single
Delight our lips would mingle,
With kisses glad as birds are
    That get sweet rain at noon;
If I were what the words are,
    And love were like the tune.

If you were life, my darling,
    And I your love were death,
We'd shine and snow together
Ere March made sweet the weather   20
With daffodil and starling
    And hours of fruitful breath;
If you were life, my darling,
    And I your love were death.

If you were thrall to sorrow,
   And I were page to joy,
We'd play for lives and seasons
With loving looks and treasons
And tears of night and morrow
   And laughs of maid and boy;   30
If you were thrall to sorrow,
   And I were page to joy.

If you were April's lady,
   And I were lord in May,
We'd throw with leaves for hours
And draw for days with flowers,
Till day like night were shady
   And night were bright like day;
If you were April's lady,
   And I were lord in May.   40

If you were queen of pleasure,
And I were king of pain,
We'd hunt down love together,
Pluck out his flying-feather,
And teach his feet a measure,
   And find his mouth a rein;
If you were queen of pleasure,
   And I were king of pain.

Faustine

> *Ave Faustina Imperatrix, morituri te salutant.**

Lean back, and get some minutes' peace;
   Let your head lean

---

  * Adapted from the traditional words of the Roman gladiators: "Hail Caesar, Emperor! those about to die salute you!"

Back to the shoulder with its fleece
   Of locks, Faustine.

The shapely silver shoulder stoops,
   Weighed over clean
With state of splendid hair that droops
   Each side, Faustine.

Let me go over your good gifts
   That crown you queen;   10
A queen whose kingdom ebbs and shifts
   Each week, Faustine.

Bright heavy brows well gathered up:
   White gloss and sheen;
Carved lips that make my lips a cup
   To drink, Faustine,

Wine and rank poison, milk and blood,
   Being mixed therein
Since first the devil threw dice with God
   For you, Faustine.   20

Your naked new-born soul, their stake,
   Stood blind between;
God said "let him that wins her take
   And keep Faustine."

But this time Satan throve, no doubt;
   Long since, I ween,
God's part in you was battered out;
   Long since, Faustine.

The die rang sideways as it fell,
   Rang cracked and thin,   30
Like a man's laughter heard in hell
   Far down, Faustine,

A shadow of laughter like a sigh,
   Dead sorrow's kin;
So rang, thrown down, the devil's die
   That won Faustine.

A suckling of his breed you were,
   One hard to wean;
But God, who lost you, left you fair,
   We see, Faustine.   40

You have the face that suits a woman
   For her soul's screen—
The sort of beauty that's called human
   In hell, Faustine.

You could do all things but be good
   Or chaste of mien;
And that you would not if you could,
   We know, Faustine.

Even he who cast seven devils out
   Of Magdalene
Could hardly do as much, I doubt,   50
   For you, Faustine.

Did Satan make you to spite God?
   Or did God mean
To scourge with scorpions for a rod
   Our sins, Faustine?

I know what queen at first you were,*
   As though I had seen
Red gold and black imperious hair
   Twice crown Faustine.   60

* Faustina, wife of the Roman emperor Antoninus, and her daughter
Faustina, wife of Marcus Aurelius, were notorious for their beauty and
licentiousness.

As if your fed sarcophagus
   Spared flesh and skin,
You come back face to face with us,
   The same Faustine.

She loved the games men played with death,
   Where death must win;
As though the slain man's blood and breath
   Revived Faustine.

Nets caught the pike, pikes tore the net;
   Lithe limbs and lean   70
From drained-out pores dripped thick red sweat
   To soothe Faustine.

She drank the steaming drift and dust
   Blown off the scene;
Blood could not ease the bitter lust
   That galled Faustine.

All round the foul fat furrows reeked,
   Where blood sank in;
The circus splashed and seethed and shrieked
   All round Faustine.   80

But these are gone now: years entomb
   The dust and din;
Yea, even the bath's fierce reek and fume
   That slew Faustine.

Was life worth living then? and now
   Is life worth sin?
Where are the imperial years? and how
   Are you, Faustine?

Your soul forgot her joys, forgot
   Her times of teen;   90

Yea, this life likewise will you not
    Forget, Faustine?

For in the time we know not of
    Did fate begin
Weaving the web of days that wove
    Your doom, Faustine.

The threads were wet with wine, and all
    Were smooth to spin;
They wove you like a Bacchanal,
    The first Faustine.   100

And Bacchus cast your mates and you
    Wild grapes to glean;
Your flower-like lips were dashed with dew
    From his, Faustine.

Your drenched loose hands were stretched to hold
    The vine's wet green,
Long ere they coined in Roman gold
    Your face, Faustine.

Then after change of soaring feather
    And winnowing fin,   110
You woke in weeks of feverish weather,
    A new Faustine.

A star upon your birthday burned,
    Whose fierce serene
Red pulseless planet never yearned
    In heaven, Faustine.

Stray breaths of Sapphic song that blew
    Through Mitylene
Shook the fierce quivering blood in you
    By night, Faustine.   120

The shameless nameless love that makes
　　Hell's iron gin
Shut on you like a trap that breaks
　　The soul, Faustine.

And when your veins were void and dead,
　　What ghosts unclean
Swarmed round the straitened barren bed
　　That hid Faustine?

What sterile growths of sexless root
　　Or epicene?　　　　　　　　　　　　　130
What flower of kisses without fruit
　　Of love, Faustine?

What adders came to shed their coats?
　　What coiled obscene
Small serpents with soft stretching throats
　　Caressed Faustine?

But the time came of famished hours,
　　Maimed loves and mean,
This ghastly thin-faced time of ours,
　　To spoil Faustine.　　　　　　　　　　140

You seem a thing that hinges hold,
　　A love-machine
With clockwork joints of supple gold
　　No more, Faustine.

Not godless, for you serve one God,
　　The Lampsacene,*
Who metes the gardens with his rod;
　　Your lord, Faustine.

---

* Lampsacene, birthplace of Priapus, the Greek god of fertility and gardens, later of lasciviousness and obscenity.

If one should love you with real love
   (Such things have been,   150
Things your fair face knows nothing of,
   It seems, Faustine);

That clear hair heavily bound back,
   The lights wherein
Shift from dead blue to burnt-up black;
   Your throat, Faustine,

Strong, heavy, throwing out the face
   And hard bright chin
And shameful scornful lips that grace
   Their shame, Faustine,   160

Curled lips, long since half kissed away,
   Still sweet and keen;
You'd give him—poison shall we say?
   Or what, Faustine?

The Leper

Nothing is better, I well think,
   Than love; the hidden well-water
Is not so delicate to drink:
   This was well seen of me and her.

I served her in a royal house;
   I served her wine and curious meat.
For will to kiss between her brows,
   I had no heart to sleep or eat.

Mere scorn God knows she had of me,
   A poor scribe, nowise great or fair,
Who plucked his clerk's hood back to see
   Her curled-up lips and amorous hair.   10

I vex my head with thinking this.
  Yea, though God always hated me,
And hates me now that I can kiss
  Her eyes, plait up her hair to see

How she then wore it on the brows,
  Yet am I glad to have her dead
Here in this wretched wattled house
  Where I can kiss her eyes and head.   20

Nothing is better, I well know,
  Than love; no amber in cold sea
Or gathered berries under snow:
  That is well seen of her and me.

Three thoughts I make my pleasure of:
  First I take heart and think of this:
That knight's gold hair she chose to love,
  His mouth she had such will to kiss.

Then I remember that sundawn
  I brought him by a privy way   30
Out at her lattice, and thereon
  What gracious words she found to say.

(Cold rushes for such little feet—
  Both feet could lie into my hand.
A marvel was it of my sweet
  Her upright body could so stand.)

"Sweet friend, God give you thank and grace;
  Now am I clean and whole of shame,
Nor shall men burn me in the face
  For my sweet fault that scandals them."   40

I tell you over word by word.
  She, sitting edgewise on her bed,

Holding her feet, said thus. The third,
    A sweeter thing than these, I said.

God, that makes time and ruins it
    And alters not, abiding God,
Changed with disease her body sweet,
    The body of love wherein she abode.

Love is more sweet and comelier
    Than a dove's throat strained out to sing.   50
All they spat out and cursed at her
    And cast her forth for a base thing.

They cursed her, seeing how God had wrought
    This curse to plague her, a curse of his.
Fools were they surely, seeing not
    How sweeter than all sweet she is.

He that had held her by the hair,
    With kissing lips blinding her eyes,
Felt her bright bosom, strained and bare,
    Sigh under him, with short mad cries   60

Out of her throat and sobbing mouth
    And body broken up with love,
With sweet hot tears his lips were loth
    Her own should taste the savour of,

Yea, he inside whose grasp all night
    Her fervent body leapt or lay,
Stained with sharp kisses red and white,
    Found her a plague to spurn away.

I hid her in this wattled house,
    I served her water and poor bread.   70
For joy to kiss between her brows
    Time upon time I was nigh dead.

Bread failed; we got but well-water
   And gathered grass with dropping seed.
I had such joy of kissing her,
   I had small care to sleep or feed.

Sometimes when service made me glad
   The sharp tears leapt between my lids,
Falling on her, such joy I had
   To do the service God forbids.   80

"I pray you let me be at peace,
   Get hence, make room for me to die."
She said that: her poor lip would cease,
   Put up to mine, and turn to cry.

I said, "Bethink yourself how love
   Fared in us twain, what either did;
Shall I unclothe my soul thereof?
   That I should do this, God forbid."

Yea, though God hateth us, he knows
   That hardly in a little thing   90
Love faileth of the work it does
   Till it grow ripe for gathering.

Six months, and now my sweet is dead
   A trouble takes me; I know not
If all were done well, all well said,
   No word or tender deed forgot.

Too sweet, for the least part in her,
   To have shed life out by fragments; yet,
Could the close mouth catch breath and stir,
   I might see something I forget.   100

Six months, and I sit still and hold
   In two cold palms her cold two feet.

Her hair, half grey half ruined gold,
    Thrills me and burns me in kissing it.

Love bites and stings me through, to see
    Her keen face made of sunken bones.
Her worn-off eyelids madden me,
    That were shot through with purple once.

She said, "Be good with me; I grow
    So tired for shame's sake, I shall die   110
If you say nothing:" even so.
    And she is dead now, and shame put by.

Yea, and the scorn she had of me
    In the old time, doubtless vexed her then.
I never should have kissed her. See
    What fools God's anger makes of men!

She might have loved me a little too,
    Had I been humbler for her sake.
But that new shame could make love new
    She saw not—yet her shame did make.   120

I took too much upon my love,
    Having for such mean service done
Her beauty and all the ways thereof,
    Her face and all the sweet thereon.

Yea, all this while I tended her,
    I know the old love held fast his part:
I know the old scorn waxed heavier,
    Mixed with sad wonder, in her heart.

It may be all my love went wrong—
    A scribe's work writ awry and blurred,   130
Scrawled after the blind evensong—
    Spoilt music with no perfect word.

But surely I would fain have done
   All things the best I could. Perchance
Because I failed, came short of one,
   She kept at heart that other man's.

I am grown blind with all these things:
   It may be now she hath in sight
Some better knowledge; still there clings
   The old question. Will not God do right?   140

❧ ☙

Before the Mirror
*(VERSES WRITTEN UNDER A PICTURE)**

Inscribed to J. A. Whistler

I

White rose in red rose-garden
   Is not so white;
Snowdrops that plead for pardon
   And pine for fright
Because the hard East blows
Over their maiden rows
   Grow not as this face grows from pale to bright.

Behind the veil, forbidden,
   Shut up from sight,
Love, is there sorrow hidden,   10
   Is there delight?
Is joy thy dower or grief,
White rose of weary leaf,
   Late rose whose life is brief, whose loves are light?

Soft snows that hard winds harden
   Till each flake bite

   * "Little White Girl, Symphony No. 2."

Fill all the flowerless garden
  Whose flowers took flight
Long since when summer ceased,
And men rose up from feast,   20
  And warm west wind grew east, and warm day night.

    2
"Come snow, come wind or thunder
  High up in air,
I watch my face, and wonder
  At my bright hair;
Nought else exalts or grieves
The rose at heart, that heaves
  With love of her own leaves and lips that pair.

"She knows not loves that kissed her
  She knows not where.   30
Art thou the ghost, my sister,
  White sister there,
Am I the ghost, who knows?
My hand, a fallen rose,
  Lies snow-white on white snows, and takes no care.

"I cannot see what pleasures
  Or what pains were;
What pale new loves and treasures
  New years will bear;
What beam will fall, what shower,   40
What grief or joy for dower;
  But one thing knows the flower; the flower is fair."

    3
Glad, but not flushed with gladness,
  Since joys go by;
Sad, but not bent with sadness,
  Since sorrows die;
Deep in the gleaming glass

She sees all past things pass,
    And all sweet life that was lie down and lie.

There glowing ghosts of flowers   50
    Draw down, draw nigh;
And wings of swift spent hours
    Take flight and fly;
She sees by formless gleams,
She hears across cold streams,
    Dead mouths of many dreams that sing and sigh.

Face fallen and white throat lifted,
    With sleepless eye
She sees old loves that drifted,
    She knew not why,   60
Old loves and faded fears
Float down a stream that hears
    The flowing of all men's tears beneath the sky.

Dolores
(*NOTRE-DAME DES SEPT DOULEURS*)

Cold eyelids that hide like a jewel
    Hard eyes that grow soft for an hour;
The heavy white limbs, and the cruel
    Red mouth like a venomous flower;
When these are gone by with their glories,
    What shall rest of thee then, what remain,
O mystic and sombre Dolores,
    Our Lady of Pain?

Seven sorrows the priests give their Virgin;
    But thy sins, which are seventy times seven,   10
Seven ages would fail thee to purge in,
    And then they would haunt thee in heaven:

Fierce midnights and famishing morrows,
    And the loves that complete and control
All the joys of the flesh, all the sorrows
    That wear out the soul.

O garment not golden but gilded,*
    O garden where all men may dwell,
O tower not of ivory, but builded
    By hands that reach heaven from hell;   20
O mystical rose of the mire,
    O house not of gold but of gain,
O house of unquenchable fire,
    Our Lady of Pain!

O lips full of lust and of laughter,
    Curled snakes that are fed from my breast,
Bite hard, lest remembrance come after
    And press with new lips where you pressed.
For my heart too springs up at the pressure,
    Mine eyelids too moisten and burn;   30
Ah, feed me and fill me with pleasure,
    Ere pain come in turn.

In yesterday's reach and to-morrow's,
    Out of sight though they lie of to-day,
There have been and there yet shall be sorrows
    That smite not and bite not in play.
The life and the love thou despisest,
    These hurt us indeed, and in vain,
O wise among women, and wisest,
    Our Lady of Pain.   40

Who gave thee thy wisdom? what stories
    That stung thee, what visions that smote?
Wert thou pure and a maiden, Dolores,
    When desire took thee first by the throat?

   * Inverted imagery from the Litany of the Blessed Virgin and *The
Song of Solomon* 7:4: "Thy neck is as a tower of ivory."

What bud was the shell of a blossom
    That all men may smell to and pluck?
What milk fed thee first at what bosom?
    What sins gave thee suck?

We shift and bedeck and bedrape us,
    Thou art noble and nude and antique;   50
Libitina* thy mother, Priapus
    Thy father, a Tuscan and Greek.
We play with light loves in the portal,
    And wince and relent and refrain;
Loves die, and we know thee immortal,
    Our Lady of Pain.

Fruits fail and love dies and time ranges;
    Thou art fed with perpetual breath,
And alive after infinite changes,
    And fresh from the kisses of death;   60
Of languors rekindled and rallied,
    Of barren delights and unclean,
Things monstrous and fruitless, a pallid
    And poisonous queen.

Could you hurt me, sweet lips, though I hurt you?
    Men touch them, and change in a trice
The lilies and languors of virtue
    For the raptures and roses of vice;
Those lie where thy foot on the floor is,
    These crown and caress thee and chain,   70
O splendid and sterile Dolores,
    Our Lady of Pain.

There are sins it may be to discover,
    There are deeds it may be to delight.
What new work wilt thou find for thy lover,
    What new passions for daytime or night?

---

    * Goddess of gardens, voluptuous pleasures, fertility, and death—
the Roman counterpart of the Greek god Priapus.

What spells that they know not a word of
   Whose lives are as leaves overblown?
What tortures undreamt of, unheard of,
   Unwritten, unknown?   80

Ah beautiful passionate body
   That never has ached with a heart!
On thy mouth though the kisses are bloody,
   Though they sting till it shudder and smart,
More kind than the love we adore is,
   They hurt not the heart or the brain,
O bitter and tender Dolores,
   Our Lady of Pain.

As our kisses relax and redouble,
   From the lips of the foam and the fangs   90
Shall no new sin be born for men's trouble,
   No dream of impossible pangs?
With the sweet of the sins of old ages
   Wilt thou satiate thy soul as of yore?
Too sweet is the rind, say the sages,
   Too bitter the core.

Hast thou told all thy secrets the last time,
   And bared all thy beauties to one?
Ah, where shall we go then for pastime,
   If the worst that can be has been done?   100
But sweet as the rind was the core is;
   We are fain of thee still, we are fain,
O sanguine and subtle Dolores,
   Our Lady of Pain.

By the hunger of change and emotion,
   By the thirst of unbearable things,
By despair, the twin-born of devotion,
   By the pleasure that winces and stings,
The delight that consumes the desire,
   The desire that outruns the delight,   110

By the cruelty deaf as a fire
   And blind as the night,

By the ravenous teeth that have smitten
   Through the kisses that blossom and bud,
By the lips intertwisted and bitten
   Till the foam has a savour of blood,
By the pulse as it rises and falters,
   By the hands as they slacken and strain,
I adjure thee, respond from thine altars,
   Our Lady of Pain.   120

Wilt thou smile as a woman disdaining
   The light fire in the veins of a boy?
But he comes to thee sad, without feigning,
   Who has wearied of sorrow and joy;
Less careful of labour and glory
   Than the elders whose hair has uncurled;
And young, but with fancies as hoary
   And grey as the world.

I have passed from the outermost portal
   To the shrine where a sin is a prayer;   130
What care though the service be mortal?
   O our Lady of Torture, what care?
All thine the last wine that I pour is,
   The last in the chalice we drain,
O fierce and luxurious Dolores,
   Our Lady of Pain.

All thine the new wine of desire,
   The fruit of four lips as they clung
Till the hair and the eyelids took fire,
   The foam of a serpentine tongue,   140
The froth of the serpents of pleasure,
   More salt than the foam of the sea,
Now felt as a flame, now at leisure
   As wine shed for me.

Ah thy people, thy children, thy chosen,
    Marked cross from the womb and perverse!
They have found out the secret to cozen
    The gods that constrain us and curse;
They alone, they are wise, and none other;
    Give me place, even me, in their train,   150
O my sister, my spouse, and my mother,
    Our Lady of Pain.

For the crown of our life as it closes
    Is darkness, the fruit thereof dust;
No thorns go as deep as a rose's,
    And love is more cruel than lust.
Time turns the old days to derision,
    Our loves into corpses or wives;
And marriage and death and division
    Make barren our lives.   160

And pale from the past we draw nigh thee,
    And satiate with comfortless hours;
And we know thee, how all men belie thee,
    And we gather the fruit of thy flowers;
The passion that slays and recovers,
    The pangs and the kisses that rain
On the lips and the limbs of thy lovers,
    Our Lady of Pain.

The desire of thy furious embraces
    Is more than the wisdom of years,   170
On the blossom though blood lie in traces,
    Though the foliage be sodden with tears.
For the lords in whose keeping the door is
    That opens on all who draw breath
Gave the cypress to love, my Dolores,
    The myrtle to death.

And they laughed, changing hands in the measure,
    And they mixed and made peace after strife;

Pain melted in tears, and was pleasure;
   Death tingled with blood, and was life. 180
Like lovers they melted and tingled,
   In the dusk of thine innermost fane;
In the darkness they murmured and mingled,
   Our Lady of Pain.

In a twilight where virtues are vices,
   In thy chapels, unknown of the sun,
To a tune that enthralls and entices,
   They were wed, and the twain were as one.
For the tune from thine altar hath sounded
   Since God bade the world's work begin, 190
And the fume of thine incense abounded,
   To sweeten the sin.

Love listens, and paler than ashes,
   Through his curls as the crown on them slips,
Lifts languid wet eyelids and lashes,
   And laughs with insatiable lips.
Thou shalt hush him with heavy caresses,
   With music that scares the profane;
Thou shalt darken his eyes with thy tresses,
   Our Lady of Pain. 200

Thou shalt blind his bright eyes though he wrestle,
   Thou shalt chain his light limbs though he strive;
In his lips all thy serpents shall nestle,
   In his hands all thy cruelties thrive.
In the daytime thy voice shall go through him,
   In his dreams he shall feel thee and ache;
Thou shalt kindle by night and subdue him
   Asleep and awake.

Thou shalt touch and make redder his roses
   With juice not of fruit nor of bud; 210
When the sense in the spirit reposes,
   Thou shalt quicken the soul through the blood.

Thine, thine the one grace we implore is,
   Who would live and not languish or feign,
O sleepless and deadly Dolores,
   Our Lady of Pain.

Dost thou dream, in a respite of slumber,
   In a lull of the fires of thy life,
Of the days without name, without number,
   When thy will stung the world into strife;   220
When, a goddess, the pulse of thy passion
   Smote kings as they revelled in Rome;
And they hailed thee re-risen, O Thalassian,*
   Foam-white, from the foam?

When thy lips had such lovers to flatter;
   When the city lay red from thy rods,
And thine hands were as arrows to scatter
   The children of change and their gods;
When the blood of thy foemen made fervent
   A sand never moist from the main,   230
As one smote them, their lord and thy servant,
   Our Lady of Pain.

On sands by the storm never shaken,
   Nor wet from the washing of tides;
Nor by foam of the waves overtaken,
   Nor winds that the thunder bestrides;
But red from the print of thy paces,
   Made smooth for the world and its lords,
Ringed round with a flame of fair faces,
   And splendid with swords.   240

There the gladiator, pale for thy pleasure,
   Drew bitter and perilous breath;
There torments laid hold on the treasure
   Of limbs too delicious for death;

* An epithet applied to Venus and meaning *born of the sea.*

When thy gardens were lit with live torches;
  When the world was a steed for thy rein;
When the nations lay prone in thy porches,
  Our Lady of Pain.

When, with flame all around him aspirant,
  Stood flushed, as a harp-player stands,   250
The implacable beautiful tyrant,*
  Rose-crowned, having death in his hands;
And a sound as the sound of loud water
  Smote far through the flight of the fires,
And mixed with the lightning of slaughter
  A thunder of lyres.

Dost thou dream of what was and no more is,
  The old kingdoms of earth and the kings?
Dost thou hunger for these things, Dolores,
  For these, in a world of new things?   260
But thy bosom no fasts could emaciate,
  No hunger compel to complain
Those lips that no bloodshed could satiate,
  Our Lady of Pain.

As of old when the world's heart was lighter,
  Through thy garments the grace of thee glows,
The white wealth of thy body made whiter
  By the blushes of amorous blows,
And seamed with sharp lips and fierce fingers,
  And branded by kisses that bruise;   270
When all shall be gone that now lingers,
  Ah, what shall we lose?

Thou wert fair in the fearless old fashion,
  And thy limbs are as melodies yet,
And move to the music of passion
  With lithe and lascivious regret.

---

* Nero, who is said to have illuminated his gardens with burning Christians.

What ailed us, O gods, to desert you
    For creeds that refuse and restrain?
Come down and redeem us from virtue,
    Our Lady of Pain.   280

All shrines that were Vestal are flameless,
    But the flame has not fallen from this;
Though obscure be the god, and though nameless
    The eyes and the hair that we kiss;
Low fires that love sits by and forges
    Fresh heads for his arrows and thine;
Hair loosened and soiled in mid orgies
    With kisses and wine.

Thy skin changes country and colour,
    And shrivels or swells to a snake's.   290
Let it brighten and bloat and grow duller,
    We know it, the flames and the flakes,
Red brands on it smitten and bitten,
    Round skies where a star is a stain,
And the leaves with thy litanies written,
    Our Lady of Pain.

On thy bosom though many a kiss be,
    There are none such as knew it of old.
Was it Alciphron once or Arisbe,*
    Male ringlets or feminine gold,   300
That thy lips met with under the statue,
    Whence a look shot out sharp after thieves
From the eyes of the garden-god at you
    Across the fig-leaves?

Then still, through dry seasons and moister,
    One god had a wreath to his shrine;

---

* Alciphron: Greek rhetorician and author of letters supposedly composed by celebrated courtesans. Arisbe: a wife of King Priam of Troy. The "garden-god" refers to Priapus, whose phallic image adorned gardens as an emblem of fertility.

Then love was the pearl of his oyster,
    And Venus rose red out of wine.
We have all done amiss, choosing rather
    Such loves as the wise gods disdain; 310
Intercede for us thou with thy father,
    Our Lady of Pain.

In spring he had crowns of his garden,
    Red corn in the heat of the year,
Then hoary green olives that harden
    When the grape-blossom freezes with fear;
And milk-budded myrtles with Venus
    And vine-leaves with Bacchus he trod;
And ye said, "We have seen, he hath seen us,
    A visible God." 320

What broke off the garlands that girt you?
    What sundered you spirit and clay?
Weak sins yet alive are as virtue
    To the strength of the sins of that day.
For dried is the blood of thy lover,
    Ipsithilla,* contracted the vein;
Cry aloud, "Will he rise and recover,
    Our Lady of Pain?"

Cry aloud; for the old world is broken:
    Cry out; for the Phrygian is priest,** 330
And rears not the bountiful token
    And spreads not the fatherly feast.
From the midmost of Ida, from shady
    Recesses that murmur at morn,
They have brought and baptized her, Our Lady,
    A goddess new-born.

* A lover mentioned by Catullus in *Carmina*, XXXII.
** Cybele, goddess of generation, was worshipped more restrainedly than Venus in Phrygia, Asia Minor. Mt. Ida was a seat of her worship; Dindymus, a mountain sacred to her from which she traveled in a chariot drawn by lions (see lines 333, 345–6, below).

And the chaplets of old are above us,
 And the oyster-bed teems out of reach;
Old poets outsing and outlove us,
 And Catullus makes mouths at our speech. 340
Who shall kiss, in thy father's own city,
 With such lips as he sang with, again?
Intercede for us all of thy pity,
 Our Lady of Pain.

Out of Dindymus heavily laden
 Her lions draw bound and unfed
A mother, a mortal, a maiden,
 A queen over death and the dead.
She is cold, and her habit is lowly,
 Her temple of branches and sods; 350
Most fruitful and virginal, holy,
 A mother of gods.

She hath wasted with fire thine high places,
 She hath hidden and marred and made sad
The fair limbs of the Loves, the fair faces
 Of gods that were goodly and glad.
She slays, and her hands are not bloody;
 She moves as a moon in the wane,
White-robed, and thy raiment is ruddy,
 Our Lady of Pain. 360

They shall pass and their places be taken,
 The gods and the priests that are pure.
They shall pass, and shalt thou not be shaken?
 They shall perish, and shalt thou endure?
Death laughs, breathing close and relentless
 In the nostrils and eyelids of lust,
With a pinch in his fingers of scentless
 And delicate dust.

But the worm shall revive thee with kisses;
 Thou shalt change and transmute as a god, 370

As the rod to a serpent that hisses,*
   As the serpent again to a rod.
Thy life shall not cease though thou doff it;
   Thou shalt live until evil be slain,
And good shall die first, said thy prophet,
   Our Lady of Pain.

Did he lie? did he laugh? does he know it,
   Now he lies out of reach, out of breath,
Thy prophet, thy preacher, thy poet,
   Sin's child by incestuous Death?   380
Did he find out in fire at his waking,
   Or discern as his eyelids lost light,
When the bands of the body were breaking
   And all came in sight?

Who has known all the evil before us,
   Or the tyrannous secrets of time?
Though we match not the dead men that bore us
   At a song, at a kiss, at a crime—
Though the heathen outface and outlive us,
   And our lives and our longings are twain—   390
Ah, forgive us our virtues, forgive us,
   Our Lady of Pain.

Who are we that embalm and embrace thee
   With spices and savours of song?
What is time, that his children should face thee?
   What am I, that my lips do thee wrong?
I could hurt thee—but pain would delight thee;
   Or caress thee—but love would repel;
And the lovers whose lips would excite thee
   Are serpents in hell.   400

Who now shall content thee as they did,
   Thy lovers, when temples were built

    * Cf. Aaron's rod, *Exodus* 7:9: "Take thy rod, and cast it before Pharaoh, and it shall become a serpent."

And the hair of the sacrifice braided
    And the blood of the sacrifice spilt,
In Lampsacus fervent with faces,
    In Aphaca* red from thy reign,
Who embraced thee with awful embraces,
    Our Lady of Pain?

Where are they, Cotytto or Venus,
    Astarte or Ashtaroth, where? **   410
Do their hands as we touch come between us?
    Is the breath of them hot in thy hair?
From their lips have thy lips taken fever,
    With the blood of their bodies grown red?
Hast thou left upon earth a believer
    If these men are dead?

They were purple of raiment and golden,
    Filled full of thee, fiery with wine,
Thy lovers, in haunts unbeholden,
    In marvellous chambers of thine.   420
They are fled, and their footprints escape us,
    Who appraise thee, adore, and abstain,
O daughter of Death and Priapus,
    Our Lady of Pain.

What ails us to fear overmeasure,
    To praise thee with timorous breath,
O mistress and mother of pleasure,
    The one thing as certain as death?
We shall change as the things that we cherish,
    Shall fade as they faded before,   430
As foam upon water shall perish,
    As sand upon shore.

* Aphaca and Lampsacus: centers of worship of Priapus and Venus.
** Cotytto: Thracian goddess worshipped in licentious rites. Astarte
and Ashtaroth: Middle-Eastern counterpart of Venus.

We shall know what the darkness discovers,
   If the grave-pit be shallow or deep;
And our fathers of old, and our lovers,
   We shall know if they sleep not or sleep.
We shall see whether hell be not heaven,
   Find out whether tares be not grain,*
And the joys of thee seventy times seven,
   Our Lady of Pain.   440

The Garden of Proserpine

Here, where the world is quiet;
   Here, where all trouble seems
Dead winds' and spent waves' riot
   In doubtful dreams of dreams;
I watch the green field growing
For reaping folk and sowing,
For harvest-time and mowing,
   A sleepy world of streams.

I am tired of tears and laughter,
   And men that laugh and weep;   10
Of what may come hereafter
   For men that sow to reap:
I am weary of days and hours,
Blown buds of barren flowers,
Desires and dreams and powers
   And everything but sleep.

Here life has death for neighbour,
   And far from eye or ear
Wan waves and wet winds labour,
   Weak ships and spirits steer;   20

    * An allusion to the parable of the tares and wheat, *Matthew*
13:25–40.

They drive adrift, and whither
They wot not who make thither;
But no such winds blow hither,
   And no such things grow here.

No growth of moor or coppice,
   No heather-flower or vine,
But bloomless buds of poppies,
   Green grapes of Proserpine,
Pale beds of blowing rushes
Where no leaf blooms or blushes   30
Save this whereout she crushes
   For dead men deadly wine.

Pale, without name or number,
   In fruitless fields of corn,
They bow themselves and slumber
   All night till light is born;
And like a soul belated,
In hell and heaven unmated,
By cloud and mist abated
   Comes out of darkness morn.   40

Though one were strong as seven,
   He too with death shall dwell,
Nor wake with wings in heaven,
   Nor weep for pains in hell;
Though one were fair as roses,
His beauty clouds and closes;
And well though love reposes,
   In the end it is not well.

Pale, beyond porch and portal,
   Crowned with calm leaves, she stands   50
Who gathers all things mortal
   With cold immortal hands;
Her languid lips are sweeter
Than love's who fears to greet her

To men that mix and meet her
  From many times and lands.

She waits for each and other,
  She waits for all men born;
Forgets the earth her mother,
  The life of fruits and corn;   60
And spring and seed and swallow
Take wing for her and follow
Where summer song rings hollow
  And flowers are put to scorn.

There go the loves that wither,
  The old loves with wearier wings;
And all dead years draw thither,
  And all disastrous things;
Dead dreams of days forsaken,
Blind buds that snows have shaken,   70
Wild leaves that winds have taken,
  Red strays of ruined springs.

We are not sure of sorrow,
  And joy was never sure;
To-day will die to-morrow;
  Time stoops to no man's lure;
And love, grown faint and fretful,
With lips but half regretful
Sighs, and with eyes forgetful
  Weeps that no loves endure.   80

From too much love of living,
  From hope and fear set free,
We thank with brief thanksgiving
  Whatever gods may be
That no life lives for ever;
That dead men rise up never;
That even the weariest river
  Winds somewhere safe to sea.

Then star nor sun shall waken,
  Nor any change of light: 90
Nor sound of waters shaken,
  Nor any sound or sight:
Nor wintry leaves nor vernal,
Nor days nor things diurnal;
Only the sleep eternal
  In an eternal night.

Before Parting

A month or twain to live on honeycomb
Is pleasant; but one tires of scented time,
Cold sweet recurrence of accepted rhyme,
And that strong purple under juice and foam
Where the wine's heart has burst;
Nor feel the latter kisses like the first.

Once yet, this poor one time; I will not pray
Even to change the bitterness of it,
The bitter taste ensuing on the sweet,
To make your tears fall where your soft hair lay   10
All blurred and heavy in some perfumed wise
Over my face and eyes.

And yet who knows what end the scythèd wheat
Makes of its foolish poppies' mouths of red?
These were not sown, these are not harvested,
They grow a month and are cast under feet
And none has care thereof,
As none has care of a divided love.

I know each shadow of your lips by rote,
Each change of love in eyelids and eyebrows;   20
The fashion of fair temples tremulous
With tender blood, and colour of your throat;

I know not how love is gone out of this,
Seeing that all was his.

Love's likeness there endures upon all these:
But out of these one shall not gather love.
Day hath not strength nor the night shade enough
To make love whole and fill his lips with ease,
As some bee-builded cell
Feels at filled lips the heavy honey swell.   30

I know not how this last month leaves your hair
Less full of purple colour and hid spice,
And that luxurious trouble of closed eyes
Is mixed with meaner shadow and waste care;
And love, kissed out by pleasure, seems not yet
Worth patience to regret.

The Sundew

A little marsh-plant, yellow green,
And pricked at lip with tender red.
Tread close, and either way you tread
Some faint black water jets between
Lest you should bruise the curious head.

A live thing maybe; who shall know?
The summer knows and suffers it;
For the cool moss is thick and sweet
Each side, and saves the blossom so
That it lives out the long June heat.   10

The deep scent of the heather burns
About it; breathless though it be,
Bow down and worship; more than we
Is the least flower whose life returns,
Least weed renascent in the sea.

We are vexed and cumbered in earth's sight
With wants, with many memories;
These see their mother what she is,
Glad-growing, till August leave more bright
The apple-coloured cranberries.   20

Wind blows and bleaches the strong grass,
Blown all one way to shelter it
From trample of strayed kine, with feet
Felt heavier than the moorhen was,
Strayed up past patches of wild wheat.

You call it sundew: how it grows,
If with its colour it have breath,
If life taste sweet to it, if death
Pain its soft petal, no man knows:
Man has no sight or sense that saith.   30

My sundew, grown of gentle days,
In these green miles the spring begun
Thy growth ere April had half done
With the soft secret of her ways
Or June made ready for the sun.

O red-lipped mouth of marsh-flower,
I have a secret halved with thee.
The name that is love's name to me
Thou knowest, and the face of her
Who is my festival to see.   40

The hard sun, as thy petals knew,
Coloured the heavy moss-water:
Thou wert not worth green midsummer
Nor fit to live to August blue,
O sundew, not remembering her.

*Hendecasyllabics**

In the month of the long decline of roses
I, beholding the summer dead before me,
Set my face to the sea and journeyed silent,
Gazing eagerly where above the sea-mark
Flame as fierce as the fervid eyes of lions
Half divided the eyelids of the sunset;
Till I heard as it were a noise of waters
Moving tremulous under feet of angels
Multitudinous, out of all the heavens;
Knew the fluttering wind, the fluttered foliage,   10
Shaken fitfully, full of sound and shadow;
And saw, trodden upon by noiseless angels,
Long mysterious reaches fed with moonlight,
Sweet sad straits in a soft subsiding channel,
Blown about by the lips of winds I knew not,
Winds not born in the north nor any quarter,
Winds not warm with the south nor any sunshine;
Heard between them a voice of exultation,
"Lo, the summer is dead, the sun is faded,
Even like as a leaf the year is withered,   20
All the fruits of the day from all her branches
Gathered, neither is any left to gather.
All the flowers are dead, the tender blossoms,
All are taken away; the season wasted,
Like an ember among the fallen ashes.
Now with light of the winter days, with moonlight,
Light of snow, and the bitter light of hoarfrost,
We bring flowers that fade not after autumn,
Pale white chaplets and crowns of latter seasons,
Fair false leaves (but the summer leaves were falser),   30
Woven under the eyes of stars and planets
When low light was upon the windy reaches
Where the flower of foam was blown, a lily

* Lines of eleven syllables.

Dropt among the sonorous fruitless furrows
And green fields of the sea that make no pasture:
Since the winter begins, the weeping winter,
All whose flowers are tears, and round his temples
Iron blossom of frost is bound for ever."

Love and Sleep

Lying asleep between the strokes of night
   I saw my love lean over my sad bed,
   Pale as the duskiest lily's leaf or head,
Smooth-skinned and dark, with bare throat made to bite,
Too wan for blushing and too warm for white,
   But perfect-coloured without white or red.
   And her lips opened amorously, and said—
I wist not what, saving one word—Delight.
And all her face was honey to my mouth,
   And all her body pasture to mine eyes;   10
     The long lithe arms and hotter hands than fire,
The quivering flanks, hair smelling of the south,
   The bright light feet, the splendid supple thighs
     And glittering eyelids of my soul's desire.

After Death

The four boards of the coffin lid
Heard all the dead man did.

The first curse was in his mouth,
Made of grave's mould and deadly drouth.

The next curse was in his head,
Made of God's work discomfited.

The next curse was in his hands,
Made out of two grave-bands.

The next curse was in his feet,
Made out of a grave-sheet. 10

"I had fair coins red and white,
And my name was as great light;

I had fair clothes green and red,
And strong gold bound round my head.

But no meat comes in my mouth,
Now I fare as the worm doth;

And no gold binds in my hair,
Now I fare as the blind fare.

My live thews were of great strength,
Now am I waxen a span's length; 20

My live sides were full of lust,
Now are they dried with dust."

The first board spake and said:
"Is it best eating flesh or bread?"

The second answered it:
"Is wine or honey the more sweet?"

The third board spake and said:
"Is red gold worth a girl's gold head?"

The fourth made answer thus:
"All these things are as one with us." 30

The dead man asked of them:
"Is the green land stained brown with flame?

Have they hewn my son for beasts to eat,
And my wife's body for beasts' meat?

Have they boiled my maid in a brass pan,
And built a gallows to hang my man?"

The boards said to him:
"This is a lewd thing that ye deem.

Your wife has gotten a golden bed,
All the sheets are sewn with red.   40

Your son has gotten a coat of silk,
The sleeves are soft as curded milk.

Your maid has gotten a kirtle new,
All the skirt has braids of blue.

Your man has gotten both ring and glove,
Wrought well for eyes to love."

The dead man answered thus:
"What good gift shall God give us?"

The boards answered him anon:
"Flesh to feed hell's worm upon."   50

Super Flumina Babylonis *

By the waters of Babylon we sat down and wept,
   Remembering thee,
That for ages of agony hast endured, and slept,
   And wouldst not see.

 * Cf. *Psalms* 137:1: "By the rivers of Babylon, there we sat down, yea, we wept, when we remembered Zion."

By the waters of Babylon we stood up and sang,
      Considering thee,
That a blast of deliverance in the darkness rang,
      To set thee free.

And with trumpets and thunderings and with morning
    song
      Came up the light;   10
And thy spirit uplifted thee to forget thy wrong
      As day doth night.

And thy sons were dejected not any more, as then
      When thou wast shamed;
When thy lovers went heavily without heart, as men
      Whose life was maimed.

In the desolate distances, with a great desire,
      For thy love's sake,
With our hearts going back to thee, they were filled
    with fire,
      Were nigh to break.   20

It was said to us: "Verily ye are great of heart,
      But ye shall bend;
Ye are bondmen and bondwomen, to be scourged
    and smart,
      To toil and tend."

And with harrows men harrowed us, and subdued
    with spears,
      And crushed with shame:
And the summer and winter was, and the length of years,
      And no change came.

By the rivers of Italy, by the sacred streams,
      By town, by tower,   30
There was feasting with revelling, there was sleep with
    dreams,
      Until thine hour.

And they slept and they rioted on their rose-hung beds,
      With mouths on flame,
And with love-locks vine-chapleted, and with rose-
   crowned heads
      And robes of shame.

And they knew not their forefathers, nor the hills and
   streams
      And words of power,
Nor the gods that were good to them, but with songs
   and dreams
      Filled up their hour.   40

By the rivers of Italy, by the dry streams' beds,
      When thy time came,
There was casting of crowns from them, from their
   your men's heads,
      The crowns of shame.

By the horn of Eridanus, by the Tiber mouth,
      As thy day rose,
They arose up and girded them to the north and south,
      By seas, by snows.

As a water in January the frost confines,
      Thy kings bound thee;   50
As a water in April is, in the new-blown vines,
      Thy sons made free.

And thy lovers that looked for thee, and that mourned
   from far,
      For thy sake dead,
We rejoiced in the light of thee, in the signal star
      Above thine head.

In thy grief had we followed thee, in thy passion loved,
      Loved in thy loss;

In thy shame we stood fast to thee, with thy pangs were
    moved,
        Clung to thy cross.   60

By the hillside of Calvary we beheld thy blood,
        Thy bloodred tears,
As a mother's in bitterness, an unebbing flood,
        Years upon years.

And the north was Gethsemane, without leaf or bloom,
        A garden sealed;
And the south was Aceldama,* for a sanguine fume
        Hid all the field.

By the stone of the sepulchre we returned to weep,
        From far, from prison;   70
And the guards by it keeping it we beheld asleep,
        But thou wast risen.

And an angel's similitude by the unsealed grave,
        And by the stone:
And the voice was angelical, to whose words God gave
        Strength like his own.

"Lo, the graveclothes of Italy that are folded up
        In the grave's gloom!
And the guards as men wrought upon with a charmèd
    cup,
        By the open tomb.   80

"And her body most beautiful, and her shining head,
        These are not here;
For your mother, for Italy, is not surely dead:
        Have ye no fear.

"As of old time she spake to you, and you hardly heard,
        Hardly took heed,

    * The "Field of Blood," scene of Judas' suicide.

So now also she saith to you, yet another word,
      Who is risen indeed.

"By my saying she saith to you, in your ears she saith,
      Who hear these things,   90
Put no trust in men's royalties, nor in great men's breath,
      Nor words of kings.

"For the life of them vanishes and is no more seen,
      Nor no more known;
Nor shall any remember him if a crown hath been,
      Or where a throne.

"Unto each man his handiwork, unto each his crown,
      The just Fate gives;
Whoso takes the world's life on him and his own lays
    down,
      He, dying so, lives.*   100

"Whoso bears the whole heaviness of the wronged
    world's weight
      And puts it by,
It is well with him suffering, though he face man's fate;
      How should he die?

"Seeing death has no part in him any more, no power
      Upon his head;
He has bought his eternity with a little hour,
      And is not dead.

"For an hour, if ye look for him, he is no more found,
      For one hour's space;   110
Then ye lift up your eyes to him and behold him
    crowned,
      A deathless face.

---

   * Cf. *Matthew* 16:25: "For whosoever will save his life shall lose it:
and whosoever will lose his life for my sake shall find it."

"On the mountains of memory, by the world's well-
    springs,
        In all men's eyes,
Where the light of the life of him is on all past things,
        Death only dies.

"Not the light that was quenched for us, nor the deeds
    that were,
        Nor the ancient days,
Nor the sorrows not sorrowful, nor the face most fair
        Of perfect praise."   120

So the angel of Italy's resurrection said,
        So yet he saith;
So the son of her suffering, that from breasts nigh dead
        Drew life, not death.

That the pavement of Golgotha should be white as snow,
        Not red, but white;
That the waters of Babylon should no longer flow,
        And men see light.

Hertha*

        I am that which began;
           Out of me the years roll;
        Out of me God and man;
           I am equal and whole;
God changes, and man, and the form of them bodily;
        I am the soul.

    * Germanic goddess of earth, fertility and growth, here transmuted
by Swinburne into a kind of generative world-soul. "Of all that I have
done," he wrote, "I rate *Hertha* highest as a single piece, finding in
it the most of lyric force and music combined with the most condensed
and clarified thought."

Before ever land was,
    Before ever the sea,
Or soft hair of the grass,
    Or fair limbs of the tree,
Or the flesh-coloured fruit of my branches, I was,   10
    and thy soul was in me.

    First life on my sources
        First drifted and swam;
    Out of me are the forces
        That save it or damn;
Out of me man and woman, and wild-beast and bird;
    before God was, I am.*

    Beside or above me
        Nought is there to go;
    Love or unlove me,
        Unknow me or know,
I am that which unloves me and loves; I am stricken,   20
    and I am the blow.

    I the mark that is missed
        And the arrows that miss,
    I the mouth that is kissed
        And the breath in the kiss,
The search, and the sought, and the seeker, the soul
    and the body that is.

    I am that thing which blesses
        My spirit elate;
    That which caresses
        With hands uncreate
My limbs unbegotten that measure the length of the   30
    measure of fate.

    But what thing dost thou now,
        Looking Godward, to cry

---

   * Cf. *Exodus* 3:14: "And God said unto Moses, I AM THAT
I AM." Cf. also *John* 8:58: "Before Abraham was, I am."

"I am I, thou art thou,
    I am low, thou art high"?
I am thou, whom thou seekest to find him; find thou
    but thyself, thou art I.

I the grain and the furrow,
    The plough-cloven clod
And the ploughshare drawn thorough,
    The germ and the sod,
The deed and the doer, the seed and the sower, the   40
    dust which is God.

Hast thou known how I fashioned thee,*
    Child, underground?
Fire that impassioned thee,
    Iron that bound,
Dim changes of water, what thing of all these hast
    thou known of or found?

Canst thou say in thine heart
    Thou hast seen with thine eyes
With what cunning of art
    Thou wast wrought in what wise,
By what force of what stuff thou wast shapen, and   50
    shown on my breast to the skies?

Who hath given, who hath sold it thee,
    Knowledge of me?
Hath the wilderness told it thee?
    Hast thou learnt of the sea?
Hast thou communed in spirit with night? have the
    winds taken counsel with thee?

Have I set such a star
    To show light on thy brow

* This stanza and the next four loosely paraphrase, and are intended
implicitly to refute, the Voice out of the Whirlwind, *Job* 38–9.

That thou sawest from afar
        What I show to thee now?
Have ye spoken as brethren together, the sun and   60
    the mountains and thou?

        What is here, dost thou know it?
        What was, hast thou known?
        Prophet nor poet
        Nor tripod nor throne
Nor spirit no flesh can make answer, but only thy
    mother alone.

        Mother, not maker,
        Born, and not made;
        Though her children forsake her,
        Allured or afraid,
Praying prayers to the God of their fashion, she stirs   70
    not for all that have prayed.

        A creed is a rod,
        And a crown is of night;
        But this thing is God,
        To be man with thy might,
To grow straight in the strength of thy spirit, and
    live out thy life as the light.

        I am in thee to save thee,
        As my soul in thee saith;
        Give thou as I gave thee,
        Thy life-blood and breath,
Green leaves of thy labour, white flowers of thy   80
    thought, and red fruit of thy death.

        Be the ways of thy giving
        As mine were to thee;

The free life of thy living,
    Be the gift of it free;
Not as servant to lord, nor as master to slave, shalt
    thou give thee to me.

    O children of banishment,
        Souls overcast,
    Were the lights ye see vanish meant
        Alway to last,
Ye would know not the sun overshining the shadows   90
    and stars overpast.

    I that saw where ye trod
        The dim paths of the night
    Set the shadow called God
        In your skies to give light;
But the morning of manhood is risen, and the shadow-
    less soul is in sight.

    The tree many-rooted *
        That swells to the sky
    With frondage red-fruited,
        The life-tree am I;
In the buds of your lives is the sap of my leaves: ye   100
    shall live and not die.

    But the Gods of your fashion
        That take and that give,
    In their pity and passion
        That scourge and forgive,
They are worms that are bred in the bark that falls
    off; they shall die and not live.

    My own blood is what stanches
        The wounds in my bark;

---

* The great ash tree Yggdrasil, in Norse mythology, supposed to
sustain the universe.

Stars caught in my branches
Make day of the dark,
And are worshipped as suns till the sunrise shall   110
tread out their fires as a spark.

Where dead ages hide under
The live roots of the tree,
In my darkness the thunder
Makes utterance of me;
In the clash of my boughs with each other ye hear
the waves sound of the sea.

That noise is of Time,
As his feathers are spread
And his feet set to climb
Through the boughs overhead,
And my foliage rings round him and rustles, and   120
branches are bent with his tread.

The storm-winds of ages
Blow through me and cease,
The war-wind that rages,
The spring-wind of peace,
Ere the breath of them roughen my tresses, ere one
of my blossoms increase.

All sounds of all changes,
All shadows and lights
On the world's mountain-ranges
And stream-riven heights,
Whose tongue is the wind's tongue and language of   130
storm-clouds on earth-shaking nights;

All forms of all faces,
All works of all hands

In unsearchable places
Of time-stricken lands,
All death and all life, and all reigns and all ruins,
drop through me as sands.

Though sore be my burden
And more than ye know,
And my growth have no guerdon
But only to grow,
Yet I fail not of growing for lightnings above me or 140
deathworms below.

These too have their part in me,
As I too in these;
Such fire is at heart in me,
Such sap is this tree's,
Which hath in it all sounds and all secrets of infinite
lands and of seas.

In the spring-coloured hours
When my mind was as May's,
There brake forth of me flowers
By centuries of days,
Strong blossoms with perfume of manhood, shot out 150
from my spirit as rays.

And the sound of them springing
And smell of their shoots
Were as warmth and sweet singing
And strength to my roots;
And the lives of my children made perfect with freedom
of soul were my fruits.

I bid you but be;
I have need not of prayer;

I have need of you free
    As your mouths of mine air;
That my heart may be greater within me, beholding   160
    the fruits of me fair.

    More fair than strange fruit is
      Of faiths ye espouse;
    In me only the root is
      That blooms in your boughs;
Behold now your God that ye made you, to feed him
    with faith of your vows.

    In the darkening and whitening
      Abysses adored,
    With dayspring and lightning
      For lamp and for sword,
God thunders in heaven, and his angels are red with   170
    the wrath of the Lord.

    O my sons, O too dutiful
      Toward Gods not of me,
    Was not I enough beautiful?
      Was it hard to be free?
For behold, I am with you, am in you and of you; look
    forth now and see.

    Lo, winged with world's wonders,
      With miracles shod,
    With the fires of his thunders
      For raiment and rod,
God trembles in heaven, and his angels are white with   180
    the terror of God.

    For his twilight is come on him,
      His anguish is here;
    And his spirits gaze dumb on him,

> Grown grey from his fear;
> And his hour taketh hold on him stricken, the last of his
> infinite year.

> Thought made him and breaks
> him,
> Truth slays and forgives;
> But to you, as time takes him,
> This new thing it gives,
> Even love, the beloved Republic, that feeds upon free-
> dom and lives.

190

> For truth only is living,
> Truth only is whole,
> And the love of his giving
> Man's polestar and pole;
> Man, pulse of my centre, and fruit of my body, and
> seed of my soul.

> One birth of my bosom;
> One beam of mine eye;
> One topmost blossom
> That scales the sky;
> Man, equal and one with me, man that is made of
> me, man that is I.

200

Before a Crucifix

Here, down between the dusty trees,
    At this lank edge of haggard wood,
Women with labour-loosened knees,
    With gaunt backs bowed by servitude,

Stop, shift their loads, and pray, and fare
Forth with souls easier for the prayer.

The suns have branded black, the rains
   Striped grey this piteous God of theirs;
The face is full of prayers and pains,
   To which they bring their pains and prayers;   10
Lean limbs that shew the labouring bones,
And ghastly mouth that gapes and groans.

God of this grievous people, wrought
   After the likeness of their race,
By faces like thine own besought,
   Thine own blind helpless eyeless face,
I too, that have nor tongue nor knee
For prayer, I have a word to thee.

It was for this then, that thy speech
   Was blown about the world in flame   20
And men's souls shot up out of reach
   Of fear or lust or thwarting shame—
That thy faith over souls should pass
As sea-winds burning the grey grass?

It was for this, that prayers like these
   Should spend themselves about thy feet,
And with hard overlaboured knees
   Kneeling, these slaves of men should beat
Bosoms too lean to suckle sons
And fruitless as their orisons?   30

It was for this, that men should make
   Thy name a fetter on men's necks,
Poor men's made poorer for thy sake,
   And women's withered out of sex?
It was for this, that slaves should be,
Thy word was passed to set men free?

The nineteenth wave of the ages rolls
   Now deathward since thy death and birth.
Hast thou fed full men's starved-out souls?
   Hast thou brought freedom upon earth?   40
Or are there less oppressions done
In this wild world under the sun?

Nay, if indeed thou be not dead,
   Before thy terrene shrine be shaken,
Look down, turn usward, bow thine head;
   O thou that wast of God forsaken,*
Look on thine household here, and see
These that have not forsaken thee.

Thy faith is fire upon their lips,
   Thy kingdom golden in their hands;   50
They scourge us with thy words for whips,
   They brand us with thy words for brands;
The thirst that made thy dry throat shrink
To their moist mouths commends the drink.

The toothèd thorns that bit thy brows
   Lighten the weight of gold on theirs;
Thy nakedness enrobes thy spouse
   With the soft sanguine stuff she wears
Whose old limbs use for ointment yet
Thine agony and bloody sweat.   60

The blinding buffets on thine head
   On their crowned heads confirm the crown;
Thy scourging dyes their raiment red,
   And with thy bands they fasten down
For burial in the blood-bought field
The nations by thy stripes unhealed.

* Cf. Jesus' last words: "My God, my God, why hast thou forsaken me?" (*Matthew* 27:46).

With iron for thy linen bands
   And unclean cloths for winding-sheet
They bind the people's nail-pierced hands,
   They hide the people's nail-pierced feet;   70
And what man or what angel known
Shall roll back the sepulchral stone?

But these have not the rich man's grave
   To sleep in when their pain is done.
These were not fit for God to save.
   As naked hell-fire is the sun
In their eyes living, and when dead
These have not where to lay their head.*

They have no tomb to dig, and hide;
   Earth is not theirs, that they should sleep.   80
On all these tombless crucified
   No lovers' eyes have time to weep.
So still, for all man's tears and creeds,
The sacred body hangs and bleeds.

Through the left hand a nail is driven,
   Faith, and another through the right,
Forged in the fires of hell and heaven,
   Fear that puts out the eye of light:
And the feet soiled and scarred and pale
Are pierced with falsehood for a nail.   90

And priests against the mouth divine
   Push their sponge full of poison yet
And bitter blood for myrrh and wine,
   And on the same reed is it set
Wherewith before they buffeted
The people's disanointed head.

O sacred head, O desecrate,
   O labour-wounded feet and hands,

* Cf. *Matthew* 8:20: "Foxes have holes, and the birds of the air
have nests; but the Son of man hath not where to lay his head."

O blood poured forth in pledge to fate
   Of nameless lives in divers lands,   100
O slain and spent and sacrificed
People, the grey-grown speechless Christ!

Is there a gospel in the red
   Old witness of thy wide-mouthed wounds?
From thy blind stricken tongueless head
   What desolate evangel sounds
A hopeless note of hope deferred?
What word, if there be any word?

O son of man, beneath man's feet
   Cast down, O common face of man   110
Whereon all blows and buffets meet,
   O royal, O republican
Face of the people bruised and dumb
And longing till thy kingdom come!

The soldiers and the high priests part
   Thy vesture: all thy days are priced,
And all the nights that eat thine heart.
   And that one seamless coat of Christ,
The freedom of the natural soul,
They cast their lots for to keep whole.   120

No fragment of it save the name
   They leave thee for a crown of scorns
Wherewith to mock thy naked shame
   And forehead bitten through with thorns
And, marked with sanguine sweat and tears,
The stripes of eighteen hundred years.

And we seek yet if God or man
   Can loosen thee as Lazarus,
Bid thee rise up republican
   And save thyself and all of us;   130
But no disciple's tongue can say
When thou shalt take our sins away.

And mouldering now and hoar with moss
　　Between us and the sunlight swings
The phantom of a Christless cross
　　Shadowing the sheltered heads of kings
And making with its moving shade
The souls of harmless men afraid.

It creaks and rocks to left and right
　　Consumed of rottenness and rust,　　　　　　140
Worm-eaten of the worms of night,
　　Dead as their spirits who put trust,
Round its base muttering as they sit,
In the time-cankered name of it.

Thou, in the day that breaks thy prison,
　　People, though these men take thy name,
And hail and hymn thee rearisen,
　　Who made songs erewhile of thy shame,
Give thou not ear; for these are they
Whose good day was thine evil day.　　　　　　150

Set not thine hand unto their cross.
　　Give not thy soul up sacrificed.
Change not the gold of faith for dross
　　Of Christian creeds that spit on Christ.
Let not thy tree of freedom be
Regrafted from that rotting tree.

This dead God here against my face
　　Hath help for no man; who hath seen
The good works of it, or such grace
　　As thy grace in it, Nazarene,　　　　　　　160
As that from thy live lips which ran
For man's sake, O thou son of man?

The tree of faith ingraffed by priests
　　Put its foul foliage out above thee,
And round it feed man-eating beasts

Because of whom we dare not love thee;
Though hearts reach back and memories ache,
We cannot praise thee for their sake.

O hidden face of man, whereover
   The years have woven a viewless veil,   170
If thou wast verily man's lover,
   What did thy love or blood avail?
Thy blood the priests make poison of,
And in gold shekels coin thy love.

So when our souls look back to thee
   They sicken, seeing against thy side,
Too foul to speak of or to see,
   The leprous likeness of a bride,
Whose kissing lips through his lips grown
Leave their God rotten to the bone.   180

When we would see thee man, and know
   What heart thou hadst toward men indeed,
Lo, thy blood-blackened altars; lo,
   The lips of priests that pray and feed
While their own hell's worm curls and licks
The poison of the crucifix.

Thou bad'st let children come to thee;
   What children now but curses come?
What manhood in that God can be
   Who sees their worship, and is dumb?   190
No soul that lived, loved, wrought, and died,
Is this their carrion crucified.

Nay, if their God and thou be one,
   If thou and this thing be the same,
Thou shouldst not look upon the sun;
   The sun grows haggard at thy name.
Come down, be done with, cease, give o'er;
Hide thyself, strive not, be no more.

Genesis

In the outer world that was before this earth,
  That was before all shape or space was born,
Before the blind first hour of time had birth,
  Before night knew the moonlight or the morn;

Yea, before any world had any light,
  Or anything called God or man drew breath,
Slowly the strong sides of the heaving night
  Moved, and brought forth the strength of life and death.

And the sad shapeless horror increate
  That was all things and one thing, without fruit,   10
Limit, or law; where love was none, nor hate,
  Where no leaf came to blossom from no root;

The very darkness that time knew not of,
  Nor God laid hand on, nor was man found there,
Ceased, and was cloven in several shapes; above
  Light, and night under, and fire, earth, water, and air.

Sunbeams and starbeams, and all coloured things,
  All forms and all similitudes began;
And death, the shadow cast by life's wide wings,
  And God, the shade cast by the soul of man.   20

Then between shadow and substance, night and light,
  Then between birth and death, and deeds and days,
The illimitable embrace and the amorous fight
  That of itself begets, bears, rears, and slays,

The immortal war of mortal things, that is
  Labour and life and growth and good and ill,

The mild antiphonies that melt and kiss,
    The violent symphonies that meet and kill,

All nature of all things began to be.
    But chiefliest in the spirit (beast or man,   30
Planet of heaven or blossom of earth or sea)
    The divine contraries of life began.

For the great labour of growth, being many, is one;
    One thing the white death and the ruddy birth;
The invisible air and the all-beholden sun,
    And barren water and many-childed earth.

And these things are made manifest in men
    From the beginning forth unto this day:
Time writes and life records them, and again
    Death seals them lest the record pass away.   40

For if death were not, then should growth not be,
    Change, nor the life of good nor evil things;
Nor were there night at all nor light to see,
    Nor water of sweet nor water of bitter springs.

For in each man and each year that is born
    Are sown the twin seeds of the strong twin powers;
The white seed of the fruitful helpful morn,
    The black seed of the barren hurtful hours.

And he that of the black seed eateth fruit,
    To him the savour as honey shall be sweet;   50
And he in whom the white seed hath struck root,
    He shall have sorrow and trouble and tears for meat.

And him whose lips the sweet fruit hath made red
    In the end men loathe and make his name a rod;
And him whose mouth on the unsweet fruit hath fed
    In the end men follow and know for very God.

And of these twain, the black seed and the white,
   All things come forth, endured of men and done;
And still the day is great with child of night,
   And still the black night labours with the sun.   60

And each man and each year that lives on earth
   Turns hither or thither, and hence or thence is fed;
And as a man before was from his birth,
   So shall a man be after among the dead.

To Walt Whitman in America

Send but a song oversea for us,
   Heart of their hearts who are free,
Heart of their singer, to be for us
   More than our singing can be;
Ours, in the tempest at error,
With no light but the twilight of terror;
   Send us a song oversea!

Sweet-smelling of pine-leaves and grasses,
   And blown as a tree through and through
With the winds of the keen mountain-passes,   10
   And tender as sun-smitten dew;
Sharp-tongued as the winter that shakes
The wastes of your limitless lakes,
   Wide-eyed as the sea-line's blue.

O strong-winged soul with prophetic
   Lips hot with the bloodbeats of song,
With tremor of heartstrings magnetic,
   With thoughts as thunders in throng,
With consonant ardours of chords
That pierce men's souls as with swords   20
   And hale them hearing along,

Make us too music, to be with us
  As a word from a world's heart warm,
To sail the dark as a sea with us,
  Full-sailed, outsinging the storm,
A song to put fire in our ears
Whose burning shall burn up tears,
  Whose sign bid battle reform;

A note in the ranks of a clarion,
  A word in the wind of cheer,   30
To consume as with lightning the carrion
  That makes time foul for us here;
In the air that our dead things infest
A blast of the breath of the west,
  Till east way as west way is clear.

Out of the sun beyond sunset,
  From the evening whence morning shall be,
With the rollers in measureless onset,
  With the van of the storming sea,
With the world-wide wind, with the breath   40
That breaks ships driven upon death,
  With the passion of all things free,

With the sea-steeds footless and frantic,
  White myriads for death to bestride
In the charge of the ruining Atlantic
  Where deaths by regiments ride,
With clouds and clamours of waters,
With a long note shriller than slaughter's
  On the furrowless fields world-wide,

With terror, with ardour and wonder,   50
  With the soul of the season that wakes
When the weight of a whole year's thunder
  In the tidestream of autumn breaks,
Let the flight of the wide-winged word

Come over, come in and be heard,
   Take form and fire for our sakes.

For a continent bloodless with travail
   Here toils and brawls as it can,
And the web of it who shall unravel
   Of all that peer on the plan;   60
Would fain grow men, but they grow not,
And fain be free, but they know not
   One name for freedom and man?

One name, not twain for division;
   One thing, not twain, from the birth;
Spirit and substance and vision,
   Worth more than worship is worth;
Unbeheld, unadored, undivined,
The cause, the centre, the mind,
   The secret and sense of the earth.   70

Here as a weakling in irons,
   Here as a weanling in bands,
As a prey that the stake-net environs,
   Our life that we looked for stands;
And the man-child naked and dear,
Democracy, turns on us here
   Eyes trembling with tremulous hands.

It sees not what season shall bring to it
   Sweet fruit of its bitter desire;
Few voices it hears yet sing to it,   80
   Few pulses of hearts reaspire;
Foresees not time, nor forehears
The noises of imminent years,
   Earthquake, and thunder, and fire:

When crowned and weaponed and curbless
   It shall walk without helm or shield
The bare burnt furrows and herbless

Of war's last flame-stricken field,
Till godlike, equal with time,
It stand in the sun sublime,   90
    In the godhead of man revealed.

Round your people and over them
    Light like raiment is drawn,
Close as a garment to cover them
    Wrought not of mail nor of lawn;
Here, with hope hardly to wear,
Naked nations and bare
    Swim, sink, strike out for the dawn.

Chains are here, and a prison,
    Kings, and subjects, and shame;   100
If the God upon you be arisen,
    How should our songs be the same?
How, in confusion of change,
How shall we sing, in a strange
    Land, songs praising his name?*

God is buried and dead to us,
    Even the spirit of earth,
Freedom; so have they said to us,
    Some with mocking and mirth,
Some with heartbreak and tears;   110
And a God without eyes, without ears,
    Who shall sing of him, dead in the birth?

The earth-god Freedom, the lonely
    Face lightening, the footprint unshod,
Not as one man crucified only
    Nor scourged with but one life's rod;
The soul that is substance of nations,
Reincarnate with fresh generations;
    The great god Man, which is God.

* Cf. *Psalms* 137:4: "How shall we sing the Lord's song in a strange
land?"

But in weariest of years and obscurest   120
    Doth it live not at heart of all things,
The one God and one spirit, a purest
    Life, fed from unstanchable springs?
Within love, within hatred it is,
And its seed in the stripe as the kiss,
    And in slaves is the germ, and in kings.

Freedom we call it, for holier
    Name of the soul's there is none;
Surelier it labours, if slowlier,
    Than the metres of star or of sun;   130
Slowlier than life into breath,
Surelier than time into death,
    It moves till its labour be done.

Till the motion be done and the measure
    Circling through season and clime,
Slumber and sorrow and pleasure,
    Vision of virtue and crime;
Till consummate with conquering eyes,
A soul disembodied, it rise
    From the body transfigured of time.   140

Till it rise and remain and take station
    With the stars of the worlds that rejoice;
Till the voice of its heart's exultation
    Be as theirs an invariable voice;
By no discord of evil estranged,
By no pause, by no breach in it changed,
    By no clash in the chord of its choice.

It is one with the world's generations,
    With the spirit, the star, and the sod;
With the kingless and king-stricken nations,   150
    With the cross, and the chain, and the rod;
The most high, the most secret, most lonely,

The earth-soul Freedom, that only
    Lives, and that only is God.

❧ ❧

Cor Cordium *

O heart of hearts, the chalice of love's fire,
    Hid round with flowers and all the bounty of bloom;
    O wonderful and perfect heart, for whom
The lyrist liberty made life a lyre;
O heavenly heart, at whose most dear desire
    Dead love, living and singing, cleft his tomb,
    And with him risen and regent in death's room
All day thy choral pulses rang full choir;
O heart whose beating blood was running song,
    O sole thing sweeter than thine own songs were,
      Help us for thy free love's sake to be free,
True for thy truth's sake, for thy strength's sake strong,
    Till very liberty make clean and fair
      The nursing earth as the sepulchral sea.

❧ ❧

Tiresias

PART I

It is an hour before the hour of dawn.
    Set in mine hand my staff and leave me here
    Outside the hollow house that blind men fear,
More blind than I who live on life withdrawn
    And feel on eyes that see not but foresee
    The shadow of death which clothes Antigone.

Here lay her living body that here lies
    Dead, if man living know what thing is death,

* "Heart of Hearts," inscribed on Shelley's tomb in Rome.

If life be all made up of blood and breath,
And no sense be save as of ears and eyes.   10
   But heart there is not, tongue there is not found,
   To think or sing what verge hath life or bound.

In the beginning when the powers that made
   The young child man a little loved him, seeing
   His joy of life and fair face of his being,
And bland and laughing with the man-child played,
   As friends they saw on our divine one day
   King Cadmus take to queen Harmonia.*

The strength of soul that builds up as with hands
   Walls spiritual and towers and towns of thought   20
   Which only fate, not force, can bring to nought,
Took then to wife the light of all men's lands,
   War's child and love's, most sweet and wise and strong,
   Order of things and rule and guiding song.

It was long since: yea, even the sun that saw
   Remembers hardly what was, nor how long.
   And now the wise heart of the worldly song
Is perished, and the holy hand of law
   Can set no tune on time, nor help again
   The power of thought to build up life for men.   30

Yea, surely are they now transformed or dead,
   And sleep below this world, where no sun warms,
   Or move about it now in formless forms
Incognizable, and all their lordship fled;
   And where they stood up singing crawl and hiss,
   With fangs that kill behind their lips that kiss.

   * When Cadmus, founder of Thebes and progenitor of Oedipus and
Antigone, married Harmonia, daughter of Ares and Aphrodite (line 23),
the gods attended their wedding. The gods later transformed the once
blessed couple into serpents (line 35) and plagued their progeny with
disaster.

Yet though her marriage-garment, seeming fair,
   Was dyed in sin and woven of jealousy
   To turn their seed to poison, time shall see
The gods reissue from them, and repair   40
   Their broken stamp of godhead, and again
   Thought and wise love sing words of law to men.

I, Tiresias the prophet, seeing in Thebes
   Much evil, and the misery of men's hands
   Who sow with fruitless wheat the stones and sands,
With fruitful thorns the fallows and warm glebes,
   Bade their hands hold lest worse hap came to pass;
   But which of you had heed of Tiresias?

I am as Time's self in mine own wearied mind,
   Whom the strong heavy-footed years have led   50
   From night to night and dead men unto dead,
And from the blind hope to the memory blind;
   For each man's life is woven, as Time's life is,
   Of blind young hopes and old blind memories.

I am a soul outside of death and birth.
   I see before me and afterward I see,
   O child, O corpse, the live dead face of thee,
Whose life and death are one thing upon earth
   Where day kills night and night again kills day
   And dies; but where is that Harmonia?   60

O all-beholden light not seen of me,
   Air, and warm winds that under the sun's eye
   Stretch your strong wings at morning; and thou, sky,
Whose hollow circle engirdling earth and sea
   All night the set stars limit, and all day
   The moving sun remeasures; ye, I say,

Ye heights of hills, and thou Dircean spring
   Inviolable, and ye towers that saw cast down

Seven kings keen-sighted toward your seven-faced town
And quenched the red seed of one sightless king;*   70
   And thou, for death less dreadful than for birth,
   Whose wild leaves hide the horror of the earth,

O mountain whereon gods made chase of kings,
   Cithæron, thou that sawest on Pentheus dead
   Fangs of a mother fasten and wax red
And satiate with a son thy swollen springs,**
   And heardst her cry fright all thine eyries' nests
   Who gave death suck at sanguine-suckling breasts;

Yea, and a grief more grievous, without name,
   A curse too grievous for the name of grief,   80
   Thou sawest, and heardst the rumour scare belief
Even unto death and madness, when the flame
   Was lit whose ashes dropped about the pyre
   That of two brethren made one sundering fire;

O bitter nurse, that on thine hard bare knees
   Rear'dst for his fate the bloody-footed child ***
   Whose hands should be more bloodily defiled
And the old blind feet walk wearier ways than these,
   Whose seed, brought forth in darkness unto doom,
   Should break as fire out of his mother's womb;   90

I bear you witness as ye bear to me,
   Time, day, night, sun, stars, life, death, air, sea, earth,
   And ye that round the human house of birth
Watch with veiled heads and weaponed hands, and see
   Good things and evil, strengthless yet and dumb,
   Sit in the clouds with cloudlike hours to come;

* The Seven Against Thebes included Oedipus' son Polynices, who died in single combat with his brother Eteocles, the Theban king. The single funeral pyre of the brothers burned with a divided flame (line 84).

** Pentheus, grandson of Cadmus, was torn to pieces on Mt. Cithaeron by his mother Agave, who was maddened by Dionysus.

*** Oedipus was abandoned as a child on Mt. Cithaeron, with his feet spiked together.

Ye forces without form and viewless powers
   That have the keys of all our years in hold,
   That prophesy too late with tongues of gold,
In a strange speech whose words are perished hours,   100
   I witness to you what good things ye give
   As ye to me what evil while I live.

What should I do to blame you, what to praise,
   For floral hours and hours funereal?
   What should I do to curse or bless at all
For winter-woven or summer-coloured days?
   Curse he that will and bless you whoso can,
   I have no common part in you with man.

I hear a springing water, whose quick sound
   Makes softer the soft sunless patient air,   110
   And the wind's hand is laid on my thin hair
Light as a lover's, and the grasses round
   Have odours in them of green bloom and rain
   Sweet as the kiss wherewith sleep kisses pain.

I hear the low sound of the spring of time
   Still beating as the low live throb of blood,
   And where its waters gather head and flood
I hear change moving on them, and the chime
   Across them of reverberate wings of hours
   Sounding, and feel the future air of flowers.   120

The wind of change is soft as snow, and sweet
   The sense thereof as roses in the sun,
   The faint wind springing with the springs that run,
The dim sweet smell of flowering hopes, and heat
   Of unbeholden sunrise; yet how long
   I know not, till the morning put forth song.

I prophesy of life, who live with death;
   Of joy, being sad; of sunlight, who am blind;
   Of man, whose ways are alien from mankind

And his lips are not parted with man's breath;   130
 I am a word out of the speechless years,
  The tongue of time, that no man sleeps who hears.

I stand a shadow across the door of doom,
 Athwart the lintel of death's house, and wait;
 Nor quick nor dead, nor flexible by fate,
Nor quite of earth nor wholly of the tomb;
 A voice, a vision, light as fire or air,
  Driven between days that shall be and that were. . . .

On the Downs

 A faint sea without wind or sun;
 A sky like flameless vapour dun;
  A valley like an unsealed grave
 That no man cares to weep upon,
  Bare, without boon to crave,
   Or flower to save.

 And on the lip's edge of the down,
 Here where the bent-grass burns to brown
  In the dry sea-wind, and the heath
 Crawls to the cliff-side and looks down,   10
  I watch, and hear beneath
   The low tide breathe.

 Along the long lines of the cliff,
 Down the flat sea-line without skiff
  Or sail or back-blown fume for mark,
 Through wind-worn heads of heath and stiff
  Stems blossomless and stark
   With dry sprays dark,

 I send mine eyes out as for news
 Of comfort that all these refuse,   20

Tidings of light or living air
From windward where the low clouds muse
  And the sea blind and bare
    Seems full of care.

So is it now as it was then,
And as men have been such are men.
  There as I stood I seem to stand,
Here sitting chambered, and again
  Feel spread on either hand
    Sky, sea, and land.   30

As a queen taken and stripped and bound
Sat earth, discoloured and discrowned;
  As a king's palace empty and dead
The sky was, without light or sound;
  And on the summer's head
    Were ashes shed.

Scarce wind enough was on the sea,
Scarce hope enough there moved in me,
  To sow with live blown flowers of white
The green plain's sad serenity,   40
  Or with stray thoughts of light
    Touch my soul's sight.

By footless ways and sterile went
My thought unsatisfied, and bent
  With blank unspeculative eyes
On the untracked sands of discontent
  Where, watched of helpless skies,
    Life hopeless lies.

East and west went my soul to find
Light, and the world was bare and blind   50
  And the soil herbless where she trod
And saw men laughing scourge mankind,

Unsmitten by the rod
   Of any God.

Out of time's blind old eyes were shed
Tears that were mortal, and left dead
   The heart and spirit of the years,
And on man's fallen and helmless head
   Time's disanointing tears
     Fell cold as fears.   60

Hope flowering had but strength to bear
The fruitless fruitage of despair;
   Grief trod the grapes of joy for wine,
Whereof love drinking unaware
   Died as one undivine
     And made no sign.

And soul and body dwelt apart;
And weary wisdom without heart
   Stared on the dead round heaven and sighed,
"Is death too hollow as thou art,   70
   Or as man's living pride?"
     And saying so died.

And my soul heard the songs and groans
That are about and under thrones,
   And felt through all time's murmur thrill
Fate's old imperious semitones
   That made of good and ill
     One same tune still.

Then "Where is God? and where is aid?
Or what good end of these?" she said;   80
   "Is there no God or end at all,
Nor reason with unreason weighed,
   Nor force to disenthral
     Weak feet that fall?

"No light to lighten and no rod
To chasten men? Is there no God?"
   So girt with anguish, iron-zoned,
Went my soul weeping as she trod
    Between the men enthroned
      And men that groaned.   90

O fool, that for brute cries of wrong
Heard not the grey glad mother's song
   Ring response from the hills and waves,
But heard harsh noises all day long
    Of spirits that were slaves
      And dwelt in graves.

The wise word of the secret earth
Who knows what life and death are worth,
   And how no help and no control
Can speed or stay things come to birth,   100
    Nor all worlds' wheels that roll
      Crush one born soul.

With all her tongues of life and death,
With all her bloom and blood and breath,
   From all years dead and all things done,
In the ear of man the mother saith,
    "There is no God, O son,
      If thou be none."

So my soul sick with watching heard
That day the wonder of that word,   110
   And as one springs out of a dream
Sprang, and the stagnant wells were stirred
    Whence flows through gloom and gleam
      Thought's soundless stream.

Out of pale cliff and sunburnt heath,
Out of the low sea curled beneath
   In the land's bending arm embayed,

Out of all lives that thought hears breathe
   Life within life inlaid,
      Was answer made.   120

A multitudinous monotone
Of dust and flower and seed and stone,
   In the deep sea-rock's mid-sea sloth,
In the live water's trembling zone,
   In all men love and loathe,
      One God at growth.

One forceful nature uncreate
That feeds itself with death and fate,
   Evil and good, and change and time,
That within all men lies at wait   130
   Till the hour shall bid them climb
      And live sublime.

For all things come by fate to flower
At their unconquerable hour,
   And time brings truth, and truth makes free,
And freedom fills time's veins with power,
   As, brooding on that sea,
      My thought filled me.

And the sun smote the clouds and slew,
And from the sun the sea's breath blew,   140
   And white waves laughed and turned and fled
The long green heaving sea-field through,
   And on them overhead
      The sky burnt red.

Like a furled flag that wind sets free,
On the swift summer-coloured sea
   Shook out the red lines of the light,
The live sun's standard, blown to lee
   Across the live sea's white
      And green delight.   150

And with divine triumphant awe
My spirit moved within me saw,
   With burning passion of stretched eyes,
Clear as the light's own firstborn law,
   In the windless wastes of skies
     Time's deep dawn rise.

"Non Dolet" *

It does not hurt. She looked along the knife
   Smiling, and watched the thick drops mix and run
   Down the sheer blade; not that which had been done
Could hurt the sweet sense of the Roman wife,
But that which was to do yet ere the strife
   Could end for each for ever, and the sun:
   Nor was the palm yet nor was peace yet won
While pain had power upon her husband's life.

It does not hurt, Italia. Thou art more
   Than bride to bridegroom; how shalt thou not take
   The gift love's blood has reddened for thy sake?
Was not thy lifeblood given for us before?
   And if love's heartblood can avail thy need,
   And thou not die, how should it hurt indeed?

  * Paetus Caecina, ordered to kill himself by Emperor Claudius I, hesitated until his wife took the dagger from him, stabbed herself and returned it to him, saying, "Paete, non dolet"—"it does not hurt."

Dirae *

I

A DEAD KING

[*Ferdinand II. entered* Malebolge *May 22nd, 1859.*]

Go down to hell. This end is good to see;
  The breath is lightened and the sense at ease
  Because thou art not; sense nor breath there is
In what thy body was, whose soul shall be
Chief nerve of hell's pained heart eternally.
  Thou art abolished from the midst of these
  That are what thou wast: Pius from his knees
Blows off the dust that flecked them, bowed for thee.
Yea, now the long-tongued slack-lipped litanies
  Fail, and the priest has no more prayer to sell—
Now the last Jesuit found about thee is
  The beast that made thy fouler flesh his cell—
Time lays his finger on thee, saying, "Cease;
  Here is no room for thee; go down to hell."

VI

*LOCUSTA***

Come close and see her and hearken. This is she.
  Stop the ways fast against the stench that nips
  Your nostril as it nears her. Lo, the lips
That between prayer and prayer find time to be
Poisonous, the hands holding a cup and key,
  Key of deep hell, cup whence blood reeks and drips;
  The loose lewd limbs, the reeling hingeless hips,

---

* Curses or execrations.
** Famous for her skill in poisons, in the time of Nero and Claudius.

The scurf that is not skin but leprosy.
This haggard harlot grey of face and green
With the old hand's cunning mixes her new priest
The cup she mixed her Nero, stirred and spiced.
She lisps of Mary and Jesus Nazarene
With a tongue tuned, and head that bends to the east,
Praying. There are who say she is bride of Christ.

XIII

THE SAVIOUR OF SOCIETY

I

O son of man, but of what man who knows?
   That broughtest healing on thy leathern wings
   To priests, and under them didst gather kings,
And madest friends to thee of all man's foes;
Before thine incarnation, the tale goes,
   Thy virgin mother, pure of sensual stings,
   Communed by night with angels of chaste things,
And, full of grace, untimely felt the throes
Of motherhood upon her, and believed
   The obscure annunciation made when late
   A raven-feathered raven-throated dove
   Croaked salutation to the mother of love
Whose misconception was immaculate,
And when her time was come she misconceived.

Erechtheus *

CHORUS

Out of the north wind grief came forth,   [*Str.* 1.
   And the shining of a sword out of the sea.

---

   * This chorus from the second of Swinburne's Hellenic dramas
recounts the rape by Boreas, the north wind, of Oreithyia, daughter of
the Athenian king Erechtheus.

Yea, of old the first-blown blast blew the prelude of this
    last,
  The blast of his trumpet upon Rhodope.
Out of the north skies full of his cloud,
With the clamour of his storms as of a crowd
At the wheels of a great king crying aloud,
At the axle of a strong king's car
That has girded on the girdle of war—
With hands that lightened the skies in sunder   10
And feet whose fall was followed of thunder,
  A God, a great God strange of name,
  With horse-yoke fleeter-hoofed than flame,
To the mountain bed of a maiden came,
Oreithyia, the bride mismated,
Wofully wed in a snow-strewn bed
With a bridegroom that kisses the bride's mouth dead;
Without garland, without glory, without song,
As a fawn by night on the hills belated,
Given over for a spoil unto the strong.   20
From lips how pale so keen a wail   [*Ant.* 1.
  At the grasp of a God's hand on her she gave,
When his breath that darkens air made a havoc of her
    hair,
   It rang from the mountain even to the wave;
Rang with a cry, *Woe's me, woe is me!*
From the darkness upon Hæmus to the sea:
And with hands that clung to her new lord's knee,
As a virgin overborne with shame,
She besought him by her spouseless fame,   30
By the blameless breasts of a maid unmarried,
And locks unmaidenly rent and harried,
  And all her flower of body, born
  To match the maidenhood of morn,
With the might of the wind's wrath wrenched and
    torn.
Vain, all vain as a dead man's vision
Falling by night in his old friends' sight,
To be scattered with slumber and slain ere light;

Such a breath of such a bridegroom in that hour
Of her prayers made mock, of her fears derision, 40
And a ravage of her youth as of a flower.
With a leap of his limbs as a lion's, a cry from his
     lips as of thunder, [*Str*. 2.
  In a storm of amorous godhead filled with fire,
From the height of the heaven that was rent with
     the roar of his coming in sunder,
  Sprang the strong God on the spoil of his desire.
And the pines of the hills were as green reeds shattered,
And their branches as buds of the soft spring scattered,
And the west wind and east, and the sound of the south,
Fell dumb at the blast of the north wind's mouth,
  At the cry of his coming out of heaven. 50
And the wild beasts quailed in the rifts and hollows
Where hound nor clarion of huntsman follows,
And the depths of the sea were aghast, and whitened,
And the crowns of their waves as flame that
     lightened,
  And the heart of the floods thereof was riven.
But she knew not him coming for terror, she felt not
     her wrong that he wrought her, [*Ant*. 2.
  When her locks as leaves were shed before his
     breath,
And she heard not for terror his prayer, though the
     cry was a God's that besought her,
  Blown from lips that strew the world-wide seas
     with death.
For the heart was molten within her to hear, 60
And her knees beneath her were loosened for fear,
And her blood fast bound as a frost-bound water,
And the soft new bloom of the green earth's daughter
  Wind-wasted as blossom of a tree;
As the wild God rapt her from earth's breast lifted,
On the strength of the stream of his dark breath drifted,
From the bosom of earth as a bride from the mother,
With storm for bridesman and wreck for brother,
  As a cloud that he sheds upon the sea.

Of this hoary-headed woe　　　　　　　　　　　*[Epode.*
Song made memory long ago;
Now a younger grief to mourn
Needs a new song younger born.
Who shall teach our tongues to reach
What strange height of saddest speech,
For the new bride's sake that is given to be
A stay to fetter the foot of the sea,
Lest it quite spurn down and trample the town,
Ere the violets be dead that were plucked for its crown,
　　Or its olive-leaf whiten and wither?　　　　　80
　　Who shall say of the wind's way
　　That he journeyed yesterday,
Or the track of the storm that shall sound tomorrow,
If the new be more than the grey-grown sorrow?
For the wind of the green first season was keen,
And the blast shall be sharper than blew between
　　That the breath of the sea blows hither.

A Forsaken Garden

In a coign of the cliff between lowland and highland,
　　At the sea-down's edge between windward and lee,
Walled round with rocks as an inland island,
　　The ghost of a garden fronts the sea.
A girdle of brushwood and thorn encloses
　　The steep square slope of the blossomless bed
Where the weeds that grew green from the graves of
　　　　its roses
　　　　　Now lie dead.

The fields fall southward, abrupt and broken,
　　To the low last edge of the long lone land.　　10
If a step should sound or a word be spoken,
　　Would a ghost not rise at the strange guest's hand?
So long have the grey bare walks lain guestless,

Through branches and briars if a man make way,
He shall find no life but the sea-wind's, restless
      Night and day.

The dense hard passage is blind and stifled
   That crawls by a track none turn to climb
To the strait waste place that the years have rifled
   Of all but the thorns that are touched not of time.   20
The thorns he spares when the rose is taken;
   The rocks are left when he wastes the plain.
The wind that wanders, the weeds wind-shaken,
      These remain.

Not a flower to be pressed of the foot that falls not;
   As the heart of a dead man the seed-plots are dry;
From the thicket of thorns whence the nightingale calls
     not,
   Could she call, there were never a rose to reply.
Over the meadows that blossom and wither
   Rings but the note of a sea-bird's song;   30
Only the sun and the rain come hither
      All year long.

The sun burns sere and the rain dishevels
   One gaunt bleak blossom of scentless breath.
Only the wind here hovers and revels
   In a round where life seems barren as death.
Here there was laughing of old, there was weeping,
   Haply, of lovers none ever will know,
Whose eyes went seaward a hundred sleeping
      Years ago.   40

Heart handfast in heart as they stood, "Look thither,"
   Did he whisper? "look forth from the flowers to the
     sea;
For the foam-flowers endure when the rose-blossoms
     wither,
   And men that love lightly may die—but we?"

And the same wind sang and the same waves whitened,
  And or ever the garden's last petals were shed,
In the lips that had whispered, the eyes that had
     lightened,
        Love was dead.

Or they loved their life through, and then went whither?
  And were one to the end—but what end who knows?   50
Love deep as the sea as a rose must wither,
  As the rose-red seaweed that mocks the rose.
Shall the dead take thought for the dead to love them?
  What love was ever as deep as a grave?
They are loveless now as the grass above them
      Or the wave.

All are at one now, roses and lovers,
  Not known of the cliffs and the fields and the sea.
Not a breath of the time that has been hovers
  In the air now soft with a summer to be.   60
Not a breath shall there sweeten the seasons hereafter
  Of the flowers or the lovers that laugh now or weep,
When as they that are free now of weeping and laughter
      We shall sleep.

Here death may deal not again for ever;
  Here change may come not till all change end.
From the graves they have made they shall rise up
     never,
  Who have left nought living to ravage and rend.
Earth, stones, and thorns of the wild ground growing,
  While the sun and the rain live, these shall be;
Till a last wind's breath upon all these blowing   70
      Roll the sea.

Till the slow sea rise and the sheer cliff crumble,
  Till terrace and meadow the deep gulfs drink,
Till the strength of the waves of the high tides humble
  The fields that lessen, the rocks that shrink,

Here now in his triumph where all things falter,
    Stretched out on the spoils that his own hand spread,
As a god self-slain on his own strange altar,
        Death lies dead.   80

At a Month's End

The night last night was strange and shaken:
    More strange the change of you and me.
Once more, for the old love's love forsaken,
    We went out once more toward the sea.

For the old love's love-sake dead and buried,
    One last time, one more and no more,
We watched the waves set in, the serried
    Spears of the tide storming the shore.

Hardly we saw the high moon hanging,
    Heard hardly through the windy night   10
Far waters ringing, low reefs clanging,
    Under wan skies and waste white light.

With chafe and change of surges chiming,
    The clashing channels rocked and rang
Large music, wave to wild wave timing,
    And all the choral water sang.

Faint lights fell this way, that way floated,
    Quick sparks of sea-fire keen like eyes
From the rolled surf that flashed, and noted
    Shores and faint cliffs and bays and skies.   20

The ghost of sea that shrank up sighing
    At the sand's edge, a short sad breath
Trembling to touch the goal, and dying
    With weak heart heaved up once in death—

The rustling sand and shingle shaken
   With light sweet touches and small sound—
These could not move us, could not waken
   Hearts to look forth, eyes to look round.

Silent we went an hour together,
   Under grey skies by waters white.   30
Our hearts were full of windy weather,
   Clouds and blown stars and broken light.

Full of cold clouds and moonbeams drifted
   And streaming storms and straying fires,
Our souls in us were stirred and shifted
   By doubts and dreams and foiled desires.

Across, aslant, a scudding sea-mew
   Swam, dipped, and dropped, and grazed the sea:
And one with me I could not dream you;
   And one with you I could not be.   40

As the white wing the white wave's fringes
   Touched and slid over and flashed past—
As a pale cloud a pale flame tinges
   From the moon's lowest light and last—

As a star feels the sun and falters,
   Touched to death by diviner eyes—
As on the old gods' untended altars
   The old fire of withered worship dies—

(Once only, once the shrine relighted
   Sees the last fiery shadow shine,   50
Last shadow of flame and faith benighted,
   Sees falter and flutter and fail the shrine)

So once with fiery breath and flying
   Your winged heart touched mine and went,

And the swift spirits kissed, and sighing,
   Sundered and smiled and were content.

That only touch, that feeling only,
   Enough we found, we found too much;
For the unlit shrine is hardly lonely
   As one the old fire forgets to touch.   60

Slight as the sea's sight of the sea-mew,
   Slight as the sun's sight of the star:
Enough to show one must not deem you
   For love's sake other than you are.

Who snares and tames with fear and danger
   A bright beast of a fiery kin,
Only to mar, only to change her
   Sleek supple soul and splendid skin?

Easy with blows to mar and maim her,
   Easy with bonds to bind and bruise;   70
What profit, if she yield her tamer
   The limbs to mar, the soul to lose?

Best leave or take the perfect creature,
   Take all she is or leave complete;
Transmute you will not form or feature,
   Change feet for wings or wings for feet.

Strange eyes, new limbs, can no man give her;
   Sweet is the sweet thing as it is.
No soul she hath, we see, to outlive her;
   Hath she for that no lips to kiss?   80

So may one read his weird, and reason,
   And with vain drugs assuage no pain.
For each man in his loving season
   Fools and is fooled of these in vain.

Charms that allay not any longing,
   Spells that appease not any grief,
Time brings us all by handfuls, wronging
   All hurts with nothing of relief.

Ah, too soon shot, the fool's bolt misses!
   What help? the world is full of loves;   90
Night after night of running kisses,
   Chirp after chirp of changing doves.

Should Love disown or disesteem you
   For loving one man more or less?
You could not tame your light white sea-mew,
   Nor I my sleek black pantheress.

For a new soul let whoso please pray,
   We are what life made us, and shall be.
For you the jungle and me the sea-spray,
   And south for you and north for me.   100

But this one broken foam-white feather
   I throw you off the hither wing,
Splashed stiff with sea-scurf and salt weather,
   This song for sleep to learn and sing—

Sing in your ear when, daytime over,
   You, couched at long length on hot sand
With some sleek sun-discoloured lover,
   Wince from his breath as from a brand:

Till the acrid hour aches out and ceases,
   And the sheathed eyeball sleepier swims,   110
The deep flank smoothes its dimpling creases,
   And passion loosens all the limbs:

Till dreams of sharp grey north-sea weather
   Fall faint upon your fiery sleep,
As on strange sands a strayed bird's feather
   The wind may choose to lose or keep.

But I, who leave my queen of panthers,
   As a tired honey-heavy bee
Gilt with sweet dust from gold-grained anthers
   Leaves the rose-chalice, what for me?   120

From the ardours of the chaliced centre,
   From the amorous anthers' golden grime,
That scorch and smutch all wings that enter,
   I fly forth hot from honey-time.

But as to a bee's gilt thighs and winglets
   The flower-dust with the flower-smell clings;
As a snake's mobile rampant ringlets
   Leave the sand marked with print of rings;

So to my soul in surer fashion
   Your savage stamp and savour hangs;   130
The print and perfume of old passion,
   The wild-beast mark of panther's fangs.

❦ ❦

Ave Atque Vale *

IN MEMORY OF CHARLES BAUDELAIRE

> Nous devrions pourtant lui porter quelques fleurs;
> Et quand Octobre souffle, émondeur des vieux arbres,
> Les morts, les pauvres morts, ont de grandes douleurs,
> Son vent mélancolique à l'entour de leurs marbres,
> Certe, ils doivent trouver les vivants bien ingrats.
>
> *Les Fleurs du Mal*

I

Shall I strew on thee rose or rue or laurel,
   Brother, on this that was the veil of thee?

---

* The title, "Hail and Farewell," alludes to Catullus' elegy to his
brother: *Frater ave atque vale*. The epigraph reads:
    Yet we should bring him a few flowers;
    the dead, the miserable dead, have great sorrows,
    and when October, pruner of old trees, blows
    its melancholy wind around their marble stones,
    they must find the living indeed ungrateful.

Or quiet sea-flower moulded by the sea,
Or simplest growth of meadow-sweet or sorrel,
     Such as the summer-sleepy Dryads weave,
     Waked up by snow-soft sudden rains at eve?
Or wilt thou rather, as on earth before,
     Half-faded fiery blossoms, pale with heat
     And full of bitter summer, but more sweet
To thee than gleanings of a northern shore   10
     Trod by no tropic feet?

                    2

For always thee the fervid languid glories
     Allured of heavier suns in mightier skies;
     Thine ears knew all the wandering watery sighs
Where the sea sobs round Lesbian promontories,*
     The barren kiss of piteous wave to wave
     That knows not where is that Leucadian grave
Which hides too deep the supreme head of song.
     Ah, salt and sterile as her kisses were,
     The wild sea winds her and the green gulfs bear   20
Hither and thither, and vex and work her wrong,
     Blind gods that cannot spare.

                    3

Thou sawest, in thine old singing season, brother,
     Secrets and sorrows unbeheld of us:
     Fierce loves, and lovely leaf-buds poisonous,
Bare to thy subtler eye, but for none other
     Blowing by night in some unbreathed-in clime;
     The hidden harvest of luxurious time,
Sin without shape, and pleasure without speech;
     And where strange dreams in a tumultuous sleep   30
     Make the shut eyes of stricken spirits weep;
And with each face thou sawest the shadow on each,
     Seeing as men sow men reap.**

---

* Baudelaire's "Lesbos" tells of the death of Sappho, who threw
herself from the cliffs of Leucas into the sea.
** Cf. *Galatians* 6:7: "Be not deceived; God is not mocked: for
whatsoever a man soweth, that shall he also reap."

4

O sleepless heart and sombre soul unsleeping,
    That were athirst for sleep and no more life
    And no more love, for peace and no more strife!
Now the dim gods of death have in their keeping
    Spirit and body and all the springs of song,
    Is it well now where love can do no wrong,
Where stingless pleasure has no foam or fang   40
    Behind the unopening closure of her lips?
    Is it not well where soul from body slips
And flesh from bone divides without a pang
    As dew from flower-bell drips?

5

It is enough; the end and the beginning
    Are one thing to thee, who art past the end.
    O hand unclasped of unbeholden friend,
For thee no fruits to pluck, no palms for winning,
    No triumph and no labour and no lust,
    Only dead yew-leaves and a little dust.   50
O quiet eyes wherein the light saith nought,
    Whereto the day is dumb, nor any night
    With obscure finger silences your sight,
Nor in your speech the sudden soul speaks thought,
    Sleep, and have sleep for light.

6

Now all strange hours and all strange loves are over,
    Dreams and desires and sombre songs and sweet,
    Hast thou found place at the great knees and feet
Of some pale Titan-woman* like a lover,
    Such as thy vision here solicited,   60
    Under the shadow of her fair vast head,
The deep division of prodigious breasts,
    The solemn slope of mighty limbs asleep,

---

* The features of the Titan-woman are drawn from Baudelaire's "La Géante."

The weight of awful tresses that still keep
The savour and shade of old-world pine-forests
 Where the wet hill-winds weep?

7

Hast thou found any likeness for thy vision?
 O gardener of strange flowers, what bud, what bloom,
 Hast thou found sown, what gathered in the gloom?
What of despair, of rapture, of derision,   70
 What of life is there, what of ill or good?
 Are the fruits grey like dust or bright like blood?
Does the dim ground grow any seed of ours,
 The faint fields quicken any terrene root,
 In low lands where the sun and moon are mute
And all the stars keep silence? Are there flowers
 At all, or any fruit?

8

Alas, but though my flying song flies after,
 O sweet strange elder singer, thy more fleet
 Singing, and footprints of thy fleeter feet,   80
Some dim derision of mysterious laughter
 From the blind tongueless warders of the dead,
 Some gainless glimpse of Proserpine's veiled head,
Some little sound of unregarded tears
 Wept by effaced unprofitable eyes,
 And from pale mouths some cadence of dead sighs—
These only, these the hearkening spirit hears,
 Sees only such things rise.

9

Thou art far too far for wings of words to follow,
 Far too far off for thought or any prayer.   90
 What ails us with thee, who art wind and air?
What ails us gazing where all seen is hollow?
 Yet with some fancy, yet with some desire,
 Dreams pursue death as winds a flying fire,
Our dreams pursue our dead and do not find.

Still, and more swift than they, the thin flame flies,
   The low light fails us in elusive skies,
Still the foiled earnest ear is deaf, and blind
   Are still the eluded eyes.

10

Not thee, O never thee, in all time's changes,   100
   Not thee, but this the sound of thy sad soul,
   The shadow of thy swift spirit, this shut scroll
I lay my hand on, and not death estranges
   My spirit from communion of thy song—
   These memories and these melodies that throng
Veiled porches of a Muse funereal—
   These I salute, these touch, these clasp and fold
   As though a hand were in my hand to hold,
Or through mine ears a mourning musical
   Of many mourners rolled.   110

11

I among these, I also, in such station
   As when the pyre was charred, and piled the sods,
   And offering to the dead made, and their gods,
The old mourners had, standing to make libation,
   I stand, and to the gods and to the dead
   Do reverence without prayer or praise, and shed
Offering to these unknown, the gods of gloom,
   And what of honey and spice my seedlands bear,
   And what I may of fruits in this chilled air,
And lay, Orestes-like,* across the tomb   120
   A curl of severed hair.

12

But by no hand nor any treason stricken,
   Not like the low-lying head of Him, the King,
   The flame that made of Troy a ruinous thing,
Thou liest, and on this dust no tears could quicken

---

   * Orestes laid a lock of his hair as a sacrifice on the tomb of his
father, Agamemnon, murdered on his return from the siege of Troy.

There fall no tears like theirs that all men hear
 Fall tear by sweet imperishable tear
Down the opening leaves of holy poets' pages.
 Thee not Orestes, not Electra mourns;
 But bending us-ward with memorial urns   130
The most high Muses that fulfil all ages
 Weep, and our God's heart yearns.

13

For, sparing of his sacred strength, not often
 Among us darkling here the lord of light
 Makes manifest his music and his might
In hearts that open and in lips that soften
 With the soft flame and heat of songs that shine.
 Thy lips indeed he touched with bitter wine,
And nourished them indeed with bitter bread;
 Yet surely from his hand thy soul's food came,   140
 The fire that scarred thy spirit at his flame
Was lighted, and thine hungering heart he fed
 Who feeds our hearts with fame.

14

Therefore he too now at thy soul's sunsetting,
 God of all suns and songs, he too bends down
 To mix his laurel with thy cypress crown,
And save thy dust from blame and from forgetting.
 Therefore he too, seeing all thou wert and art,
 Compassionate, with sad and sacred heart,
Mourns thee of many his children the last dead,   150
 And hallows with strange tears and alien sighs
 Thine unmelodious mouth and sunless eyes,
And over thine irrevocable head
 Sheds light from the under skies.

15

And one weeps with him in the ways Lethean,
 And stains with tears her changing bosom chill:

That obscure Venus of the hollow hill,*
That thing transformed which was the Cytherean,
 With lips that lost their Grecian laugh divine
 Long since, and face no more called Erycine;   160
A ghost, a bitter and luxurious god.
 Thee also with fair flesh and singing spell
 Did she, a sad and second prey, compel
Into the footless places once more trod,
 And shadows hot from hell.

16

And now no sacred staff shall break in blossom,
 No choral salutation lure to light
 A spirit sick with perfume and sweet night
And love's tired eyes and hands and barren bosom.
 There is no help for these things; none to mend   170
 And none to mar; not all our songs, O friend,
Will make death clear or make life durable.
 Howbeit with rose and ivy and wild vine
 And with wild notes about this dust of thine
At least I fill the place where white dreams dwell
 And wreathe an unseen shrine.

17

Sleep; and if life was bitter to thee, pardon,
 If sweet, give thanks; thou hast no more to live;
 And to give thanks is good, and to forgive.
Out of the mystic and the mournful garden   180
 Where all day through thine hands in barren braid
 Wove the sick flowers of secrecy and shade,
Green buds of sorrow and sin, and remnants grey,
 Sweet-smelling, pale with poison, sanguine-hearted,
 Passions that sprang from sleep and thoughts that started,

---

* The fallen medieval Venus of the Tannhäuser legend in Swinburne's "Laus Veneris," Cytherean refers to the site of Venus' birth, amidst the sea-foam off Cythera; Erycine, to Mt. Eryx in Sicily (modern Erice), where she was worshipped.

Shall death not bring us all as thee one day
   Among the days departed?

18

For thee, O now a silent soul, my brother,
   Take at my hands this garland, and farewell.
   Thin is the leaf, and chill the wintry smell,   190
And chill the solemn earth, a fatal mother,
   With sadder than the Niobean womb,
   And in the hollow of her breasts a tomb.
Content thee, howsoe'er, whose days are done;
   There lies not any troublous thing before,
   Nor sight nor sound to war against thee more,
For whom all winds are quiet as the sun,
   All waters as the shore.

Inferiae *

Spring, and the light and sound of things on earth
Requickening, all within our green sea's girth;
A time of passage or a time of birth
   Fourscore years since as this year, first and last.

The sun is all about the world we see,
The breath and strength of very spring; and we
Live, love, and feed on our own hearts; but he
   Whose heart fed mine has passed into the past.

Past, all things born with sense and blood and breath;
The flesh hears nought that now the spirit saith.   10
If death be like as birth and birth as death,
   The first was fair—more fair should be the last.

---

  * Sacrifices in honor of the dead; the occasion is the death of the
poet's father, Admiral Swinburne.

Fourscore years since, and come but one month more
The count were perfect of his mortal score
Whose sail went seaward yesterday from shore
    To cross the last of many an unsailed sea.

Light, love and labour up to life's last height,
These three were stars unsetting in his sight;
Even as the sun is life and heat and light
    And sets not nor is dark when dark are we.   20

The life, the spirit, and the work were one
That here—ah, who shall say, that here are done?
Not I, that know not; father, not thy son,
    For all the darkness of the night and sea.
                     MARCH 5, 1877.

Cyril Tourneur *

A sea that heaves with horror of the night,
    As maddened by the moon that hangs aghast
    With strain and torment of the ravening blast,
Haggard as hell, a bleak blind bloody light;
No shore but one red reef of rock in sight,
    Whereon the waifs of many a wreck were cast
    And shattered in the fierce nights overpast
Wherein more souls toward hell than heaven took flight;
And 'twixt the shark-toothed rocks and swallowing shoals
A cry as out of hell from all these souls
    Sent through the sheer gorge of the slaughtering sea,
Whose thousand throats, full-fed with life by death,
Fill the black air with foam and furious breath;
    And over all these one star—Chastity.

    * Elizabethan dramatist, the lurid atmosphere of whose *Revenger's Tragedy* Swinburne's sonnet evokes.

A Vision of Spring in Winter

1

O tender time that love thinks long to see,
   Sweet foot of spring that with her footfall sows
   Late snowlike flowery leavings of the snows,
Be not too long irresolute to be;
O mother-month,* where have they hidden thee?
   Out of the pale time of the flowerless rose
I reach my heart out toward the springtime lands,
   I stretch my spirit forth to the fair hours,
     The purplest of the prime;
I lean my soul down over them, with hands   10
   Made wide to take the ghostly growths of flowers;
     I send my love back to the lovely time.

2

Where has the greenwood hid thy gracious head?
   Veiled with what visions while the grey world grieves,
   Or muffled with what shadows of green leaves,
What warm intangible green shadows spread
To sweeten the sweet twilight for thy bed?
   What sleep enchants thee? what delight deceives?
Where the deep dreamlike dew before the dawn
   Feels not the fingers of the sunlight yet   20
     Its silver web unweave,
Thy footless ghost on some unfooted lawn
   Whose air the unrisen sunbeams fear to fret
     Lives a ghost's life of daylong dawn and eve.

3

Sunrise it sees not, neither set of star,
   Large nightfall, nor imperial plenilune,
   Nor strong sweet shape of the full-breasted noon;

---

* April, the month of Swinburne's birth.

But where the silver-sandalled shadows are,
Too soft for arrows of the sun to mar,
  Moves with the mild gait of an ungrown moon: 30
Hard overhead the half-lit crescent swims,
  The tender-coloured night draws hardly breath,
    The light is listening;
They watch the dawn of slender-shapen limbs,
  Virginal, born again of doubtful death,
    Chill foster-father of the weanling spring.

  4

As sweet desire of day before the day,
  As dreams of love before the true love born,
  From the outer edge of winter overworn
The ghost arisen of May before the May   40
Takes through dim air her unawakened way,
  The gracious ghost of morning risen ere morn.
With little unblown breasts and child-eyed looks
  Following, the very maid, the girl-child spring,
    Lifts windward her bright brows,
Dips her light feet in warm and moving brooks,
  And kindles with her own mouth's colouring
    The fearful firstlings of the plumeless boughs.

  5

I seek thee sleeping, and awhile I see,
  Fair face that art not, how thy maiden breath   50
  Shall put at last the deadly days to death
And fill the fields and fire the woods with thee
And seaward hollows where my feet would be
  When heaven shall hear the word that April saith
To change the cold heart of the weary time,
  To stir and soften all the time to tears,
    Tears joyfuller than mirth;
As even to May's clear height the young days climb
  With feet not swifter than those fair first years
    Whose flowers revive not with thy flowers on earth.   60

6

I would not bid thee, though I might, give back
  One good thing youth has given and borne away;
  I crave not any comfort of the day
That is not, nor on time's retrodden track
Would turn to meet the white-robed hours or black
  That long since left me on their mortal way;
Nor light nor love that has been, nor the breath
  That comes with morning from the sun to be
    And sets light hope on fire;
No fruit, no flower thought once too fair for death,   70
  No flower nor hour once fallen from life's green tree,
    No leaf once plucked or once fulfilled desire.

7

The morning song beneath the stars that fled
  With twilight through the moonless mountain air,
  While youth with burning lips and wreathless hair
Sang toward the sun that was to crown his head,
Rising; the hopes that triumphed and fell dead,
  The sweet swift eyes and songs of hours that were;
These may'st thou not give back for ever; these,
  As at the sea's heart all her wrecks lie waste,   80
    Lie deeper than the sea;
But flowers thou may'st, and winds, and hours of ease,
  And all its April to the world thou may'st
    Give back, and half my April back to me.

A Ballad of François Villon

PRINCE OF ALL BALLAD-MAKERS

Bird of the bitter bright grey golden morn*
  Scarce risen upon the dusk of dolorous years,

  * Villon (1431–63?) as herald of the early Renaissance, risen from
the "dusk" of medieval song. For Swinburne's recurrent characterization
of Villon as "our sad bad glad mad" brother, see p. xxxii, n.19.

First of us all and sweetest singer born
　　Whose far shrill note the world of new men hears
　　Cleave the cold shuddering shade as twilight clears;
When song new-born put off the old world's attire
And felt its tune on her changed lips expire,
　　Writ foremost on the roll of them that came
Fresh girt for service of the latter lyre,
　　Villon, our sad bad glad mad brother's name!   10

Alas the joy, the sorrow, and the scorn,
　　That clothed thy life with hopes and sins and fears,
And gave thee stones for bread and tares for corn
　　And plume-plucked gaol-birds for thy starveling peers
　　Till death clipt close their flight with shameful shears;
Till shifts came short and loves were hard to hire,
When lilt of song nor twitch of twangling wire
　　Could buy thee bread or kisses; when light fame
Spurned like a ball and haled through brake and briar,
　　Villon, our sad bad glad mad brother's name!   20

Poor splendid wings so frayed and soiled and torn!
　　Poor kind wild eyes so dashed with light quick tears!
Poor perfect voice, most blithe when most forlorn,
　　That rings athwart the sea whence no man steers
　　Like joy-bells crossed with death-bells in our ears!
What far delight has cooled the fierce desire
That like some ravenous bird was strong to tire
　　On that frail flesh and soul consumed with flame,
But left more sweet than roses to respire,
　　Villon, our sad bad glad mad brother's name?   30

Envoi

Prince of sweet songs made out of tears and fire,
A harlot was thy nurse, a God thy sire;
　　Shame soiled thy song, and song assoiled thy shame.
But from thy feet now death has washed the mire,
Love reads out first at head of all our quire,
　　Villon, our sad bad glad mad brother's name.

❧ ❧

Translations from the French of Villon
THE COMPLAINT OF THE FAIR ARMOURESS *

1

Meseemeth I heard cry and groan
  That sweet who was the armourer's maid;
For her young years she made sore moan,
  And right upon this wise she said;
  "Ah fierce old age with foul bald head,
To spoil fair things thou art over fain;
  Who holdeth me? who? would God I were dead!
Would God I were well dead and slain!

2

"Lo, thou hast broken the sweet yoke
  That my high beauty held above
All priests and clerks and merchant-folk;   10
  There was not one but for my love
  Would give me gold and gold enough,
Though sorrow his very heart had riven,
  To win from me such wage thereof
As now no thief would take if given.

3

"I was right chary of the same,
  God wot it was my great folly,
For love of one sly knave of them,
  Good store of that same sweet had he;   20
  For all my subtle wiles, perdie,
God wot I loved him well enow;
  Right evilly he handled me,
But he loved well my gold, I trow.

* Lines 54–56 and 70, omitted because of their supposed indecency
from the 1904 edition of the *Poems*, have been restored.

4

"Though I gat bruises green and black,
    I loved him never the less a jot;
Though he bound burdens on my back,
    If he said 'Kiss me and heed it not'
    Right little pain I felt, God wot,
When that foul thief's mouth, found so sweet,   30
    Kissed me—Much good thereof I got!
I keep the sin and the shame of it.

5

"And he died thirty year agone.
    I am old now, no sweet thing to see;
By God, though, when I think thereon,
    And of that good glad time, woe's me,
    And stare upon my changed body
Stark naked, that has been so sweet,
    Lean, wizen, like a small dry tree,
I am nigh mad with the pain of it.   40

6

"Where is my faultless forehead's white,
    The lifted eyebrows, soft gold hair,
Eyes wide apart and keen of sight,
    With subtle skill in the amorous air;
    The straight nose, great nor small, but fair,
The small carved ears of shapeliest growth,
    Chin dimpling, colour good to wear,
And sweet red splendid kissing mouth?

7

"The shapely slender shoulders small,
    Long arms, hands wrought in glorious wise,   50
Round little breasts, the hips withal
    High, full of flesh, not scant of size,
    Fit for all amorous masteries;
The large loins, and the flower that was

Planted above my strong, round thighs
In a small garden of soft grass?

8

"A writhled forehead, hair gone grey,
　　Fallen eyebrows, eyes gone blind and red,
Their laughs and looks all fled away,
　　Yea, all that smote men's hearts are fled;　　　　　60
　　The bowed nose, fallen from goodlihead;
Foul flapping ears like water-flags;
　　Peaked chin, and cheeks all waste and dead,
And lips that are two skinny rags:

9

"Thus endeth all the beauty of us.
　　The arms made short, the hands made lean,
The shoulders bowed and ruinous,
　　The breasts, alack! all fallen in;
　　The flanks too, like the breasts, grown thin;
As for the sweet place, out on it!　　　　　70
　　For the lank thighs, no thighs but skin,
They are specked with spots like sausage-meat.

10

"So we make moan for the old sweet days,
　　Poor old light women, two or three
Squatting above the straw-fire's blaze,
　　The bosom crushed against the knee,
　　Like faggots on a heap we be,
Round fires soon lit, soon quenched and done;
　　And we were once so sweet, even we!
Thus fareth many and many an one."　　　　　80

*THE BALLAD OF VILLON AND FAT MADGE**

" 'Tis no sin for a man to labour in his vocation." Falstaff
"The night cometh, when no man can work."

　　* Reprinted with the generous permission of Cecil Y. Lang and the
Syracuse University Press from *New Writings by Swinburne,* Syracuse,

What though the beauty I love and serve be cheap,
　　Ought you to take me for a beast or fool?
All things a man could wish are in her keep;
　　For her I turn swashbuckler in love's school.
　　When folk drop in, I take my pot and stool
And fall to drinking with no more ado.
I fetch them bread, fruit, cheese, and water, too;
　　I say all's right so long as I'm well paid;
"Look in again when your flesh troubles you,
　　Inside this brothel where we drive our trade."　　　10

But soon the devil's among us flesh and fell,
　　When penniless to bed comes Madge my whore;
I loathe the very sight of her like hell.
　　I snatch gown, girdle, surcoat, all she wore,
　　And tell her, these shall stand against her score.
She grips her hips with both hands, cursing God,
Swearing by Jesus' body, bones, and blood,
　　That they shall not. Then I, no whit dismayed,
Cross her cracked nose with some stray shiver of wood
　　Inside this brothel where we drive our trade.　　　20

When all's made up she drops me a windy word,
　　Bloat like a beetle puffed and poisonous:
Grins, thumps my pate, and calls me dickey-bird,
　　And cuffs me with a fist that's ponderous.
　　We sleep like logs, being drunken both of us;
Then when we wake her womb begins to stir;
To save her seed she gets me under her
　　Wheezing and whining, flat as planks are laid:
And thus she spoils me for a whoremonger
　　Inside this brothel where we drive our trade.　　　30

Blow, hail or freeze, I've bread here baked rent free!
Whoring's my trade, and my whore pleases me;

1964. Swinburne never published his translation of Villon's "Ballade de la Grosse Margot" because, as he put it, the poem "has not six decent lines (nor a single bad or weak one) in it from beginning to end." The outrageously apt second epigraph is from *John* 9:4.

Bad cat, bad rat; we're just the same if weighed.
We that love filth, filth follows us, you see;
Honour flees from us, as from her we flee
    Inside this brothel where we drive our trade.

THE EPITAPH IN FORM OF A BALLAD

*Which Villon made for himself and his comrades,
expecting to be hanged along with them*

Men, brother men, that after us yet live,
    Let not your hearts too hard against us be;
For if some pity of us poor men ye give,
    The sooner God shall take of you pity.
    Here are we five or six strung up, you see,
And here the flesh that all too well we fed
Bit by bit eaten and rotten, rent and shred,
    And we the bones grow dust and ash withal;
Let no man laugh at us discomforted,
    But pray to God that he forgive us all.   10

If we call on you, brothers, to forgive,
    Ye should not hold our prayer in scorn, though we
Were slain by law; ye know that all alive
    Have not wit alway to walk righteously;
    Make therefore intercession heartily
With him that of a virgin's womb was bred,
That his grace be not as a dry well-head
    For us, nor let hell's thunder on us fall;
We are dead, let no man harry or vex us dead,
    But pray to God that he forgive us all.   20

The rain has washed and laundered us all five,
    And the sun dried and blackened; yea, perdie,
Ravens and pies with beaks that rend and rive
    Have dug our eyes out, and plucked off for fee
    Our beards and eyebrows; never are we free,
Not once, to rest; but here and there still sped,

Drive at its wild will by the wind's change led,
   More pecked of birds than fruits on garden-wall;
Men, for God's love, let no gibe here be said,
   But pray to God that he forgive us all.   30

Prince Jesus, that of all art lord and head,
Keep us, that hell be not our bitter bed;
   We have nought to do in such a master's hall.
Be not ye therefore of our fellowhead,
   But pray to God that he forgive us all.

Thalassius *

Upon the flowery forefront of the year,
One wandering by the grey-green April sea
Found on a reach of shingle and shallower sand
Inlaid with starrier glimmering jewellery
Left for the sun's love and the light wind's cheer
Along the foam-flowered strand
Breeze-brightened, something nearer sea than land
Though the last shoreward blossom-fringe was near,
A babe asleep with flower-soft face that gleamed
To sun and seaward as it laughed and dreamed,   10
Too sure of either love for either's fear,
Albeit so birdlike slight and light, it seemed
Nor man nor mortal child of man, but fair
As even its twin-born tenderer spray-flowers were,
That the wind scatters like an Oread's hair.

   For when July strewed fire on earth and sea
The last time ere that year,
Out of the flame of morn Cymothoe
Beheld one brighter than the sunbright sphere

---

   * "From the sea": the poem, a veiled autobiography, opens with
Swinburne's birth as the spiritual child of sun and sea, of Apollo the
god of light and music, and Cymothoe the sea-nymph.

Move toward her from its fieriest heart, whence trod   20
The live sun's very God,
Across the foam-bright water-ways that are
As heavenlier heavens with star for answering star,
And on her eyes and hair and maiden mouth
Felt a kiss falling fierier than the South
And heard above afar
A noise of songs and wind-enamoured wings
And lutes and lyres of milder and mightier strings,
And round the resonant radiance of his car
Where depth is one with height,   30
Light heard as music, music seen as light.
And with that second moondawn of the spring's
That fosters the first rose,
A sun-child whiter than the sunlit snows
Was born out of the world of sunless things
That round the round earth flows and ebbs and flows.

 But he that found the sea-flower by the sea*
And took to foster like a graft of earth
Was born of man's most highest and heavenliest birth,
Free-born as winds and stars and waves are free;   40
A warrior grey with glories more than years,
Though more of years than change the quick to dead
Had rained their light and darkness on his head;
A singer that in time's and memory's ears
Should leave such words to sing as all his peers
Might praise with hallowing heat of rapturous tears
Till all the days of human flight were fled.
And at his knees his fosterling was fed
Not with man's wine and bread
Nor mortal mother-milk of hopes and fears,   50
But food of deep memorial days long sped;
For bread with wisdom and with song for wine
Clear as the full calm's emerald hyaline.
And from his grave glad lips the boy would gather

 * Probably Walter Savage Landor (1775–1864), whom Swinburne
reverenced as one of his "demi-gods."

Fine honey of song-notes goldener than gold,
More sweet than bees make of the breathing heather,
That he, as glad and bold,
Might drink as they, and keep his spirit from cold.
And the boy loved his laurel-laden hair
As his own father's risen on the eastern air,   60
And that less white brow-binding bayleaf bloom
More than all flowers his father's eyes relume;
And those high songs he heard,
More than all notes of any landward bird,
More than all sounds less free
Than the wind's quiring to the choral sea.

High things the high song taught him; how the breath
Too frail for life may be more strong than death;
And this poor flash of sense in life, that gleams
As a ghost's glory in dreams,   70
More stabile than the world's own heart's root seems,
By that strong faith of lordliest love which gives
To death's own sightless-seeming eyes a light
Clearer, to death's bare bones a verier might,
Than shines or strikes from any man that lives.
How he that loves life overmuch shall die
The dog's death, utterly:
And he that much less loves it than he hates
All wrongdoing that is done
Anywhere always underneath the sun   80
Shall live a mightier life than time's or fate's.
One fairer thing he shewed him, and in might
More strong than day and night
Whose strengths build up time's towering period:
Yea, one thing stronger and more high than God,
Which if man had not, then should God not be:
And that was Liberty.
And gladly should man die to gain, he said,
Freedom; and gladlier, having lost, lie dead.*

---

* An adaptation of a Latin inscription written by Landor for the
Spanish patriots who died resisting the Napoleonic invasion of 1811–12.

For man's earth was not, nor the sweet sea-waves   90
His, nor his own land, nor its very graves,
Except they bred not, bore not, hid not slaves:
But all of all that is,
Were one man free in body and soul, were his.

   And the song softened, even as heaven by night
Softens, from sunnier down to starrier light,
And with its moonbright breath
Blessed life for death's sake, and for life's sake death.
Till as the moon's own beam and breath confuse
In one clear hueless haze of glimmering hues   100
The sea's line and the land's line and the sky's,
And light for love of darkness almost dies,
As darkness only lives for light's dear love,
Whose hands the web of night is woven of,
So in that heaven of wondrous words were life
And death brought out of strife;
Yea, by that strong spell of serene increase
Brought out of strife to peace.

   And the song lightened, as the wind at morn
Flashes, and even with lightning of the wind   110
Night's thick-spun web is thinned
And all its weft unwoven and overworn
Shrinks, as might love from scorn.
And as when wind and light on water and land
Leap as twin gods from heavenward hand in hand,
And with the sound and splendour of their leap
Strike darkness dead, and daunt the spirit of sleep,
And burn it up with fire;
So with the light that lightened from the lyre
Was all the bright heat in the child's heart stirred   120
And blown with blasts of music into flame
Till even his sense became
Fire, as the sense that fires the singing bird
Whose song calls night by name.
And in the soul within the sense began

The manlike passion of a godlike man,
And in the sense within the soul again
Thoughts that make men of gods and gods of men.

For love the high song taught him: love that turns
God's heart toward man as man's to Godward; love   130
That life and death and life are fashioned of,
From the first breath that burns
Half kindled on the flowerlike yeanling's lip,
So light and faint that life seems like to slip,
To that yet weaklier drawn
When sunset dies of night's devouring dawn.
But the man dying not wholly as all men dies
If aught be left of his in live men's eyes
Out of the dawnless dark of death to rise;
If aught of deed or word   140
Be seen for all time or of all time heard.
Love, that though body and soul were overthrown
Should live for love's sake of itself alone,
Though spirit and flesh were one thing doomed and dead,
Not wholly annihilated.
Seeing even the hoariest ash-flake that the pyre
Drops, and forgets the thing was once afire
And gave its heart to feed the pile's full flame
Till its own heart its own heat overcame,
Outlives its own life, though by scarce a span,   150
As such men dying outlive themselves in man,
Outlive themselves for ever; if the heat
Outburn the heart that kindled it, the sweet
Outlast the flower whose soul it was, and flit
Forth of the body of it
Into some new shape of a strange perfume
More potent than its light live spirit of bloom,
How shall not something of that soul relive,
That only soul that had such gifts to give
As lighten something even of all men's doom   160
Even from the labouring womb
Even to the seal set on the unopening tomb?

And these the loving light of song and love
Shall wrap and lap round and impend above,
Imperishable; and all springs born illume
Their sleep with brighter thoughts than wake the dove
To music, when the hillside winds resume
The marriage-song of heather-flower and broom
And all the joy thereof.

And hate the song too taught him: hate of all   170
That brings or holds in thrall
Of spirit or flesh, free-born ere God began,
The holy body and sacred soul of man.
And wheresoever a curse was or a chain,
A throne for torment or a crown for bane
Rose, moulded out of poor men's molten pain,
There, said he, should man's heaviest hate be set
Inexorably, to faint not or forget
Till the last warmth bled forth of the last vein
In flesh that none should call a king's again,   180
Seeing wolves and dogs and birds that plague-strike air
Leave the last bone of all the carrion bare.

And hope the high song taught him: hope whose eyes
Can sound the seas unsoundable, the skies
Inaccessible of eyesight; that can see
What earth beholds not, hear what wind and sea
Hear not, and speak what all these crying in one
Can speak not to the sun.
For in her sovereign eyelight all things are
Clear as the closest seen and kindlier star   190
That marries morn and even and winter and spring
With one love's golden ring.
For she can see the days of man, the birth
Of good and death of evil things on earth
Inevitable and infinite, and sure
As present pain is, or herself is pure.
Yea, she can hear and see, beyond all things
That lighten from before Time's thunderous wings

Through the awful circle of wheel-winged periods,
The tempest of the twilight of all Gods: 200
And higher than all the circling course they ran
The sundawn of the spirit that was man.

   And fear the song too taught him; fear to be
Worthless the dear love of the wind and sea
That bred him fearless, like a sea-mew reared
In rocks of man's foot feared,
Where nought of wingless life may sing or shine.
Fear to wax worthless of that heaven he had
When all the life in all his limbs was glad
And all the drops in all his veins were wine   210
And all the pulses music; when his heart,
Singing, bade heaven and wind and sea bear part
In one live song's reiterance, and they bore:
Fear to go crownless of the flower he wore
When the winds loved him and the waters knew,
The blithest life that clove their blithe life through
With living limbs exultant, or held strife
More amorous than all dalliance aye anew
With the bright breath and strength of their large life,
With all strong wrath of all sheer winds that blew,   220
All glories of all storms of the air that fell
Prone, ineluctable,
With roar from heaven of revel, and with hue
As of a heaven turned hell.
For when the red blast of their breath had made
All heaven aflush with light more dire than shade,
He felt it in his blood and eyes and hair
Burn as if all the fires of the earth and air
Had laid strong hold upon his flesh, and stung
The soul behind it as with serpent's tongue,   230
Forked like the loveliest lightnings: nor could bear
But hardly, half distraught with strong delight,
The joy that like a garment wrapped him round
And lapped him over and under
With raiment of great light

And rapture of great sound
At every loud leap earthward of the thunder
From heaven's most furthest bound:
So seemed all heaven in hearing and in sight,
Alive and mad with glory and angry joy,   240
That something of its marvellous mirth and might
Moved even to madness, fledged as even for flight,
The blood and spirit of one but mortal boy.

So, clothed with love and fear that love makes great,
And armed with hope and hate,
He set first foot upon the spring-flowered ways
That all feet pass and praise.
And one dim dawn between the winter and spring,
In the sharp harsh wind harrying heaven and earth
To put back April that had borne his birth   250
From sunward on her sunniest shower-struck wing,
With tears and laughter for the dew-dropt thing,
Slight as indeed a dew-drop, by the sea
One met him lovelier than all men may be,
God-featured, with god's eyes; and in their might
Somewhat that drew men's own to mar their sight,
Even of all eyes drawn toward him: and his mouth
Was as the very rose of all men's youth,
One rose of all the rose-beds in the world:
But round his brows the curls were snakes that curled,   260
And like his tongue a serpent's; and his voice
Speaks death, and bids rejoice.
Yet then he spake no word, seeming as dumb,
A dumb thing mild and hurtless; nor at first
From his bowed eyes seemed any light to come,
Nor his meek lips for blood or tears to thirst:
But as one blind and mute in mild sweet wise
Pleading for pity of piteous lips and eyes,
He strayed with faint bare lily-lovely feet
Helpless, and flowerlike sweet: 270
Nor might man see, not having word hereof,
That this of all gods was the great god Love.

And seeing him lovely and like a little child
That wellnigh wept for wonder that it smiled
And was so feeble and fearful, with soft speech
The youth bespake him softly; but there fell
From the sweet lips no sweet word audible
That ear or thought might reach:
No sound to make the dim cold silence glad,
No breath to thaw the hard harsh air with heat;   280
Only the saddest smile of all things sweet,
Only the sweetest smile of all things sad.

And so they went together one green way
Till April dying made free the world for May;
And on his guide suddenly Love's face turned,
And in his blind eyes burned
Hard light and heat of laughter; and like flame
That opens in a mountain's ravening mouth
To blear and sear the sunlight from the south,
His mute mouth opened, and his first word came: 290
'Knowest thou me now by name?'
And all his stature waxed immeasurable,
As of one shadowing heaven and lightening hell;
And statelier stood he than a tower that stands
And darkens with its darkness far-off sands
Whereon the sky leans red;
And with a voice that stilled the winds he said:
'I am he that was thy lord before thy birth,
I am he that is thy lord till thou turn earth:
I make the night more dark, and all the morrow   300
Dark as the night whose darkness was my breath:
O fool, my name is sorrow;
Thou fool, my name is death.'

And he that heard spake not, and looked right on
Again, and Love was gone.

Through many a night toward many a wearier day
His spirit bore his body down its way.

Through many a day toward many a wearier night
His soul sustained his sorrows in her sight.
And earth was bitter, and heaven, and even the sea　　　310
Sorrowful even as he.
And the wind helped not, and the sun was dumb;
And with too long strong stress of grief to be
His heart grew sere and numb.

　　And one bright eve ere summer in autumn sank
At stardawn standing on a grey sea-bank
He felt the wind fitfully shift and heave
As toward a stormier eve;
And all the wan wide sea shuddered; and earth
Shook underfoot as toward some timeless birth,　　　320
Intolerable and inevitable; and all
Heaven, darkling, trembled like a stricken thrall.
And far out of the quivering east, and far
From past the moonrise and its guiding star,
Began a noise of tempest and a light
That was not of the lightning; and a sound
Rang with it round and round
That was not of the thunder; and a flight
As of blown clouds by night,
That was not of them; and with songs and cries　　　330
That sang and shrieked their soul out at the skies
A shapeless earthly storm of shapes began
From all ways round to move in on the man,
Clamorous against him silent; and their feet
Were as the wind's are fleet,
And their shrill songs were as wild birds' are sweet.

　　And as when all the world of earth was wronged
And all the host of all men driven afoam
By the red hand of Rome,
Round some fierce amphitheatre overthronged　　　340
With fair clear faces full of bloodier lust
Than swells and stings the tiger when his mood
Is fieriest after blood

And drunk with trampling of the murderous must
That soaks and stains the tortuous close-coiled wood
Made monstrous with its myriad-mustering brood,
Face by fair face panted and gleamed and pressed,
And breast by passionate breast
Heaved hot with ravenous rapture, as they quaffed
The red ripe full fume of the deep live draught,   350
The sharp quick reek of keen fresh bloodshed, blown
Through the dense deep drift up to the emperor's throne
From the under steaming sands
With clamour of all-applausive throats and hands,
Mingling in mirthful time
With shrill blithe mockeries of the lithe-limbed mime:
So from somewhence far forth of the unbeholden,
Dreadfully driven from over and after and under,
Fierce, blown through fifes of brazen blast and golden,
With sound of chiming waves that drown the thunder   360
Or thunder that strikes dumb the sea's own chimes,
Began the bellowing of the bull-voiced mimes,
Fulfilled with clamour and clangour and storms of psalms;
Even at the breathless blast as of a breeze
Fulfilled with clamour and clangour of storms of psalms;
Red hands rent up the roots of old-world trees,
Thick flames of torches tossed as tumbling seas
Made mad the moonless and infuriate air
That, ravening, revelled in the riotous hair
And raiment of the furred Bassarides.   370

    So came all those in on him; and his heart,
As out of sleep suddenly struck astart,*
Danced, and his flesh took fire of theirs, and grief
Was as a last year's leaf
Blown dead far down the wind's way; and he set
His pale mouth to the brightest mouth it met
That laughed for love against his lips, and bade
Follow; and in following all his blood grew glad

    * The paragraph suggests the temper in which Swinburne wrote the
first series of *Poems and Ballads*.

And as again a sea-bird's; for the wind
Took him to bathe him deep round breast and brow   380
Not as it takes a deaf leaf drained and thinned,
But as the brightest bay-flower blown on bough,
Set springing toward it singing: and they rode
By many a vine-leafed, many a rose-hung road,
Exalt with exultation; many a night
Set all its stars upon them as for spies
On many a moon-bewildering mountain-height
Where he rode only by the fierier light
Of his dread lady's hot sweet hungering eyes.
For the moon wandered witless of her way,   390
Spell-stricken by strong magic in such wise
As wizards use to set the stars astray.
And in his ears the music that makes mad
Beat always; and what way the music bade,
That alway rode he; nor was any sleep
His, nor from height nor deep.
But heaven was as red iron, slumberless,
And had no heart to bless;
And earth lay sere and darkling as distraught,
And help in her was nought.   400

Then many a midnight, many a morn and even,
His mother, passing forth of her fair heaven,
With goodlier gifts than all save gods can give
From earth or from the heaven where sea-things live,
With shine of sea-flowers through the bay-leaf braid
Woven for a crown her foam-white hands had made
To crown him with land's laurel and sea-dew,
Sought the sea-bird that was her boy: but he
Sat panther-throned beside Erigone,*
Riding the red ways of the revel through   410
Midmost of pale-mouthed passion's crownless crew.

* Erigone, a suicide, was taught the culture of the grape by Dionysus,
to whom the panther was sacred. The next several verse paragraphs allude
to Swinburne's recovery from the "soul-sick," dissipated days which found
him near death in 1879.

Till on some winter's dawn of some dim year
He let the vine-bit on the panther's lip
Slide, and the green rein slip,
And set his eyes to seaward, nor gave ear
If sound from landward hailed him, dire or dear;
And passing forth of all those fair fierce ranks
Back to the grey sea-banks,
Against a sea-rock lying, aslant the steep,
Fell after many sleepless dreams on sleep.   420

    And in his sleep the dun green light was shed
Heavily round his head
That through the veil of sea falls fathom-deep,
Blurred like a lamp's that when the night drops dead
Dies; and his eyes gat grace of sleep to see
The deep divine dark dayshine of the sea,
Dense water-walls and clear dusk water-ways,
Broad-based, or branching as a sea-flower sprays
That side or this dividing; and anew
The glory of all her glories that he knew.   430
And in sharp rapture of recovering tears
He woke on fire with yearnings of old years,
Pure as one purged of pain that passion bore,
Ill child of bitter mother; for his own
Looked laughing toward him from her midsea throne,
Up toward him there ashore.

    Thence in his heart the great same joy began,
Of child that made him man:
And turned again from all hearts else on quest,
He communed with his own heart, and had rest.   440
And like sea-winds upon loud waters ran
His days and dreams together, till the joy
Burned in him of the boy.
Till the earth's great comfort and the sweet sea's breath
Breathed and blew life in where was heartless death,
Death spirit-stricken of soul-sick days, where strife
Of thought and flesh made mock of death and life.

And grace returned upon him of his birth
Where heaven was mixed with heavenlike sea and earth;
And song shot forth strong wings that took the sun   450
From inward, fledged with might of sorrow and mirth
And father's fire made mortal in his son.
Nor was not spirit of strength in blast and breeze
To exalt again the sun's child and the sea's;
For as wild mares in Thessaly grow great
With child of ravishing winds, that violate
Their leaping length of limb with manes like fire*
And eyes outburning heaven's
With fires more violent than the lightning levin's**
And breath drained out and desperate of desire,   460
Even so the spirit in him, when winds grew strong,
Grew great with child of song.
Nor less than when his veins first leapt for joy
To draw delight in such as burns a boy,
Now too the soul of all his senses felt
The passionate pride of deep sea-pulses dealt
Through nerve and jubilant vein
As from the love and largess of old time,
And with his heart again
The tidal throb of all the tides keep rhyme   470
And charm him from his own soul's separate sense
With infinite and invasive influence
That made strength sweet in him and sweetness strong,
Being now no more a singer, but a song.

Till one clear day when brighter sea-wind blew
And louder sea-shine lightened, for the waves
Were full of godhead and the light that saves,
His father's, and their spirit had pierced him through,
He felt strange breath and light all round him shed
That bowed him down with rapture; and he knew   480

---

* Boreas fell in love with a herd of beautiful mares on the plain of Thessaly and, assuming the form of an azure–maned steed, sired twelve fillies.
** *Levin's:* flash's.

His father's hand, hallowing his humbled head,
And the old great voice of the old good time, that said:

"Child of my sunlight and the sea, from birth
A fosterling and fugitive on earth;
Sleepless of soul as wind or wave or fire,
A manchild with an ungrown God's desire;
Because thou hast loved nought mortal more than me,
Thy father, and thy mother-hearted sea;
Because thou hast set thine heart to sing, and sold
Life and life's love for song, God's living gold;   490
Because thou hast given thy flower and fire of youth
To feed men's hearts with visions, truer than truth;
Because thou hast kept in those world-wandering eyes
The light that makes me music of the skies;
Because thou hast heard with world-unwearied ears
The music that puts light into the spheres;
Have therefore in thine heart and in thy mouth
The sound of song that mingles north and south,
The song of all the winds that sing of me,
And in thy soul the sense of all the sea."   500

On the Cliffs*

Between the moondawn and the sundown here
The twilight hangs half starless; half the sea
Still quivers as for love or pain or fear
Or pleasure mightier than these all may be
A man's live heart might beat
Wherein a God's with mortal blood should meet
And fill its pulse too full to bear the strain
With fear or love or pleasure's twin-born, pain.
Fiercely the gaunt woods to the grim soil cling

* This densely difficult, deeply personal poem was composed in the summer of 1879, just after Swinburne's total collapse in London and before he took up residence with Watts-Dunton at "The Pines."

That bears for all fair fruits 　　　　　　　　　　10
Wan wild sparse flowers of windy and wintry spring
Between the tortive serpent-shapen roots
Wherethrough their dim growth hardly strikes and
　　　shoots
And shews one gracious thing
Hardly, to speak for summer one sweet word
Of summer's self scarce heard.
But higher the steep green sterile fields, thick-set
With flowerless hawthorn even to the upward verge
Whence the woods gathering watch new cliffs emerge
Higher than their highest of crowns that sea-winds fret, 　20
Hold fast, for all that night or wind can say,
Some pale pure colour yet,
Too dim for green and luminous for grey.
Between the climbing inland cliffs above
And these beneath that breast and break the bay,
A barren peace too soft for hate or love
Broods on an hour too dim for night or day.

O wind, O wingless wind that walk'st the sea,
Weak wind, wing-broken, wearier wind than we,
Who are yet not spirit-broken, maimed like thee, 　　30
Who wail not in our inward night as thou
In the outer darkness now,
What word has the old sea given thee for mine ear
From thy faint lips to hear?
For some word would she send me, knowing not how.

Nay, what far other word
Than ever of her was spoken, or of me
Or all my winged white kinsfolk of the sea
Between fresh wave and wave was ever heard,
Cleaves the clear dark enwinding tree with tree 　　40
Too close for stars to separate and to see
Enmeshed in multitudinous unity?
What voice of what strong God hath stormed and
　　　stirred

The fortressed rock of silence, rent apart
Even to the core Night's all-maternal heart?
What voice of God grown heavenlier in a bird,
Made keener of edge to smite
Than lightning—yea, thou knowest, O mother Night,
Keen as that cry from thy strange children sent
Wherewith the Athenian judgment-shrine was rent,*   50
For wrath that all their wrath was vainly spent,
Their wrath for wrong made right
By justice in her own divine despite
That bade pass forth unblamed
The sinless matricide and unashamed?
Yea, what new cry is this, what note more bright
Than their song's wing of words was dark of flight,
What word is this thou hast heard,
Thine and not thine or theirs, O Night, what word
More keen than lightning and more sweet than light?   60
As all men's hearts grew godlike in one bird
And all those hearts cried on thee, crying with might,
Hear us, O mother Night.

Dumb is the mouth of darkness as of death:
Light, sound and life are one
In the eyes and lips of dawn that draw the sun
To hear what first child's word with glimmering breath
Their weak wan weanling child the twilight saith;
But night makes answer none.

God, if thou be God,—bird, if bird thou be,—**   70
Do thou then answer me.
For but one word, what wind soever blow,
Is blown up usward ever from the sea.

* The Erinyes or Furies, daughters of Night, demanded of Athena
the punishment of Orestes for killing his mother, Clytemnestra—a "sinless
matricide" because he slew her, at Apollo's behest, for murdering his
father Agamemnon. (See the Furies' cry to Night in Aeschylus' *Oresteia:*
"The Eumenides," lines 321 ff.)

** Swinburne seems to hear in the song of the nightingale (see note
to "Itylus," p. 111) the voice of Sappho.

In fruitless years of youth dead long ago
And deep beneath their own dead leaves and snow
Buried, I heard with bitter heart and sere
The same sea's word unchangeable, nor knew
But that mine own life-days were changeless too
And sharp and salt with unshed tear on tear
And cold and fierce and barren; and my soul,   80
Sickening, swam weakly with bated breath
In a deep sea like death,
And felt the wind buffet her face with brine
Hard, and harsh thought on thought in long bleak roll
Blown by keen gusts of memory sad as thine
Heap the weight up of pain, and break, and leave
Strength scarce enough to grieve
In the sick heavy spirit, unmanned with strife
Of waves that beat at the tired lips of life.

Nay, sad may be man's memory, sad may be   90
The dream he weaves him as for shadow of thee,
But scarce one breathing-space, one heartbeat long,
Wilt thou take shadow of sadness on thy song.
Not thou, being more than man or man's desire,
Being bird and God in one,
With throat of gold and spirit of the sun;
The sun whom all our souls and songs call sire,*
Whose godhead gave thee, chosen of all our quire,
Thee only of all that serve, of all that sing
Before our sire and king,   100
Borne up some space on time's world-wandering wing,
This gift, this doom, to bear till time's wing tire—
Life everlasting of eternal fire.

Thee only of all; yet can no memory say
How many a night and day
My heart has been as thy heart, and my life

* Apollo, the source of poetry, whom Swinburne (line 352) associates
as a kind of triune deity with Sappho and the nightingale.

As thy life is, a sleepless hidden thing,
Full of the thirst and hunger of winter and spring,
That seeks its food not in such love or strife
As fill men's hearts with passionate hours and rest.   110
From no loved lips and on no loving breast
Have I sought ever for such gifts as bring
Comfort, to stay the secret soul with sleep.
The joys, the loves, the labours, whence men reap
Rathe fruit of hopes and fears,
I have made not mine; the best of all my days
Have been as those fair fruitless summer strays,
Those water-waifs that but the sea-wind steers,
Flakes of glad foam or flowers on footless ways
That take the wind in season and the sun,   120
And when the wind wills is their season done.

For all my days as all thy days from birth
My heart as thy heart was in me as thee,
Fire; and not all the fountains of the sea
Have waves enough to quench it, nor on earth
Is fuel enough to feed,
While day sows night and night sows day for seed.

We were not marked for sorrow, thou nor I,
For joy nor sorrow, sister, were we made,
To take delight and grief to live and die,   130
Assuaged by pleasures or by pains affrayed
That melt men's hearts and alter; we retain
A memory mastering pleasure and all pain,
A spirit within the sense of ear and eye,
A soul behind the soul, that seeks and sings
And makes our life move only with its wings
And feed but from its lips, that in return
Feed of our hearts wherein the old fires that burn
Have strength not to consume
Nor glory enough to exalt us past our doom.   140

Ah, ah, the doom (thou knowest whence rang that
    wail)*
Of the shrill nightingale!
(From whose wild lips, thou knowest, that wail was
    thrown)
For round about her have the great gods cast
A wing-borne body, and clothed her close and fast
With a sweet life that hath no part in moan.
But me, for me (how hadst thou heart to hear?)
Remains a sundering with the two-edged spear.

Ah, for her doom! so cried in presage then
The bodeful bondslave of the king of men,   150
And might not win her will.
Too close the entangling dragnet woven of crime,**
The snare of ill new-born of elder ill,
The curse of new time for an elder time,
Had caught, and held her yet,
Enmeshed intolerably in the intolerant net,
Who thought with craft to mock the God most high,***
And win by wiles his crown of prophecy
From the Sun's hand sublime,
As God were man, to spare or to forget.   160

But thou,—the gods have given thee and forgiven thee
More than our master gave
That strange-eyed spirit-wounded strange-tongued slave
There questing houndlike where the roofs red-wet

---

    * The words of the maddened, captive Cassandra, "pale princess-priest of Priam's seed," prophesying her own death by the two-edged sword with which Clytemnestra kills Agamemnon and her, when he returns from Troy with Cassandra. See note to "Itylus" for the doom of Philomela preferred by Cassandra.
    ** Clytemnestra threw a net around Agamemnon before stabbing him. The entangling net, as Swinburne suggests, symbolizes the inescapable curse that binds the generations.
    *** Cassandra, given the gift of prophecy by Apollo, afterwards refused in turn to submit to him, whereupon he spit in her mouth as he kissed her so that her prophecies should never be believed.

Reeked as a wet red grave.
Life everlasting has their strange grace given thee,
Even hers whom thou wast wont to sing and serve
With eyes, but not with song, too swift to swerve;
Yet might not even thine eyes estranged estrange her,
Who seeing thee too, but inly, burn and bleed   170
Like that pale princess-priest of Priam's seed,
For stranger service gave thee guerdon stranger;
If this indeed be guerdon, this indeed
Her mercy, this thy meed—
That thou, being more than all we born, being higher
Than all heads crowned * of him that only gives
The light whereby man lives,
The bay that bids man moved of God's desire
Lay hand on lute or lyre,
Set lip to trumpet or deflowered green reed—   180
If this were given thee for a grace indeed,
That thou, being first of all these, thou alone
Shouldst have the grace to die not, but to live
And lose nor change one pulse of song, one tone
Of all that were thy lady's and thine own,
Thy lady's whom thou criedst on to forgive,
Thou, priest and sacrifice on the altar-stone
Where none may worship not of all that live,
Love's priestess, errant on dark ways diverse;
If this were grace indeed for Love to give,   190
If this indeed were blessing and no curse.

Love's priestess, mad with pain and joy of song,
Song's priestess, mad with joy and pain of love,
Name above all names that are lights above,
We have loved, praised, pitied, crowned and done
      thee wrong,
O thou past praise and pity; thou the sole
Utterly deathless, perfect only and whole
Immortal, body and soul.

* Apollo, who crowns singers with bay. Sappho's gift of prophecy,
like Cassandra's, is not ordinary song: it is both a "blessing and a curse."

For over all whom time hath overpast
The shadow of sleep inexorable is cast,   200
The implacable sweet shadow of perfect sleep
That gives not back what life gives death to keep;
Yea, all that lived and loved and sang and sinned
Are all borne down death's cold sweet soundless wind
That blows all night and knows not whom its breath,
Darkling, may touch to death:
But one that wind hath touched and changed not,—one
Whose body and soul are parcel of the sun;
One that earth's fire could burn not, nor the sea
Quench; nor might human doom take hold on thee;   210
All praise, all pity, all dreams have done thee wrong,
All love, with eyes love-blinded from above;
Song's priestess, mad with joy and pain of love,
Love's priestess, mad with pain and joy of song.

Hast thou none other answer then for me
Than the air may have of thee,
Or the earth's warm woodlands girdling with green
        girth
Thy secret sleepless burning life on earth,
Or even the sea that once, being woman crowned   220
And girt with fire and glory of anguish round,
Thou wert so fain to seek to, fain to crave
If she would hear thee and save
And give thee comfort of thy great green grave?
Because I have known thee always who thou art,
Thou knowest, have known thee to thy heart's own
        heart,
Nor ever have given light ear to storied song
That did thy sweet name sweet unwitting wrong,
Nor ever have called thee nor would call for shame,
Thou knowest, but inly by thine only name,   230
Sappho—because I have known thee and loved, hast
        thou
None other answer now?

As brother and sister were we, child and bird,
Since thy first Lesbian word
Flamed on me, and I knew not whence I knew
This was the song that struck my whole soul through,
Pierced my keen spirit of sense with edge more keen,
Even when I knew not,—even ere sooth was seen,—
When thou wast but the tawny sweet winged thing
Whose cry was but of spring.   240

And yet even so thine ear should hear me—yea,
Hear me this nightfall by this northland bay,
Even for their sake whose loud good word I had,
Singing of thee in the all-beloved clime
Once, where the windy wine of spring makes mad
Our sisters of Majano, who kept time
Clear to my choral rhyme.
Yet was the song acclaimed of these aloud
Whose praise had made mute humbleness misproud,
The song with answering song applauded thus,   250
But of that Daulian dream of Itylus.
So but for love's love haply was it—nay,
How else?—that even their song took my song's part,
For love of love and sweetness of sweet heart,
Or god-given glorious madness of mid May
And heat of heart and hunger and thirst to sing,
Full of the new wine of the wind of spring.

Or if this were not, and it be not sin
To hold myself in spirit of thy sweet kin,
In heart and spirit of song;   260
If this my great love do thy grace no wrong,
Thy grace that gave me grace to dwell therein;
If thy gods thus be my gods, and their will
Made my song part of thy song—even such part
As man's hath of God's heart—
And my life like as thy life to fulfil;
What have our gods then given us? Ah, to thee,

Sister, much more, much happier than to me,
Much happier things they have given, and more of
    grace
Than falls to man's light race;　　　　　　　　　　　270
For lighter are we, all our love and pain
Lighter than thine, who knowest of time or place
Thus much, that place nor time
Can heal or hurt or lull or change again
The singing soul that makes his soul sublime
Who hears the far fall of its fire-fledged rhyme
Fill darkness as with bright and burning rain
Till all the live gloom inly glows, and light
Seems with the sound to cleave the core of night.

The singing soul that moves thee, and that moved　　280
When thou wast woman, and their songs divine
Who mixed for Grecian mouths heaven's lyric wine
Fell dumb, fell down reproved
Before one sovereign Lesbian song of thine.
That soul, though love and life had fain held fast,
Wind-winged with fiery music, rose and past
Through the indrawn hollow of earth and heaven and
    hell,
As through some strait sea-shell
The wide sea's immemorial song,—the sea
That sings and breathes in strange men's ears of thee　　290
How in her barren bride-bed, void and vast,
Even thy soul sang itself to sleep at last.

To sleep? Ah, then, what song is this, that here
Makes all the night one ear,
One ear fulfilled and mad with music, one
Heart kindling as the heart of heaven, to hear
A song more fiery than the awakening sun
Sings, when his song sets fire
To the air and clouds that build the dead night's pyre?
*O thou of divers-coloured mind, O thou**　　　　300

   * Atthis, beloved of Sappho, addressed directly in line 327.

Deathless, God's daughter subtle-souled—lo, now,
Now too the song above all songs, in flight
Higher than the day-star's height,
And sweet as sound the moving wings of night!
Thou of the divers-coloured seat—behold,
Her very song of old!—
O deathless, O God's daughter subtle-souled!
That same cry through this boskage overhead
Rings round reiterated,
Palpitates as the last palpitated,   310
The last that panted through her lips and died
Not down this grey north sea's half sapped cliff-side
That crumbles toward the coastline, year by year
More near the sands and near;
The last loud lyric fiery cry she cried,
Heard once on heights Leucadian,*—heard not here.

Not here; for this that fires our northland night,
This is the song that made
Love fearful, even the heart of love afraid,
With the great anguish of its great delight.   320
No swan-song, no far-fluttering half-drawn breath,
No word that love of love's sweet nature saith,
No dirge that lulls the narrowing lids of death,
No healing hymn of peace-prevented strife,—
This is her song of life.

I loved thee,—hark, one tenderer note than all—
Atthis, of old time, once—one low long fall,
Sighing—one long low lovely loveless call,
Dying—one pause in song so flamelike fast—
Atthis, long since in old time overpast—   330
One soft first pause and last.
One,—then the old rage of rapture's fieriest rain
Storms all the music-maddened night again.

* Sappho is said to have leaped from the cliffs of Leucadia into the
sea.

Child of God, close craftswoman, I beseech thee,
Bid not ache nor agony break nor master,
Lady, my spirit—
O thou her mistress, might her cry not reach thee?
Our Lady of all men's loves, could Love go past her,
Pass, and not hear it?

She hears not as she heard not; hears not me,   340
O treble-natured mystery,—how should she
Hear, or give ear?—who heard and heard not thee;
Heard, and went past, and heard not; but all time
Hears all that all the ravin of his years
Hath cast not wholly out of all men's ears
And dulled to death with deep dense funeral chime
Of their reiterate rhyme.
An now of all songs uttering all her praise,
All hers who had thy praise and did thee wrong,
Abides one song yet of her lyric days,   350
Thine only, this thy song.

O soul triune, woman and god and bird,
Man, man at least has heard.
All ages call thee conqueror, and thy cry
The mightiest as the least beneath the sky
Whose heart was ever set to song, or stirred
With wind of mounting music blown more high
Than wildest wing may fly,
Hath heard or hears,—even Æschylus as I.

But when thy name was woman, and thy word   360
Human,—then haply, surely then meseems
This thy bird's note was heard on earth of none,
Of none save only in dreams.
In all the world then surely was but one
Song; as in heaven at highest one sceptred sun
Regent, on earth here surely without fail
One only, one imperious nightingale.
Dumb was the field, the woodland mute, the lawn
Silent; the hill was tongueless as the vale

Even when the last fair waif of cloud that felt 370
Its heart beneath the colouring moonrays melt,
At high midnoon of midnight half withdrawn,
Bared all the sudden deep divine moondawn.
Then, unsaluted by her twin-born tune,
That latter timeless morning of the moon
Rose past its hour of moonrise; clouds gave way
To the old reconquering ray,
But no song answering made it more than day;
No cry of song by night
Shot fire into the cloud-constraining light. 380
One only, one Æolian island heard
Thrill, but through no bird's throat,
In one strange manlike maiden's godlike note,
The song of all these as a single bird.
Till the sea's portal was as funeral gate
For that sole singer in all time's ageless date
Singled and signed for so triumphal fate,
All nightingales but one in all the world
All her sweet life were silent; only then,
When her life's wing of womanhood was furled, 390
Their cry, this cry of thine was heard again,
As of me now, of any born of men.

Through sleepless clear spring nights filled full of thee,
Rekindled here, thy ruling song has thrilled
The deep dark air and subtle tender sea
And breathless hearts with one bright sound fulfilled.
Or at midnoon to me
Swimming, and birds about my happier head
Skimming, one smooth soft way by water and air,
To these my bright born brethren and to me 400
Hath not the clear wind borne or seemed to bear
A song wherein all earth and heaven and sea
Were molten in one music made of thee
To enforce us, O our sister of the shore,
Look once in heart back landward and adore?
For songless were we sea-mews, yet had we

More joy than all things joyful of thee—more,
Haply, than all things happiest; nay, save thee,
In thy strong rapture of imperious joy
Too high for heart of sea-borne bird or boy,   410
What living things were happiest if not we?
But knowing not love nor change nor wrath nor
    wrong,
No more we knew of song.

Song, and the secrets of it, and their might,
What blessings curse it and what curses bless,
I know them since my spirit had first in sight,
Clear as thy song's words or the live sun's light,
The small dark body's Lesbian loveliness
That held the fire eternal; eye and ear
Were as a god's to see, a god's to hear,   420
Through all his hours of daily and nightly chime,
The sundering of the two-edged spear of time:
The spear that pierces even the sevenfold shields
Of mightiest Memory, mother of all songs made,
And wastes all songs as roseleaves kissed and frayed
As here the harvest of the foam-flowered fields;
But thine the spear may waste not that he wields
Since first the God whose soul is man's live breath,
The sun whose face hath our sun's face for shade,
Put all the light of life and love and death   430
Too strong for life, but not for love too strong,
Where pain makes peace with pleasure in thy song,
And in thine heart, where love and song make strife,
Fire everlasting of eternal life.

Evening on the Broads

Over two shadowless waters, adrift as a pinnace in peril,
   Hangs as in heavy suspense, charged with irresolute
     light,

Softly the soul of the sunset upholden awhile on the
    sterile
  Waves and wastes of the land, half repossessed by
    the night.
Inland glimmer the shallows asleep and afar in the
    breathless
  Twilight: yonder the depths darken afar and asleep.
Slowly the semblance of death out of heaven descends on
    the deathless
  Waters: hardly the light lives on the face of the deep—
Hardly, but here for awhile. All over the grey soft
    shallow
  Hover the colours and clouds of the twilight, void of   10
    a star.
As a bird unfledged is the broad-winged night, whose
    winglets are callow
  Yet, but soon with their plumes will she cover her
    brood from afar,
Cover the brood of her worlds that cumber the skies
    with their blossom
  Thick as the darkness of leaf-shadowed spring is
    encumbered with flowers.
World upon world is enwound in the bountiful girth
    of her bosom,
  Warm and lustrous with life lovely to look on as ours.
Still is the sunset adrift as a spirit in doubt that
    dissembles
  Still with itself, being sick of division and dimmed
    by dismay—
Nay, not so; but with love and delight beyond passion
    it trembles,
  Fearful and fain of the night, lovely with love of the   20
    day:
Fain and fearful of rest that is like unto death, and
    begotten
  Out of the womb of the tomb, born of the seed of
    the grave:

Lovely with shadows of loves that are only not wholly
  forgotten,
  Only not wholly suppressed by the dark as a wreck
    by the wave.
Still there linger the loves of the morning and noon,
  in a vision
  Blindly beheld, but in vain: ghosts that are tired,
    and would rest.
But the glories beloved of the night rise all too dense
  for division,
  Deep in the depth of her breast sheltered as doves
    in a nest.
Fainter the beams of the loves of the daylight season
  enkindled
  Wane, and the memories of hours that were fair   30
    with the love of them fade:
Loftier, aloft of the lights of the sunset stricken and
  dwindled,
  Gather the signs of the love at the heart of the night
    new-made.
New-made night, new-born of the sunset, immeasur-
  able, endless,
  Opens the secret of love hid from of old in her heart,
In the deep sweet heart full-charged with faultless love
  of the friendless
  Spirits of men that are eased when the wheels of the
    sun depart.
Still is the sunset afloat as a ship on the waters
  upholden
  Full-sailed, wide-winged, poised softly for ever
    asway—
Nay, not so, but at least for a little, awhile at the
  golden
  Limit of arching air fain for an hour to delay.   40
Here on the bar of the sand-bank, steep yet aslope
  to the gleaming
  Waste of the water without, waste of the water
    within,

Lights overhead and lights underneath seem doubt-
    fully dreaming
  Whether the day be done, whether the night may
    begin.
Far and afar and farther again they falter and hover,
  Warm on the water and deep in the sky and pale
    on the cloud:
Colder again and slowly remoter, afraid to recover
  Breath, yet fain to revive, as it seems, from the
    skirt of the shroud.
Faintly the heartbeats shorten and pause of the light
    in the westward
  Heaven, as eastward quicken the paces of star   50
    upon star
Hurried and eager of life as a child that strains to
    the breast-ward
  Eagerly, yearning forth of the deeps where the
    ways of them are,
Glad of the glory of the gift of their life and the
    wealth of its wonder,
  Fain of the night and the sea and the sweet wan
    face of the earth.
Over them air grows deeper, intense with delight in
    them: under
  Things are thrilled in their sleep as with sense of
    a sure new birth.
But here by the sand-bank watching, with eyes on
    the sea-line, stranger
  Grows to me also the weight of the sea-ridge
    gazed on of me,
Heavily heaped up, changefully changeless, void
    though of danger
  Void not of menace, but full of the might of the   60
    dense dull sea.
Like as the wave is before me, behind is the bank
    deep-drifted;
  Yellow and thick as the bank is behind me in front
    is the wave.

As the wall of a prison imprisoning the mere is the
    girth of it lifted:
  But the rampire of water in front is erect as the
    wall of a grave.
And the crests of it crumble and topple and change,
    but the wall is not broken:
  Standing still dry-shod, I see it as higher than my
    head,
Moving inland alway again, reared up as in token
  Still of impending wrath still in the foam of it shed.
And even in the pauses between them, dividing the
    rollers in sunder,
  High overhead seems ever the sea-line fixed as a
    mark,   70
And the shore where I stand as a valley beholden of
    hills whence thunder
  Cloud and torrent and storm, darkening the depths
    of the dark.
Up to the sea, not upon it or over it, upward from
    under
  Seems he to gaze, whose eyes yearn after it here
    from the shore:
A wall of turbid water, aslope to the wide sky's
    wonder
  Of colour and cloud, it climbs, or spreads as a
    slanted floor.
And the large lights change on the face of the mere
    like things that were living,
  Winged and wonderful, beams like as birds are
    that pass and are free:
But the light is dense as darkness, a gift withheld in
    the giving,
  That lies as dead on the fierce dull face of the land-   80
    ward sea.
Stained and stifled and soiled, made earthier than
    earth is and duller,
  Grimly she puts back light as rejected, a thing put
    away:

No transparent rapture, a molten music of colour;
  No translucent love taken and given of the day.
Fettered and marred and begrimed is the light's live
      self on her falling,
    As the light of a man's life lighted the fume of a
      dungeon mars:
Only she knows of the wind, when her wrath gives
      ear to him calling;
    The delight of the light she knows not, nor answers
      the sun or the stars.
Love she hath none to return for the luminous love
      of their giving:
    None to reflect from the bitter and shallow response   90
      of her heart.
Yearly she feeds on her dead, yet herself seems dead
      and not living,
    Or confused as a soul heavy-laden with trouble
      that will not depart.
In the sound of her speech to the darkness the moan
      of her evil remorse is,
    Haply, for strong ships gnawed by the dog-toothed
      sea-bank's fang
And trampled to death by the rage of the feet of her
      foam-lipped horses
    Whose manes are yellow as plague, and as ensigns
      of pestilence hang,
That wave in the foul faint air of the breath of a
      death-stricken city;
    So menacing heaves she the manes of her rollers
      knotted with sand,
Discoloured, opaque, suspended in sign as of strength
      without pity,
    That shake with flameless thunder the low long   100
      length of the strand.
Here, far off in the farther extreme of the shore as it
      lengthens
    Northward, lonely for miles, ere ever a village begin,

On the lapsing land that recedes as the growth of
    the strong sea strengthens
  Shoreward, thrusting further and further its out-
    works in,
Here in Shakespeare's vision,* a flower of her kin
    forsaken,
  Lay in her golden raiment alone on the wild wave's
    edge,
Surely by no shore else, but here on the bank storm-
    shaken,
  Perdita, bright as a dew-drop engilt of the sun on
    the sedge.
Here on a shore unbeheld of his eyes in a dream he
    beheld her
  Outcast, fair as a fairy, the child of a far-off king: 110
And over the babe-flower gently the head of a pastoral
    elder
  Bowed, compassionate, hoar as the hawthorn-
    blossom in spring,
And kind as harvest in autumn: a shelter of shade
    on the lonely
  Shelterless unknown shore scourged of implacable
    waves:
Here, where the wind walks royal, alone in his
    kingdom, and only
  Sounds to the sedges a wail as of triumph that
    conquers and craves.
All these waters and wastes are his empire of old,
    and awaken
  From barren and stagnant slumber at only the
    sound of his breath:
Yet the hunger is eased not that aches in his heart,
    nor the goal overtaken
  That his wide wings yearn for and labour as hearts   120
    that yearn after death.

* *The Winter's Tale*, Act III, Scene 3.

All the solitude sighs and expects with a blind expectation
    Somewhat unknown of its own sad heart, grown
heartsick of strife:
Till sometime its wild heart maddens, and moans,
and the vast ululation
    Takes wing with the clouds on the waters, and
wails to be quit of its life.
For the spirit and soul of the waste is the wind, and
his wings with their waving
    Darken and lighten the darkness and light of it
thickened or thinned;
But the heart that impels them is even as a conqueror's
insatiably craving
    That victory can fill not, as power cannot satiate
the want of the wind.
All these moorlands and marshes are full of his might,
and oppose not
    Aught of defence nor of barrier, of forest or preci-
pice piled: 130
But the will of the wind works ever as his that desires
what he knows not,
    And the wail of his want unfulfilled is as one
making moan for her child.
And the cry of his triumph is even as the crying of
hunger that maddens
    The heart of a strong man aching in vain as the
wind's heart aches
And the sadness itself of the land for its infinite
solitude saddens
    More for the sound than the silence athirst for the
sound that slakes.
And the sunset at last and the twilight are dead:
and the darkness is breathless
    With fear of the wind's breath rising that seems
and seems not to sleep:
But a sense of the sound of it alway, a spirit unsleeping and deathless,

Ghost or God, evermore moves on the face of the   140
    deep.*

By the North Sea**

    i

A land that is lonelier than ruin;
    A sea that is stranger than death:
Far fields that a rose never blew in,
    Wan waste where the winds lack breath;
Waste endless and boundless and flowerless
    But of marsh-blossoms fruitless as free:
Where earth lies exhausted, as powerless
                To strive with the sea.

Far flickers the flight of the swallows,
    Far flutters the weft of the grass   10
Spun dense over desolate hollows
    More pale than the clouds as they pass:
Thick woven as the weft of a witch is
    Round the heart of a thrall that hath sinned,
Whose youth and the wrecks of its riches
                Are waifs on the wind.

The pastures are herdless and sheepless,
    No pasture or shelter for herds:
The wind is relentless and sleepless,

---

* Cf. *Genesis* 1:2: "Darkness was upon the face of the deep. And the Spirit of God moved upon the face of the waters."

** In the "Dedicatory Epistle" to his *Poems,* Swinburne describes "By the North Sea" as an evocation of "the dreary beauty, inhuman if not unearthly in its desolation, of the innumerable creeks and inlets, lined and paven with sea-flowers, which make of the salt marshes a fit and funereal setting, a fatal and appropriate foreground, for the supreme desolation of the relics of Dunwich; the beautiful and awful solitude of a wilderness on which the sea has forbidden man to build or live, overtopped and bounded by the tragic and ghastly solitude of a headland on which the sea has forbidden the works of human charity and piety to survive."

And restless and songless the birds;   20
  Their cries from afar fall breathless,
    Their wings are as lightnings that flee;
For the land has two lords that are deathless:
          Death's self, and the sea.

These twain, as a king with his fellow,
  Hold converse of desolate speech:
And her waters are haggard and yellow
    And crass with the scurf of the beach:
And his garments are grey as the hoary
  Wan sky where the day lies dim;   30
And his power is to her, and his glory,
          As hers unto him.

In the pride of his power she rejoices,
  In her glory he glows and is glad:
In her darkness the sound of his voice is,
    With his breath she dilates and is mad:
"If thou slay me, O death, and outlive me,
  Yet thy love hath fulfilled me of thee."
"Shall I give thee not back if thou give me,
          O sister, O sea?"   40

And year upon year dawns living,
  And age upon age drops dead:
And his hand is not weary of giving,
    And the thirst of her heart is not fed:
And the hunger that moans in her passion,
  And the rage in her hunger that roars,
As a wolf's that the winter lays lash on,
          Still calls and implores.

Her walls have no granite for girder,
  No fortalice fronting her stands: 50
But reefs the bloodguiltiest of murder
    Are less than the banks of her sands:

These number their slain by the thousand;
  For the ship hath no surety to be,
When the bank is abreast of her bows and
           Aflush with the sea.

No surety to stand, and no shelter
  To dawn out of darkness but one,
Out of waters that hurtle and welter
  No succour to dawn with the sun,   60
But a rest from the wind as it passes,
  Where, hardly redeemed from the waves,
Lie thick as the blades of the grasses
           The dead in their graves.

A multitude noteless of numbers,
  As wild weeds cast on an heap:
And sounder than sleep are their slumbers,
  And softer than song is their sleep;
And sweeter than all things and stranger
  The sense, if perchance it may be,   70
That the wind is divested of danger
           And scatheless the sea.

That the roar of the banks they breasted
  Is hurtless as bellowing of herds,
And the strength of his wings that invested
  The wind, as the strength of a bird's;
As the sea-mew's might or the swallow's
  That cry to him back if he cries,
As over the graves and their hollows
           Days darken and rise.   80

As the souls of the dead men disburdened
  And clean of the sins that they sinned,
With a lovelier than man's life guerdoned
  And delight as a wave's in the wind,
And delight as the wind's in the billow,
  Birds pass, and deride with their glee

The flesh that has dust for its pillow
   As wrecks have the sea.

When the ways of the sun wax dimmer,
 Wings flash through the dusk like beams;   90
As the clouds in the lit sky glimmer,
 The bird in the graveyard gleams;
As the cloud at its wing's edge whitens
 When the clarions of sunrise are heard,
The graves that the bird's note brightens
   Grow bright for the bird.

As the waves of the numberless waters
 That the wind cannot number who guides
Are the sons of the shore and the daughters
 Here lulled by the chime of the tides: 100
And here in the press of them standing
 We know not if these or if we
Live truliest, or anchored to landing
   Or drifted to sea.

In the valley he named of decision*
 No denser were multitudes met
When the soul of the seer in her vision
 Saw nations for doom of them set;
Saw darkness in dawn, and the splendour
 Of judgment, the sword and the rod;   110
But the doom here of death is more tender
   And gentler the god.

And gentler the wind from the dreary
 Sea-banks by the waves overlapped,
Being weary, speaks peace to the weary
 From slopes that the tide-stream hath sapped;
And sweeter than all that we call so

---

 * An allusion to the prophecy of God's vengeance upon the enemies
of Israel, when "multitudes, multitudes in the valley of decision" shall
perish (*Joel* 3:14).

The seal of their slumber shall be
Till the graves that embosom them also
          Be sapped of the sea.   120

iii

Miles, and miles, and miles of desolation!
   Leagues on leagues on leagues without a change!
Sign or token of some eldest nation
   Here would make the strange land not so strange.
Time-forgotten, yea since time's creation,
   Seem these borders where the sea-birds range.

Slowly, gladly, full of peace and wonder
   Grows his heart who journeys here alone.
Earth and all its thoughts of earth sink under
   Deep as deep in water sinks a stone.   130
Hardly knows it if the rollers thunder,
   Hardly whence the lonely wind is blown.

Tall the plumage of the rush-flower tosses,
   Sharp and soft in many a curve and line
Gleam and glow the sea-coloured marsh-mosses
   Salt and splendid from the circling brine.
Streak on streak of glimmering seashine crosses
   All the land sea-saturate as with wine.

Far, and far between, in divers orders,
   Clear grey steeples cleave the low grey sky;   140
Fast and firm as time-unshaken warders,
   Hearts made sure by faith, by hope made high.
These alone in all the wild sea-borders
   Fear no blast of days and nights that die.

All the land is like as one man's face is,
   Pale and troubled still with change of cares.
Doubt and death pervade her clouded spaces:
   Strength and length of life and peace are theirs;

Theirs alone amid these weary places,
    Seeing not how the wild world frets and fares.   150

Firm and fast where all is cloud that changes
    Cloud-clogged sunlight, cloud by sunlight thinned,
Stern and sweet, above the sand-hill ranges
    Watch the towers and tombs of men that sinned
Once, now calm as earth whose only change is
    Wind, and light, and wind, and cloud, and wind.

Out and in and out the sharp straits wander,
    In and out and in the wild way strives,
Starred and paved and lined with flowers that squander
    Gold as golden as the gold of hives,   160
Salt and moist and multiform: but yonder
    See, what sign of life or death survives?

Seen then only when the songs of olden
    Harps were young whose echoes yet endure,
Hymned of Homer when his years were golden,
    Known of only when the world was pure,
Here is Hades, manifest, beholden,
    Surely, surely here, if aught be sure!

Where the border-line was crossed, that, sundering
    Death from life, keeps weariness from rest,   170
None can tell, who fares here forward wondering;
    None may doubt but here might end his quest.
Here life's lightning joys and woes once thundering
    Sea-like round him cease like storm suppressed.

Here the wise wave-wandering steadfast-hearted
    Guest of many a lord of many a land *
Saw the shape or shade of years departed,
    Saw the semblance risen and hard at hand,

---

* Odysseus, who, in the eleventh book of the *Odyssey,* visits the
Underworld. There, he vainly seeks to embrace the shade of his mother,
who had died of grief for her long-absent son.

Saw the mother long from love's reach parted,
  Anticleia, like a statue stand.   180

Statue? nay, nor tissued image woven
  Fair on hangings in his father's hall;
Nay, too fast her faith of heart was proven,
  Far too firm her loveliest love of all;
Love wherethrough the loving heart was cloven,
  Love that hears not when the loud Fates call.

Love that lives and stands up re-created
  Then when life has ebbed and anguish fled;
Love more strong than death or all things fated,
  Child's and mother's, lit by love and led;   190
Love that found what life so long awaited
  Here, when life came down among the dead.

Here, where never came alive another,
  Came her son across the sundering tide
Crossed before by many a warrior brother
  Once that warred on Ilion at his side;
Here spread forth vain hands to clasp the mother
  Dead, that sorrowing for his love's sake died.

Parted, though by narrowest of divisions,
  Clasp he might not, only might implore,   200
Sundered yet by bitterest of derisions,
  Son, and mother from the son she bore—
Here? But all dispeopled here of visions
  Lies, forlorn of shadows even, the shore.

All too sweet such men's Hellenic speech is,
  All too fain they lived of light to see,
Once to see the darkness of these beaches,
  Once to sing this Hades found of me
Ghostless, all its gulfs and creeks and reaches,
  Sky, and shore, and cloud, and waste, and sea.   210

vi

Death, and change, and darkness everlasting,
   Deaf, that hears not what the daystar saith,
Blind, past all remembrance and forecasting,
   Dead, past memory that it once drew breath;
These, above the washing tides and wasting,
   Reign, and rule this land of utter death.

Change of change, darkness of darkness, hidden,
   Very death of very death, begun
When none knows,—the knowledge is forbidden—
   Self-begotten, self-proceeding, one,*   220
Born, not made—abhorred, unchained, unchidden,
   Night stands here defiant of the sun.

Change of change, and death of death begotten,
   Darkness born of darkness, one and three,
Ghostly godhead of a world forgotten,
   Crowned with heaven, enthroned on land and sea,
Here, where earth with dead men's bones is rotten,
   God of Time, thy likeness worships thee.

Lo, thy likeness of thy desolation,
   Shape and figure of thy might, O Lord,   230
Formless form, incarnate miscreation,
   Served of all things living and abhorred;
Earth herself is here thine incarnation,
   Time, of all things born on earth adored.

All that worship thee are fearful of thee;
   No man may not worship thee for fear:
Prayers nor curses prove not nor disprove thee,
   Move nor change thee with our change of cheer:

---

   *Cf. the description of Christ in *The Book of Common Prayer* as "the only-begotten Son of God; Begotten of his Father before all worlds, God of God, Light of Light, very God of very God; Begotten, not made; Being of one substance with the Father; by whom all things were made." (The Nicene Creed.)

All at last, though all abhorred thee, love thee,
   God, the sceptre of whose throne is here.   240

Here thy throne and sceptre of thy station,
   Here the palace paven for thy feet;
Here thy sign from nation unto nation
   Passed as watchword for thy guards to greet,
Guards that go before thine exaltation,
   Ages, clothed with bitter years and sweet.

Here, where sharp the sea-bird shrills his ditty,
   Flickering flame-wise through the clear live calm,
Rose triumphal, crowning all a city,
   Roofs exalted once with prayer and psalm,   250
Built of holy hands for holy pity,
   Frank and fruitful as a sheltering palm.

Church and hospice wrought in faultless fashion,
   Hall and chancel bounteous and sublime,
Wide and sweet and glorious as compassion,
   Filled and thrilled with force of choral chime,
Filled with spirit of prayer and thrilled with passion,
   Hailed a God more merciful than Time.

Ah, less mighty, less than Time prevailing,
   Shrunk, expelled, made nothing at his nod,   260
Less than clouds across the sea-line sailing,
   Lies he, stricken by his master's rod.
"Where is man?" the cloister murmurs wailing;
   Back the mute shrine thunders—"Where is God?"

Here is all the end of all his glory—
   Dust, and grass, and barren silent stones.
Dead, like him, one hollow tower and hoary
   Naked in the sea-wind stands and moans,
Filled and thrilled with its perpetual story:
   Here, where earth is dense with dead men's bones.   270

Low and loud and long, a voice for ever,
  Sounds the wind's clear story like a song.
Tomb from tomb the waves devouring sever,
  Dust from dust as years relapse along;
Graves where men made sure to rest, and never
  Lie dismantled by the seasons' wrong.

Now displaced, devoured and desecrated,
  Now by Time's hands darkly disinterred,
These poor dead that sleeping here awaited
  Long the archangel's re-creating word,   280
Closed about with roofs and walls high-gated
  Till the blast of judgment should be heard,

Naked, shamed, cast out of consecration,
  Corpse and coffin, yea the very graves,
Scoffed at, scattered, shaken from their station,
  Spurned and scourged of wind and sea like slaves,
Desolate beyond man's desolation,
  Shrink and sink into the waste of waves.

Tombs, with bare white piteous bones protruded,
  Shroudless, down the loose collapsing banks,   290
Crumble, from their constant place detruded,
  That the sea devours and gives not thanks.
Graves where hope and prayer and sorrow brooded
  Gape and slide and perish, ranks on ranks.

Rows on rows and line by line they crumble,
  They that thought for all time through to be.
Scarce a stone whereon a child might stumble
  Breaks the grim field paced alone of me.
Earth, and man, and all their gods wax humble
  Here, where Time brings pasture to the sea.   300

⊷❦ ❦⊷

*The Higher Pantheism in a Nutshell**

One, who is not, we see: but one, whom we see not, is:
Surely this is not that: but that is assuredly this.

What, and wherefore, and whence? for under is over and
　　under:
If thunder could be without lightning, lightning could
　　be without thunder.

Doubt is faith in the main: but faith, on the whole, is
　　doubt:
We cannot believe by proof: but could we believe
　　without?

Why, and whither, and how? for barley and rye are
　　not clover:
Neither are straight lines curves: yet over is under and
　　over.

Two and two may be four: but four and four are not
　　eight:
Fate and God may be twain: but God is the same thing　　10
　　as fate.

Ask a man what he thinks, and get from a man what
　　he feels:
God, once caught in the fact, shows you a fair pair of
　　heels.

Body and spirit are twins: God only knows which is
　　which:
The soul squats down in the flesh, like a tinker drunk
　　in a ditch.

* A parody of Tennyson's "The Higher Pantheism."

More is the whole than a part: but half is more than
 the whole:
Clearly, the soul is the body: but is not the body the
 soul?

One and two are not one: but one and nothing is
 two:
Truth can hardly be false, if falsehood cannot be
 true.

Once the mastodon was: pterodactyls were common as
 cocks:
Then the mammoth was God: now is He a prize ox.   20

Parallels all things are: yet many of these are askew:
You are certainly I: but certainly I am not you.

Springs the rock from the plain, shoots the stream
 from the rock:
Cocks exist for the hen: but hens exist for the cock.

God, whom we see not, is: and God, who is not, we
 see:
Fiddle, we know, is diddle: and diddle, we take it, is
 dee.

*Nephelidia**

From the depth of the dreamy decline of the dawn
 through a notable nimbus of nebulous noonshine,
 Pallid and pink as the palm of the flag-flower that
  flickers with fear of the flies as they float,
Are they looks of our lovers that lustrously lean from
 a marvel of mystic miraculous moonshine,
 These that we feel in the blood of our blushes that

* "Cloudlets," Swinburne's self-parody.

  thicken and threaten with throbs through the
   throat?
Thicken and thrill as a theatre thronged at appeal of
   an actor's appalled agitation,
  Fainter with fear of the fires of the future than pale
   with the promise of pride in the past;
Flushed with the famishing fullness of fever that
   reddens with radiance of rathe recreation,
  Gaunt as the ghastliest of glimpses that gleam
   through the gloom of the gloaming when ghosts
   go aghast?
Nay, for the nick of the tick of the time is a tremulous
   touch on the temples of terror,
  Strained as the sinews yet strenuous with strife of 10
   the dead who is dumb as the dust-heaps of death:
Surely no soul is it, sweet as the spasm of erotic emo-
   tional exquisite error,
  Bathed in the balms of beautified bliss, beatific itself
   by beatitude's breath.
Surely no spirit or sense of a soul that was soft to the
   spirit and soul of our senses
  Sweetens the stress of suspiring suspicion that sobs
   in the semblance and sound of a sigh;
Only this oracle opens Olympian, in mystical moods
   and triangular tenses—
  "Life is the lust of a lamp for the light that is dark
   till the dawn of the day when we die."
Mild is the mirk and monotonous music of memory,
   melodiously mute as it may be,
  While the hope in the heart of a hero is bruised by
   the breach of men's rapiers, resigned to the rod;
Made meek as a mother whose bosom-beats bound
   with the bliss-bringing bulk of a balm-breathing
   baby,
  As they grope through the grave-yard of creeds, 20
   under skies growing green at a groan for the
   grimness of God.

Blank is the book of his bounty beholden of old, and
      its binding is blacker than bluer:
  Out of blue into black is the scheme of the skies,
        and their dews are the wine of the bloodshed of
        things;
Till the darkling desire of delight shall be free as a
      fawn that is freed from the fangs that pursue her,
  Till the heart-beats of hell shall be hushed by a
      hymn from the hunt that has harried the kennel
      of kings.

Prelude

Tristram and Iseult

Love, that is first and last of all things made,
The light that has the living world for shade,
The spirit that for temporal veil has on
The souls of all men woven in unison,
One fiery raiment with all lives inwrought
And lights of sunny and starry deed and thought,
And alway through new act and passion new
Shines the divine same body and beauty through,
The body spiritual of fire and light
That is to worldly noon as noon to night;   10
Love, that is flesh upon the spirit of man
And spirit within the flesh whence breath began;
Love, that keeps all the choir of lives in chime;
Love, that is blood within the veins of time;
That wrought the whole world without stroke of hand,
Shaping the breadth of sea, the length of land,
And with the pulse and motion of his breath
Through the great heart of the earth strikes life and
      death,
The sweet twain chords that make the sweet tune live

Through day and night of things alternative,   20
Through silence and through sound of stress and strife,
And ebb and flow of dying death and life;
Love, that sounds loud or light in all men's ears,
Whence all men's eyes take fire from sparks of tears,
That binds on all men's feet or chains or wings;
Love, that is root and fruit of terrene things;
Love, that the whole world's waters shall not drown,
The whole world's fiery forces not burn down;
Love, that what time his own hands guard his head
The whole world's wrath and strength shall not strike   30
    dead;
Love, that if once his own hands make his grave
The whole world's pity and sorrow shall not save;
Love, that for very life shall not be sold,
Nor bought nor bound with iron nor with gold;
So strong that heaven, could love bid heaven farewell,
Would turn to fruitless and unflowering hell;
So sweet that hell, to hell could love be given,
Would turn to splendid and sonorous heaven;
Love that is fire within thee and light above,
And lives by grace of nothing but of love;   40
Through many and lovely thoughts and much desire
Led these twain to the life of tears and fire;
Through many and lovely days and much delight
Led these twain to the lifeless life of night. . . .

Canto 2

THE QUEEN'S PLEASANCE *

Out of the night arose the second day,
And saw the ship's bows break the shoreward spray.

* In Canto I, "The Sailing of the Swallow," Tristram escorts Iseult
to King Mark, her bridegroom. Tristram and Iseult meet at dawn on deck
and, unknowing, drink the love potion intended for her wedding night:

> Their heads neared, and their hands were drawn in one,
> And they saw dark, though still the unsunken sun
> Far through fine rain shot fire into the south;
> And their four lips became one burning mouth.

As the sun's boat of gold and fire began
To sail the sea of heaven unsailed of man,
And the soft waves of sacred air to break
Round the prow launched into the morning's lake,
They saw the sign of their sea-travel done.
　　Ah, was not something seen of yester-sun,
When the sweet light that lightened all the skies
Saw nothing fairer than one maiden's eyes,   10
That whatsoever in all time's years may be
To-day's sun nor to-morrow's sun shall see?
Not while she lives, not when she comes to die,
Shall she look sunward with that sinless eye.
　　Yet fairer now than song may show them stand
Tristram and Iseult, hand in amorous hand,
Soul-satisfied, their eyes made great and bright
With all the love of all the livelong night;
With all its hours yet singing in their ears
No mortal music made of thoughts and tears,   20
But such a song, past conscience of man's thought,
As hearing he grows god and knows it not.
Nought else they saw nor heard but what the night
Had left for seal upon their sense and sight,
Sound of past pulses beating, fire of amorous light.
Enough, and overmuch, and never yet
Enough, though love still hungering feed and fret,
To fill the cup of night which dawn must overset.
For still their eyes were dimmer than with tears
And dizzier from diviner sounds their ears   30
Than though from choral thunders of the quiring spheres.
They heard not how the landward waters rang,
Nor saw where high into the morning sprang,
Riven from the shore and bastioned with the sea,
Toward summits where the north wind's nest might be,
A wave-walled palace with its eastern gate
Full of the sunrise now and wide at wait,
And on the mighty-moulded stairs that clomb
Sheer from the fierce lip of the lapping foam
The knights of Mark that stood before the wall.   40

So with loud joy and storm of festival
They brought the bride in up the towery way
That rose against the rising front of day,
Stair based on stair, between the rocks unhewn,
To those strange halls wherethrough the tidal tune
Rang loud or lower from soft or strengthening sea,
Tower shouldering tower, to windward and to lee,
With change of floors and stories, flight on flight,
That clomb and curled up to the crowning height
Whence men might see wide east and west in one   50
And on one sea waned moon and mounting sun.
And severed from the sea-rock's base, where stand
Some worn walls yet they saw the broken strand,
The beachless cliff that in the sheer sea dips,
The sleepless shore inexorable to ships,
And the straight causeway's bare gaunt spine between
The sea-spanned walls and naked mainland's green.
   On the mid stairs, between the light and dark,
Before the main tower's portal stood King Mark,
Crowned: and his face was as the face of one   60
Long time athirst and hungering for the sun
In barren thrall of bitter bonds, who now
Thinks here to feel its blessing on his brow.
A swart lean man, but kinglike, still of guise,
With black streaked beard and cold unquiet eyes,
Close-mouthed, gaunt-cheeked, wan as a morning moon,
Though hardly time on his worn hair had strewn
The thin first ashes from a sparing hand:
Yet little fire there burnt upon the brand,
And way-worn seemed he with life's wayfaring.   70
So between shade and sunlight stood the king,
And his face changed nor yearned not toward his bride;
But fixed between mild hope and patient pride
Abode what gift of rare or lesser worth
This day might bring to all his days on earth.
But at the glory of her when she came
His heart endured not: very fear and shame
Smote him, to take her by the hand and kiss,

Till both were molten in the burning bliss,
And with a thin flame flushing his cold face   80
He led her silent to the bridal place.
There were they wed and hallowed of the priest;
And all the loud time of the marriage feast
One thought within three hearts was as a fire,
Where craft and faith took counsel with desire.
For when the feast had made a glorious end
They gave the new queen for her maids to tend
At dawn of bride-night, and thereafter bring
With marriage music to the bridegroom king.
Then by device of craft between them laid   90
To him went Brangwain* delicately, and prayed
That this thing even for love's sake might not be,
But without sound or light or eye to see
She might come in to bride-bed: and he laughed,
As one that wist not well of wise love's craft,
And bade all bridal things be as she would.
Yet of his gentleness he gat not good;
For clothed and covered with the nuptial dark
Soft like a bride came Brangwain to King Mark,
And to the queen came Tristram; and the night   100
Fled, and ere danger of detective light
From the king sleeping Brangwain slid away,
And where had lain her handmaid Iseult lay,
And the king waking saw beside his head
That face yet passion-coloured, amorous red
From lips not his, and all that strange hair shed
Across the tissued pillows, fold on fold,
Innumerable, incomparable, all gold,
To fire men's eyes with wonder, and with love
Men's hearts; so shone its flowering crown above   110
The brows enwound with that imperial wreath,
And framed with fragrant radiance round the face
      beneath.
    And the king marvelled, seeing with sudden start
Her very glory, and said out of his heart;

* Iseult's handmaid.

"What have I done of good for God to bless
That all this he should give me, tress on tress,
All this great wealth and wondrous? Was it this
That in mine arms I had all night to kiss,
And mix with me this beauty? this that seems
More fair than heaven doth in some tired saint's   120
    dreams,
Being part of that same heaven? yea, more, for he,
Though loved of God so, yet but seems to see,
But to me sinful such great grace is given
That in mine hands I hold this part of heaven,
Not to mine eyes lent merely. Doth God make
Such things so godlike for man's mortal sake?
Have I not sinned, that in this fleshly life
Have made of her a mere man's very wife?"
    So the king mused and murmured; and she heard
The faint sound trembling of each breathless word,   130
And laughed into the covering of her hair.
    And many a day for many a month as fair
Slid over them like music; and as bright
Burned with love's offerings many a secret night.
And many a dawn to many a fiery noon
Blew prelude, when the horn's heart-kindling tune
Lit the live woods with sovereign sound of mirth
Before the mightiest huntsman hailed on earth
Lord of its lordliest pleasure, where he rode
Hard by her rein whose peerless presence glowed   140
Not as that white queen's of the virgin hunt *
Once, whose crown-crescent braves the night-wind's brunt,
But with the sun for frontlet of a queenlier front.
For where the flashing of her face was turned
As lightning was the fiery light that burned
From eyes and brows enkindled more with speed
And rapture of the rushing of her steed
Than once with only beauty; and her mouth
Was as a rose athirst that pants for drouth
Even while it laughs for pleasure of desire,   150

* Artemis or Diana, virgin goddess of the hunt and of the moon.

And all her heart was as a leaping fire.
Yet once more joy they took of woodland ways
Than came of all those flushed and fiery days
When the loud air was mad with life and sound,
Through many a dense green mile, of horn and hound
Before the king's hunt going along the wind,
And ere the timely leaves were changed or thinned,
Even in mid maze of summer. For the knight
Forth was once ridden toward some frontier fight
Against the lewd folk of the Christless lands   160
That warred with wild and intermittent hands
Against the king's north border; and there came
A knight unchristened yet of unknown name,
Swart Palamede, upon a secret quest,
To high Tintagel, and abode as guest
In likeness of a mistrel with the king.
Nor was there man could sound so sweet a string,
Save Tristram only, of all held best on earth.
And one loud eve, being full of wine and mirth,
Ere sunset left the walls and waters dark,   170
To that strange minstrel strongly swore King Mark,
By all that makes a knight's faith firm and strong
That he for guerdon of his harp and song
Might crave and have his liking. Straight there came
Up the swart cheek a flash of swarthier flame,
And the deep eyes fulfilled of glittering night
Laughed out in lightnings of triumphant light
As the grim harper spake: "O king, I crave
No gift of man that king may give to slave,
But this thy crowned queen only, this thy wife,   180
Whom yet unseen I loved, and set my life
On this poor chance to compass, even as here,
Being fairer famed than all save Guenevere."
Then as the noise of seaward storm that mocks
With roaring laughter from reverberate rocks
The cry from ships near shipwreck, harsh and high
Rose all the wrath and wonder in one cry
Through all the long roof's hollow depth and length

That hearts of strong men kindled in their strength
May speak in laughter lion-like, and cease, 190
Being wearied: only two men held their peace
And each glared hard on other: but King Mark
Spake first of these: "Man, though thy craft be dark
And thy mind evil that begat this thing,
Yet stands the word once plighted of a king
Fast: and albeit less evil it were for me
To give my life up than my wife, or be
A landless man crowned only with a curse,
Yet this in God's and all men's sight were worse,
To live soul-shamed, a man of broken troth, 200
Abhorred of men as I abhor mine oath
Which yet I may forswear not." And he bowed
His head, and wept: and all men wept aloud,
Save one, that heard him weeping: but the queen
Wept not: and statelier yet than eyes had seen
That ever looked upon her queenly state
She rose, and in her eyes her heart was great
And full of wrath seen manifest and scorn
More strong than anguish to go thence forlorn
Of all men's comfort and her natural right. 210
And they went forth into the dawn of night.
Long by wild ways and clouded light they rode,
Silent; and fear less keen at heart abode
With Iseult than with Palamede: for awe
Constrained him, and the might of love's high law,
That can make lewd men loyal; and his heart
Yearned on her, if perchance with amorous art
And soothfast skill of very love he might
For courtesy find favour in her sight
And comfort of her mercies: for he wist 220
More grace might come of that sweet mouth unkissed
Than joy for violence done it, that should make
His name abhorred for shame's disloyal sake.
And in the stormy starlight clouds were thinned
And thickened by short gusts of changing wind
That panted like a sick man's fitful breath:

And like a moan of lions hurt to death
Came the sea's hollow noise along the night.
But ere its gloom from aught but foam had light
They halted, being aweary: and the knight   230
As reverently forbore her where she lay
As one that watched his sister's sleep till day.
Nor durst he kiss or touch her hand or hair
For love and shamefast pity, seeing how fair
She slept, and fenceless from the fitful air.
And shame at heart stung nigh to death desire,
But grief at heart burned in him like a fire
For hers and his own sorrowing sake, that had
Such grace for guerdon as makes glad men sad,
To have their will and want it. And the day   240
Sprang: and afar along the wild waste way
They heard the pulse and press of hurrying horse-
    hoofs play:
And like the rushing of a ravenous flame
Whose wings make tempest of the darkness, came
Upon them headlong as in thunder borne
Forth of the darkness of the labouring morn
Tristram: and up forthright upon his steed
Leapt, as one blithe of battle, Palamede,
And mightily with shock of horse and man
They lashed together: and fair that fight began   250
As fair came up that sunrise: to and fro,
With knees nigh staggered and stout heads bent low
From each quick shock of spears on either side,
Reeled the strong steeds heavily, haggard-eyed
And heartened high with passion of their pride
As sheer the stout spears shocked again, and flew
Sharp-splintering: then, his sword as each knight drew,
They flashed and foined full royally, so long
That but to see so fair a strife and strong
A man might well have given out of his life   260
One year's void space forlorn of love or strife.
As when a bright north-easter, great of heart,
Scattering the strengths of squadrons, hurls apart

Ship from ship labouring violently, in such toil
As earns but ruin—with even so strong recoil
Back were the steeds hurled from the spear-shock, fain
And foiled of triumph: then with tightened rein
And stroke of spur, inveterate, either knight
Bore in again upon his foe with might,
Heart-hungry for the hot-mouthed feast of fight   270
And all athirst of mastery: but full soon
The jarring notes of that tempestuous tune
Fell, and its mighty music made of hands
Contending, clamorous through the loud waste lands,
Broke at once off; and shattered from his steed
Fell, as a mainmast ruining, Palamede,
Stunned: and those lovers left him where he lay,
And lightly through green lawns they rode away.
    There was a bower beyond man's eye more fair
Than ever summer dews and sunniest air   280
Fed full with rest and radiance till the boughs
Had wrought a roof as for a holier house
Than aught save love might breathe in; fairer far
Than keeps the sweet light back of moon and star
From high king's chambers: there might love and sleep
Divide for joy the darkling hours, and keep
With amorous alternation of sweet strife
The soft and secret ways of death and life
Made smooth for pleasure's feet to rest and run
Even from the moondawn to the kindling sun,   290
Made bright for passion's feet to run and rest
Between the midnight's and the morning's breast,
Where hardly though her happy head lie down
It may forget the hour that wove its crown;
Where hardly though her joyous limbs be laid
They may forget the mirth that midnight made.
And thither, ere sweet night had slain sweet day,
Iseult and Tristram took their wandering way,
And rested, and refreshed their hearts with cheer
In hunters' fashion of the woods; and here   300
More sweet it seemed, while this might be, to dwell

And take of all world's weariness farewell
Than reign of all world's lordship queen and king.
Nor here would time for three moons' changes bring
Sorrow nor thought of sorrow; but sweet earth
Fostered them like her babes of eldest birth,
Reared warm in pathless woods and cherished well.
And the sun sprang above the sea and fell,
And the stars rose and sank upon the sea;
And outlaw-like, in forest wise and free,   310
The rising and the setting of their lights
Found those twain dwelling all those days and nights.
And under change of sun and star and moon
Flourished and fell the chaplets woven of June,
And fair through fervours of the deepening sky
Panted and passed the hours that lit July,
And each day blessed them out of heaven above,
And each night crowned them with the crown of love.
Nor till the might of August overhead
Weighed on the world was yet one roseleaf shed   320
Of all their joy's warm coronal, nor aught
Touched them in passing ever with a thought
That ever this might end on any day
Or any night not love them where they lay;
But like a babbling tale of barren breath
Seemed all report and rumour held of death,
And a false bruit the legend tear-impearled
That such a thing as change was in the world.
And each bright song upon his lips that came,
Mocking the powers of change and death by name,   330
Blasphemed their bitter godhead, and defied
Time, though clothed round with ruin as kings with
     pride,
To blot the glad life out of love: and she
Drank lightly deep of his philosophy
In that warm wine of amorous words which is
Sweet with all truths of all philosophies.
For well he wist all subtle ways of song,
And in his soul the secret eye was strong

That burns in meditation, till bright words
Break flamelike forth as notes from fledgeling birds   340
That feel the soul speak through them of the spring.
So fared they night and day as queen and king
Crowned of a kingdom wide as day and night.
Nor ever cloudlet swept or swam in sight
Across the darkling depths of their delight
Whose stars no skill might number, nor man's art
Sound the deep stories of its heavenly heart.
Till, even for wonder that such life should live,
Desires and dreams of what death's self might give
Would touch with tears and laughter and wild speech   350
The lips and eyes of passion, fain to reach,
Beyond all bourne of time or trembling sense,
The verge of love's last possible eminence.
Out of the heaven that storm nor shadow mars,
Deep from the starry depth beyond the stars,
A yearning ardour without scope or name
Fell on them, and the bright night's breath of flame
Shot fire into their kisses; and like fire
The lit dews lightened on the leaves, as higher
Night's heart beat on toward midnight. Far and fain   360
Somewhiles the soft rush of rejoicing rain
Solaced the darkness, and from steep to steep
Of heaven they saw the sweet sheet lightning leap
And laugh its heart out in a thousand smiles,
When the clear sea for miles on glimmering miles
Burned as though dawn were strewn abroad astray,
Or, showering out of heaven, all heaven's array
Had paven instead the waters: fain and far
Somewhiles the burning love of star for star
Spake words that love might wellnigh seem to hear   370
In such deep hours as turn delight to fear
Sweet as delight's self ever. So they lay
Tranced once, nor watched along the fiery bay
The shine of summer darkness palpitate and play.
She had nor sight nor voice; her swooning eyes
Knew not if night or light were in the skies;

Across her beauty sheer the moondawn shed
Its light as on a thing as white and dead;
Only with stress of soft fierce hands she prest
Between the throbbing blossoms of her breast   380
His ardent face, and through his hair her breath
Went quivering as when life is hard on death;
And with strong trembling fingers she strained fast
His head into her bosom; till at last,
Satiate with sweetness of that burning bed,
His eyes afire with tears, he raised his head
And laughed into her lips; and all his heart
Filled hers; then face from face fell, and apart
Each hung on each with panting lips, and felt
Sense into sense and spirit in spirit melt.   390
    "Hast thou no sword? I would not live till day;
O love, this night and we must pass away,
It must die soon, and let not us die late."
    "Take then my sword and slay me; nay, but wait
Till day be risen; what, wouldst thou think to die
Before the light take hold upon the sky?"
    "Yea, love; for how shall we have twice, being
        twain,
This very night of love's most rapturous reign?
Live thou and have thy day, and year by year
Be great, but what shall I be? Slay me here;   400
Let me die not when love lies dead, but now
Strike through my heart: nay, sweet, what heart hast
        thou?
Is it so much I ask thee, and spend my breath
In asking? nay, thou knowest it is but death.
Hadst thou true heart to love me, thou wouldst give
This: but for hate's sake thou wilt let me live."
    Here he caught up her lips with his, and made
The wild prayer silent in her heart that prayed,
And strained her to him till all her faint breath sank
And her bright light limbs palpitated and shrank   410
And rose and fluctuated as flowers in rain
That bends them and they tremble and rise again

And heave and straighten and quiver all through with
　　　bliss
And turn afresh their mouths up for a kiss,
Amorous, athirst of that sweet influent love;
So, hungering towards his hovering lips above,
Her red-rose mouth yearned silent, and her eyes
Closed, and flashed after, as through June's darkest
　　　skies
The divine heartbeats of the deep live light
Make open and shut the gates of the outer night.　　　420
　　Long lay they still, subdued with love, nor knew
If cloud or light changed colour as it grew,
If star or moon beheld them; if above
The heaven of night waxed fiery with their love,
Or earth beneath were moved at heart and root
To burn as they, to burn and bring forth fruit
Unseasonable for love's sake; if tall trees
Bowed, and close flowers yearned open, and the breeze
Failed and fell silent as a flame that fails:
And all that hour unheard the nightingales　　　430
Clamoured, and all the woodland soul was stirred,
And depth and height were one great song unheard,
As though the world caught music and took fire
From the instant heart alone of their desire.
　　So sped their night of nights between them: so,
For all fears past and shadows, shine and snow,
That one pure hour all-golden where they lay
Made their life perfect and their darkness day.
And warmer waved its harvest yet to reap,
Till in the lovely fight of love and sleep　　　440
At length had sleep the mastery; and the dark
Was lit with soft live gleams they might not mark,
Fleet butterflies, each like a dead flower's ghost,
White, blue, and sere leaf-coloured; but the most
White as the sparkle of snow-flowers in the sun
Ere with his breath they lie at noon undone
Whose kiss devours their tender beauty, and leaves
But raindrops on the grass and sere thin leaves

That were engraven with traceries of the snow
Flowerwise ere any flower of earth's would blow;   450
So swift they sprang and sank, so sweet and light
They swam the deep dim breathless air of night.
Now on her rose-white amorous breast half bare,
Now on her slumberous love-dishevelled hair,
The white wings lit and vanished, and afresh
Lit soft as snow lights on her snow-soft flesh,
On hand or throat or shoulder; and she stirred
Sleeping, and spake some tremulous bright word,
And laughed upon some dream too sweet for truth,
Yet not so sweet as very love and youth   460
That there had charmed her eyes to sleep at last.
Nor woke they till the perfect night was past,
And the soft sea thrilled with blind hope of light.
But ere the dusk had well the sun in sight
He turned and kissed her eyes awake and said,
Seeing earth and water neither quick nor dead
And twilight hungering toward the day to be,
"As the dawn loves the sunlight I love thee."
And even as rays with cloudlets in the skies
Confused in brief love's bright contentious wise,   470
Sleep strove with sense rekindling in her eyes;
And as the flush of birth scarce overcame
The pale pure pearl of unborn light with flame
Soft as may touch the rose's heart with shame
To break not all reluctant out of bud,
Stole up her sleeping cheek her waking blood;
And with the lovely laugh of love that takes
The whole soul prisoner ere the whole sense wakes,
Her lips for love's sake bade love's will be done.
And all the sea lay subject to the sun.   480

On the Russian Persecution of the Jews

O son of man, by lying tongues adored,
  By slaughterous hands of slaves with feet red-shod
  In carnage deep as ever Christian trod
Profaned with prayer and sacrifice abhorred
And incense from the trembling tyrant's horde,
  Brute worshippers or wielders of the rod,
  Most murderous even of all that call thee God,
Most treacherous even that ever called thee Lord;
Face loved of little children long ago,
  Head hated of the priests and rulers then,
    If thou see this, or hear these hounds of thine
    Run ravening as the Gadarean swine,*
Say, was not this thy Passion, to foreknow
  In death's worst hour the works of Christian men?

        January 23, 1882.

Sonnets on English Dramatic Poets

CHRISTOPHER MARLOWE

Crowned, girdled, garbed and shod with light and fire,
  Son first-born of the morning, sovereign star!
  Soul nearest ours of all, that wert most far,
Most far off in the abysm of time, thy lyre
Hung highest above the dawn-enkindled quire
  Where all ye sang together,** all that are,
  And all the starry songs behind thy car
Rang sequence, all our souls acclaim thee sire.

---

  * A herd of swine, possessed by devils, which "ran violently down
a steep place into the sea, and perished in the waters" (*Matthew* 8:32).
  ** Cf. *Job* 38:7: "[Where wast thou] when the morning stars sang
together, and all the sons of God shouted for joy?"

"If all the pens that ever poets held
  Had fed the feeling of their masters' thoughts," *
  And as with rush of hurtling chariots
The flight of all their spirits were impelled
  Toward one great end, thy glory—nay, not then,
Not yet might'st thou be praised enough of men.

The Roundel

A roundel is wrought as a ring or a starbright sphere,
With craft of delight and with cunning of sound unsought,
That the heart of the hearer may smile if to pleasure his
    ear
           A roundel is wrought.

Its jewel of music is carven of all or of aught—
Love, laughter, or mourning—remembrance of rapture
  or fear—
That fancy may fashion to hang in the ear of thought.

As a bird's quick song runs round, and the hearts in us
    hear
Pause answer to pause, and again the same strain caught,
So moves the device whence, round as a pearl or tear,
           A roundel is wrought.

Envoi

Fly, white butterflies, out to sea,
Frail pale wings for the winds to try,
Small white wings that we scarce can see
  Fly.

    * Lines from Marlowe's great apostrophe to beauty in *Tamburlaine,*
Part I, Act V, Scene 1.

Here and there may a chance-caught eye
Note in a score of you twain or three
Brighter or darker of tinge or dye.

Some fly light as a laugh of glee,
Some fly soft as a low long sigh:
All to the haven where each would be
   Fly.

Neap-Tide *

Far off is the sea, and the land is afar:
   The low banks reach at the sky,
    Seen hence, and are heavenward high;
Though light for the leap of a boy they are,
   And the far sea late was nigh.

The fair wild fields and the circling downs,
   The bright sweet marshes and meads
    All glorious with flowerlike weeds,
The great grey churches, the sea-washed towns,
   Recede as a dream recedes.   10

The world draws back, and the world's light wanes,
   As a dream dies down and is dead;
    And the clouds and the gleams overhead
Change, and change; and the sea remains,
   A shadow of dreamlike dread.

Wild, and woful, and pale, and grey,
   A shadow of sleepless fear,
    A corpse with the night for bier,

   * The lowest tide of the month.

The fairest thing that beholds the day
    Lies haggard and hopeless here.   20

And the wind's wings, broken and spent, subside;
    And the dumb waste world is hoar,
    And strange as the sea the shore;
And shadows of shapeless dreams abide
    Where life may abide no more.

A sail to seaward, a sound from shoreward,
    And the spell were broken that seems
    To reign in a world of dreams
Where vainly the dreamer's feet make forward
    And vainly the low sky gleams.   30

The sea-forsaken forlorn deep-wrinkled
    Salt slanting stretches of sand
    That slope to the seaward hand,
Were they fain of the ripples that flashed and twinkled
    And laughed as they struck the strand?

As bells on the reins of the fairies ring
    The ripples that kissed them rang,
    The light from the sundawn sprang,
And the sweetest of songs that the world may sing
    Was theirs when the full sea sang.   40

Now no light is in heaven; and now
    Not a note of the sea-wind's tune
    Rings hither: the bleak sky's boon
Grants hardly sight of a grey sun's brow—
    A sun more sad than the moon.

More sad than a moon that clouds beleaguer
    And storm is a scourge to smite,
    The sick sun's shadowlike light
Grows faint as the clouds and the waves wax eager,
    And withers away from sight.   50

The day's heart cowers, and the night's heart quickens:
    Full fain would the day be dead
    And the stark night reign in his stead:
The sea falls dumb as the sea-fog thickens
    And the sunset dies for dread.

Outside of the range of time, whose breath
    Is keen as the manslayer's knife
    And his peace but a truce for strife,
Who knows if haply the shadow of death
    May be not the light of life?   60

For the storm and the rain and the darkness borrow
    But an hour from the suns to be,
    But a strange swift passage, that we
May rejoice, who have mourned not to-day, to-morrow,
    In the sun and the wind and the sea.

❦ ❧

A Lyke-Wake Song*

Fair of face, full of pride,
Sit ye down by a dead man's side.

Ye sang songs a' the day:
Sit down at night in the red worm's way.

Proud ye were a' day long:
Ye'll be but lean at evensong.

Ye had gowd kells** on your hair:
Nae man kens what ye were.

Ye set scorn by the silken stuff:
Now the grave is clean enough.

    * Sung at a vigil over a dead body.
    ** *gowd kells:* gold hairnets.

Ye set scorn by the rubis ring:
Now the worm is a saft sweet thing.

Fine gold and blithe fair face,
Ye are come to a grimly place.

Gold hair and glad grey een,
Nae man kens if ye have been.

A Jacobite's Farewell
1716

There's nae mair lands to tyne,* my dear,
   And nae mair lives to gie:
Though a man think sair to live nae mair,
   There's but one day to die.

For a' things come and a' days gane,
   What needs ye rend your hair?
But kiss me till the morn's morrow,
   Then I'll kiss ye nae mair.

O lands are lost and life's losing,
   And what were they to gie?
Fu' mony a man gives all he can,
   But nae man else gives ye.

Our king wons** ower the sea's water,
   And I in prison sair:
But I'll win out the morn's morrow,
   And ye'll see me nae mair.

    * *tyne:* lose.
    ** *wons:* dwells.

Duriesdyke *

The rain rains sair[1] on Duriesdyke
    Both the winter through and the spring;
And she that will gang to get broom thereby
    She shall get an ill thing.

The rain rains sair on Duriesdyke
    Both the winter and the summer day;
And he that will steek[2] his sheep thereby
    He shall go sadly away.

"Between Crossmuir and Duriesdyke
    The fieldhead is full green;   10
The shaws[3] are thick in the fair summer,
    And three wellheads[4] between.

"Flower of broom is a fair flower,
    And heather is good to play."
O she went merry to Duriesdyke,
    But she came heavy away.

"It's I have served you, Burd [5] Maisry,
    These three months through and mair;
And the little ae kiss I gat of you,
    It pains me aye and sair.   20

"This is the time of heather-blowing,
    And that was syne in the spring;

* This ballad was first published in its present, completed form in
1958 and is here reprinted with the kind permission of the *Harvard
Library Bulletin* from the text established by Anne Henry Ehrenpreis.
    [1] Sorely, hard.
    [2] Shut, close.
    [3] Thickets.
    [4] Springs.
    [5] Lady.

And the little ae leaf comes aye to red,
    And the corn to harvesting."

The first kiss their twa mouths had,
    Sae fain she was to greet;[6]
The neist kiss their twa mouths had,
    I wot she laughed fu' sweet.

"Cover my head with a silken hood,
    My feet with a yellow claith;   30
For to stain my body wi' the dyke-water
    God wot I were fu' laith."

He's happit[7] her head about wi' silk,
    Her feet with a gowden claith;
The red sendal [8] that was of price
    He's laid between them baith.

The grass was low by Duriesdyke,
    The high heather was red;
And between the grass and the high heather
    He's tane her maidenhead.   40

They did not kiss in a noble house,
    Nor yet in a lordly bed;
But their mouths kissed in the high heather
    Between the green side and the red.

"I have three sailing ships, Maisry,
    For red wheat and for wine;
The maintopmast is a bonny mast,
    Three furlongs off to shine.

"The foremast shines like new lammer,[9]
    The mizen-mast like steel: 50

[6] Weep, grieve.
[7] Wrapped.
[8] Thin silk fabric.
[9] Amber.

Gin ye wad sail wi' me, Maisry,
    The warst should carry ye weel."

"Gin I should sail wi' you, Lord John,
    Out under the rocks red,
It's wha wad be my mither's bower-maiden
    To hap saft her feet in bed?

"Gin I should sail wi' you, Lord John,
    Out under the rocks white,
There's nane wad do her a very little ease
    To hap her left and right."   60

It fell upon the midwinter
    She gat mickle scaith[10] and blame;
She's bound hersell by the white water
    To see his ships come hame.

She's leaned hersell against the wind,
    To see upon the middle tide;
The faem was fallen in the running wind,
    The wind was fallen in the waves wide.

"There's nae moon by the white water
    To do me ony good the day;   70
And but this wind a little slacken,
    They shall have a sair seaway.

"O stir not for this med,[11] baby,
    O stir not at my side;
Ye'll have the better birth, baby,
    Gin ye wad but a little abide.

"Gin ye winna cease for the pity of him
    O cease for the pity of me;

[10] *Mickle scaith*: much harm, injury.
[11] *med*: commotion, tumult.

There was never bairn born of a woman
    Between the sea-wind and the sea: 80
There was never bairn born of a woman
    That was born so bitterly."

The ship drove hard upon the wind,
    I wot it drove full mightily;
But the fair gold sides upon the ship
    They were bursten with the sea.

"O I am sae fain for you, Lord John,
    Gin ye be no sae fain
How shall I bear wi' my body,
    It is sae full of pain?"   90

"O I am sae fain of your body,
    Ye are no sae fain of me;
But the sails are riven wi' the wind
    And the sides are full of sea."

O when she saw the sails riven
    The sair pain bowed her back;
But when she saw the sides bursten
    I wot her very heart brak.

The wind waxed in the sea between,
    The rain waxed in the land;   100
Lord John was happit wi' saut sea-faem,
    Lady Maisry wi' sea-sand:
And the little bairn between them twa
    That was to her right hand.

The rain rains sair on Duriesdyke
    To the land side and the sea;
There was never bairn born of a woman
    That was born mair bitterly.

A Nympholept*

Summer, and noon, and a splendour of silence, felt,
    Seen, and heard of the spirit within the sense.
Soft through the frondage the shades of the sunbeams
        melt,
    Sharp through the foliage the shafts of them, keen
        and dense,
    Cleave, as discharged from the string of the God's
        bow, tense
As a war-steed's girth, and bright as a warrior's belt.
    Ah, why should an hour that is heaven for an hour
        pass hence?

I dare not sleep for delight of the perfect hour,
    Lest God be wroth that his gift should be scorned
        of man.
The face of the warm bright world is the face of a   10
        flower,
    The word of the wind and the leaves that the light
        winds fan
    As the word that quickened at first into flame, and
        ran,
Creative and subtle and fierce with invasive power,
    Through darkness and cloud, from the breath of the
        one God, Pan.

The perfume of earth possessed by the sun pervades
    The chaster air that he soothes but with sense of
        sleep.
Soft, imminent, strong as desire that prevails and fades,
    The passing noon that beholds not a cloudlet weep

---

* Literally, "caught by the nymphs"; inspired by ecstasy or violent
enthusiasm for an unattainable ideal. See p. xxxiii, n. 19, for Swinburne's
comment on the poem.

Imbues and impregnates life with delight more deep
Than dawn or sunset or moonrise on lawns or glades   20
  Can shed from the skies that receive it and may not
      keep.

The skies may hold not the splendour of sundown fast;
  It wanes into twilight as dawn dies down into day.
And the moon, triumphant when twilight is overpast,
  Takes pride but awhile in the hours of her stately
      sway.
  But the might of the noon, though the light of it pass
    away,
Leaves earth fulfilled of desires and of dreams that last;
  But if any there be that hath sense of them none can
    say.

For if any there be that hath sight of them, sense, or
    trust
  Made strong by the might of a vision, the strength   30
    of a dream,
His lips shall straiten and close as a dead man's must,
  His heart shall be sealed as the voice of a frost-
    bound stream.
  For the deep mid mystery of light and of heat that
    seem
To clasp and pierce dark earth, and enkindle dust,
  Shall a man's faith say what it is? or a man's guess
    deem?

Sleep lies not heavier on eyes that have watched all
    night
  Than hangs the heat of the noon on the hills and
    trees.
Why now should the haze not open, and yield to sight
  A fairer secret than hope or than slumber sees?
  I seek not heaven with submission of lips and knees,   40
With worship and prayer for a sign till it leap to light:
  I gaze on the gods about me, and call on these.

I call on the gods hard by, the divine dim powers
    Whose likeness is here at hand, in the breathless air,
In the pulseless peace of the fervid and silent flowers,
    In the faint sweet speech of the waters that whisper
        there.
    Ah, what should darkness do in a world so fair?
The bent-grass heaves not, the couch-grass quails not
    or cowers;
    The wind's kiss frets not the rowan's or aspen's hair.

But the silence trembles with passion of sound sup-   50
    pressed,
    And the twilight quivers and yearns to the sunward,
        wrung
With love as with pain; and the wide wood's motion-
    less breast
    Is thrilled with a dumb desire that would fain find
        tongue
    And palpitates, tongueless as she whom a man-
        snake stung,
Whose heart now heaves in the nightingale, never at
    rest
    Nor satiated ever with song till her last be sung.

Is it rapture or terror that circles me round, and
    invades
    Each vein of my life with hope—if it be not fear?
Each pulse that awakens my blood into rapture fades,
    Each pulse that subsides into dread of a strange   60
        thing near
    Requickens with sense of a terror less dread than
        dear.
Is peace not one with light in the deep green glades
    Where summer at noonday slumbers? Is peace not
        here?

The tall thin stems of the firs, and the roof sublime
    That screens from the sun the floor of the steep
        still wood,

Deep, silent, splendid, and perfect and calm as time,
　　Stand fast as ever in sight of the night they stood,
　　When night gave all that moonlight and dewfall
　　　　could.
The dense ferns deepen, the moss glows warm as the
　　　　thyme:
　　The wild heath quivers about me: the world is　　　　70
　　　　good.

Is it Pan's breath, fierce in the tremulous maidenhair,
　　That bids fear creep as a snake through the wood-
　　　　lands, felt
In the leaves that it stirs not yet, in the mute bright air,
　　In the stress of the sun? For here has the great God
　　　　dwelt:
　　For hence were the shafts of his love or his anger
　　　　dealt.
For here has his wrath been fierce as his love was fair,
　　When each was as fire to the darkness its breath
　　　　bade melt.

Is it love, is it dread, that enkindles the trembling noon,
　　That yearns, reluctant in rapture that fear has fed,
As man for woman, as woman for man? Full soon,　　　80
　　If I live, and the life that may look on him drop
　　　　not dead,
　　Shall the ear that hears not a leaf quake hear his
　　　　tread,
The sense that knows not the sound of the deep day's
　　　　tune
　　Receive the God, be it love that he brings or dread.

The naked noon is upon me: the fierce dumb spell,
　　The fearful charm of the strong sun's imminent
　　　　might,
Unmerciful, steadfast, deeper than seas that swell,
　　Pervades, invades, appals me with loveless light,

With harsher awe than breathes in the breath of
    night.
Have mercy, God who art all! For I know thee well,   90
    How sharp is thine eye to lighten, thine hand to
        smite.

The whole wood feels thee, the whole air fears thee:
        but fear
    So deep, so dim, so sacred, is wellnigh sweet.
For the light that hangs and broods on the wood-
        lands here,
    Intense, invasive, intolerant, imperious, and meet
    To lighten the works of thine hands and the ways
        of thy feet,
Is hot with the fire of the breath of thy life, and dear
    As hope that shrivels or shrinks not for frost or
        heat.

Thee, thee the supreme dim godhead, approved afar,
    Perceived of the soul and conceived of the sense of   100
        man,
We scarce dare love, and we dare not fear: the star
    We call the sun, that lit us when life began
    To brood on the world that is thine by his grace
        for a span,
Conceals and reveals in the semblance of things that
        are
    Thine immanent presence, the pulse of thy heart's
        life, Pan.

The fierce mid noon that wakens and warms the
        snake
    Conceals thy mercy, reveals thy wrath: and again
The dew-bright hour that assuages the twilight brake
    Conceals thy wrath and reveals thy mercy: then
    Thou art fearful only for evil souls of men   110
That feel with nightfall the serpent within them wake,
    And hate the holy darkness on glade and glen.

Yea, then we know not and dream not if ill things be,
  Or if aught of the work of the wrong of the world
    be thine.
We hear not the footfall of terror that treads the sea,
  We hear not the moan of winds that assail the pine:
  We see not if shipwreck reign in the storm's dim
    shrine;
If death do service and doom bear witness to thee
  We see not,—know not if blood for thy lips be wine.

But in all things evil and fearful that fear may scan,   120
  As in all things good, as in all things fair that fall,
We know thee present and latent, the lord of man;
  In the murmuring of doves, in the clamouring of
    winds that call
  And wolves that howl for their prey; in the mid-
    night's pall,
In the naked and nymph-like feet of the dawn, O Pan,
  And in each life living, O thou the God who art all.

Smiling and singing, wailing and wringing of hands,
  Laughing and weeping, watching and sleeping, still
Proclaim but and prove but thee, as the shifted sands
  Speak forth and show but the strength of the sea's   130
    wild will
  The sifts and grinds them as grain in the storm-
    wind's mill.
In thee is the doom that falls and the doom that
    stands:
  The tempests utter thy word, and the stars fulfil.

Where Etna shudders with passion and pain volcanic
  That rend her heart as with anguish that rends a
    man's,
Where Typho labours, and finds not his thews Titanic,*

* Typho, last and largest of the monster sons of Earth, was buried
by Zeus under Mt. Etna.

In breathless torment that ever the flame's breath
    fans,
Men felt and feared thee of old, whose pastoral
    clans
Were given to the charge of thy keeping; and
    soundless panic
    Held fast the woodland whose depths and whose   140
    heights were Pan's.

And here, though fear be less than delight, and awe
    Be one with desire and with worship of earth and
    thee,
So mild seems now thy secret and speechless law,
    So fair and fearless and faithful and godlike she,
    So soft the spell of thy whisper on stream and sea,
Yet man should fear lest he see what of old men saw
    And withered: yet shall I quail if thy breath smite me.

Lord God of life and of light and of all things fair,
    Lord God of ravin and ruin and all things dim,
Death seals up life, and darkness the sunbright air,   150
    And the stars that watch blind earth in the deep
    night swim
    Laugh, saying, "What God is your God, that ye call
    on him?
What is man, that the God who is guide of our way
    should care
    If day for a man be golden, or night be grim?"

But thou, dost thou hear? Stars too but abide for a
    span,
    Gods too but endure for a season; but thou, if thou
    be
God, more than shadows conceived and adored of man,
    Kind Gods and fierce, that bound him or made him
    free,
    The skies that scorn us are less in thy sight than
    we,

Whose souls have strength to conceive and perceive   160
   thee, Pan,
  With sense more subtle than senses that hear and
    see.

Yet may not it say, though it seek thee and think to
   find
  One soul of sense in the fire and the frost-bound
    clod,
What heart is this, what spirit alive or blind,
   That moves thee: only we know that the ways we
    trod
  We tread, with hands unguided, with feet unshod,
With eyes unlightened; and yet, if with steadfast mind,
   Perchance may we find thee and know thee at last
    for God.

Yet then should God be dark as the dawn is bright,
   And bright as the night is dark on the world—no   170
    more.
Light slays not darkness, and darkness absorbs not
    light;
  And the labour of evil and good from the years of
    yore
  Is even as the labour of waves on a sunless shore.
And he who is first and last, who is depth and height,
   Keeps silence now, as the sun when the woods wax
    hoar.

The dark dumb godhead innate in the fair world's life
   Imbues the rapture of dawn and of noon with dread,
Infects the peace of the star-shod night with strife,
   Informs with terror the sorrow that guards the dead.
   No service of bended knee or of humbled head   180
May soothe or subdue the God who has change to wife:
   And life with death is as morning with evening wed.

And yet, if the light and the life in the light that here
   Seem soft and splendid and fervid as sleep may seem

Be more than the shine of a smile or the flash of a tear,
 Sleep, change, and death are less than a spell-struck
  dream,
 And fear than the fall of a leaf on a starlit stream.
And yet, if the hope that hath said it absorb not fear,
 What helps it man that the stars and the waters gleam?

What helps it man, that the noon be indeed intense,   190
 The night be indeed worth worship? Fear and pain
Were lords and masters yet of the secret sense,
 Which now dares deem not that light is as darkness,
  fain
 Though dark dreams be to declare it, crying in vain.
For whence, thou God of the light and the darkness,
  whence
 Dawns now this vision that bids not the sunbeams
  wane?

What light, what shadow, diviner than dawn or night,
 Draws near, makes pause, and again—or I dream—
  draws near?
More soft than shadow, more strong than the strong
  sun's light,
 More pure than moonbeams—yea, but the rays run   200
  sheer
 As fire from the sun through the dusk of the pinewood,
  clear
And constant; yea, but the shadow itself is bright
 That the light clothes round with love that is one
  with fear.

Above and behind it the noon and the woodland lie,
 Terrible, radiant with mystery, superb and subdued,
Triumphant in silence; and hardly the sacred sky
 Seems free from the tyrannous weight of the dumb
  fierce mood
 Which rules as with fire and invasion of beams that
  brood

The breathless rapture of earth till its hour pass by
    And leave her spirit released and her peace renewed.   210

I sleep not: never in sleep has a man beholden
    This. From the shadow that trembles and yearns with
        light
Suppressed and elate and reluctant—obscure and golden
    As water kindled with presage of dawn or night—
    A form, a face, a wonder to sense and sight,
Grows great as the moon through the month; and her
        eyes embolden
    Fear, till it change to desire, and desire to delight.

I sleep not: sleep would die of a dream so strange;
    A dream so sweet would die as a rainbow dies,
As a sunbow laughs and is lost on the waves that range   220
    And reck not of light that flickers or spray that flies.
    But the sun withdraws not, the woodland shrinks not
        or sighs,
No sweet thing sickens with sense or with fear of change;
    Light wounds not, darkness blinds not, my steadfast
        eyes.

Only the soul in my sense that receives the soul
    Whence now my spirit is kindled with breathless bliss
Knows well if the light that wounds it with love makes
        whole,
    If hopes that carol be louder than fears that hiss,
    If truth be spoken of flowers and of waves that kiss,
Of clouds and stars that contend for a sunbright goal.   230
    And yet may I dream that I dream not indeed of this?

An earth-born dreamer, constrained by the bonds of
        birth,
    Held fast by the flesh, compelled by his veins that beat
And kindle to rapture or wrath, to desire or to mirth,
    May hear not surely the fall of immortal feet,
    May feel not surely if heaven upon earth be sweet;

And here is my sense fulfilled of the joys of earth,
  Light, silence, bloom, shade, murmur of leaves that
      meet.

Bloom, fervour, and perfume of grasses and flowers aglow,
  Breathe and brighten about me: the darkness gleams,   240
The sweet light shivers and laughs on the slopes below,
  Made soft by leaves that lighten and change like
      dreams;
  The silence thrills with the whisper of secret streams
That well from the heart of the woodland: these I know:
  Earth bore them, heaven sustained them with showers
      and beams.

I lean my face to the heather, and drink the sun
  Whose flame-lit odour satiates the flowers: mine eyes
Close, and the goal of delight and of life is one:
  No more I crave of earth or her kindred skies.
  No more? But the joy that springs from them smiles   250
      and flies:
The sweet work wrought of them surely, the good work
      done,
  If the mind and the face of the season be loveless, dies.

Thee, therefore, thee would I come to, cleave to, cling,
  If haply thy heart be kind and thy gifts be good,
Unknown sweet spirit, whose vesture is soft in spring,
  In summer splendid, in autumn pale as the wood
  That shudders and wanes and shrinks as a shamed
      thing should,
In winter bright as the mail of a war-worn king
  Who stands where foes fled far from the face of him
      stood.

My spirit or thine is it, breath of thy life or of mine,   260
  Which fills my sense with a rapture that casts out
      fear?

Pan's dim frown wanes, and his wild eyes brighten as
      thine,
  Transformed as night or as day by the kindling year.
  Earth-born, or mine eye were withered that sees, mine
      ear
That hears were stricken to death by the sense divine,
  Earth-born I know thee: but heaven is about me here.

The terror that whispers in darkness and flames in light,
  The doubt that speaks in the silence of earth and sea,
The sense, more fearful at noon than in midmost night,
  Of wrath scarce hushed and of imminent ill to be,   270
  Where are they? Heaven is as earth, and as heaven
      to me
Earth: for the shadows that sundered them here take
      flight;
  And nought is all, as am I, but a dream of thee.

The Lake of Gaube

The sun is lord and god, sublime, serene,
  And sovereign on the mountains: earth and air
Lie prone in passion, blind with bliss unseen
  By force of sight and might of rapture, fair
  As dreams that die and know not what they were.
The lawns, the gorges, and the peaks, are one
Glad glory, thrilled with sense of unison
In strong compulsive silence of the sun.

Flowers dense and keen as midnight stars aflame
  And living things of light like flames in flower*   10
That glance and flash as though no hand might tame
  Lightnings whose life outshone their stormlit hour

---

    * Salamanders, fabled to live unharmed in fire; the lake itself is
set deep in the heart of the Pyrenees.

And played and laughed on earth, with all their power
Gone, and with all their joy of life made long
And harmless as the lightning life of song,
Shine sweet like stars when darkness feels them strong.

The deep mild purple flaked with moonbright gold
　　That makes the scales seem flowers of hardened light,
The flamelike tongue, the feet that noon leaves cold,
　　The kindly trust in man, when once the sight　　20
　　Grew less than strange, and faith bade fear take flight,
Outlive the little harmless life that shone
And gladdened eyes that loved it, and was gone
Ere love might fear that fear had looked thereon.

Fear held the bright thing hateful, even as fear,
　　Whose name is one with hate and horror, saith
That heaven, the dark deep heaven of water near,
　　Is deadly deep as hell and dark as death.
　　The rapturous plunge that quickens blood and breath
With pause more sweet than passion, ere they strive　　30
To raise again the limbs that yet would dive
Deeper, should there have slain the soul alive.

As the bright salamander in fire of the noonshine exults
　　　　and is glad of his day,
The spirit that quickens my body rejoices to pass from
　　　　the sunlight away,
To pass from the glow of the mountainous flowerage, the
　　　　high multitudinous bloom,
Far down through the fathomless night of the water, the
　　　　gladness of silence and gloom.
Death-dark and delicious as death in the dream of a lover
　　　　and dreamer may be,
It clasps and encompasses body and soul with delight to
　　　　be living and free:
Free utterly now, though the freedom endure but the
　　　　space of a perilous breath,

And living, though girdled about with the darkness and   40
    coldness and strangeness of death:

Each limb and each pulse of the body rejoicing, each
    nerve of the spirit at rest,
All sense of the soul's life rapture, a passionate peace
    in its blindness blest.
So plunges the downward swimmer, embraced of the
    water unfathomed of man,
The darkness unplummeted, icier than seas in mid-
    winter, for blessing or ban;
And swiftly and sweetly, when strength and breath fall
    short, and the dive is done,
Shoots up as a shaft from the dark depth shot, sped
    straight into sight of the sun;
And sheer through the snow-soft water, more dark than
    the roof of the pines above,
Strikes forth, and is glad as a bird whose flight is impelled
    and sustained of love.
As a sea-mew's love of the sea-wind breasted and ridden
    for rapture's sake
Is the love of his body and soul for the darkling delight   50
    of the soundless lake:
As the silent speed of a dream too living to live for a
    thought's space more
Is the flight of his limbs through the still strong chill of
    the darkness from shore to shore.
Might life be as this is and death be as life that casts off
    time as a robe,
The likeness of infinite heaven were a symbol revealed
    of the lake of Gaube.

    Whose thought has fathomed and measured
      The darkness of life and of death,
    The secret within them treasured,
      The spirit that is not breath?
    Whose vision has yet beholden
      The splendour of death and of life?   60

Though sunset as dawn be golden,
　　Is the word of them peace, not strife?
Deep silence answers: the glory
　　We dream of may be but a dream,
And the sun of the soul wax hoary
　　As ashes that show not a gleam.
But well shall it be with us ever
　　Who drive through the darkness here,
If the soul that we live by never,
　　For aught that a lie saith, fear.

70

Prose

Notes on Poems and Reviews*

It is by no wish of my own that I accept the task now proposed to me. To vindicate or defend myself from the assault or the charge of men whom, but for their attacks, I might never have heard of, is an office which I, or any writer who respects his work, cannot without reluctance stoop to undertake. As long as the attacks on my books—I have seen a few, I am told there are many—were confined within the usual limits of the anonymous press, I let them pass without the notice to which they appeared to aspire. Sincere or insincere, insolent or respectful, I let my assailants say out their say unheeded.

I have now undertaken to write a few words on this affair, not by way of apology or vindication, of answer or appeal. I have none such to offer. Much of the criticism I have seen is as usual, in the words of Shakespeare's greatest follower,

> As if a man should spit against the wind;
> The filth returns in's face.**

In recognition of his fair dealing with me in this matter, I am bound by my own sense of right to accede to the wish of my present publisher, and to the wishes of friends whose advice I value, that on his account, if not on mine, I should make some reply to the charges brought against me—as far as I understand them. The work is not fruitful of pleasure, of honour, or of profit; but, like other such tasks, it may be none the less useful and necessary. I am aware that it cannot be accomplished with-

* Published in 1866 in answer to the violent attacks upon *Poems and Ballads,* First Series, and upon Swinburne himself as "the libidinous laureate of a pack of satyrs."

** John Webster, *The White Devil,* Act III, Scene 2, lines 149–50.

out some show of egotism; and I am perforce prepared to incur
the consequent charge of arrogance. The office of commentator
of my own works has been forced upon me by circumstances
connected with the issue and re-issue of my last book. I am
compelled to look sharply into it, and inquire what passage,
what allusion, or what phrase can have drawn down such sudden thunder from the serene heavens of public virtue. A mere
libeller I have no wish to encounter; I leave it to saints to fight
with beasts at Ephesus or nearer. 'For in these strifes, and on
such persons, it were as wretched to affect a victory, as it is unhappy to be committed with them.' *

Certain poems of mine, it appears, have been impugned by
judges, with or without a name, as indecent or as blasphemous.
To me, as I have intimated, their verdict is a matter of infinite
indifference: it is of equally small moment to me whether in
such eyes as theirs I appear moral or immoral, Christian or
pagan. But, remembering that science must not scorn to in-
vestigate animalcules and infusoria, I am ready for once to play
the anatomist.

With regard to any opinion implied or expressed throughout
my book, I desire that one thing should be remembered: the
book is dramatic, many-faced, multifarious; and no utterance of
enjoyment or despair, belief or unbelief, can properly be assumed as the assertion of its author's personal feeling or faith.
Were each poem to be accepted as the deliberate outcome and
result of the writer's conviction, not mine alone but most other
men's verses would leave nothing behind them but a sense of
cloudy chaos and suicidal contradiction. Byron and Shelley,
speaking in their own persons, and with what sublime effect we
know, openly and insultingly mocked and reviled what the
English of their day held most sacred. I have not done this. I
do not say that, if I chose, I would not do so to the best of my
power; I do say that hitherto I have seen fit to do nothing of
the kind.

It remains then to inquire what in that book can be reason-
ably offensive to the English reader. In order to resolve this
problem, I will not fish up any of the ephemeral scurrilities born

* Ben Jonson, Epilogue "To the Reader," *The Poetaster*.

only to sting if they can, and sink as they must. I will take the one article that lies before me; the work (I admit) of an enemy, but the work (I acknowledge) of a gentleman. I cannot accept it as accurate; but I readily and gladly allow that it neither contains nor suggests anything false or filthy. To him therefore, rather than to another, I address my reclamation. Two among my poems, it appears, are in his opinion 'especially horrible.' Good. Though the phrase be somewhat 'inexpressive,' I am content to meet him on this ground. It is something —nay, it is much—to find an antagonist who has sufficient sense of honesty and honour to mark out the lists in which he, the challenger, is desirous to encounter the challenged.

The first, it appears, of these especially horrible poems is 'Anactoria.' I am informed, and have not cared to verify the assertion, that this poem has excited, among the chaste and candid critics of the day or hour or minute, a more vehement reprobation, a more virtuous horror, a more passionate appeal, than any other of my writing. Proud and glad as I must be of this distinction, I must yet, however reluctantly, inquire what merit or demerit has incurred such unexpected honour. I was not ambitious of it; I am not ashamed of it; but I am overcome by it. I have never lusted after the praise of reviewers; I have never feared their abuse; but I would fain know why the vultures should gather here of all places; what congenial carrion they smell, who can discern such (it is alleged) in any rosebed. And after a little reflection I do know, or conjecture. Virtue, as she appears incarnate in British journalism and voluble through that unsavoury organ, is something of a compound creature:

> A lump neither alive nor dead,
> Dog-headed, bosom-eyed, and bird-footed;*

nor have any dragon's jaws been known to emit or occasion stronger and stranger sounds and odours. But having, not without astonishment and disgust, inhaled these odours, I find myself at last able to analyse their component parts. What my poem means, if any reader should want that explained, I am ready to explain, though perplexed by the hint that explanation

---

* Shelley, *The Witch of Atlas*, XI, 7–8.

may be required. What certain reviewers have imagined it to imply, I am incompetent to explain, and unwilling to imagine. I am evidently not virtuous enough to understand them. I thank Heaven that I am not. *Ma corruption rougirait de leur pudeur.* I have not studied in those schools whence that full-fledged phœnix, the 'virtue' of professional pressmen, rises chuckling and crowing from the dunghill, its birthplace and its deathbed. But there are birds of alien feather, if not of higher flight; and these I would now recall into no hencoop or preserve of mine, but into the open and general field where all may find pasture and sunshine and fresh air; into places whither the prurient prudery and the virulent virtue of pressmen and prostitutes cannot follow; into an atmosphere where calumny cannot speak, and fatuity cannot breathe; in a word, where backbiters and imbeciles become impossible. I neither hope nor wish to change the unchangeable, to purify the impure. To conciliate them, to vindicate myself in their eyes, is a task which I should not condescend to attempt, even were I sure to accomplish.

In this poem I have simply expressed, or tried to express, that violence of affection between one and another which hardens into rage and deepens into despair. The keynote which I have here touched was struck long since by Sappho. We in England are taught, are compelled under penalties to learn, to construe, and to repeat, as schoolboys, the imperishable and incomparable verses of that supreme poet; and I at least am grateful for the training. I have wished, and I have even ventured to hope, that I might be in time competent to translate into a baser and later language the divine words which even as a boy I could not but recognise as divine. That hope, if indeed I dared ever entertain such a hope, I soon found fallacious. To translate the two odes and the remaining fragments of Sappho is the one impossible task; and as witness of this I will call up one of the greatest among poets. Catullus 'translated'—or as his countrymen would now say 'traduced'—the 'Ode to Anactoria'—a more beautiful translation there never was and will never be; but compared with the Greek, it is colourless and bloodless, puffed out by additions and enfeebled by alterations. Let any one set against

---

* My depravity blushes at their modesty.

each other the two first stanzas, Latin and Greek, and pronounce. (This would be too much to ask of all of my critics; but some among the journalists of England may be capable of achieving the not exorbitant task.) Where Catullus failed I could not hope to succeed; I tried instead to reproduce in a diluted and dilated form the spirit of a poem which could not be reproduced in the body.

Now the 'Ode to Anactoria' (as it is named by tradition)—the poem which English boys have to get by heart—the poem (and this is more important) which has in the whole world of verse no companion and no rival but the 'Ode to Aphrodite,' has been twice at least translated or 'traduced.' I am not aware that Mr. Ambrose Phillips, or M. Nicolas Boileau–Despréaux, was ever impeached before any jury of moralists for his sufficiently grievous offence. By any jury of poets both would assuredly have been convicted. Now, what they did I have not done. To the best (and bad is the best) of their ability, they have 'done into' bad French and bad English the very words of Sappho. Feeling that although I might do it better I could not do it well, I abandoned the idea of translation.

I tried, then, to write some paraphrase of the fragment which the Fates and the Christians have spared us. I have not said, as Boileau and Phillips have, that the speaker sweats and swoons at sight of her favourite by the side of a man. I have abstained from touching on such details, for this reason: that I felt myself incompetent to give adequate expression in English to the literal and absolute words of Sappho; and would not debase and degrade them into a viler form. No one can feel more deeply than I do the inadequacy of my work. 'That is not Sappho,' a friend said once to me. I could only reply, 'It is as near as I can come; and no man can come close to her.' Her remaining verses are the supreme success, the final achievement, of the poetic art.

But this, it may be, is not to the point. I will try to draw thither; though the descent is immeasurable from Sappho's verse to mine, or to any man's. I have striven to cast my spirit into the mould of hers, to express and represent not the poem but the poet. I did not think it requisite to disfigure the page with a footnote wherever I had fallen back upon the original text. Here and there, I need not say, I have rendered into English the very words of Sappho. I have tried also to work into words of my own some expression of their effect: to bear witness how, more than any other's, her verses strike and sting the memory in lonely places, or at sea, among all loftier sights and sounds— how they seem akin to fire and air, being themselves 'all air and fire'; other element there is none in them. As to the angry appeal against the supreme mystery of oppressive heaven, which I have ventured to put into her mouth at that point only where pleasure culminates in pain, affection in anger, and desire in despair—as to the 'blasphemies' * against God or Gods of which here and elsewhere I stand accused—they are to be taken as the first outcome or outburst of foiled and fruitless passion recoiling on itself. After this, the spirit finds time to breathe and repose above all vexed senses of the weary body, all bitter labours of the revolted soul; the poet's pride of place is resumed, the lofty conscience of invincible immortality in the memories and the mouths of men.

What is there now of horrible in this? the expressions of fierce fondness, the ardours of passionate despair? Are these so unnatural as to affright or disgust? Where is there an unclean detail? where an obscene allusion? A writer as impure as my critics might of course have written, on this or on any subject, an impure poem; I have not. And if to translate or paraphrase Sappho be an offence, indict the heavier offenders who have handled and rehandled this matter in their wretched versions of

* As I shall not return to this charge of 'blasphemy,' I will here cite a notable instance of what does seem permissible in that line to the English reader. (I need not say that I do not question the right, which hypocrisy and servility would deny, of author and publisher to express and produce what they please. I do not deprecate, but demand for all men freedom to speak and freedom to hear. It is the line of demarcation which admits, if offence there be, the greater offender and rejects the less—it is this that I do not understand.) After many alternate curses and denials of God, a great poet talks of Christ 'veiling his horrible Godhead,' of his 'malignant soul,' his 'godlike malice.' Shelley outlived all this and much more; but Shelley wrote all this and much more. Will no Society for the Suppression of Common Sense, no Committee for the Propagation of Cant, see to it a little? or have they not already tried their hands at it and broken down? For the poem which contains the words above quoted continues at this day to bring credit to its publishers, Messrs. Moxon and Co. [Swinburne's note.]

the ode. Is my poem more passionate in detail, more unmistakable in subject? I affirm that it is less; and what I affirm I have proved.

Next on the list of accusation stands the poem of Dolores. The gist and bearing of this I should have thought evident enough, viewed by the light of others which precede and follow it. I have striven here to express that transient state of spirit through which a man may be supposed to pass, foiled in love and weary of loving, but not yet in sight of rest; seeking refuge in those 'violent delights' which 'have violent ends,' * in fierce and frank sensualities which at least profess to be no more than they are. This poem, like *Faustine*, is so distinctly symbolic and fanciful that it cannot justly be amenable to judgment as a study in the school of realism. The spirit, bowed and discoloured by suffering and by passion (which are indeed the same thing and the same word), plays for awhile with its pleasures and its pains, mixes and distorts them with a sense half-humorous and half-mournful, exults in bitter and doubtful emotions:

Moods of fantastic sadness, nothing worth.**

It sports with sorrow, and jests against itself; cries out for freedom and confesses the chain; decorates with the name of goddess, crowns anew as the mystical Cotytto, some woman, real or ideal, in whom the pride of life with its companion lusts is incarnate. In her lover's half-shut eyes, her fierce unchaste beauty is transfigured, her cruel sensual eyes have a meaning and a message; there are memories and secrets in the kisses of her lips. She is the darker Venus, fed with burnt-offering and blood-sacrifice; the veiled image of that pleasure which men impelled by satiety and perverted by power have sought through ways as strange as Nero's before and since his time; the daughter of lust and death, and holding of both her parents; Our Lady of Pain, antagonist alike of trivial sins and virtues; no Virgin, and unblessed of men; no mother of the Gods or God; no Cybele, served by sexless priests or monks, adored of Origen or Atys; no likeness of her in Dindymus or Loreto.

* *Romeo and Juliet*, Act II, Scene 6, line 9.
** Matthew Arnold, "To a Gypsy Child by the Seashore."

The next act in this lyrical monodrama of passion represents a new stage and scene. The worship of desire has ceased; the mad commotion of sense has stormed itself out; the spirit, clear of the old regret that drove it upon such violent ways for a respite, healed of the fever that wasted it in the search for relief among fierce fancies and tempestuous pleasures, dreams now of truth discovered and repose attained. Not the martyr's ardour of selfless love, an unprofitable flame that burnt out and did no service—not the rapid rage of pleasure that seemed for a little to make the flesh divine, to clothe the naked senses with the fiery raiment of faith; but a stingless love, an innocuous desire. 'Hesperia,' the tenderest type of woman or of dream, born in the westward 'islands of the blest,' where the shadows of all happy and holy things live beyond the sunset a sacred and a sleepless life, dawns upon his eyes a western dawn, risen as the fiery day of passion goes down, and risen where it sank. Here, between moonrise and sunset, lives the love that is gentle and faithful, neither giving too much nor asking—a bride rather than a mistress, a sister rather than a bride. But not at once, or not for ever, can the past be killed and buried; hither also the huntress follows her flying prey, wounded and weakened, still fresh from the fangs of passion; the cruel hands, the amorous eyes, still glitter and allure. *Qui a bu boira**: the feet are drawn back towards the ancient ways. Only by lifelong flight, side by side with the goddess that redeems, shall her slave of old escape from the goddess that consumes: if even thus one may be saved, even thus distance the bloodhounds.

This is the myth or fable of my poem; and it is not without design that I have slipped in, between the first and the second part, the verses called *The Garden of Proserpine,* expressive, as I meant they should be, of that brief total pause of passion and of thought, when the spirit, without fear or hope of good things or evil, hungers and thirsts only after the perfect sleep. Now, what there is in all this unfit to be written—what there is here indecent in manner or repulsive in matter—I at least do not yet see; and before I can see it, my eyes must be purged with the euphrasy and rue which keep clear the purer eyes of

* He who has drunk will drink.

professional virtue. The insight into evil of chaste and critical
pressmen, their sharp scent for possible or impossible impurities,
their delicate ear for a sound or a whisper of wrong—all this
knowledge 'is too wonderful and excellent for me; I cannot
attain unto it.' * In one thing, indeed, it seems I have erred: I
have forgotten to prefix to my work the timely warning of a
great poet and humorist**:

> J'en préviens les mères des familles,
> Ce que j'écris n'est pas pour les petites filles
> Dont on coupe le pain en tartines; mes vers
> Sont des vers de jeune homme.

I have overlooked the evidence which every day makes clearer,
that our time has room only for such as are content to write
for children and girls. But this oversight is the sum of my
offence.

It would seem indeed as though to publish a book were
equivalent to thrusting it with violence into the hands of every
mother and nurse in the kingdom as fit and necessary food for
female infancy. Happily there is no fear that the supply of milk
for babes will fall short of the demand for some time yet. There
are moral milkmen enough, in all conscience, crying their ware
about the streets and byways; fresh or stale, sour or sweet, the
requisite fluid runs from a sufficiently copious issue. In due time,
perhaps, the critical doctors may prescribe a stronger diet for
their hypochondriac patient, the reading world; or the gigantic
malade imaginaire called the public may rebel against the
weekly draught or the daily drug of MM. Purgon and Diafoirus.
We, meanwhile, who profess to deal neither in poison nor in
pap, may not unwillingly stand aside. Let those read who will,
and let those who will abstain from reading. *Caveat emptor.* No
one wishes to force men's food down the throats of babes and
sucklings. The verses last analysed were assuredly written with
no moral or immoral design; but the upshot seems to me moral
rather than immoral, if it must needs be one or the other, and

---

* *Psalms* 139:6.
** Gautier's warning to mothers that he does not write for little girls
but for young men.

if (which I cannot be sure of) I construe aright those somewhat misty and changeable terms.

These poems thus disposed of are (I am told) those which have given most offence and scandal to the venal virtue of journalism. As I have not to review my reviewers, I need not be at pains to refute at length every wilful error or unconscious lie which a workman that way inclined might drag into light. To me, as to all others who may read what I write, the whole matter must continue to seem too pitiable and trivial to waste a word or thought on it which we can help wasting. But having begun this task, I will add yet a word or two of annotation. I have heard that even the little poem of 'Faustine' has been to some readers a thing to make the scalp creep and the blood freeze. It was issued with no such intent. Nor do I remember that any man's voice or heel was lifted against it when it first appeared, a new-born and virgin poem, in the *Spectator* newspaper for 1862. Virtue, it would seem, has shot up surprisingly in the space of four years or less—a rank and rapid growth, barren of blossom and rotten at root. 'Faustine' is the reverie of a man gazing on the bitter and vicious loveliness of a face as common and as cheap as the morality of reviewers, and dreaming of past lives in which this fair face may have held a nobler or fitter station; the imperial profile may have been Faustina's, the thirsty lips a Mænad's, when first she learnt to drink blood or wine, to waste the loves and ruin the lives of men; through Greece and again through Rome she may have passed with the same face which now comes before us dishonoured and discrowned. Whatever of merit or demerit there may be in the verses, the idea that gives them such life as they have is simple enough: the transmigration of a single soul, doomed as though by accident from the first to all evil and no good, through many ages and forms, but clad always in the same type of fleshly beauty. The chance which suggested to me this poem was one which may happen any day to any man—the sudden sight of a living face which recalled the well-known likeness of another dead for centuries: in this instance, the noble and faultless type of the elder Faustina, as seen in coin and bust.

Out of that casual glimpse and sudden recollection these verses sprang and grew.

Of the poem [*Laus Veneris*] in which I have attempted once more to embody the legend of Venus and her knight, I need say only that my first aim was to rehandle the old story in a new fashion. To me it seemed that the tragedy began with the knight's return to Venus—began at the point where hitherto it had seemed to leave off. The immortal agony of a man lost after all repentance—cast down from fearful hope into fearless despair —believing in Christ and bound to Venus—desirous of penitential pain, and damned to joyless pleasure—this, in my eyes, was the kernel and nucleus of a myth comparable only to that of the foolish virgins and bearing the same burden. The tragic touch of the story is this: that the knight who has renounced Christ believes in him; the lover who has embraced Venus disbelieves in her. Vainly and in despair would he make the best of that which is the worst—vainly remonstrate with God, and argue on the side he would fain desert. Once accept or admit the least admixture of pagan worship, or of modern thought, and the whole story collapses into froth and smoke. It was not till my poem was completed that I received from the hands of its author the admirable pamphlet of Charles Baudelaire on Wagner's *Tannhäuser*. If any one desires to see, expressed in better words than I can command, the conception of the mediæval Venus which it was my aim to put into verse, let him turn to the magnificent passage in which M. Baudelaire describes the fallen goddess, grown diabolic among ages that would not accept her as divine. In another point, as I then found, I concur with the great musician and his great panegyrist. I have made Venus the one love of her knight's whole life, as Mary Stuart of Chastelard's; I have sent him, poet and soldier, fresh to her fierce embrace. Thus only both legend and symbol appear to me noble and significant. Light loves and harmless errors must not touch the elect of heaven or of hell. Th queen of evil, the lady of lust, will endure no rival but God; and when the vicar of God rejects him, to her only can he return to abide the day of judgment in weariness and sorrow and fear.

These poems do not seem to me condemnable, unless it be on the ground of bad verse; and to any charge of that kind I should of course be as unable as reluctant to reply. But I certainly was even less prepared to hear the batteries of virtue open fire in another quarter. Sculpture I knew was a dead art, buried centuries deep out of sight, with no angel keeping watch over the sepulchre; its very grave-clothes divided by wrangling and impotent sectaries, and no chance anywhere visible of a resurrection. I knew that belief in the body was the secret of sculpture, and that a past age of ascetics could no more attempt or attain it than the present age of hypocrites; I knew that modern moralities and recent religions were, if possible, more averse and alien to this purely physical and pagan art than to the others; but how far averse I did not know. There is nothing lovelier, as there is nothing more famous, in later Hellenic art, than the statue of Hermaphroditus. No one would compare it with the greatest works of Greek sculpture. No one would lift Keats on a level with Shakespeare. But the Fates have allowed us to possess at once Othello and Hyperion, Theseus and Hermaphroditus. At Paris, at Florence, at Naples, the delicate divinity of this work has always drawn towards it the eyes of artists and poets.*
A creature at once foul and dull enough to extract from a sight so lovely, from a thing so noble, the faintest, the most fleeting idea of impurity, must be, and must remain, below comprehension and below remark. It is incredible that the meanest of men

* Witness Shelley's version:

> A sexless thing it was, and in its growth
> It seemed to have developed no defect
> Of either sex, yet all the grace of both;
> In gentleness and strength its limbs were decked;
> The bosom lightly swelled with its full youth,
> The countenance was such as might select
> Some artist, that his skill should never die,
> Imaging forth such perfect purity.
> *Witch of Atlas*, st. xxxvi.

But Shelley had not studied purity in the school of reviewers. It is well for us that we have teachers able to enlighten our darkness, or Heaven knows into what error such as he, or such as I, might not fall. We might even, in time, come to think it possible to enjoy the naked beauty of a statue or a picture without any virtuous vision behind it of a filthy fancy; which would be immoral. [Swinburne's note.]

should derive from it any other than the sense of high and grateful pleasure. Odour and colour and music are not more tender or more pure. How favourite and frequent a vision among the Greeks was this of the union of sexes in one body of perfect beauty, none need be told. In Plato the legend has fallen into a form coarse, hard, and absurd. The theory of God splitting in two the double archetype of man and woman, the original hermaphrodite which had to get itself bisected into female and male, is repulsive and ridiculous enough. But the idea thus incarnate, literal or symbolic, is merely beautiful. I am not the first who has translated into written verse this sculptured poem: another before me, as he says, has more than once 'caressed it with a sculptor's love.' It is, indeed, among statues as a lyric among tragedies; it stands below the Niobe as Simonides below Æschylus, as Correggio beneath Titian. The sad and subtle moral of this myth, which I have desired to indicate in verse, is that perfection once attained on all sides is a thing thenceforward barren of use or fruit; whereas the divided beauty of separate woman and man—a thing inferior and imperfect— can serve all turns of life. Ideal beauty, like ideal genius, dwells apart, as though by compulsion; supremacy is solitude. But leaving this symbolic side of the matter, I cannot see why this statue should not be the text for yet another poem. Treated in the grave and chaste manner as a serious 'thing of beauty,' to be for ever applauded and enjoyed, it can give no offence but to the purblind and the prurient. For neither of these classes have I ever written or will I ever write. 'Loathsome and abominable' and full of 'unspeakable foulnesses' must be that man's mind who could here discern evil; unclean and inhuman the animal which could suck from this mystical rose of ancient loveliness the foul and rancid juices of an obscene fancy. It were a scavenger's office to descend with torch or spade into such depths of mental sewerage, to plunge or peer into subterranean sloughs of mind impossible alike to enlighten or to cleanse.

I have now gone over the poems which, as I hear, have incurred most blame; whether deservedly or not, I have shown. For the terms in which certain critics have clothed their sentiments I bear them no ill-will: they are welcome for me to write unmolested, as long as they keep to simple ribaldry. I hope it gives them amusement; I presume it brings them profit; I know it does not affect me. Absolute falsehood may, if it be worth while, draw down contradiction and disproof; but the mere calling of bad names is a child's trick, for which the small fry of the press should have a child's correction at the hands of able editors; standing as these gentlemen ought to do in a parental or pedagogic relation to their tender charges. They have, by all I see and hear, been sufficiently scurrilous—one or two in particular:

> However, from one crime they are exempt;
> They do not strike a brother, striking *me*.*

I will only throw them one crumb of advice in return; I fear the alms will be of no avail, but it shall not be withheld:

> Why grudge them lotus-leaf and laurel,
>   O toothless mouth or swinish maw,
> Who never grudged you bells and coral,
>   Who never grudged you troughs and straw?
>
> Lie still in kennel, sleek in stable,
>   Good creatures of the stall or sty;
> Shove snouts for crumbs below the table;
>   Lie still; and rise not up to lie.

To all this, however, there is a grave side. The question at issue is wider than any between a single writer and his critics, or it might well be allowed to drop. It is this: whether or not the first and last requisite of art is to give no offence; whether or not all that cannot be lisped in the nursery or fingered in the schoolroom is therefore to be cast out of the library; whether or not the domestic circle is to be for all men and writers the outer limit and extreme horizon of their world of work. For to this we have come; and all students of art must face the matter as it stands. Who has not heard it asked, in a final and triumphant tone, whether this book or that can be read aloud by her mother

---

* Landor, *Appendix to the Hellenics*. The two doggerel stanzas that follow are by Swinburne.

to a young girl? whether such and such a picture can properly be exposed to the eyes of young persons? If you reply that this is nothing to the point, you fall at once into the ranks of the immoral. Never till now, and nowhere but in England, could so monstrous an absurdity rear for one moment its deformed and eyeless head. In no past century were artists ever bidden to work on these terms; nor are they now, except among us. The disease, of course, afflicts the meanest members of the body with most virulence. Nowhere is cant at once so foul-mouthed and so tight-laced as in the penny, twopenny, threepenny, or sixpenny press. Nothing is so favourable to the undergrowth of real indecency as this overshadowing foliage of fictions, this artificial network of proprieties. *L'Arioste rit au soleil, l'Arétin ricane à l'ombre.** The whiter the sepulchre without, the ranker the rottenness within. Every touch of plaster is a sign of advancing decay. The virtue of our critical journals is a dowager of somewhat dubious antecedents: every day that thins and shrivels her cheek thickens and hardens the paint on it; she consumes more chalk and ceruse than would serve a whole courtful of crones. 'It is to be presumed,' certainly, that in her case 'all is not sweet, all is not sound.' ** The taint on her fly-blown reputation is hard to overcome by patches and perfumery. Literature, to be worthy of men, must be large, liberal, sincere; and cannot be chaste if it be prudish. Purity and prudery cannot keep house together. Where free speech and fair play are interdicted, foul hints and evil suggestions are hatched into fetid life. And if literature indeed is not to deal with the full life of man and the whole nature of things, let it be cast aside with the rods and rattles of childhood. Whether it affect to teach or to amuse, it is equally trivial and contemptible to us; only less so than the charge of immorality. Against how few really great names has not this small and dirt-encrusted pebble been thrown! A reputation seems imperfect without this tribute also: one jewel is wanting to the crown. It is good to be praised by those whom all men should

---

* Ariosto laughs in the sun, Aretino (author of lascivious sonnets as well as a book about Christ) sneers in the shade.
   ** From the song "Still to be neat, still to be drest," in Ben Jonson's *Epicoene*.

praise; it is better to be reviled by those whom all men should scorn.

Various chances and causes must have combined to produce a state of faith or feeling which would turn all art and literature 'into the line of children.' One among others may be this: where the heaven of invention holds many stars at once, there is no fear that the highest and largest will either efface or draw aside into its orbit all lesser lights. Each of these takes its own way and sheds its proper lustre. But where one alone is dominant in heaven, it is encircled by a pale procession of satellite moons, filled with shallow and stolen radiance. Thus, with English versifiers now, the idyllic form is alone in fashion. The one great and prosperous poet of the time has given out the tune, and the hoarser choir takes it up. His highest lyrical work remains unimitated, being in the main inimitable. But the trick of tone which suits an idyl is easier to assume; and the note has been struck so often that the shrillest songsters can affect to catch it up. We have idyls good and bad, ugly and pretty; idyls of the farm and the mill; idyls of the dining-room and the deanery; idyls of the gutter and the gibbet. If the Muse of the minute will not feast with 'gig-men' * and their wives, she must mourn with costermongers and their trulls. I fear the more ancient Muses are guests at neither house of mourning nor house of feasting.

For myself, I begrudge no man his taste or his success; I can enjoy and applaud all good work, and would always, when possible, have the workman paid in full. There is much excellent and some admirable verse among the poems of the day: to none has it given more pleasure than to me, and from none, had I been a man of letters to whom the ways were open, would it have won heartier applause. I have never been able to see what should attract men to the profession of criticism but the noble pleasure of praising. But I have no right to claim a place in the silver flock of idyllic swans. I have never worked for praise or pay, but simply by impulse, and to please myself; I must therefore, it is to be feared, remain where I am, shut out from the

---

* Philistines, whose respectability is measured by their keeping a gig.

communion of these. At all events, I shall not be hounded into emulation of other men's work by the baying of unleashed beagles. There are those with whom I do not wish to share the praise of their praisers. I am content to abide a far different judgment:

> I write as others wrote
> On Sunium's height.*

I need not be over-careful to justify my ways in other men's eyes; it is enough for me that they also work after their kind, and earn the suffrage, as they labour after the law, of their own people. The idyllic form is best for domestic and pastoral poetry. It is naturally on a lower level than that of tragic or lyric verse. Its gentle and maidenly lips are somewhat narrow for the stream and somewhat cold for the fire of song. It is very fit for the sole diet of girls; not very fit for the sole sustenance of men.

When England has again such a school of poetry, so headed and so followed, as she has had at least twice before, or as France has now; when all higher forms of the various art are included within the larger limits of a stronger race; then, if such a day should ever rise or return upon us, it will be once more remembered that the office of adult art is neither puerile nor feminine, but virile; that its purity is not that of the cloister or the harem; that all things are good in its sight, out of which good work may be produced. Then the press will be as impotent as the pulpit to dictate the laws and remove the landmarks of art; and those will be laughed at who demand from one thing the qualities of another—who seek for sermons in sonnets and morality in music. Then all accepted work will be noble and chaste in the wider masculine sense, not truncated and curtailed, but outspoken and fullgrown; art will be pure by instinct and fruitful by nature, no clipped and forced growth of unhealthy heat and unnatural air; all baseness and all triviality will fall off from it, and be forgotten; and no one will then need to assert, in defence of work done for the work's sake, the simple laws of his art which no one will then be permitted to impugn.

* Landor, "Poems on Books and Writers."

Byron*

The most delicate and thoughtful of English critics has charged the present generation of Englishmen with forgetfulness of Byron. It is not a light charge: and it is not ungrounded. Men born when this century was getting into its forties were baptized into another church than his with the rites of another creed. Upon their ears, first after the cadences of elder poets, fell the faultless and fervent melodies of Tennyson. To them, chief among the past heroes of the younger century, three men appeared as predominant in poetry; Coleridge, Keats, and Shelley. Behind these were effaced, on either hand, the two great opposing figures of Byron and Wordsworth. No man under twenty can just now be expected to appreciate these. The time was when all boys and girls who paddled in rhyme and dabbled in sentiment were wont to adore the presence or the memory of Byron with foolish faces of praise. It is of little moment to him or to us that they have long since ceased to cackle and begun to hiss. They have become used to better verse and carefuller workmen; and must be forgiven if after such training they cannot at once appreciate the splendid and imperishable excellence which covers all his offences and outweighs all his defects: the excellence of sincerity and strength. Without these no poet can live; but few have ever had so much of them as Byron. His sincerity indeed is difficult to discover and define; but it does in effect lie at the root of all his good works:

* First published in 1866 as the preface to Swinburne's selection of Byron's poems. The English critic of the opening line is very likely Matthew Arnold, who had written in his essay on Heine, "Look at Byron, that Byron whom the present generation of Englishmen are forgetting."

deformed by pretension and defaced by assumption, masked by folly and veiled by affectation; but perceptible after all, and priceless.

It is no part of my present office to rewrite the history of a life in which every date and event that could be given would now seem trite and stale to all possible readers. If, after so many promises and hints, something at once new and true shall at length be unearthed or extricated, which may affect for the better or the worse our judgment of the man, it will be possible and necessary to rewrite it. Meantime this among other chances 'lies on the lap of the gods'; and especially on the lap of a goddess who still treads our earth. Until she speaks, we cannot guess what she may have to say; and can only pass by with reverent or with sceptical reticence.*

Thus much however we may safely assert: that no man's work was ever more influenced by his character; and that no man's character was ever more influenced by his circumstances. Rather from things without than from things within him did the spirit of Byron assume colour and shape. His noblest verse leapt on a sudden into life after the heaviest evils had fallen

---

* It will be evident that these lines were written before the appearance of the book in which Madame de Boissy [formerly, Countess Teresa Guiccioli, Byron's mistress from 1819 until his death] thought fit to let the world know that she had nothing to tell worth its hearing with regard to the man whose love had made her famous, but was not the less willing to put forth that nothing in two leaden volumes of verbiage. The worst consequence of this miscarriage was not the collapse of such faint hopes or surmises as we might yet have cherished of some benefit to be received in the way of biography, some new and kindly light to be thrown on the life and character of Byron; it was the opportunity given to a filthy female moralist and novelist [Harriet Beecher Stowe, whose lectures in England were partisan to Lady Byron and helped to fan the rumors of an incestuous relationship between Byron and his half-sister Augusta] who was not slow to avail herself of such an occasion 'to expound her beastly mind to all.' Evidently the laurels of Mrs. [Aphra] Behn [1640–89] had long kept her successor from sleeping; it was not enough to have copied the authoress of *Oroonoko* in the selection of a sable and a servile hero; her American imitator was bent on following her down fouler ways than this. But I feel that an apology is due to the virtuous memory of the chaste Aphra; she was indeed the first 'nigger novelist,' and she was likewise a vendor and purveyor of obscene fiction; but here the parallel ends; for I am not aware that she ever applied her unquestionable abilities in that unlovely line of business to the defamation at second hand of the illustrious and defenceless dead. [Swinburne's note.]

upon him which even he ever underwent. From the beginning indeed he had much to fight against; and three impediments hung about him at starting, the least of which would have weighed down a less strong man: youth, and genius, and an ancient name.* In spite of all three he made his way; and suffered for it. At the first chance given or taken, every obscure and obscene thing that lurks for pay or prey among the fouler shallows and thickets of literature flew against him; every hound and every hireling lavished upon him the loathsome tribute of their abuse; all nameless creatures that nibble and prowl, upon whom the serpent's curse has fallen, to go upon his belly and eat dust all the days of his life, assailed him with their foulest venom and their keenest fangs. And the promise given of old to their kind was now at least fulfilled: they did bruise his heel. But the heads of such creatures are so small that it is hard to bruise them in return; it would first be necessary to discern them.

That Byron was able to disregard and to outlive the bark and the bite of such curs as these is small praise enough: the man who cannot do as much is destructible, and therefore contemptible. He did far more than this; he withstood the weight of circumstances to the end; not always without complaint, but always without misgiving. His glorious courage, his excellent contempt for things contemptible, and hatred of hateful men, are enough of themselves to embalm and endear his memory in the eyes of all who are worthy to pass judgment upon him. And these qualities gave much of their own value to verse not otherwise or not always praiseworthy. Even at its best, the serious poetry of Byron is often so rough and loose, so weak in the screws and joints which hold together the framework of verse, that it is not easy to praise it enough without seeming to condone or to extenuate such faults as should not be overlooked or

---

* That his youth and his rank were flung in his face with vulgar insolence on the publication of his first little book it can hardly be necessary to remind any reader of Byron: but possibly even these offences might have been condoned in a scribbler whose work had given no offensive promise of greatness yet to be. In the verses on Lochnagar at least an ominous threat or presage of something new and splendid must have been but too perceptible to the discerning eye of criticism. [Swinburne's note.]

forgiven. No poet is so badly represented by a book of selections. It must show something of his weakness; it cannot show all of his strength. Often, after a noble overture, the last note struck is either dissonant or ineffectual. His magnificent masterpiece, which must endure for ever among the precious relics of the world, will not bear dissection or extraction. The merit of 'Don Juan' does not lie in any part, but in the whole. There is in that great poem an especial and exquisite balance and sustenance of alternate tones which cannot be expressed or explained by the utmost ingenuity of selection. Haidée is supplanted by Dudù, the shipwreck by the siege, the Russian court by the English household; and this perpetual change, this tidal variety of experience and emotion, gives to the poem something of the breadth and freshness of the sea. Much of the poet's earlier work is or seems unconsciously dishonest; this, if not always or wholly unaffected, is as honest as the sunlight, as frank as the sea-wind. Here, and here alone, the student of his work may recognise and enjoy the ebb and flow of actual life. Here the pulse of vital blood may be felt in tangible flesh. Here for the first time the style of Byron is beyond all praise or blame: a style at once swift and supple, light and strong, various and radiant. Between 'Childe Harold' and 'Don Juan' the same difference exists which a swimmer feels between lake-water and sea-water: the one is fluent, yielding, invariable; the other has in it a life and pulse, a sting and a swell, which touch and excite the nerves like fire or like music. Across the stanzas of 'Don Juan' we swim forward as over 'the broad backs of the sea'; they break and glitter, hiss and laugh, murmur and move, like waves that sound or that subside. There is in them a delicious resistance, an elastic motion, which salt water has and fresh water has not. There is about them a wide wholesome air, full of vivid light and constant wind, which is only felt at sea. Life undulates and death palpitates in the splendid verse which resumes the evidence of a brave and clear-sighted man concerning life and death. Here, as at sea, there is enough and too much of fluctuation and intermission; the ripple flags and falls in loose and lazy lines: the foam flies wide of any mark, and the breakers collapse here and there in sudden ruin and violent failure. But the violence and weakness of the sea are preferable to the smooth sound and equable security of a lake: its buoyant and progressive impulse sustains and propels those who would sink through weariness in the flat and placid shallows. There are others whom it sickens, and others whom it chills; these will do well to steer inshore.

It is natural in writing of Byron to slide into remembrances of what is likest to his verse. His work and Shelley's, beyond that of all our other poets, recall or suggest the wide and high things of nature; the large likeness of the elements; the immeasurable liberty and the stormy strength of waters and winds. They are strongest when they touch upon these; and it is worth remark how few are the poets of whom this can be said. Here, as elsewhere, Shakespeare is supreme when it pleased him; but it pleased him rarely. No poetry of shipwreck and the sea has ever equalled the great scene of 'Pericles'; no such note of music was ever struck out of the clash and contention of tempestuous elements. In Milton the sublimity is chiefly of sound; the majesty of melodies unsurpassed from all time wellnigh excludes and supplants all other motives of material beauty. In the minds of mediæval poets there was no width or depth to receive and contain such emotion. In Spenser, despite his fertile and fluent ingenuity, his subtle and sleepy graces the effeminacy of colour no less than the monotony of metre makes it hopeless to look for any trace of that passionate sense of power and delight in great outer things of which we speak here. Among later men, Coleridge and Keats used nature mainly as a stimulant or a sedative; Wordsworth as a vegetable fit to shred into his pot and pare down like the outer leaves of a lettuce for didactic and culinary purposes.* All these doubtless in their own fashion

* I remember some critical cackling over this phrase when it first appeared as over a senseless insult offered to the name and genius of a great poet. Insult is no habit of mine; and the term here used implies no more than he that runs may read in the text of Wordsworth; in whom, after the somewhat early subsidence of that 'simple, sensuous, and passionate' delight in nature of which in two of his most famous poems he has for ever embalmed his recollection, the place of this rapturous instinct of submission and absorption which other poets have been who never have ceased to feel in sight of natural glory and beauty, was taken by a meditative and moralising spirit too apt to express itself in the tone of a preacher to whom all the divine life of things outside man is but as raw material for philosophic or theological cookery. [Swinburne's note.]

loved her, for her beauties, for her uses, for her effects; hardly one for herself.

Turn now to Byron or to Shelley. These two at least were not content to play with her skirts and paddle in her shallows. Their passion is perfect, a fierce and blind desire which exalts and impels their verse into the high places of emotion and expression. They feed upon nature with a holy hunger, follow her with a divine lust as of gods chasing the daughters of men. Wind and fire, the cadences of thunder and the clamours of the sea, gave to them no less of sensual pleasure than of spiritual sustenance. These things they desired as others desire music or wine or the beauty of women. This outward and indifferent nature of things, cruel in the eyes of all but her lovers, and even in theirs not loving, became as pliant to their grasp and embrace as any Clymene or Leucothea to Apollo's. To them the large motions and the remote beauties of space were tangible and familiar as flowers. Of this poetry, where description melts into passion and contemplation takes fire from delight, the highest sample is Shelley's 'Ode to the West Wind.' An imperfect mastery of his materials keeps the best things of Byron some few degrees below an equal rank. One native and incurable defect grew up and strengthened side by side with his noblest qualities: a feeble and faulty sense of metre. No poet of equal or inferior rank ever had so bad an ear. His smoother cadences are often vulgar and facile; his fresher notes are often incomplete and inharmonious. His verse stumbles and jingles, stammers and halts, where there is most need for a swift and even pace of musical sound. The rough sonorous changes of the songs in 'The Deformed Transformed' rise far higher in harmony and strike far deeper into the memory than the lax easy lines in which he at first indulged; but they slip too readily into notes as rude and weak as the rhymeless tuneless verse in which they are so loosely set, as in a cheap and casual frame. The magnificent lyric measures of 'Heaven and Earth' are defaced by the coarse obtrusion of short lines with jagged edges: no small offence in a writer of verse. Otherwise these choral scenes are almost as blameless as they are brilliant. The poet who above others took delight in the sense of sounding storms and shaken waters could not but exult over the vision of deluge with all his strength and breadth of wing. Tempest and rebellion and the magnificence of anguish were as the natural food and fire to kindle and sustain his indomitable and sleepless spirit. The godless martyrdom of rebels; the passion that cannot redeem; the Thebaid whose first hermit was Cain, the Calvary whose first martyr was Satan; these, time after time, allured and inspired him. Here for once this inner and fiery passion of thought found outer clothing and expression in the ruin of a world. Both without and within, the subject was made for him, and lay ready shapen for the strong impressure of his hand. His love of wide and tempestuous waters fills his work throughout as with the broad breath of a sea-wind. Even the weakest of his poems, a thing still-born and shapeless, is redeemed and revived by one glorious verse:—

When the Poles crashed, and water was the world.*

This passion and power in dealing with the higher things of nature, with her large issues and remote sources, has been bestowed upon Victor Hugo alone among our contemporaries. He also can pass beyond the idyllic details of landscape, and put out from shore into the wide waste places of the sea. And this of course is the loftiest form of such poetry as deals with outward nature and depends upon the forms of things. In Byron the power given by this passion is the more conspicuous through his want of dramatic capacity. Except in the lighter and briefer scenes of 'Don Juan,' he was never able to bring two speakers face to face and supply them with the right words. In structure as in metre his elaborate tragedies are wholly condemnable; filled as they are in spirit with the overflow of his fiery energy. 'Cain' and 'Manfred' are properly monologues decorated and set off by some slight appendage of ornament or explanation. In the later and loftier poem there is no difference perceptible, except in strength and knowledge, between Lucifer and Cain. Thus incompetent to handle the mysteries and varieties of character, Byron turns always with a fresh delight and a fresh confidence thither where he feels himself safe and strong. No

* "The Island," Canto IV, line 150.

part of his nature was more profound and sincere than the vigorous love of such inanimate things as were in tune with his own spirit and senses. His professions of contempt were too loud to express it; scorn is brief or silent; anger alone finds vent in violent iteration and clamorous appeal. He had too much of fury and not enough of contempt; he foams at things and creatures not worth a glance or a blow. But when once clear of men and confronted with elements, he casts the shell of pretence and drops the veil of habit; then, as in the last and highest passage of a poem which has suffered more from praise than any other from dispraise, his scorn of men caught in the nets of nature and necessity has no alloy of untruth; his spirit is mingled with the sea's, and overlooks with a superb delight the ruins and the prayers of men.

This loftiest passage in 'Childe Harold' has been so often mouthed and mauled by vulgar admiration that it now can scarcely be relished. Like a royal robe worn out, or a royal wine grown sour, it seems the worse for having been so good. But in fact, allowing for one or two slips and blots, we must after all replace it among the choice and high possessions of poetry. After the first there is hardly a weak line; many have a wonderful vigour and melody; and the deep and glad disdain of the sea for men and the works of men passes into the verse in music and fills it with a weighty and sonorous harmony grave and sweet as the measured voice of heavy remote waves. No other passage in the fourth canto will bear to be torn out from the text; and this one suffers by extraction. The other three cantos are more loosely built and less compact of fabric; but in the first two there is little to remember or to praise. Much of the poem is written throughout in falsetto; there is a savour in many places as of something false and histrionic. This singular and deep defect, which defaces so much of Byron's work, seems also to have deformed his personal character, to have given a twist to his enmities and left a taint upon his friendships. He was really somewhat sombre and sad at heart, and it pleased him to seem sadder than he was. He was impressible and susceptible of pleasure, able to command and enjoy it; and of this also it pleased him to make the most in public. But in fact he was neither a Harold nor a Juan; he was better than these in his own way, and assumed their parts and others with a hypocrisy but half insincere. The fault was probably in great part unconscious, and transparent as a child's acting. To the keen eye and cool judgment of Stendhal it was at once perceptible. Byron's letter to him in defence of Scott was doubtless not insincere; yet it is evident that the writer felt himself to be playing a graceful part to advantage. This fretful and petulant appetite for applause, the proper apanage of small poets and lowly aspirants, had in Byron's case to wrestle with the just pride of place and dignity of genius; no man ever had more of these; yet they did not always support him; he fell even into follies and vulgarities unworthy of a meaner name than his. In effect, when his errors were gravest, he erred through humility and not through pride. Pride would have sustained him far above the remarks and reviews of his day, the praise or dispraise of his hour. As it was, he was vulnerable even by creeping things; and at times their small stings left a poison behind which turned his blood. The contagion of their touch infected him; and he strove under its influence to hiss and wound as they. Here and there in his letters and reflections, in the loose records of his talk and light fragments of his work, the traces of infection are flagrant.

But these defects were only as scars on the skin, superficial and removable; they are past and done with; while all of him that was true and good remains, as it will to all time. Justice cannot be done to it here or now. It is enough if after careful selection as little injustice be done as possible. His few sonnets, unlike Shelley's, are all good; the best is that on Bonnivard, one of his noblest and completest poems. The versified narratives which in their day were so admirable and famous have yielded hardly a stray sheaf to the gleaner. They have enough of vigour and elasticity to keep life in them yet; but once chipped or broken their fabric would crumble and collapse. The finest among them is certainly either 'The Giaour' or 'The Siege of Corinth'; the weakest is probably either 'Parisina' or 'The Bride of Abydos.' But in none of these is there even a glimpse of Byron's higher and rarer faculty. All that can be said for them is that they gave tokens of a talent singularly fertile, rapid and vivid; a certain power of action and motion which redeems them from the complete stagnation of dead verses; a command over words and rhymes never of the best and never of the worst. In 'The Giaour,' indeed, there is something of a fiery sincerity which in its successors appears diluted and debased.*

The change began in Byron when he first found out his comic power, and rose at once beyond sight or shot of any rival. His early satires are wholly devoid of humour, wit, or grace; the verse of 'Beppo', bright and soft and fluent, is full at once of all. The sweet light music of its few and low notes was perfect as a prelude to the higher harmonies of laughter and tears, of scorn and passion, which as yet lay silent in the future. It is mere folly to seek in English or Italian verse a precedent or a parallel. The scheme of metre is Byron's alone; no weaker hand than his could ever bend that bow, or ever will. Even the Italian poets, working in a language more flexible and ductile than ours, could never turn their native metre to such uses, could never handle their national weapon with such grace and strength. The *terza rima* remains their own, after all our efforts to adapt it; it bears here only forced flowers and crude fruits; but the *ottava rima* Byron has fairly conquered and wrested from them. Before the appearance of 'Beppo' no one could foresee what a master's hand might make of the instrument; and no one could predict its further use and its dormant powers before the advent of 'Don Juan.' In 'The Vision of Judgment' it appears finally perfected;

* Remembering the success of these stories, we may believe that Byron's contempt for the critical fashions of a time which extolled his worst work was not wholly affected or assumed; and understand how the instincts of opposition and reaction drove him back into that open idolatry of Pope and his school which he expressed loudly and foolishly enough. Probably at heart he did really prefer Pope to all men. His critical faculty, if I may steal one phrase from a treasury that may well spare me the loan, was 'zero, or even a frightful *minus* quantity'; his judgment never worth the expense of a thought or a word. Besides, he had striven to emulate or at least to copy the exquisite manner of Pope in his satires, and must have seen how great and impassable a gulf lay between the master and his pupil. This would naturally lead him to over-estimate what he could not attain: the delicate merit, the keen perfection, the equable balance of force and finish, of sense and style, which raised his favourite so high among writers, if they left him somewhat low among poets; and having himself so bad an ear for metre, he may even have imagined that Pope's verse was musical. [Swinburne's note.]

the metre fits the sense as with close and pliant armour, the perfect panoply of Achilles. A poem so short and hasty, based on a matter so worthy of brief contempt and long oblivion as the funeral and the fate of George III, bears about it at first sight no great sign or likelihood of life. But this poem which we have by us stands alone, not in Byron's work only, but in the work of the world. Satire in earlier times had changed her rags for robes; Juvenal had clothed with fire, and Dryden with majesty, that wandering and bastard Muse. Byron gave her wings to fly with, above the reach even of these. Others have had as much of passion and as much of humour; Dryden had perhaps as much of both combined. But here and not elsewhere a third quality is apparent: the sense of a high and clear imagination. The grave and great burlesque of King George and St. Peter is relieved and sustained by the figures of Michael and Satan. These two, confronted and corresponding as noon and night, lift and light up the background of satire, blood-red or black according to the point of view. Above all, the balance of thought and passion is admirable; human indignation and divine irony are alike understood and expressed: the pure and fiery anger of men at sight of wrongdoing, the tacit inscrutable derision of heaven. Upon this light and lofty poem a commentary might be written longer than the text and less worth reading; but here it shall not be. Those who read it with the due delight, not too gravely and not too lightly, will understand more than can now be set down; those who read it otherwise will not understand anything. Even these can hardly fail to admire the vigour and variety of scorn, the beauty and the bitterness of verse, which raise it beyond comparison with any other satire. There is enough and too much of violence and injustice in the lines on Southey; but it must be remembered that he was the first to strike, and with an unfair weapon. A poet by profession, he had assaulted with feeble fury another poet, not on the fair and open charge of bad verses, but under the impertinent and irrelevant plea that his work was an affliction or an offence to religion and morality—the most susceptible, as the most intangible, among the creatures of metaphor. A man less irritable and less powerful than Byron might be forgiven for any reprisals; and the excellence of his verses justifies their injustice. But that Southey, who could win and retain for life the love and the praise of Landor, was capable of conscious baseness or falsity, Byron himself in sober moments should hardly have believed. Between official adoration and not less official horror—between George deified and Byron denounced—the Laureate's position was grotesque enough. It was almost a good office to pelt him with the names of hireling and apostate; these charges he could reject and refute. The facts were surely sufficient: that, as to religion, his 'present Deity' was the paltriest maniac among kings and Cæsars; as to morality, his feelings or his faith obliged him to decry as pernicious the greatest work of his opponent.

Side by side with the growth of his comic and satiric power, the graver genius of Byron increased and flourished. As the tree grew higher it grew shapelier; the branches it put forth on all sides were fairer of leaf and fuller of fruit than its earlier offshoots had promised. But from these hardly a stray bud or twig can be plucked off by way of sample. No detached morsel of 'Don Juan,' no dismembered fragment of 'Cain,' will serve to show or to suggest the excellence of either. These poems are coherent and complete as trees or flowers; they cannot be split up and parcelled out like a mosaic of artificial jewellery, which might be taken to pieces by the same artisan who put it together. It must then be remembered that any mere selection from the verse of Byron, however much of care and of goodwill be spent upon the task, must perforce either exclude or impair his very greatest work. Cancel or select a leaf from these poems, and you will injure the whole framework equally in either case. It is not without reluctance that I have given any extracts from 'Don Juan'; it is not without a full sense of the damage done to these extracts by the very act of extraction. But I could only have left them untouched with a reluctance even greater; and this plea, if it can, must excuse me. As fragments they are exquisite and noble, like the broken hand or severed foot of a Greek statue; but here as much is lost as there. Taken with their context, they regain as much of beauty and of force as the sculptured foot or hand when, reunited to the perfect body, they resume their place and office among its vital and various limbs. This gift of life and variety is the supreme quality of Byron's chief poem; a quality which cannot be expressed by any system of extracts. Little can here be given beyond a sample or two of tragic and serious work. The buoyant beauty of surrounding verse, the 'innumerable laughter' and the profound murmur of its many measures, the fervent flow of stanzas now like the ripples and now like the gulfs of the sea, can no more be shown by process of selection than any shallow salt pool left in the sand for sunbeams to drain dry can show the depth and length of the receding tide.

It would be waste of words and time here to enlarge at all upon the excellence of the pure comedy of 'Don Juan.' From the first canto to the sixteenth; from the defence of Julia, which is worthy of Congreve or Molière, to the study of Adeline, which is worthy of Laclos or Balzac; the elastic energy of humour never falters or flags. English criticism, with a mournful murmur of unanimous virtue, did at the time, and may yet if it please, appeal against the satire which strikes home and approve the satire that flies abroad. It was said, and perhaps is still said, that the poem falls off and runs low towards the end. Those who can discover where a change for the worse begins might at least indicate the landmark, imperceptible to duller eyes, which divides the good from the bad. Others meantime will retain their belief that this cry was only raised because in these latter cantos a certain due amount of satire fell upon the false and corrupt parts of English character, its mealy-mouthed vices and its unsound virtues. Had the scene been shifted to Italy or France, we might have heard little of the poet's failing power and perverse injustice.

It is just worth a word of notice that Byron, like Fielding before him, has caught up a well-known name and prefixed it to his work, without any attempt or desire to retain the likeness or follow the tradition attached to it. With him Don Juan is simply a man somewhat handsomer and luckier than others of his age. This hero is not even a reduced copy of the great and terrible figure with which he has nothing in common but a name. The Titan of embodied evil, the likeness of sin made flesh, which grew up in the grave and bitter imagination of a Spanish poet, steeped in the dyes and heated by the flames of hell, appears even in the hands of Molière diminished, and fallen as it were from Satan to Belial; but still splendid with intellect and courage that tower above the meaner minds and weaker wills of women and of men; still inflexible to human appeal and indomitable by divine anger. To crush him, heaven is compelled to use thunder and hell-fire; and by these, though stricken, he is not subdued. The sombre background of a funereal religion is not yet effaced; but it tasked the whole strength of Molière, gigantic as that strength was, to grapple with the shadow of this giant, to transfigure upon a new stage the tragic and enormous incarnation of supreme sin. As it is, even when playing with his debtors or his peasants, the hero of Molière retains always some feature of his first likeness, some shadow of his early shape. But further than France the terrible legend has never moved. Rigid criticism would therefore say that the title of Byron's masterpiece was properly a misnomer: which is no great matter after all, since the new Juan can never be confounded with the old.

Of Byron's smaller poems there is less to say, and less space to say it. Their splendid merits and their visible defects call neither for praise nor blame. Their place and his, in the literature of England, are fixed points: no critical astronomy of the future can lower or can raise them: they have their own station for all time among the greater and the lesser stars. As a poet, Byron was surpassed, beyond all question and all comparison, by three men at least of his own time; and matched, if not now and then overmatched, by one or two others. The verse of Wordsworth, at its highest, went higher than his; the verse of Landor flowed clearer. But his own ground, where none but he could set foot, was lofty enough, fertile and various. Nothing in Byron is so worthy of wonder and admiration as the scope and range of his power. New fields and ways of work, had he lived, might have given room for exercise and matter for triumph to

that most fiery spirit.' * As it is, his work was done at Misso-
longhi; all of his work for which the fates could spare him time.
A little space was allowed him to show at least a heroic purpose,
and attest a high design; then, with all things unfinished before
him and behind, he fell asleep after many troubles and tri-
umphs. Few can ever have gone wearier to the grave; none with
less fear. He had done enough to earn his rest. Forgetful now
and set free for ever from all faults and foes, he passed through
the doorway of no ignoble death out of reach of time, out of
sight of love, out of hearing of hatred, beyond the blame of
England and the praise of Greece. In the full strength of spirit
and of body his destiny overtook him, and made an end of all
his labours. He had seen and borne and achieved more than
most men on record. 'He was a great man, good at many
things, and now he has attained this also, to be at rest.'

* The noble verses of Shelley are fitter to be spoken over Byron
than over any first or last Napoleon. To no other man could they be so
well applied: for the world indeed took more of warmth from the fire of
his spirit while alive than from any other then kindled:

> What! alive and so bold, O Earth?
>   Art thou not over bold?
>   What! leapest thou forth as of old
> In the light of thy morning mirth,
>   The last of the flock of the starry fold?
>   . . . .
>   Thou wert warming thy fingers old
>   O'er the embers covered and cold
> Of that most fiery spirit, when it fled:
> What, Mother, do you laugh now he is dead?
> [Swinburne's note.]

❧{ }❧

William Blake

I

LIFE AND DESIGNS

In the year 1827, there died, after a long dim life of labour, a man as worthy of remark and regret as any then famous. In his time he had little enough of recognition or regard from the world; and now that here and there one man and another begin to observe that after all this one was perhaps better worth notice and honour than most, the justice comes as usual somewhat late.

Between 1757 and 1827 the world, one might have thought, had time to grow aware whether or not a man were worth something. For so long there lived and laboured in more ways than one the single Englishman of supreme and simple poetic genius born before the closing years of the eighteenth century; the one man of that date fit on all accounts to rank with the old great names. A man perfect in his way, and beautifully unfit for walking in the way of any other man. We have now the means of seeing what he was like as to face in the late years of his life: for his biography* has at the head of it a clearly faithful and valuable likeness. The face is singular, one that strikes at a first sight and grows upon the observer; a brilliant eager old face, keen and gentle, with a preponderance of brow and head; clear bird-like eyes, eloquent excitable mouth, with a look of nervous and fluent power; the whole lighted through as it were from behind with a strange and pure kind of smile,

---

* Swinburne's *William Blake* (1868) was begun as a review of Alexander Gilchrist's *Life of Blake*, and traces of its earlier form are still evident in the expansion.

touched too with something of an impatient prospective rapture. The words clear and sweet seem the best made for it; it has something of fire in its composition, and something of music. If there is a want of balance, there is abundance of melody in the features; melody rather than harmony; for the mould of some is weaker and the look of them vaguer than that of others. Thought and time have played with it, and have nowhere pressed hard; it has the old devotion and desire with which men set to their work at starting. It is not the face of a man who could ever be cured of illusions; here all the medicines of reason and experience must have been spent in pure waste. We know also what sort of man he was at this time by the evidence of living friends. No one, artist or poet, of whatever school, who had any insight or any love of things noble and lovable, ever passed by this man without taking away some pleasant and exalted memory of him. Those with whom he had nothing in common but a clear kind nature and sense of what was sympathetic in men and acceptable in things—those men whose work lay quite apart from his —speak of him still with as ready affection and as full remembrance of his sweet or great qualities as those nearest and likest him. There was a noble attraction in him which came home to all people with any fervour or candour of nature in themselves. One can see, by the roughest draught or slightest glimpse of his face, the look and manner it must have put on towards children. He was about the hardest worker of his time; must have done in his day some horseloads of work. One might almost pity the poor age and the poor men he came among for having such a fiery energy cast unawares into the midst of their small customs and competitions. Unluckily for them, their new prophet had not one point they could lay hold of, not one organ or channel of expression by which to make himself comprehensible to such as they were. Shelley in his time gave enough of perplexity and offence; but even he, mysterious and rebellious as he seemed to most men, was less made up of mist and fire than Blake.

He was born and baptized into the church of rebels; we can hardly imagine a time or scheme of things in which he could have lived and worked without some interval of revolt. All that was accepted for art, all that was taken for poetry, he rejected as barren symbols, and would fain have broken up as mendacious idols. What was best to other men, and in effect excellent of its kind, was to him worst. Reynolds and Rubens were daubers and devils. The complement or corollary of this habit of mind was that he would accept and admire even small and imperfect men whose line of life and action seemed to run on the same tramway as his own. Barry, Fuseli, even such as Mortimer—these were men he would allow and approve of. The devils had not entered into them; they worked, each to himself, on the same ground as Michael Angelo. To such effect he would at times prophesy, standing revealed for a brief glimpse on the cloudy and tottering height of his theories, before the incurious eyes of a public which had no mind to inhale such oracular vapour. It is hard to conjecture how his opinions, as given forth in his 'Catalogue' or other notes on art, would have been received—if indeed they had ever got hearing at all. This they naturally never did; by no means to Blake's discouragement. He spoke with authority; not in the least like the scribes of his day.

So far one may at least see what he meant; although at sight of it many would cover their eyes and turn away. But the main part of him was, and is yet, simply inexplicable; much like some among his own designs, a maze of cloudy colour and perverse form, without a clue for the hand or a feature for the eye to lay hold of. What he meant, what he wanted, why he did this thing or not that other, no man then alive could make out. Nevertheless it was worth the trying. In a time of critical reason and definite division, he was possessed by a fervour and fury of belief; among sane men who had disproved most things and proved the rest, here was an evident madman who believed a thing, one may say, only insomuch as it was incapable of proof. He lived and worked out of all rule, and yet by law. He had a devil, and its name was Faith. No materialist has such belief in bread and meat as Blake had in the substance underlying appearance which he christened god or spectre, devil or angel, as the fit took him; or rather as he saw it from one or the other side. His faith was absolute and hard, like a pure fanatic's; there was no speculation in him. What could be made of such a man in a country fed and clothed with the teapot pieties of Cowper and the tapeyard infidelities of Paine? Neither set would have to do with him; was he not a believer? and was he not a blasphemer? His licence of thought and talk was always of the maddest, or seemed so in the ears of his generation. People remember at this day with horror and pity the impression of his daring ways of speech, but excuse him still on the old plea of madness. Now on his own ground no man was ever more sane or more reverent. His outcries on various matters of art or morals were in effect the mere expression, not of reasonable dissent, but of violent belief. No artist of equal power had ever a keener and deeper regard for the meaning and teaching— what one may call the moral—of art. He sang and painted as men write or preach. Indifference was impossible to him. Thus every shred of his work has some life, some blood, infused or woven into it. In such a vast tumbling chaos of relics as he left behind to get in time disentangled and cast into shape, there are naturally inequalities enough; rough sides and loose sides, weak points and helpless knots, before which all mere human patience or comprehension recoils and reels back. But in all, at all times, there is the one invaluable quality of actual life. . . .

The first real point in Blake's life worth marking as of especial interest is the publication of his *Poetical Sketches*; which come in date before any of his paintings or illustrative work, and are quite as much matters of art as these. Though never printed till 1783, the latest written appears to belong to 1777, or thereabouts.

Here, at a time when the very notion of poetry, as we now understand it, and as it was understood in older times, had totally died and decayed out of the minds of men; when we not only had no poetry, a thing which was bearable, but had verse in plenty, a thing which was not in the least bearable; a man, hardly twenty years old yet, turns up suddenly with work in that line already done, not simply better than any man could do then; better than all except the greatest have done since: better too than some still ranked among the greatest ever managed to do. With such a poet to bring forward it was needless to fall back upon Wordsworth for excuse or Southey for patronage. The one man of genius alive during any part of Blake's own life who has ever spoken of this poet with anything like a rational admiration is Charles Lamb, the most supremely competent judge and exquisite critic of lyrical and dramatic art that we have ever had. All other extant notices down to our own day, even when well-meaning and not offensive, are to the best of our knowledge and belief utterly futile, incapable and valueless: burdened more or less with chatter about 'madness' and such-like, obscured in some degree by mere dullness and pitiable assumption.

There is something too rough and hard, too faint and formless, in any critical language yet devised, to pay tribute with the proper grace and sufficiency to the best works of the lyrical art. One can say, indeed, that some of these earliest songs of Blake's have the scent and sound of Elizabethan times upon them; that the song of forsaken love—'My silks and fine array'—is sweet enough to recall the lyrics of Beaumont and Fletcher, and strong enough to hold its own even beside such as that one of Aspatia—'Lay a garland on my hearse'—which was cut (so to speak) out of the same yew; that Webster might have signed the *Mad Song,* which falls short only (as indeed do all other things of the sort) of the two great Dirges in that poet's two chief plays; that certain verses among those headed *To Spring,* and *To the Evening Star,* are worthy even of Tennyson for tender supremacy of style and noble purity of perfection; but when we have to drop comparison and cease looking back or forward for verses to match with these, we shall hardly find words to suit our sense of their beauty. We speak of the best among them only; for, small as the pamphlet is (seventy pages long, with title-page and prefatory leaf), it contains a good deal of chaff and bran besides the pure grain and sifted honey-meal. But these best things are as wonderful as any work of Blake's. They have a fragrance of sound, a melody of colour, in a time when the best verses produced had merely the arid perfume of powder, the twang of dry wood and adjusted strings; when here the painting was laid on in patches, and there the music meted out by precedent; colour and sound never mixed together into the perfect scheme of poetry. The texture of these songs has the softness of flowers; the touch of them has nothing metallic or mechanical, such as one feels in much excellent and elaborate verse of this day as well as of that. The sound of many verses of Blake's cleaves to the sense long after conscious thought of the meaning has passed from one: a sound like running of water or ringing of bells in a long lull of the wind. . . .

That too much of Blake's written work while at Felpham* is wanting in executive quality, and even in decent coherence of verbal dress, is undeniable. The Pythoness who delivers these stormy and sonorous oracles is at once exposed and hampered as it were by her loose and heavy raiment; the prophetic robe here slips or gapes, there muffles and impedes; is now a tatter that hardly hides the contorted limbs, and now an encumbrance that catches or trips up the reeling feet. Everything now written in the fitful impatient intervals of the day's work bears the stamp of an overheated brain and of nerves too intensely strung. Everything may well appear to confirm the suggestion that, as high latitudes and climates of rarefied air affect the physical structure of inhabitants or travellers, so in this case did the sudden country life, the taste and savour of the sea, touch sharply and irritate deliciously the more susceptible and intricate organs of mind and nature. How far such passive capacity of excitement differs from insanity; how in effect a temperament so sensuous, so receptive, and so passionate, is further off from any risk of turning unsound than hardier natures carrying heavier weight and tougher in the nerves; need scarcely be indicated. For the rest, our concern at present shall still be mainly with the letters of this date; and by their light we may be enabled to see light shed upon many things hitherto hope-

---

* From 1800 to 1803 Blake lived at Felpham, under the patronage of William Hayley, for whom he was engraving illustrations for a life of Cowper and other works. During this period he was also probably working on *Milton,* the first of his more obscure prophetic books, and on *Vala, or the Four Zoas.*

lessly dark. As no other samples of Blake's correspondence worth mention have been allowed us by the jealousy of fate and divine parsimony, we must be duly grateful and careful in dealing with all we have; gathering the fragments into commodious baskets, and piecing the shreds into available patchwork.

These letters bear upon them the common stamp of all Blake's doings and writings; the fiery and lyrical tone of mind and speech, the passionate singleness of aim, the heat and flame of faith in himself, the violence of mere words, the lust of paradox, the loud and angry habits of expression which abound in his critical or didactic work, are not here missing; neither are clear indications wanting of his noblest qualities; the great love of great things, the great scorn of small men, the strong tenderness of heart, the tender strength of spirit, which won for him honour from all that were honourable. Ready even in a too fervent manner to accept, to praise, to believe in worth and return thanks for it, he will have no man or thing impede or divert him, either for love's sake or hate's. Small friends with feeble counsels to suggest must learn to suppress their small feelings and graceful regrets, or be cleared out of his way with all their powers to help or hinder; lucky if they get off without some label of epigram on the forehead or sting of epigram in the flesh. . . .

Other points and shades of character not less singular it is essential here to take notice of. These are not matters of accident, like the errors of opinion or perversities of expresssion which may distort or disfigure the notes and studies on purely artistic matters; they compose the vital element and working condition of Blake's talent. From the fifth to the tenth letter especially, it becomes evident that the writer was passing through strange struggles of spirit and passionate stages of faith. As early as the fourth letter, dated almost exactly a year later than the first written on his arrival at Felpham, Blake refers in a tone of regret and perplexity to the 'abstract folly' which makes him incapable of direct practical work, though not of earnest and continuous labour. This action of the nerves or of the mind he was plainly unable to regulate or modify. It hurries him while yet at work into 'lands of abstraction'; he 'takes the world with him in his flight.' Distress he knows would make the world heavier to him, which seems now 'lighter than a ball of wool rolled by the wind'; and this distress material philosophies or methodical regulations would 'prescribe as a medicinal potion' for a mind impaired or diseased merely by the animal superflux of spirits and childlike excess of spiritual health. But this medicine the strange and strong faculty of faith innate in the man precludes him from taking. Physical distress 'is his mock and scorn; mental no man can give; and if Heaven inflicts it, all such distress is a mercy.' It is not easy, but it is requisite, to realise the perpetual freshness and fulness of belief, the inalterable vigour and fervour of spirit with which Blake, heretic and mystic as he may have been, worshipped and worked; by which he was throughout life possessed and pursued. Above all gods or dæmons of creation and division, he beheld by faith in a perfect man a supreme God. 'Though I have been very unhappy, I am so no longer. I am again emerged into the light of day; I still (and shall to eternity) embrace Christianity, and adore Him who is the express image of God.' In the light of his especial faith all visible things were fused into the intense heat and sharpened into the keen outline of vision. He walked and laboured under other heavens, on another earth, than the earth and the heaven of material life:

> With a blue sky spread over with wings,
> And a mild sun that mounts and sings;
> With trees and fields full of fairy elves
> And little devils who fight for themselves;
> With angels planted in hawthorn bowers,
> And God Himself in the passing hours.

All this was not a mere matter of creed or opinion, much less of decoration or ornament to his work. It was, as we said, his element of life, inhaled at every breath with the common air, mixed into his veins with their natural blood. It was an element almost painfully tangible and actual; an absolute medium or state of existence, inevitable, inexplicable, insuperable. To

him the veil of outer things seemed always to tremble with some
breath behind it: seemed at times to be rent in sunder with
clamour and sudden lightning. All the void of earth and air
seemed to quiver with the passage of sentient wings and palpitate under the pressure of conscious feet. Flowers and weeds,
stars and stones, spoke with articulate lips and gazed with
living eyes. Hands were stretched towards him from beyond
the darkness of material nature, to tempt or to support, to guide
or to restrain. His hardest facts were the vaguest allegories of
other men. To him all symbolic things were literal, all literal
things symbolic. About his path and about his bed, around his
ears and under his eyes, an infinite play of spiritual life seethed
and swarmed or shone and sang. Spirits imprisoned in the husk
and shell of earth consoled or menaced him. Every leaf bore a
growth of angels; the pulse of every minute sounded as the
falling foot of God; under the rank raiment of weeds, in the
drifting down of thistles, strange faces frowned and white hair
fluttered; tempters and allies, wraiths of the living and phan-
toms of the dead, crowded and made populous the winds that
blew about him, the fields and hills over which he gazed. Even
upon earth his vision was 'twofold always'; singleness of vision
he scorned and feared as the sign of mechanical intellect, of
talent that walks while the soul sleeps, with the mere activity
of a blind somnambulism. It was fourfold in the intervals of
keenest inspiration and subtlest rapture; threefold in the paradise of dreams lying between earth and heaven, lulled by
lighter airs and lit by fainter stars; land of night and moonlight, spectral and serene. These strange divisions of spirit and
world according to some dim and mythologic hierarchy were
with Blake matters at once serious and commonplace. The
worlds of Beulah and Jerusalem, the existence of Los god of
Time and Enitharmon goddess of Space, the fallen manhood of
Theotormon, the imprisoned womanhood of Oothoon, were
more to him even than significant names; to the reader they
must needs seem less. This monstrous nomenclature, this jargon
of miscreated things in chaos, rose as by nature of his lips,
flowed from them as by instinct. Time, an incarnate spirit

clothed with fire, stands before him in the sun's likeness; he is
threatened with poverty, tempted to make himself friends of
this world; and makes answer as though to a human tempter:

> My hands are laboured day and night
> And rest comes never in my sight;
> My wife has no indulgence given
> Except what comes to her from heaven;
> We eat little, we drink less;
> This earth breeds not our happiness.

He beheld, he says, Time and Space as they were eternally, not
as they are seen upon earth; he saw nothing as man sees: his
hopes and fears were alien from all men's; and upon him and
his the light of prosperous days and the terrors of troubled time
had no power.

> When I had my defiance given
> The sun stood trembling in heaven;
> The moon, that glowed remote below,
> Became leprous and white as snow;
> And every soul of man on the earth
> Felt affliction and sorrow and sickness and dearth.

In all this we may see on one side the reflection and refraction
of outer things, on the other side the projection of his own
mind, the effusion of his individual nature, throughout the
hardest and remotest alien matter. Strangely severed from other
men, he was, or he conceived himself, more strangely inter-
woven with them. The light of his spiritual weapons, the sound
of his spiritual warfare, was seen, he believed, and was heard
in faint resonance and far reverberation among men who knew
not what such sights and sounds might mean. If, worsted in
this 'mental fight,' he should let 'his sword sleep in his hand,'
or 'refuse to do spiritual acts because of natural fears and
natural desires,' the world would be the poorer for his defection,
and himself 'called the base Judas who betrays his friend.' Fear
of this rebuke shook and wasted him day and night; he was
rent in sunder with pangs of terror and travail. Heaven was

full of the dead, coming to witness against him with blood-shedding and with shedding of tears:

> The sun was hot
> With the bows of my mind and with arrows of thought.

In this spirit he wrought at his day's work, seeing everywhere the image of his own mood, the presence of foes and friends. Nothing to him was neutral; nothing without significance. The labour and strife of soul in which he lived was a thing as earnest as any bodily warfare. Such struggles of spirit in poets or artists have been too often made the subject of public study; nay, too often the theme of chaotic versifiers. A theme more utterly improper it is of course impossible to devise. It is just that a workman should see all sides of his work, and labour with all his might of mind and dexterity of hand to make it great and perfect; but to use up the details of the process as crude material for cruder verse—to invite spectators as to the opening of a temple, and show them the unbaked bricks and untempered mortar—to expose with immodest violence and impotent satisfaction the long revolting labours of mental abortion—this no artist will ever attempt, no craftsman ever so perform as to escape ridicule. It is useless for those who can carve no statue worth the chiselling to exhibit instead six feet or nine feet of shapeless plaster or fragmentary stucco, and bid us see what sculptors work with; no man will accept that in lieu of the statue. Not less futile and not less indecent is it for those who can give expression to no great poem to disgorge masses of raw incoherent verse on the subject of verse-making: to offer, in place of a poem ready wrought out, some chaotic and convulsive story about the way in which a poet works, or does not work.

To Blake the whole thing was too grave for any such exposure of spiritual nudity. In these letters he records the result of his 'sore travail'; in these verses he commemorates the manner of his work 'under the direction of messengers from heaven daily and nightly, not without trouble or care'; but he writes in private and by pure instinct; he speaks only by the impulse of confidence, in the ardour of faith. What he has to say is said with the simple and abstract rapture of apostles or prophets; not with the laborious impertinence and vain obtrusion of tortuous analysis. For such heavy play with gossamer and straws his nature was too earnest and his genius too exalted. This is the mood in which he looks over what work he has done or has to do: and in his lips the strange scriptural language used has the sincerity of pure fire. 'I see the face of my Heavenly Father; He lays His hand upon my head, and gives a blessing to all my work. Why should I be troubled? why should my heart and flesh cry out? I will go on in the strength of the Lord; through hell will I sing forth His praises; that the dragons of the deep my praise Him, and that those who dwell in darkness and in the sea-coasts may be gathered into His kingdom.' So did he esteem of art, which indeed is not a light thing; nor is it wholly unimportant to men that they should have one capable artist more or less among them. How it may fare with artisans (be they never so pretentious) is a matter of sufficiently small moment. One blessing there assuredly was upon all Blake's work; the infinite blessing of life; the fervour of vital blood. . . .

Among these late labours of Blake the 'Dante' may take a place of some prominence. The seven published plates, though quite surprisingly various in merit, are worth more notice than has yet been spared them. Three at least, for poetical power and nobility of imaginative detail, are up to the artist's highest mark. Others have painted the episode of Francesca with more or less of vigour and beauty. . . . Blake has given nothing like this: of personal beauty and special tenderness his design has none; it starts from other ground. Often as the lovers had been painted, here first has any artist desired to paint the second circle itself. To most illustrators, as to most readers, and (one might say) to Dante himself, the rest are swallowed up in those two supreme martyrs. Here we see, not one or two, but the very circle of the souls that sinned by lust, as Dante saw it; and as Keats afterwards saw it in the dream embalmed by his sonnet; the revolution of infinite sorrowing spirits through the bitter air and grievous hurricane of hell. Through strange immense implications of snake-shaped fold beyond fold, the involved chain of figures that circle and return flickers in wan white outline upon the dense dark. Under their feet is no stay as on earth; over their heads is no light as in heaven. They have no rest, and no resting-place: they revolve like circles of curling foam or fire. The two witnesses,* who alone among all the mobile mass have ground whereon to set foot, stand apart upon a broken floor-work of roots and rocks, made rank with the slime and sprawl of rotten weed and foul flag-leaves of Lethe. Detail of drawing or other technical work is not the strong point of the design; but it does incomparably well manage to render the sense of the matter in hand, the endless measured motion, the painful and fruitless haste as of leaves or smoke upon the wind, the grey discomforted air and dividing mist. Blake has thoroughly understood and given back the physical symbols of this first punishment in Dante; the whirling motion of his figures has however more of blind violence and brute speed than the text seems to indicate: they are dashed and dragged one upon another like weed or shingle torn up in the drift of a breaking sea: overthrown or beaten down, haled or crushed together, as if by inanimate strength of iron or steam: not moved as we expect to see them, in sad rapidity of stately measure and even time of speed. The flame-like impulse of idea natural to Blake cannot absolutely match itself against Dante's divine justice and intense innate forbearance in detail; nor so comprehend, as by dint of reproduction to compete with, that supreme sense of inward and outward right which rules and attunes every word of the 'Commedia.'

Two other drawings in this series are worth remark and praise; the sixth and seventh in order. In the sixth, Dante and Virgil, standing in a niche of rifted rock faced by another cliff up and down which a reptile crowd of spirits swarms and sinks, look down on the grovelling and swine-like flocks of Malebolge; lying tumbled about the loathsome land in hateful heaps of leprous flesh and dishevelled deformity, with limbs contorted,

* Dante and his guide, Virgil.

clawing nails, and staring horror of hair and eyes: one figure thrown down in a corner of the crowded cliff-side, her form and face drowned in an overflow of ruined raining tresses. The pure grave folds of the two poets' robes, long and cleanly carved as the straight drapery of a statue, gain chastity of contrast from the swarming surge and monstrous mass of all foulest forms beneath, against the reek of which both witnesses stop their noses with their gowns. Behind and between, huge outlines of dark hill and sharp curves of crag show like stiffened ridges of solid sea, amid heaving and glaring motion of vapour and fire. Slight as the workmanship is of this design also, alien as is perhaps its structure of precipice and mountain from the Dantesque conception of descending circles and narrowing sides, it has a fiery beauty of its own; the background especially, with its climbing or crawling flames, the dark hard strength and sweep of its sterile ridges, seen by fierce fits of reflected light, washed about with surf and froth of tideless fire, and heavily laden with the lurid languor of hell. In the seventh design we reach the circle of traitors; the foot of the passenger strikes against one frost-bound face; others lie straight, with crowned congealing hair and beard taken in the tightening rivets of ice. To the right a swarm of huge and huddled figures seems gathering with moan or menace behind a veil of frozen air, a mask of hardening vapour; and from each side the bitter light of ice or steel falls grey in cruel refraction. Into the other four designs we will not enter; some indeed are too savagely reckless in their ugly and barren violation of form or law, to be redeemed by even an intenser apprehension of symbol and sense; and one at least, though with noble suggestions dropped about it, is but half sketched in. In that of the valley of serpents there is however a splendid excess of horror and prodigal agony; the ravenous delight of the closing and laughing mouths, the folded tension of every scale and ring, the horrible head caught and crushed with the last shriek between its teeth and the last strain upon its eyelids, in the serrated jaws of the erect serpent—all have the brand of Blake upon them.

III

THE PROPHETIC BOOKS

Before entering upon any system of remark or comment on the
'Prophetic Books,' we may set down in as few and distinct
words as possible the reasons which make this a thing seriously
worth doing; nay, even requisite to be done, if we would know
rather the actual facts of the man's nature than the circumstances and accidents of his life. Now, first of all, we are to
recollect that Blake himself regarded these works as his greatest,
and as containing the sum of his achieved ambitions and fulfilled desires: as in effect inspired matter, of absolute imaginative truth and eternal import. We shall not again pause to
rebut the familiar cry of response, to the effect that he was
mad and not accountable for the uttermost madness of error.
It must be enough to reply here that he was by no means
mad, in any sense that would authorise us in rejecting his
own judgment of his own aims and powers on a plea which
would be held insufficient in another man's case. Let all readers
and all critics get rid of that notion for good—clear their minds
of it utterly and with all haste; let them know and remember,
having once been told it, that in these strangest of all written
books there is purpose as well as power, meaning as well as
mystery. Doubtless, nothing quite like them was ever pitched
out headlong into the world as they were. The confusion, the
clamour, the jar of words that half suffice and thoughts that half
exist—all these and other more absolutely offensive qualities—
audacity, monotony, bombast, obscure play of licence and tortuous growth of fancy—cannot quench or even wholly conceal
the living purport and the imperishable beauty which are here
latent. . . .

Not that the thing was easy to do. If any one would realise to
himself for ever a material notion of chaos, let him take a blind
header into the midst of the whirling foam and rolling weed of
this sea of words. Indeed the sound and savour of these prophecies constantly recall some such idea or some such memory.

This poetry has the huge various monotonies, the fervent and fluent colours, the vast limits, the fresh sonorous strength, the certain confusion and tumultuous law, the sense of windy and weltering space, the intense refraction of shadow or light, the crowded life and inanimate intricacy, the patience and the passion of the sea. By no manner of argument or analysis will one be made able to look back or forward with pure confidence and comprehension. Only there are laws, strange as it must sound, by which the work is done and against which it never sins. . . . The expression shifts perpetually, the types blunder into new forms, the meaning tumbles into new types; the purpose remains, and the faith keeps its hold.

There are certain errors and eccentricities of manner and matter alike common to nearly all these books, and distinctly referable to the character and training of the man. Not educated in any regular or rational way, and by nature of an eagerly susceptible and intensely adhesive mind, in which the lyrical faculty had gained and kept a preponderance over all others visible in every scrap of his work, he had saturated his thoughts and kindled his senses with a passionate study of the forms of the Bible as translated into English, till his fancy caught a feverish contagion and his ear derived a delirious excitement from the mere sound and shape of the written words and verses. Hence the quaint and fervent imitation of style, the reproduction of peculiarities which to most men are meaningless when divested of their old sense or invested with a new. Hence the bewildering catalogues, genealogies, and divisions which (especially in such later books as the *Jerusalem*) seem at first invented only to strike any miserable reader with furious or lachrymose lunacy. Hence, though heaven knows by no fault of the originals, the insane cosmogony, blatant mythology, and sonorous aberration of thoughts and theories. Hence also much of the special force and supreme occasional loveliness or grandeur in expression. Conceive a man incomparably gifted as to the spiritual side of art, prone beyond all measure to the lyrical form of work, incredibly contemptuous of all things and people dissimilar to himself, of an intensely sensitive imagination and intolerant habit of faith, with a passionate power of peculiar belief, taking with all his might of mental nerve and strain of excitable spirit to a perusal and reperusal of such books as Job and Ezekiel. Observe too that his tone of mind was as far from being critical as from being orthodox. Thus his ecstasy of study was neither on the one side tempered and watered down by faith in established forms and external creeds, nor on the other side modified and directed by analytic judgment and the lust of facts. To Blake either form of mind was alike hateful. Like the Moses of Rabbinical tradition, he was 'drunken with the kisses of the lips of God.' Rational deism and clerical religion were to him two equally abhorrent incarnations of the same evil spirit, appearing now as negation and now as restriction. He wanted supremacy of freedom with intensity of faith. Hence he was properly neither Christian nor infidel: he was emphatically a heretic. Such men, according to the temper of the times, are burnt as demoniacs or pitied as lunatics. He believed in redemption by Christ, and in the incarnation of Satan as Jehovah. He believed that by self-sacrifice the soul should attain freedom and victorious deliverance from bodily bondage and sexual servitude; and also that the extremest fulness of indulgence in such desire and such delight as the senses can aim at or attain was absolutely good, eternally just, and universally requisite. These opinions, and stranger than these, he put forth in the cloudiest style, the wilfullest humour, and the stormiest excitement. No wonder the world let his books drift without caring to inquire what gold or jewels might be washed up as waifs from the dregs of churned foam and subsiding surf. He was the very man for fire and faggot; a mediæval inquisitor would have had no more doubt about him than a materialist or 'theophilanthropist' of his own day or of ours.

A wish is expresssed in the 'Life' that we could accompany the old man who appears entering an open door, star in hand, at the beginning of the *Jerusalem,* and thread by his light those infinite dark passages and labyrinthine catacombs of invention or thought. In default of that desirable possibility, let us make such way as we can for ourselves into this submarine world, along its slippery and unpaven ways, under its roof of hollow sound and tumbling storm.

We shall see, while above us
The waves roar and whirl,
A ceiling of amber,
A pavement of pearl.

At the entrance of the labyrinth we are met by huge mythologic
figures, created of fire and cloud. Titans of monstrous form and
yet more monstrous name obstruct the ways; sickness or sleep
never formed such savage abstractions, such fierce vanities of
vision as these: office and speech they seem at first to have none:
but to strike or clutch at the void of air with feeble fingers, to
babble with vast lax lips a dialect barren of all but noise, loud
and loose as the wind. Slowly they grow into something of
shape, assume some foggy feature and indefinite colour: word
by word the fluctuating noise condenses into music, the floating
music divides into audible notes and scales. The sound which at
first was as the mere collision of cloud with cloud is now the
recognisable voice of god or dæmon. Chaos is cloven into separate elements; air divides from water, and earth releases fire.
Upon each of these the prophet, as it were, lays hand, com-
pelling the thing into shape and speech, constraining the abstract to do service as a man might. These and such as these
make up the personal staff or executive body of his prophecies.
But it would be waste of time to conjecture how or why he
came to inflict upon them such incredible names. These hapless
energies and agencies are not simply cast into the house of
allegoric bondage, and set to make bricks without straw, to con-
struct symbols without reason; but find themselves baptized
with muddy water and fitful fire, by names inconceivable, into
a church full of storm and vapour; regenerated with a vengeance, but disembodied and disfigured in their resurrection.
Space fell into sleep, and awoke as Enitharmon: Time suffered
eclipse, and came forth as Los. The Christ or Prometheus of this
faith is Orc or Fuzon; Urizen takes the place of 'Jehovah, Jove,
or Lord.' Hardly in such chaotic sounds can one discern the
slightest element of reason gone mad, the narrowest channel of
derivation run dry. In this last word, one of incessant recurrence, there seems to flicker a thin reminiscence of such names

as Uranus, Uriel, and perhaps Urien; for the deity has a diabolic savour in him, and Blake was not incapable of mixing the Hellenic, the Miltonic, and the Celtic mythologies into one drugged and adulterated compound. He had read much and blindly; he had no leaning to verbal accuracy, and never acquired any faculty of comparison. Any sound that in the dimmest way suggested to him a notion of hell or heaven, of passion or power, was significant enough to adopt and register. Commentary was impossible to him: if his work could not be apprehended or enjoyed by an instinct of inspiration like his own, it was lost labour to dissect or expound; and here, if ever, translation would have been treason. He took the visions as they came; he let the words lie as they fell. These barbarous and blundering names are not always without a certain kind of melody and an uncertain sort of meaning. Such as they are, they must be endured; or the whole affair must be tossed aside and thrown up. Over these clamorous kingdoms of speech and dream some few ruling forces of supreme discord preside: and chiefly the lord of the world of man; Urizen, God of cloud and star, 'Father of jealousy,' clothed with a splendour of shadow, strong and sad and cruel; his planet faintly glimmers and slowly revolves, a horror in heaven; the night is a part of his thought, rain and wind are in the passage of his feet; sorrow is in all his works; he is the maker of mortal things, of the elements and sexes; in him are incarnate that jealousy which the Hebrews acknowledged and that envy which the Greeks recognised in the divine nature; in his worship faith remains one with fear. Star and cloud, the types of mystery and distance, of cold alienation and heavenly jealousy, belong of right to the God who grudges and forbids: even as the spirit of revolt is made manifest in fiery incarnation—pure prolific fire, 'the cold loins of Urizen dividing.' These two symbols of 'cruel fear' or 'starry jealousy' in the divine tyrant, of ardent love or creative lust in the rebellious saviour of man, pervade the mystical writings of Blake. Orc, the man-child, with hair and flesh like fire, son of Space and Time, a terror and a wonder from the hour of his birth, containing within himself the likeness of all passions and appetites of men, is cast out from before the face of heaven; and falling upon earth, a stronger Vulcan or Satan, fills with his fire the narrowed foreheads and the darkened eyes of all that dwell thereon; imprisoned often and fed from vessels of iron with barren food and bitter drink, a wanderer or a captive upon earth, he shall rise again when his fire has spread through all lands to inflame and to infect with a strong contagion the spirit and the sense of man, and shall prevail against the law and the commandments of his enemy. This endless myth of oppression and redemption, of revelation and revolt, runs through many forms and spills itself by strange straits and byways among the sands and shallows of prophetic speech. But in these books there is not the substantial coherence of form and reasonable unity of principle which bring within scope of apprehension even the wildest myths grown out of unconscious idealism and impulsive tradition. A single man's work, however exclusively he may look to inspiration for motive and material, must always want the breadth and variety of meaning, the supple beauty of symbol, the infectious intensity of satisfied belief, which grow out of creeds and fables native to the spirit of a nation, yet peculiar to no man or sect, common yet sacred, not invented or constructed, but found growing and kept fresh with faith. But for all the dimness and violence of expression which pervert and darken the mythology of these attempts at gospel, they have qualities great enough to be worth finding out. Only let none conceive that each separate figure in the swarming and noisy life of this populous dæmonic creation has individual meaning and vitality. Blake was often taken off his feet by the strong currents of fancy, and indulged, like a child during its first humour of invention, in wild byplay and erratic excesses of simple sound; often lost his way in a maze of wind-music, and transcribed as it were with eyes closed and open ears the notes caught by chance as they drifted across the dream of his subdued senses. Alternating between lyrical invention and gigantic allegory, it is hard to catch and hold him down to any form or plan. At one time we have mere music, chains of ringing names, scattered jewels of sound without a thread, tortuous network of harmonies without a clue; and again we have passages, not always unworthy of an Æschylean chorus, full of fate and fear;

words that are strained wellnigh in sunder by strong significance and earnest passion; words that deal greatly with great things, that strike deep and hold fast; each inclusive of some fierce apocalypse or suggestive of some obscure evangel. Now the matter in hand is touched with something of an epic style; the narrative and characters lose half their hidden sense, and the reciter passes from the prophetic tripod to the seat of a common singer; mere names, perhaps not even musical to other ears than his, allure and divert him; he plays with stately cadences, and lets the wind of swift or slow declamation steer him whither it will. Now again he falls with renewed might of will to his purpose; and his grand lyrical gift becomes an instrument not sonorous merely but vocal and articulate. To readers who can but once take their stand for a minute on the writer's footing, look for a little with his eyes and listen with his ears, even the more incoherent cadences will become not undelightful; something of his pleasure, with something of his perception, will pass into them; and understanding once the main gist of the whole fitful and high-strung tune, they will tolerate, where they cannot enjoy, the strange diversities and discords which intervene.

Among many notable eccentricities we have touched upon but two as yet; the huge windy mythology of elemental dæmons, and the capricious passion for catalogues of random names, which make obscure and hideous so much of these books. Akin to these is the habit of seeing or assuming in things inanimate or in the several limbs and divisions of one thing, separate forms of active and symbolic life. This, like many other of Blake's habits, grows and swells enormously by progressive indulgence. At first, as in *Thel,* clouds and flowers, clods and creeping things, are given speech and sense; the degree of symbolism is already excessive, owing to the strength of expression and directness of dramatic vision peculiar to Blake; but in later books everything is given a soul to feel and a tongue to speak; the very members of the body become spirits, each a type of some spiritual state. Again, in the prophecies of *Europe* and *America,* there is more fable and less allegory, more overflow of lyrical invention, more of the divine babble which sometimes takes the place of earthly speech or sense, more vague emotion with less of reducible and amenable quality than in almost any of these poems. In others, a habit of mapping out and marking down the lines of his chaotic and Titanic scenery has added to Blake's other singularities of manner this above all, that side by side with the jumbled worlds of Tharmas and Urthona, the whirling skies and plunging planets of Ololon and Beulah, the breathless student of prophecy encounters places and names absurdly familiar; London streets and suburbs make up part of the mystic antediluvian world; Fulham and Lambeth, Kentish Town and Poland Street, cross the courses and break the metres of the stars. This apparent madness of final absurdity has also its root in the deepest and soundest part of Blake's mind and faith. In the meanest place as in the meanest man he beheld the hidden spirit and significance of which the flesh or the building is but a type. If continents have a soul, shall suburbs or lanes have less? where life is, shall not the spirit of life be there also? Europe and America are vital and significant; we mean by all names somewhat more than we know of; for where there is anything visible or conceivable, there is also some invisible and inconceivable thing. This is but the rough grotesque result of the tenet that matter apart from spirit is non-existent. Launched once upon that theory, Blake never thought it worth while to shorten sail or tack about for fear of any rock or shoal. It is inadequate and even inaccurate to say that he allotted to each place as to each world a presiding dæmon or deity. He averred implicitly or directly, that each had a soul or spirit, the quintessence of its natural life, capable of change but not of death; and that of this soul the visible externals, though a native and actual part, were only a part, inseparable as yet but incomplete. Thus whenever, to his misfortune and ours, he stumbles upon the proper names of terrene men and things, he uses these names as signifying not the sensual form or body but the spirit which he supposed to animate these, to speak in them and work through them. In *America* the names of liberators, in *Jerusalem* the names of provinces, have no separate local or mundane sense whatever; throughout the prophecies 'Albion' is the mythical and typical fatherland of human life, much what the East might seem to other men: and by way of making this type actual and prominent enough, Blake seizes upon all possible divisions of the modern visible England in town or country, and turns them in his loose symbolic way into minor powers and serving spirits. That he was wholly unconscious of the intolerably laughable effect we need not believe. He had all the delight in laying snares and giving offence, which is proper to his kind. He had all the confidence in his own power and right to do such things and to get over the doing of them which accompanies in such men the subtle humour of scandalising. And unfortunately he had not by training, perhaps not by nature, the conscience which would have reminded him that whether or not an artist may allowably play with all other things in heaven and earth, one thing he must certainly not play with; the material forms of art: that levity and violence are here prohibited under grave penalties. Allowing however for this, we may notice that in the wildest passages of these books Blake merely carries into strange places or throws into strange shapes such final theories as in the dialect of calmer and smaller men have been accounted not unreasonable.

Further preface or help, however loudly the subject might seem to call for it, we have not in this place to give; and indeed . . . many voices might be heard crying in this wilderness before the paths were made straight.

◆{ }◆

Lesbia Brandon*

CHAPTER III

A Day's Work

. . . He was tired enough with various small excitements to
fall asleep while undressing; and when his sister according to
her tacit promise entered his room she found him lying back
on one side in a long arm-chair, with eyes shut fast and cheeks
warm with sleep, his hair crushed against the cushion into a
tangle of tortuous gold and flickering with fiery colours in the
reflected firelight which lit up his face from below, brightening
round the throat and chin, leaving shadows about the mouth
and glittering against the close eyelashes and rough curls that
caught its gleam and reflex. The head was curiously beautiful,
with the pure animal grace of Ampelus rather than of Cupid:
a head to be caressed by Bacchus and carved by Polycles. Something of pain still hung about the eyelids, swelled slightly and
veined with more visible blue from the morning's tears: but for
this, it might have been the face of Ampelus indeed, could the
sculptured head have taken English colour. Lying there tired
and hurt and quiet, he touched her with a new love; she bent
down and pressed her lips into his; they answered the kiss
before he woke, and clung close and hung eagerly upon hers;

---

* This second of Swinburne's novels was composed in the mid-1860's,
but Watts-Dunton blocked its publication during Swinburne's lifetime
and apparently destroyed parts of the manuscript, which was finally published, in fragmentary form, by the late Randolph Hughes in 1952. In
this excerpt, Herbert Seyton, the autobiographical hero of the novel (and
the brother of Lady Margaret Wariston), retires to his room, his senses
strained by a violent flogging he had received from his tutor earlier in
the day.

and as the eyes opened the arms went round her with a hard embrace.

"You lazy boy, you don't want me to sing you to sleep after all."

"Yes I do, and it's very jolly of you to come. Oh, I say, what a beastly time it has been."

"You got on very well with Lady Midhurst; so did I for once."

"She's a brick; but isn't old Linley a brute, just!"

"I thought he was teasing you at one time."

"I say, don't talk about it, please, it makes me so hot."

"I'm not going to talk at all. Put something on over that shirt and listen if you want to be sung to again, and then get to bed."

"You sit there and let me alone," said Herbert, pushing her into the chair and kneeling down with one of her hands between his. She beat time on his hair with the other hand, and sang low; the ballad was an older and more battered fragment of verse than her others, but a favourite with him; the dropped syllables and rough edges of ruined metre, worn half away in the passage of the poem downward into modern lips and changed accents, did not impair its charm to ears familiar with the wind on moorside and sea; and the fierce crude expressions of sorrow and anger shocked neither boy nor woman, bred up as their minds had been in border air on the fresh and strong meat of ballads, in which the lyrical tradition is not soft of speech nor demure of step. Her hand never moved in his as she sang; he hardly breathed till her voice fell, and his face seemed to absorb hers with all its features. She looked across his head into the low fallen fire, with a set face, singing.

> God send the sea sorrow,
> And all men that sail thorough.
>
> God give the wild sea woe,
> And all ships that therein go.
>
> My love went out with dawn's light;
> He went down ere it was night.

God give no live man good
That sails over the sea's flood.

God give all live men teen
That sail over the waves green.

God send for my love's sake
All their lovers' hearts break.

Many sails went over sea;
One took my heart from me.

All they saving one
Came in landward under the sun. . . .

The fire had sunk suddenly a little before she ceased, and its last long jets of light shot up sharp at short intervals. Her voice held the boy silent after she had done singing; the faint profound light in her eyes, fixed and withdrawn, touched him like music; her hair, reluctant against combs and braids, seemed to hang and vibrate like a curled cloud after sunset in a clear sky, impelled and moulded by the wind, filled and coloured by fiery light: its curling labouring mass of fervent gold made small unequal shadows on her neck and temples, as the rough and waved outline struggled and rippled outwards. Kneeling with his face lifted to hers, he inhaled the hot fragrance of her face and neck, and trembled with intense and tender delight. Her perfume thrilled and stung him; he bent down and kissed her feet, reached up and kissed her throat.

"You smell of flowers in a hot sun," he said, kissing her feet again with violent lips that felt the sweet-scented flesh pressing them back through its soft covering. She laughed and winced under the heat of his hard kiss, drawing one foot back and striking lightly with the other, which he took and pressed down upon his neck.

"Oh! I should like you to tread me to death! darling!"

She took him by the hair and shook his head to and fro, laughing as the close elastic curls rebelled against her fingers.

"I say, let your hair go," said Herbert, pressing his arms under hers: she loosened the fastenings, and it rushed downwards, a tempest and torrent of sudden tresses, heavy and tawny and riotous and radiant, over shoulders and arms and bosom; and under cover of the massive and luminous locks she drew up his face against her own and kissed him time after time with all her strength.

"Now go to bed, and sleep well," she said, putting him back. His whole spirit was moved with the passionate motion of his senses; he clung to her for a minute, and rose up throbbing from head to foot with violent love. All the day's pleasure and pain came suddenly to flower and bore fruit in him at the moment.

"I wish you would kill me some day; it would be jolly to feel you killing me. Not like it? Shouldn't I! You just hurt me, and see."

She pinched him so sharply that he laughed and panted with pleasure.

"You are the most insane child I know, and will be quite mad at this rate before you are marriageable; and Miss Brandon will have to dispense with you. Good-night and let me go, or you will be late to-morrow, and get punished again."

"I should like being swished even I think, if you were to complain of me or if I knew you liked."

"Poor old child, I'm afraid you had enough of that this morning; don't get into more trouble, for I don't happen to like it at all. Good-night, dear: I know; I love you too" (as he caressed her with signs and speechless kisses, flattering her with hands and eyes significant of love). "I know you do: and I you, and more than I can say. There, that's often enough and plain enough. Now, my dear old minor, as Wariston calls you, please let me go once for all."

"I'm glad you're not a boy though," said Herbert.

He fell asleep with her kisses burnt into his mind, and the ineffaceable brand of love upon his thoughts: and dreamed passionately of his passion till he woke; seeing her mixed with all things, seeming to lose life for her sake, suffering in dreams under her eyes or saving her from death. How far his sudden sharp delight in her beauty and her gracious habits served to change and colour his natural affection, to stimulate his devotion, and make passionate his gratitude, he never thought or felt. But the one keen and hard impression left on him by the whole day's work was this of desperate tenderness and violent submission of soul and body to her love; the day but for her would have been mere torture and trouble throughout; she had made it in part too pleasant to forget; and this he never forgot: the memory of it, and the strong fervour and spirit of love which was the fruit of it, gave in the end a new tone and colour to his life.

CHAPTER XVI

Leucadia*

Since his return from Ensdon, Herbert had been living alone in chambers, a sad and fitful sort of life. His old friend's death had hurt him for a time; but the blow fell on senses deadened and a hardening skin. Inaction and inadequacy oppressed his conscience, and a profitless repugnance against things that were: he held on to his daily life with loose and empty hands, and looked out over it with tired unhopeful eyes. He did not seem effeminate or dejected, and hoisted no signs of inward defeat; but at heart he was conscious of weakness and waste. For some months he had fared unwholesomely, taking a painful pleasure through pure indifference, and vexed in all serious moments by the shadow of a hopeless hope, the phantom of labour unperformed. Late on an afternoon, as he lounged or lay about angry and careless through mere fatigue, a note came to him. He had meant to dress early and dine out, to kill his fatigues and kindle his fancies with champagne and chatter; but the note made him cool at once and sensible of present pain. It had been posted that morning, and was pencilled in a faint thin handwriting,

* This chapter, which describes a suicide, alludes in its title to the suicide of Sappho off the island of Leucadia. Lesbia's note summoning Herbert fulfills a promise he had extracted some years earlier, when, after declaring his misplaced love, they parted as "brother and sister" and she agreed to summon him in time of need.

thus: "Come now if you like, and see me through this: I suppose you may: I have done with doctors and all friends. I should like, if you did. Don't mind if not. They have done with me, of course you see that. Goodnight, if you fail me. Dear Herbert. This may miss you, and you would like a word. L. B." He seemed to see face to face in each line the lean pallor of death. The last strokes were hardly legible, dim and rude as the scrawl of a child with shut eyes. In twenty minutes' time he was inside her house. There was no man to admit him; a maid showed him in at once to her mistress. Had he been indeed her brother it would not have seemed more simple to all concerned; in all their eyes it was natural that she should so receive him.

He had never come near the dead or dying since his tenth year, when his father died at Kirklowes: but he knew there was a savour of death in the room: something beyond the sweet strong smell of perfumes and drugs. The woman's sad and slow suicide had been with time and care duly accomplished. She had killed herself off by inches, with the help of eau-de-Cologne and doses of opium. A funereal fragrance hung about all the air. Close curtains shut out the twilight, and a covered lamp at either end filled the room with less of light than of silver shadow. Along her sofa, propped by cushions and with limbs drawn up like a tired child's, lay or leant a woman like a ghost; the living corpse of Lesbia. She was white, with grey lips; her long shapely hands were pale and faded, and the dark tender warmth of her even colour had changed into a hot and haggard hue like fever. Her beauty of form was unimpaired; she retained the distinction of noble and graceful features and attitudes. She looked like one whom death was as visibly devouring limb-meal as though fire had caught hold of her bound at a stake: like one whose life had been long sapped and undermined from the roots by some quiet fiery poison. Her eyes and hair alone had a look of life: they were brilliant and soft yet, as she reached out her worn hot hands. Herbert came to her with a sense of pressure at his heart, and something like horror and fear mixed with the bitterness of natural pain. The figure and the place were lurid in his eyes, and less fit to make one weep than to make him kindle and tremble. There was an attraction in them which shot heat into his veins instead of the chill and heaviness of terror or grief.

"I'm dying, Bertie," said Lesbia. He sat down by her, silent.

"I'm dying," she said again, playing broken tunes with her fingers in the air.

"It's very like living, do you know? If you stay with me now, mind you don't cry. I've been out of tears myself for a long time—not a sob on hand at any price; and I hate them in others. You look so very sorry."

"Is it quite a sure thing, then?" he said quietly, in a tone which pleased her.

"As sure as death, literally; I suppose the first time that was said it sounded serious. Both doctors told me—Luthrell you know and Sir Thomas Gage. It's a question of hours. I ought to have settled it before now: but I'm as bad a hand at casting up sums as you are. I'd have made an end to-day but I really care little about it and do want to see how long this will hold out—how far the life in me will go. I won't be beaten first— not till it gives in."

"Your voice is clear enough; though you look—"

"Yes, I know. I'm dying upwards. My head is as clear as my voice. I could stand only an hour since, and I can move now. But I'm very hot and weak all through, like warm water running out. There's nothing for it; only I wish I were dying in Italy. Your friend never will. All mine are there—friends I mean; which is a touch of good luck for me. My cousins— those Burleigh people, I don't know if there are any in Ireland —never were much in my way even in my poor father's time. Poor man, if there were another life I might see him. It would be curious if each knew all about the other. Old Lady Midhurst was here last week: corbaccia. I like her a little, too. It is something to be left alone and free to choose times and ways of dying. There's no one but you I should like to have by me, who would not disturb and upset me. I heard your sister had been quite ill after that shock." She reared her head and set her eyes sharply on his face.

"She was quite ill for a time; it was horrid for her," said

Herbert, in default of other words. "But ought not—" She lifted a hand and repressed him.

"One word, please. You are to let me go my way and follow if you like—I mean listen; I don't advise you to die." He noticed how she still addressed him as a woman does a boy. "For the bit of time I have to live, I want no nursing, and no guidance; I want company, and—well! I suppose, love. You care for me; sit still and be a good boy to me, and brother." She reached him her hand, and let him kiss and keep it. "Yes; do stay, if you can. I thought of dying quite alone among these women of the household. But they are servants, and I can't turn them out, and so I thought as there must be people in the house when I die there might as well be a friend." Here she raised herself and pointed, seeing a figure in the doorway about to enter. "Send her away—my maid there. I don't want you to watch to-night, Grace.—You can let yourself out when you like," turning back to Herbert as the door closed. "Are you a good watcher? don't leave me. I might be afraid. I don't know. I might think of things and hurt myself. Not that I fear or care now, or need for that matter. Give me a little of that—a spoonful in the glass: thanks. You don't mind all this? No: I know; I see so much at least; now. My poor boy; there." She touched his hair and his cheek with the hand disengaged. Seeing him visibly torn and trembling with the torment of a passion compressed for her sake, she felt deep and warm pity for him, and something of a real sister's love, sad and pure as a prayer without hope. "Do you know a clergyman wanted to see me; he knew my uncle Burleigh: a Mr. Chaplin. I did think of seeing a Catholic priest; God knows why—perhaps" she added with sceptical caution. "I told them to say I was a Catholic; for aught the man knew, I was: like my mother. I shall be past it all soon, and the less said the better: and perhaps the less thought, too." There was silence between them for a time, and when she spoke next her voice was vague and strange.

"Do you believe in anything better than sleep? for I don't. I shall be so glad to sleep and forget all the weary work of the world. I feel inclined to die talking, do you know. Last night

I had a good dream; I suppose I shan't be troubled with dreaming—at least—O, I hope not. But I wonder, I am curious to find out what it can be like to sleep sound. I'm only afraid I may not, even then. To have dreams underground and be restless after dying would be hard. Well, most things are hard. I never found out the soft side of life yet. There ought to be some soft place in one's fate, some weak point in the divine armour: never mind. Even by dying I suppose sometimes one can hardly escape what torments us, it would be too easy."

Here she began to muse heavily, and her worn eyelids to draw downwards without meeting. He had nothing to say; and after a little she began again.

"If there is such a thing as sound sleep, it must be eternal. The difficulty is to believe in sleep at all."

She stretched out her weary arms, and lifted herself from heel to shoulder, with a great sigh, bending her body like a bow, so that for a minute only the head and feet had any support: then slowly relaxed her lifted limbs, and relapsed into supine and sad prostration.

"I dreamt of the old stories; I was always fond of them. I saw Lethe; it was not dark water, nor slow. It was pale and rapid and steady; there was a smell of meadowsweet on the banks. I must have been thinking of your Ensdon woods. And when one came close there was a new smell, more faint and rank; it came from the water-flowers; many were dead and decaying, and all sickly. And opposite me just across there ran out a wharf into the water: like the end of the pier at Wansdale. I saw nothing anywhere that was not like something I had seen already. I can't get that out my head; as soon as I woke it frightened me: but I didn't wake at once. I remember the green ooze and slime on the piles of the wharf; it was all matted with dead soft stuff that smelt wet. Not like the smell of the sea, but the smell of a lock in a river. And no boat came, and I didn't want one. I felt growing deliciously cold inside my head and behind my eyelids and down to the palms of my hands and feet. I ought to have awaked with a sneeze, and found I had caught cold in fact: but I didn't. And I saw no face anywhere for hours; and that was like a beginning of rest. Then I tried to see Proserpine, and saw her. She stood up to the knees almost in full-blown poppies, single and double. She was not the old Proserpine who comes and goes up and down between Sicily and hell; she had never seen the sun. She was pale and pleased; there was nothing in her like memory or aspiration. The dead element was vital for her; she could not have breathed in higher or lower air. The poppies at her foot were red, and those in her hand white."

"Well?" said Herbert as she paused: her voice had filled him with subtle dim emotions, and he was absorbed at once by the strange sound and sense of the words.

"She had grey eyes, bluish like the mingling of mist and water; and soft hair that lay about her breast and arms in sharp pointed locks like tongues of fire. As she looked at me this hair began to vibrate with the sudden motion of her breast, and her eyes brightened into the brilliance of eyes I knew; your sister's; and I began to wonder if she would melt entirely into that likeness. All the time I knew it was impossible she should, because she was incarnate death; and the other I knew was alive. And behind her the whole place all at once became populous with pale figures, hollow all through like an empty dress set upright; stately shadows with a grey light reflected against them; and the whole world as far as I saw was not in darkness, but under a solid cloud that never moved and made the air darker and cooler than the mistiest day upon earth. And in the fields beyond the water there was a splendid harvest of aconite: no other flower anywhere; but the grass was as pale, all yellow and brown, as if the sun had burnt it. Only where the goddess stood there were poppies growing apart; and their red cups, and the big blue lamps of the aconite, all alike hung heavily without wind. I remember, when I was little, wondering whether those flowers were likest lamps or bells; I thought any light or sound that could come of them must be so like the daylight and the music of a dead world. Well, I don't remember much more: but I was haunted with the fear that there might be nothing new behind death after all; no real rest and no real change. And the flowers vexed me. Only these, and no roses; I thought that white single sort of rose might grow there well enough. And I saw no men there, and no children."

Herbert sat silent; there was nothing to be said in answer. She roamed on through strange byways of sickly thought and channels of straitened speech. Her sleepy delirious eloquence rambled and stumbled to right and left among broken fancies and memories. He saw that her dozing remembrance enlarged and explained the half forgotten dreams of which she spoke. She had not dreamt all this, but something partly like it; and beginning to remember she went on to imagine. There is nothing harder for a child or a sick person than to tell a dream truthfully; for only the clearest and soundest of full-grown minds can safely lay down the accurate landmarks of sleep. Something of this she seemed even to perceive herself as she flowed on fitfully, with sorrowful sudden pauses.

"I tried to sleep again and dream it out; I felt it all going wrong and slipping away from me before I woke; and then I shut my eyes and set my mind steadily upon the dream, but it wouldn't go on: I could only turn over in my head what was apst of it. But in a dim way I feel sure about the wharf, and the woman, and the flowers: and for the rest—well, I think it was like that. But I do hope it will not be the same thing afterwards. That would be a terrible sort of hell."

The morbid and obscure fascination of obscure disease began to tell upon her listener: his nerves trembled in harmony with hers: he felt a cruel impersonal displeasure, compound of fear and pain, in the study of her last symptoms. Then by way of reaction came a warm sudden reflux of tenderness; and he clasped one pale restless hand with a sweet acute pang of physical pity.

"My dear brother," she said sadly and softly; then changing her voice to a sudden sharp note of irony—"Bertie, you should have been my lover, sitting here like this. What else would people think if they knew?"

He wrung her hand in his, looking down silent.

"I wonder what it would have been like, to have loved you in that way. I missed of it somehow; I have missed of so many things. But mind I was always fond of you too: and never of any man else. You might give your old sister a kiss now."

A bitter taste came into his mouth and made his cheeks tremble; the bitter water rose against his teeth; he felt his throat compress, and the moist heat of thickening tears swell and beat upon his eyelids. He bowed his face upon her face, his breast across her breast; plunged his lips into hers, hot and shuddering; and devoured her fallen features with sharp sad kisses.

"Lesbia—my dearest and first love in the world—if you could love me at last—you need not die at once surely—and I will go with you.—Oh, only try to love me for five minutes!"

These words came broken between his kisses and her sobs; but as his arms fastened upon her she broke from him sideways, trembling terribly, with widened eyes and repellent hands.

"No, no, Herbert! Let me go! let me die; will you?"

There was a savage terror in her voice and gesture; the hands that thrust him back, the eyes that shone with fear of him, might but have excited him further into a passion of bitter pity and love, but for the mad repugnance, the blind absolute horror, expressed in all her struggling figure and labouring limbs. He let her go, and she cowered away against the wall, moaning and shaking like a thing stricken to death.

When she spoke next her voice was clear and low, pitched in a soft equitable key; and never varied again.

"You have done me no harm; don't be vexed. Sit down and listen quietly. Or talk to me if you have anything to say: I like your voice. There is one thing that rather troubles me, the way I shall be buried. I hate all funerals, and all the words read over us: (I feel as if I were one of them, the dead, already;) all the flutter and fuss, all the faith and hope. I have none, and no fear. And if I were to repent of anything I would repent first of my birth. It was no fault of mine. But I think people repent more of their luck than of their faults, as a rule. God knows I repent of living,—if he knows anything about us, or cares. You were very like your sister once about the mouth and eyes. No, not again; when I am dead if you like. I dreamt once that I saw her fall over a cliff. I wish I were dying out of doors, and by day. I should like my body to be burnt and the ashes thrown into the sea. It is I who have taken the leap now, not she. But in my dreams she didn't fall of herself; somebody pushed her, I think I did. My head is full of old dreams, full. I should like to see you as you were that first time.* You couldn't go and dress up now, though I have seen women with as much hair about the lips. I should like to die acting; I've heard of people dying on the stage. It would be some relief to have a good part to keep up. Here I am going out by inches, and every minute I feel more alive here, in the head, and less in the body. I think of so many things, and wish I had one to think of: nothing seems worth the trouble it gives."

"I wish to God I could give my life for yours."

"Don't; but I've no doubt you do just now and will for a day or two. I wouldn't have it as a gift."

"I know it's not worth taking," said Herbert, "but it might be worth giving—though it's not worth keeping either."

"Try," she answered smiling. "As for me, I have done with trying, thank heaven, and now I'll go to sleep."

She drank again a shorter draught and turned over lightly but painfully. But she could not sleep or die just yet. For an hour or so Herbert sat by her, watching; her limbs shuddered now and then with a slow general spasm, as though cold or out-tired; but there were no symptoms of a sharper torment. A faint savour of flowers mixed with the smell of drugs as the whitening dusk with the yellow twilight of the lamps. The place seemed ready swept and garnished for death to enter: the light had red and yellow colours as of blood and fog. The watcher felt sad and sick and half afraid; his mind was full of dim and bitter things. He was not in heart to pray; if indeed prayer could have undone things past, he might have believed it could break and remould the inevitable future growing minute by minute into the irrevocable present. The moments as they went seemed to touch him like falling drops of sand or water: as though the hourglass or the waterclock were indeed emptied by grains or gouts upon his head: a clock measuring its minutes by blood or tears instead of water or sand. He seemed in the dim hours to hear her pulses and his own. That night, as hope and trust fell away from under him, he first learnt the reality of fate: inevitable, not to be cajoled by resignation, not to be averted by

---

* Lesbia had first seen Bertie dressed as a girl at an amateur theatrical.

intercession: unlike a God, incapable of wrath as of pity, not given to preference of evil or good, not liable to repentance or to change.

It was after dawn when Lesbia spoke next. "Keep the curtains drawn," she said; "I won't see the sun again. I mean to die by lamplight." Then after a little: "The room must be dark and warm still, as I like it; though I am getting cold; at last. It will be close and dark enough soon; when I have got to bed again. Keep the light out. There: goodbye." With this she put her hand out, dropped it, turned her face into the cushion, sighing, opened her eyes, and died. He left her in half an hour to the women, having kissed her only twice.

And that was the last of Lesbia Brandon, poetess and pagan.

❦{ 3 }❦

Chronology

1837   Born in London on 5 April, the son of Admiral Charles and the highly cultured Lady Jane (née Ashburnham) Swinburne. Idyllic childhood at Bonchurch, riding and swimming with his cousins, on the Isle of Wight, with visits to ancestral estates at Capheaton, Northumberland, and Ashburnham Place, Sussex.

1849   Presented to the aged Wordsworth at Rydal Mount.

1849–53   Attends Eton; reads the Elizabethan dramatists and writes the sadomasochistic *Unhappy Revenge,* modeled on Tourneur. Develops lasting enthusiasm for Sappho, Mary Queen of Scots, Landor, and Hugo. Withdraws from Eton for reasons still undisclosed. Presented to the octogenarian poet Samuel Rogers, who blesses him and prophesies, "You will be a poet too!"

1854   Admiral Swinburne rejects his entreaties to join the Dragoons; in a remarkable feat of courage, scales Culver Cliff, Isle of Wight, to "test my nerve in face of death."

1856–59   Attends Balliol College, Oxford, and later forms a close friendship with Benjamin Jowett, the Master, who discreetly rescues Swinburne from his excesses. Becomes a founding member of Old Mortality, a literary society organized by John Nichol of Balliol, and contributes to its short-lived journal, *Undergraduate Papers.* In 1857 meets William Morris, Dante Gabriel Rossetti, and Edward Burne-Jones, all at work painting the now-faded Arthurian frescoes in the Union Debating Hall. Morris' readings from the ms. of his Pre-Raphaelite *Defence of Guenevere* deeply influence the direction of Swinburne's early verse. Erratic in studies, intemperate in habits; withdraws from Oxford provisionally in 1859, permanently, without taking a degree, in 1860.

1860 Resident in London. Mourns death at age ninety-eight of his remarkable paternal grandfather, Sir John Swinburne, educated in France, friend of Mirabeau and J. M. W. Turner, a Jacobin and bibliophile. Publishes two undergraduate dramas, *The Queen Mother* and *Rosamund,* which draw no notice whatsoever.

1861 Meets Monckton Milnes (Lord Houghton), who later introduces him to Ruskin, Browning, Arnold, Richard Burton (explorer and translator of the *Arabian Nights*), and the works of the Marquis de Sade.

1862 Reviews and spiritedly defends Baudelaire's *Les Fleurs du Mal* and Meredith's *Modern Love.* Reads Whitman's *Leaves of Grass.* Composes "Laus Veneris" immediately after reading Fitzgerald's *Rubáiyát.* Writes *A Year's Letters,* later published as *Love's Cross-Currents.* Lives with the Rossettis and Meredith at Chelsea until 1864, when his ecstatic recitations and slidings down the bannister wear thin his welcome.

1863 Visits Paris with Whistler; meets Manet. Death of his favorite sister, Edith. Begins *Atalanta in Calydon;* reads the "hounds of spring" chorus to his cousin Mary Gordon while they ride together on the Isle of Wight.

1864 Presented at Florence to Landor, then in his ninetieth year. Becomes intimate with the young artist Simeon Solomon, whose career later ends in total degeneration.

1865 Marriage of Mary Gordon, Swinburne's first love, to Colonel Disney Leith.
      Atalanta in Calydon, highly acclaimed, makes him famous: "The grandest thing ever done by a youth," Ruskin wrote, "though he is a Demoniac youth." Publishes *Chastelard,* first and finest of three dramas centering on Mary Queen of Scots.

1866 His celebrity turns to notoriety with the critics' violent denunciation of *Poems and Ballads;* undergraduates of Oxford parade through the cloistered courts chanting "Dolores."
      Publishes *Notes on Poems and Reviews* in answer to his critics. Interest begins to shift from lyric, erotic verse to songs of the Risorgimento. Commences a decade and more of intermittent dissipation and exotic gratifications that bring him close to death.

1867   Introduced, kneeling, to Mazzini; to whom he reads and dedicates *A Song of Italy*. Writes "Ave Atque Vale" on occasion of premature report of Baudelaire's death. Lives briefly, happily, but unconjugally with Adah Isaacs Menken, poetess and bareback rider.

1868   Interest in Blake, first awakened by the Rossettis, culminates in publication of *William Blake,* begun five years earlier as a review of Alexander Gilchrist's *Life of Blake.* Nearly drowns at Étretat while with his friend George Powell at a villa named Dolmancé, after the character in Sade's *La Philosophie dans le boudoir.*

1869   Publishes "Notes on the Text of Shelley" in *Fortnightly Review*. Climbs the Puy de Dôme, in the Auvergne, with Richard Burton. Writes "Prelude" to *Tristram of Lyonesse,* goaded into emulation of Tennyson's *Idylls of the King.*

1870   Favorably reviews in the *Fortnightly* Rossetti's *Poems,* the ms. of which had recently been exhumed from Mrs. Rossetti's coffin. Meets the young Edmund Gosse, who becomes his protégé and official biographer.

1871   Publication of the much-delayed *Songs before Sunrise.*

1872   Takes rooms in Great James Street, London. Meets the very steady Theodore Watts (later, Watts-Dunton), a solicitor from Huntingtonshire, who becomes his legal adviser, companion, and informal guardian. Publishes *Under the Microscope,* a pamphlet in violent and witty riposte to Robert Buchanan's "The Fleshly School of Poetry" (1871), an attack upon the Pre-Raphaelites, chiefly Rossetti, but including Morris and Swinburne.

1874   Publishes *Bothwell,* the second and largest of three plays centering on Mary Queen of Scots.

1875   *George Chapman.* (A critical study.)
      Songs of Two Nations.
      Essays and Studies. (Includes essays on Victor Hugo, Rossetti, Morris, Arnold, Shelley, Byron, Coleridge, and a curiously pre-Paterian piece on the Old Masters at Florence.)

1876   Publishes *Erechtheus,* the more purely "classic" and still-born of his two dramas on Greek myths.

1877   *A Note on Charlotte Brontë.* (A critical study.)
        Death of Admiral John Swinburne.

1878   *Poems and Ballads,* Second Series.

1879   In June taken, dying, from his London rooms by Watts, with
        whom he moves, in September, to "The Pines," Putney. Re-
        markable recovery of health in all respects, except for increasing
        deafness, a family affliction. Apart from a meeting with Victor
        Hugo and occasional visits with Watts to the sea, the external
        "events" of Swinburne's life effectively end with his removal to
        "The Pines." Swinburne's bibliography now becomes his biog-
        raphy.

1880   *A Study of Shakespeare.*
        Songs of the Springtides.
        Studies in Song.
        The Heptalogia, or The Seven Against Sense. (Parodies, some
        composed twenty years earlier.)

1881   *Mary Stuart.* (Completes the trilogy.)

1882   *Tristram of Lyonesse and Other Poems.* (*Tristram* was begun
        in 1869; many of the "Other Poems" are enthusiastic odelets to
        babies, who are the subject of much of Swinburne's later
        verse.) Dines with Victor Hugo in Paris in celebration of the
        fiftieth anniversary of *Le Roi s'amuse.*

1883   *A Century of Roundels,* dedicated to Christina Rossetti, whom
        Swinburne prized second only to Sappho among poetesses.

1884   *A Midsummer Holiday and Other Poems.*

1885   *Marino Faliero,* a blank-verse play on Italian freedom.

1886   *Miscellanies.* (Includes essays on the Romantic poets, Tenny-
        son, and Mary Queen of Scots.)
        A Study of Victor Hugo.

1887   *Gathered Songs.*
        Locrine, a rhyming play, performed in 1899.

1888   *The Whippingham Papers,* on the subject of flagellation, pri-
        vately printed, but composed much earlier.
        "Mr. Whistler's Lecture on Art," an intemperate attack upon
        Whistler's celebrated "Ten O'Clock" lecture advocating art
        for art's sake.

1889 *A Study of Ben Jonson.*
Poems and Ballads, Third Series. (The ballads, many of them from *Lesbia Brandon,* were composed much earlier.)

1892 *The Sisters,* dedicated to Mary Gordon, "a little tragedy of modern life," with sadistic overtones and dealing with incest.

1894 *Astrophel and Other Poems.*
Studies in Prose and Poetry. (Contains a fine memoir of Jowett and an egregious attack upon "Whitmania.")

1896 *The Tale of Balen,* a vigorous Arthurian narrative, set in Swinburne's beloved Northumberland.
Death of Lady Jane Swinburne.

1899 *Rosamund, Queen of the Lombards,* a blank-verse drama.

1904 *A Channel Passage and Other Poems.*
"Dedicatory Epistle" to the collected *Poems.*

1905 *Love's Cross-Currents.* (First published pseudonymously in 1877 as *A Year's Letters,* by Mrs. Horace Manners.)

1908 *The Duke of Gandia,* an unfinished drama.
The Age of Shakespeare (essays on Marlowe, Webster, Middleton, etc.).

1909 *Three Plays of Shakespeare.* (A critical study.)
Death from pneumonia, on April 10, in his seventy-third year. Burial at Bonchurch, with his request only partially honored that the Anglican Burial Service not be read by his grave.

1913 *Charles Dickens.* (A brief critical study.)

1917 *Posthumous Poems.* (Juvenilia, etc., reprinted in Bonchurch Edition.)

1925–27 *Complete Works.* (Bonchurch Edition.)

1952 *Lesbia Brandon* (composed mid-1860's).

1964 *La Sœur de la Reine* and *La Fille du Policeman* (satiric burlesques composed 1860–62).

Bibliography

Works by Swinburne

The Complete Works of Algernon Charles Swinburne. Ed. Edmund Gosse and T. J. Wise. 20 vols. ("The Bonchurch Edition.") London, Heinemann, 1925–27. [The most nearly complete edition of the poetry and prose; sumptuous but ill-edited.]

The Poems of Algernon Charles Swinburne. 6 vols. London, Chatto and Windus, 1904. (Reprinted in 2 vols. by Heinemann, 1924.) [The best available text, proofed by Swinburne himself; includes the "Dedicatory Epistle" omitted from the Bonchurch edition.]

The Swinburne Letters. Ed. Cecil Y. Lang. 6 vols. New Haven, Yale University Press, 1959–62. [Invaluable for study of the life and works.]

New Writings by Swinburne . . . Being a Medley of Poems, Critical Essays, Hoaxes and Burlesques. Ed. Cecil Y. Lang. Syracuse, Syracuse University Press, 1964.

The Novels of A. C. Swinburne: Love's Cross-Currents; Lesbia Brandon. With an Introduction by Edmund Wilson. New York, Farrar, Straus and Cudahy, 1962. [First collected edition of the novels; includes Wilson's important essay, listed below, on Swinburne as novelist *manqué.*]

Swinburne Replies. Ed. Clyde K. Hyder. Syracuse, Syracuse University Press, 1966. [Collects three essays which constitute Swinburne's informal *ars poetica: Notes on Poems and Reviews, Under the Microscope,* and the "Dedicatory Epistle."]

Works about Swinburne

Baum, Paull F. "Swinburne's 'A Nympholept,'" *South Atlantic Quarterly,* LVII (1958), 58–68.

Beerbohm, Max. "No. 2, The Pines," in *And Even Now,* New York, Dutton, 1920. [Magnificent evocation of the aging Swinburne.]

Bowra, C. M. "Atalanta in Calydon," in *The Romantic Imagination.* Cambridge, Harvard University Press, 1949.

Brown, E. K. "Swinburne: A Centenary Estimate," *University of Toronto Quarterly,* VI (1937), 215–35.

Bush, Douglas. "Swinburne," in *Mythology and the Romantic Tradition in English Poetry.* Cambridge, Harvard University Press, 1937. [A vigorous, almost entirely negative appraisal.]

Chew, Samuel C. *Swinburne.* Boston, Little, Brown, 1929. [Sound introduction; especially useful on the prose criticism.]

Drinkwater, John. *Swinburne: an Estimate.* London, Dent, 1913.

Eliot, T. S. "Swinburne as Poet," in *Selected Essays.* New York, Harcourt, Brace and World, 1950. [Misguided but masterful.]

Gosse, Edmund. *The Life of Algernon Charles Swinburne.* London, Macmillan, 1917. [Fine sense of Swinburne's unique eccentricity, but too officially reticent to be fully useful now. Reprinted in Bonchurch Edition, Vol. XIX.]

Hyder, Clyde K. *Swinburne's Literary Career and Fame.* Durham, Duke University Press, 1933.

Lafourcade, Georges. *La Jeunesse de Swinburne (1837–1867).* 2 vols. Strasbourg, Publications de la Faculté des Lettres, 1928. [The one indispensable study of Swinburne's life and verse through *Poems and Ballads,* First Series.]

———. *Swinburne: a Literary Biography.* London, Bell, 1932. [Highly useful; spans the whole career, but lacks the richness of *La Jeunesse.*]

Lang, Cecil Y. "Swinburne's Lost Love," *PMLA,* LXXIV (1959), 123–30. [Authoritatively corrects an error surrounding the biographical source of several of Swinburne's major poems.]

Nicolson, Harold. *Swinburne.* New York, Macmillan, 1926. [An uneven book, with a brilliant opening chapter.]

Peters, Robert L. *The Crowns of Apollo: Swinburne's Principles of Literature and Art.* Detroit, Wayne State University Press, 1965.

Pound, Ezra. "Swinburne versus Biographers," *Poetry,* XI (1918), 322–29. [Attacks Gosse's *Life* and pays high tribute to Swinburne's genius.]

Praz, Mario. *The Romantic Agony.* 2nd edition. London, Oxford University Press, 1951. [Swinburne, the sadomasochist.]

Reul, Paul de. *L'Oeuvre de Swinburne.* Bruxelles, Sand, 1922.

Welby, T. Earle. *A Study of Swinburne.* New York, Doran, 1926. [A splendidly original, quirky book; probably the best single study in English.]

Wilson, Edmund. "Swinburne of Capheaton and Eton," *New Yorker,* October 6, 1962, 165–200. Reprinted in *The Novels of A. C. Swinburne.*

Index of Titles

Index of First Lines

About the Author

ALGERNON CHARLES SWINBURNE was born in London in 1837. He attended Balliol College, Oxford, where he met William Morris, Dante Gabriel Rossetti and Edward Burne-Jones, Pre-Raphaelites with whom he remained associated. His classic verse tragedy, *Atalanta in Calydon,* published in 1865, made him famous, but in the following year his *Poems and Ballads* was fiercely denounced by the critics. Swinburne's ill health, worsened by years of dissipation, almost caused his death in 1879. His recovery and later retirement took place at Putney, a quiet London suburb. In addition to his fame as a poet Swinburne also played an important role among the Victorians as an early advocate of Baudelaire and Gautier, Hugo and Mallarmé, Wagner and Whitman. See the Chronology of Swinburne's life in this volume.

About the Editor

JOHN D. ROSENBERG was born in New York City in 1929. He received his A.B., M.A. and Ph.D. from Columbia. In 1951 he was awarded a Kellett Fellowship to Cambridge University, where he received an A.B. and M.A. He was a recipient of an American Council of Learned Societies Fellowship (1965–1966) for research on the Victorian poets. Mr. Rosenberg taught at the City College of New York from 1954–1962 and is now Professor of English at Columbia University. He is the author of *The Darkening Glass: A Portrait of Ruskin's Genius,* which won the Clarke F. Ansley award.